THIS
FOOTBALL
CENTURY

THIS FOOTBALL CENTURY

RUSSELL HOLMESBY
& JIM MAIN

WILKINSON BOOKS

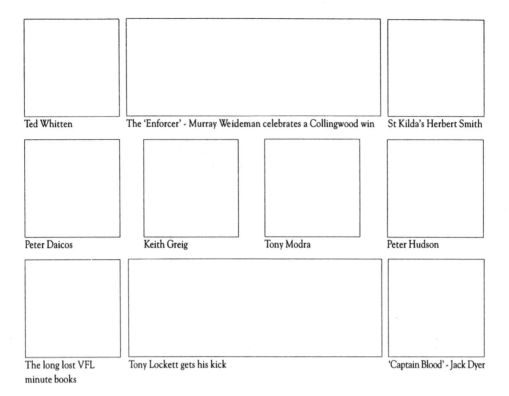

Ted Whitten

The 'Enforcer' - Murray Weideman celebrates a Collingwood win

St Kilda's Herbert Smith

Peter Daicos

Keith Greig

Tony Modra

Peter Hudson

The long lost VFL minute books

Tony Lockett gets his kick

'Captain Blood' - Jack Dyer

Cover design, Page design - Paul Martinsen

Wilkinson Books
is an imprint of

Information Australia
A.C.N. 006 042 173
45 Flinders Lane
Melbourne VIC 3000
Telephone: (03) 9654 2800
Fax: (03) 9650 5261

ISBN 1 86350 222 X

Printed and bound in Australia by Australian Print Group

The National Library of Australia
Cataloguing-in-Publication entry

Holmesby, Russell. This football century.

Includes index

ISBN 1 86350 222 X

1. Victorian Football Association - History. 2. Victorian Football League. 3. Australin football - History. I. Main, Jim, 1943- . II. Title.

796.336

FOREWORD

Growing up in Melbourne in the years after the war, I loved football almost from my first steps and dreamed of emulating the football heroes of those days.

In the streets of Prahran we kicked rolled-up paper footballs and lived and breathed footy. Every word of football was devoured in the newspapers and on the radio.

When TV came to Australia we watched the game on sets in shops and at friends' places. We couldn't get enough football. Not even Davy Crockett or the Mouseketeers were as good!

Then in 1967 the dream became a reality, moving from VFA Club Prahran to Richmond and playing mostly in the back pocket until 1979. And after a brief coaching role at Richmond crossing to Essendon as coach in 1981.

The dream and passion continue. Reading every word about the game as it now is. Watching as much football as possible on TV and on countless videos. Talking to anyone who wants to talk footy.

So This Football Century is welcome as a good read. It's not a dull history. It's packed with the action and drama of our great game, right from the first season a century ago.

You'll find you're there with the players, coaches, officials, reporters and those important people, the loyal supporters as you turn the pages. There's lots of laughs and triumphs. And yes some tragedies, despair and intrigues.

Football's been like that from day one. It'll be part of what makes it so special for another 100 years.

I hope so. Enjoy This Football Century. Russell Holmesby and Jim Main have done a top job. It doesn't matter whether you're quick, tall, short or slow...football's still got a lot of soul and spirit for all its lovers.

Kevin Sheedy

ABOUT
THE AUTHORS

*R*ussell Holmesby is recognised as one of the leading historians of Australian Rules Football. In conjunction with Jim Main he wrote the Encyclopaedia of League Footballers, acclaimed as the bible of the game, and has written three other books on football. A journalist with Leader newspapers, he has earned awards for his writing on football, cricket and basketball.

*J*im Main is a Bachelor of Arts graduate, (with a major in history) and is one of Australia's best known sports writers. He has covered major sports events ranging from the 1984 Los Angeles Olympics to Davis Cup Tennis. He is also the author of another 25 books.

CONTENTS

INTRODUCTION

*F*or millions of Australians, AFL football is as vital for survival as food and water. The game is part of the very fabric of body and soul and every winter brings its mountains of joy or valleys of despair.

This has been the case for more than 100 years, even before the Victorian Football League (now Australian Football League) was formed late in 1896 at a meeting at Buxton's Art Gallery, Melbourne.

Of course, the first VFL season was played in 1897, with just eight clubs. The competition since has experienced a multitude of highs and quite a few lows. There has been the introduction of new clubs since the first expansion in 1908 (with the admittance of Richmond and University) and the move towards a national competition with the shift of South Melbourne to Sydney in 1982 and then the introduction of the Brisbane Bears and West Coast Eagles (1987), the Adelaide Crows (1991) and the Fremantle Dockers (1995). Sadly, there also was the demise of the University club in 1915 due to the pressures of World War I.

The VFL/AFL survived both world wars without interruption and, in the process, spawned generation after generation of football heroes...the Colliers, the Coventrys, Pratt, Dyer, Bunton, Coleman, Skilton, Stewart, Farmer, Nicholls, Bartlett and, today, Williams, Lockett, Dunstall, Ablett and others.

This book encapsulates all the drama, triumph and tragedy of 100 years of football. It has not been an easy task and, in fact, the publication of this book involved five years of painstaking research through dusty volumes and archives at the Victorian State Library, the Herald and Weekly Times library and various AFL clubs.

Photographs were gleaned from a multitude of sources, including now-defunct magazines and periodicals, including The Australasian, Table Talk and Punch.

This book is a record of the first century of the greatest football code of them all. And may the game flourish for many more centuries.

Meanwhile, the authors extend their thanks to all who helped in the production of this record of the first 100 years of the game we all love.

Russell Holmesby   Jim Main

Chapter One

1890s
The origins of the League

Carlton Football Club's president tells his members the game would be improved if clubs "were allowed to spend their hard earned money in their own way" rather than have football's governing body spread income across the board.

Meanwhile there is an ongoing debate over whether there are too many clubs in Melbourne and the suggestion of mergers is floated. Nothing comes of it and the stronger clubs are chafing under the belief that they are carrying their weaker opponents.

Talk of a breakaway group simmers and there is mounting concern the competition is too big and the draw is inequitable because not all clubs meet twice. In the background players are getting huge illegal payments under the lap and the competition's chiefs seem powerless to bring it under control....

It all has a familiar ring doesn't it.

Until you discover the Carlton president's name was Gillespie and the year of his pronouncement was 1893. The mergers were proposed in 1894 and involved Collingwood with Richmond, Carlton with Fitzroy, Melbourne with St Kilda, Footscray with Williamstown, South Melbourne with Port Melbourne, and Essendon with North Melbourne. Biggest travelling problem was whether to catch a train or boat to Geelong and there wasn't a media mogul in sight to promote the concept of a "Super-league".

While the finer details of football may have been vastly different 100 years ago the same factors that dominate football in 1996 were at the core of the game's dilemmas - money and power.

Comments by the editor of *The Australasian* on football in the 1890s would be echoed in laments of later times. "Football has ceased to be a game and a pastime: it has become business." He went on to say it was "business for the players, business for the cricket clubs, and business for the regiment of barrackers who go from match to match to disgrace themselves and all near them by their vehement and biased clamour".

"The student of natural selection sees everything happen that ought to happen where the struggle to get first is severe and the motive sordid. Honor and grace have long since departed."

He compared 1890's footballers to Roman professional gladiators who "had their rich patrons, their sporting backers and their coarse, vulgar and silly noise-makers, so are some of our trained footballers countenanced by swells who dine them "at the club" after a victory; and barrackers well-dressed and otherwise, who throng the matches to shout themselves hoarse, cheering on the players and boohooing the umpire. Verily, a great game is on the downgrade, and as usual the love of money is the root of the evil."

From the time a group of young sportsmen kicked a pigskin around Yarra Park the game that became known as Australian Rules evolved at a rapid rate. In

> "Football has ceased to be a game and a pastime: it has become business."

Two of the game's famous early leaders are depicted on this poster of the early champions of the VFA which was issued in the late 1880s. "Sonny" Elms (third from left) led South Melbourne and Dave Hickinbotham (seated in the middle row) skippered Geelong.

less than 40 years it progressed from being just another form of winter recreation to the status of Melbourne's favorite sport. While it is largely true that those were simpler, less complicated times, football had plenty of problems in the 1890s. They were largely due to the fact that money had crept into the game and clubs were waving large inducements to players to sign up. The uneven nature of the competition was also a major concern, particularly in the early 1890s.

Ten games into 1894 Essendon was unbeaten and on its way to a fourth successive premiership. "The public are beginning to show apathy to the game

hitherto unknown and attendances are becoming smaller every week," said one concerned writer. He acknowledged that the economic depression was a factor, but people had managed to scrape up the admission cost whenever it looked as if Essendon may be challenged.

Player payments were a huge issue and the Victorian Football Association, the game's controlling body, kept its head well and truly in the sand despite the press's frequent calls for it to act. One reporter said, "Everybody who knows anything knows that payments of players although distinctly forbidden by the rules of the association, is in various ways carried on wholesale...This is a reprehensible state of affairs which covers a gigantic system of hypocrisy and should be reformed."

The style of football had also degenerated and most observers blamed the anachronistic "little mark" for the decline in clever running and long kicking which had previously been one of the game's features. The "little mark" was a two-yard foot pass to himself by which a player could claim a mark and a consequent free kick.

It was impossible to administer in a pack situation where players were so adept at using the rule. Umpires could not identify borderline throws and countless ball-ups destroyed the flow of play. As a result the games were frequently bogged down into ugly packs with beefy ruckmen calling the tune. The quality of football had been partly resuscitated in 1896, but it was still a long way short of the halcyon days in the 1880s.

Australian football, commonly known as Victorian Rules because of its state of origin, flourished in the second half of the nineteenth century and rivalled horse racing as the number one sports attraction in the colonies of Victoria, Tasmania, South Australia and Western Australia.

Indeed, the game had a firm foothold in New South Wales and Queensland, but club parochialism prevented the game becoming the top football code north of the Murray. In fact, the Victorian

Football Association clubs had their own problems, mainly in the equitable distribution of gate money and the relative strength and weakness of clubs. There was tremendous dissatisfaction among clubs and the general mood of unease eventually erupted into revolt. The Victorian football world was split in 1896 when a number of clubs broke away to form the Victorian Football League.

Several VFA clubs did not know of the breakaway move until well after the matter had been discussed at a protest meeting on October 2, 1896. This meeting was held at the Buxton's Art Gallery, with delegates from Carlton, Essendon, Fitzroy, Geelong, Melbourne and South Melbourne present. Former VFA delegate and life member Mr J. J. Sinn, in an article in the Sporting Globe Football Book of 1948, recalls the mood of a VFA meeting held on the same night:

"We (the VFA clubs) were a very happy family. All worked for the love of the game until one evening in the year 1896 when, on entering the meeting room, I found that the Carlton, Essendon, Fitzroy, Geelong, Melbourne and South Melbourne delegates were missing. Those present represented Footscray, North Melbourne, Port Melbourne, Richmond, St Kilda and Williamstown.

"We were consequently at a loss to explain the absence of the others until the well-known football editor of The Argus of that day, the late Mr Donald McDonald, entered the room and said: "Well boys, have you heard the news? The other fellows are holding a meeting at Buxton's Art Gallery. They are going to break away and form another body to be called the Victorian Football League."

Next day the news became public. The St Kilda club, having received an invitation to join the League, accepted the rebel offer and joined up within two weeks.

"Public opinion at the time was that we would have to disband, but our answer was emphatically 'no'. We firmly resolved to fight to the last to keep the old VFA flag flying."

Significantly, Sinn added later in the article that the League wooed Richmond to its fold in 1908 - thus depriving the Association of its last central ground. With that one phrase, added almost as an afterthought, Sinn summarised the main reason for the breakaway. The clubs closest to the inner city believed they were propping up the other clubs, some well away from the city area.

At the end of the nineteenth century, transport usually was by horse, by buggy or by cable car. Public transport was vitally important for big attendances at VFA matches. It therefore was only natural that clubs close to the city and serviced by public transport would attract the best attendances. Carlton, Collingwood, South Melbourne, Melbourne, Fitzroy and Essendon (which played at Jolimont) all had the benefit of nearby public transport.

Geelong, despite being 45 miles from Melbourne, was well serviced by rail and it was largely instrumental in the formation of the League. Geelong, which already had a proud and distinguished football history, played a vital role in the secret developments which followed the first rebel meeting. Collingwood was invited to join the movement but at first declined. In fact Collingwood came up with an alternative proposal - one that still strikes fear into the heart of all football supporters. Collingwood wanted most senior clubs to merge.

Instead, it was mooted that a breakaway body be formed. Collingwood finally agreed to join the new body and Carlton was invited to join, along with St Kilda. Significantly, both Carlton and St Kilda (with Princes Park and the Junction Oval respectively) had good grounds and excellent public transport facilities to offer the new body.

The news of the formation of the VFL was not

> "The project of forming a new football association, took definite shape last night when the representatives of six of the clubs met to discuss the matter.

The all conquering South Melbourne team which won three flags in a row from 1888 to 1890.
Top row: J. Young, J. Dunn, J. Marshall (trainer), A. Brown, E. Barrett, J. Middleton, J. Kinneburgh (trainer).
Second Row: D. McKay, G. F. Major (vice-president), J. Sloss (president), B. Morton, B. Powell, H. Steele (vice-president),
A. Evans (secretary), W. Windley, R. Doran, Third Row: W.Ellis, H. Purdy, R. Kerr, B. Page, H. Elms (captain), P. Burns (vice-
captain), H. Latchford, J. Graham, R. Talbot. Bottom Row: J. O'Meara, J. Glenn, A. McMurray, F. Waugh, W. Spence.

considered worthy of prominent display in the news-papers of October 3, 1896. *The Argus*, which first heard of the breakaway move, reported: "The project of forming a new football association, which has been quietly discussed for some time past, took definite shape last night when the representatives of six of the clubs met to discuss the matter. An alteration having been determined on, two courses were open - either to retain the association in its present form and divide the clubs into A and B sections, or to reduce the number of clubs playing, and leave the rejected to take their own course.

"The latter was the step determined on. Geelong, as a club credited with having done more for Victorian football than any other, should not, it was thought, suffer through having failed so badly this season, and will be just as well suited by the proposed alterations in rules as any in the competition. Although the residents of Carlton have not been enthusiastic about football of late, the club's glorious past, not its present feebleness, was the point considered.

"An eighth club being required the choice unani-mously fell upon St Kilda. If it be a merit to couple a good game of football with manly and decent con-duct, both on and off the field, St Kilda have every right to consideration, and its inclusion will give every general satisfaction. The new association (League) will therefore consist of Collingwood, South Melbourne, Essendon, Melbourne, Fitzroy, Geelong, St Kilda and Carlton." This left Williamstown, Footscray, Richmond, Port Melbourne and North Melbourne on their own, although the VFA hit back by admitting Brunswick to its competition in 1897 and Prahran and West Melbourne in 1899.

The assertion by *The Argus* that Geelong accepted a late invitation to join the League set the scene for a misinterpretation of history that lasts to this day. Geelong played a vital role in the formation of the League and always was going to be an original member of the new body.

The Argus report has led to countless references in football documents about the late entry of Geelong, a historical mistake that still rankles with the club and its historians. In fact, the club's official history of 1952 states: "Geelong was the club mainly instrumental in forming the Victorian Football League in 1896, and it is about time it was given the credit."

Essendon's influence was evident from the nomination of club president Alex McCracken as the inaugural VFL president. McCracken held the position until 1915 and was Essendon president from 1887-1903.

The newly formed VFL, with its eight member clubs, wasted no time in setting a program for the 1897 football season. It decided that the clubs would play each other twice over 14 home and away rounds. Semi-finals would be played by the four top sides and the winners of these two semis would play off in a grand final. That was the plan, but it did not work out that way and

Some of the VFA captains of 1895.

Arch Sykes (Essendon)

T.C. Wilson (North Melbourne)

T. Banks (Fitzroy)

T. Blake (Carlton)

the VFL decided instead to play a round-robin finals series between the four top clubs.

The last two teams invited to join the new league by the big six were St Kilda, because of its central ground at the Junction, and Carlton. The Blues had to give an assurance that they would possess their own ground and once the club found a permanent home at Princes Park it joined the new group.

One of the earliest entries in the League's first minute book is a letter from six VFL delegates to VFA secretary Thomas Marshall asking him to call a meeting of all VFA clubs on February 19, 1897, to discuss "the financial position of the VFA" and other matters. Obviously the newly formed League wanted to tie up some loose ends with its former parent body and get on with running the new competition. At that stage the League did not even have a place to hold meetings and another letter records that it placed a permanent booking for a room at the Port Phillip Hotel. The cost was a princely 15 pounds per annum.

The new League immediately scrapped the little mark rule and introduced a ten yard minimum distance. Strangely the League stuck with 20 men a side (four followers) and two seasons passed before the numbers were reduced to 18. There were no reserve or interchange players.

Everything was now in place for the new Victorian Football League to kick off. A new empire had been born.

Chapter Two

1897

A new dawn

May 8, 1897, was a cool, cloudy day on which the new competition burst into bloom. *The Herald* of the previous night announced that the St Kilda team would leave the Junction bound for Collingwood in a "four-in-hand drag" at five minutes to two. The Saints considered this was the best possible option even though The Australian Horseless Carriage Syndicate of Melbourne had exhibited its motor buggy at the cycle show in the Exhibition Building in February. The kerosene engine vehicle just managed to top 10 miles per hour.

Maybe they would have been better advised to try the new means of transport as they managed to arrive late and thus incur a five guinea penalty for "not being ready to start the game at 3.15 pm". Alighting from their horse-drawn conveyance the Saints ran into the full might of a Collingwood side celebrating the unfurling of its 1896 VFA flag. St Kilda's players had expected to "give a good account of themselves on the smooth and tuftless surface" and it was reported that the University curator had made the suggestion of removing all the little "hillocks which formerly accounted for the ball frequently beating the players". All that one pressman could find fault with was a couple of boarded up windows in the press box.

The VFL left nothing to chance and when Umpire Kendall was informed that he would umpire the Collingwood-St Kilda clash, VFL secretary Wilson added public transport details to make sure he found

his way to Victoria Park. Collingwood had too much strength and power for the Saints and ran out a comfortable winner by 23 points. The Magpies had plenty of stars and leading the charge was the brilliant Charlie Pannam, first in a long line of a family dy-

Far Left - Charlie Pannam - an early VFL star for Collingwood.

Left - Collingwood's Dick Condon - often at the centre of controversy in the League's early years.

nasty that stayed with the club through to the days of the Richards brothers.

Pannam was an exceptionally talented footballer often criticised for being sly, and exasperated opponents with his tactics. Apart from the gamesmanship he was a brilliant and dashing winger who shifted to half-forward when his pace diminished and managed to top the League's goalkicking late in his career. He was also the first man to play 100 VFL games, missing only three matches before hitting the ton. Alongside Pannam in that opening Collingwood side was Dick Condon. Richard J Condon figures largely in the Magpies' early history and he was credited with inventing the famed Collingwood "system" on a trip to Tasmania. A darker side to the gifted Condon was his vile temper and it even surfaced in later years as captain when he grappled with one of his own players on the field. He overstepped the mark when he told an umpire his daughter "is a whore" and the League suspended him for life. Collingwood didn't lift a finger to help him and he spent more than one and a half years on the sidelines before the ban was lifted.

The long lost VFL minute books which were located during research for this book and are now safely housed at the Australian Gallery of Sport.

Collingwood had the most star-studded line-up in the League with champions such as Will Proudfoot, Jack Monohan and Fred "Charger" Hailwood, but Essendon was to be the side which would win the honor of the first League premiership. The Dons or "Same Old" as they were known, opened their 1897 campaign with a 23-point win over Geelong at Corio Oval. Geelong's oval was described as "flintlike and none too smooth" and the unfortunately surnamed Umpire Crapp apparently had trouble judging the new 10-yard marking rule.

Essendon bristled with talent and one of the team's leading performers was veteran ruckman Charles "Tracker" Forbes. The tall, moustachioed Forbes had a sense of humor on the field which once led to him hoisting a particularly noisy opposition rover over the fence and sitting him on a seat outside the arena. "Get out of this, you little pest," admonished Forbes as the scene dissolved into laughter.

Essendon's first captain was George Stuckey, an all-rounder in the truest sense who represented Victoria at football and cricket, and just to prove his versatility won the Stawell Gift in 1897. Stuckey tried to retire from the game at the start of 1899, but was plucked from the crowd when Essendon was a man short and went on to play for another four years. George Vautin was another who played state football and cricket, and was part of that famous first premiership side.

Geelong was not short of stars either and included Ted Rankin, patriarch of a famous clan, and the three McShane brothers in the first side.

Melbourne and South played the most rugged game in the opening round and the "Fuschias" as Melbourne was called, won by 17 points after establishing an early break. One of Melbourne's best players was Fred McGinis, an ill-starred player who became one of the League's first champions until stricken with an eye injury that forced him out of the game at an early age.

Highest score of the day was Fitzroy's 6.13-49. The Maroons were one of the major powers in the early days of the VFL and Carlton struggled from the kick-off. Fitzroy had a big, strong side with men like Pat Hickey (an uncle of Reg, the Geelong great of later years) and the strong-marking Grace brothers Jim and Mick. Hickey was an iron willed player whose tactics so upset a Collingwood crowd in one game that he had to receive a police escort from the ground. Hickey had earlier been struck by an umbrella wielding woman, and incensed the mob when he emerged from the dressing rooms with a beaming grin.

Jim Grace was an acknowledged champion, but he angered club officials on the next two Saturdays when he and Mick opted to be part of his local cricket team's grand final rather than line up for the Maroons. One reporter sneered "they are playing for second place in a second rate cricket competition", but the Graces' attitude typified the laid-back approach to VFL football at the time. On another occasion Fitzroy kept a place open for one of the Graces and started one short in the match against Melbourne. The opposition rattled on two quick goals in the meantime which set up a win in the low-scoring match.

It wasn't unusual for League teams to lose out where a man's sporting loyalties were divided. In a vital match between the two top sides Essendon and Geelong, the red and blacks were still two men short not long before the scheduled start. They urgently summoned Gus Kearney from a tennis tournament at Albert Park and he arrived just in time to run out on the field. It wasn't just a case of making up the numbers as Kearney was the side's vice-captain! Yet there was no explanation in the press of why the vice-captain should be playing tennis in preference to a League match. Kearney was no slouch on the tennis court as he won the Victorian singles title six times.

The VFL was careful with the pennies and when a combined side travelled to Ballarat, Wilson wrote to Geelong secretary Charles Brownlow saying that the expenses required to send one of the Geelong players were too much . . . "As it will cost so much to bring McCallum it would be best to get a Melbourne man to take his place."

McCallum must have been a heck of a player and it is said that he once kicked a goal after eluding 12 St Kilda opponents in an 1898 match! Later in his career he put in a shocker and spectators wondered at his apparent lethargy. It turned out that he had been working in Lorne and had missed a ride that would have connected him with the train from Birregurra to Geelong. His only alternative had been to walk 40 kilometres across the Otway Ranges!

From the earliest days the VFL was in no doubt

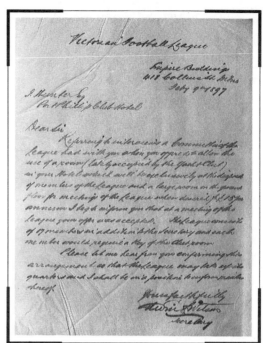

First entry in the League's minute book. The secretary seeks to rent the meeting rooms at the Port Phillip Club Hotel.

that it was the guiding light for the Australian game. Letters pontificating on the laws of the game were fired off to all and sundry. Wilson told the South Australians: "The League are entirely with you in your concern to have the game made more open". Apparently the Croweaters were more willing to accept Victorian edicts than they are now.

It may have been almost a century before marketing departments and the like, but the League had a spark of entrepreneurial flair when approaching a representative match against the Bendigo League. Wilson sent the Bendigo League a list of players "and other information which will doubtless be useful in advertising". Fitzroy's Mick Grace was described lyrically as clean, cool and clever, and Essendon's "Son" Barry was said to be accomplished, active and artful.

On the same Saturday as the Bendigo game, Collingwood journeyed to South Australia and the disturbing news is recorded that umpire Coffey had lodged complaints against certain Collingwood players. No details of the hearing are recorded and it seems that the VFL was content to let the matter fizzle out.

There was still money owing to the League clubs from the VFA days and of the 87 pound dividend Collingwood did best with 22 pounds three shillings. St Kilda's return from the VFA was a meagre two pounds 10 shillings. Onfield skirmishes occasionally sought administrative settlement and a vital match between South Melbourne and Essendon resulted in a protest being lodged.

Goal umpire Franks was informed: "Your score is 2 goals 3 behinds and the other umpire says it was 2 goals 4. Please let me know if you have made a mistake". It was subsequently found that poor Franks had made a mistake and he was chastised by Wilson. "The League does not take cognisance of the scoreboard or the newspaper reports, either or both of which may be inaccurate, but relies on the official reports which have been furnished by the umpires and I must ask you to be always very careful." Despite all that some observers thought South Melbourne's protest was born out of frustration at being superior to the Dons everywhere except on the scoreboard.

It wasn't just the goal umpires who were tardy and Wilson admonished South Melbourne for taking too long to forward match receipts: "It is now 11 days since the match was played and I cannot understand why a cheque has not been forwarded 'ere this".

Football these days is virtually a 12-month-a-year business, but it wasn't the same then. On October 9 Wilson informed the Ovens and Murray League's secretary that "the League has virtually shut

BATTLE DRESS

The original Registration of colors for each club:

- **Adelaide** (1991) - Navy, blue, red and gold hoops, navy blue shorts and navy, blue, red and gold hooped socks.
- **Brisbane Bears** (1987) - gold with maroon yoke and maroon stylised map of Queensland with extended line depicting BB for Brisbane Bears and featuring a bear's head.
- **Carlton** (1897) - dark navy blue with chamois collars, dark blue knickers and blue and white stockings .
- **Collingwood** (1897) - black and white striped jersey, black knickers and black stockings.
- **Essendon** (1897) - black jersey with red sash, blue knickers, with red and black hose.
- **Fitzroy** (1897) - maroon jersey, blue knickers and maroon hose.
- **Footscray** (1925) - blue, with one red and one white band.
- **Fremantle** (1995) - purple guernsey with one red, one green chest panel separated by a white anchor. Purple socks with green, white and red hoops around top. Purple shorts.
- **Geelong** (1897) - navy blue and white jersey and hose, blue knickers.
- **Hawthorn** (1925) - brown with gold vee.
- **Melbourne** (1897) - dark navy blue jersey and knickers and scarlet hose.
- **North Melbourne** (1925) - royal blue with white vee
- **Richmond** (1908) - black and yellow stripes.
- **St Kilda** (1897) - red, black and white jersey, white knickers, red and black stockings.
- **South Melbourne** (now Sydney Swans) (1897) - red and white jersey, blue knickers and red and white hose.
- **University** (1908) - black with blue vee.
- **West Coast Eagles** (1987) - gold with royal blue eagle wings and monogram, royal blue socks with gold trim, royal blue shorts.

up shop for the year and I was only waiting for a meeting to have your appeals considered".

Wilson was clearly a man who dotted the "i's" and crossed the "t's". That probably stemmed from his job and in the midst of the VFL correspondence is a rather testy personal letter to the Town Clerk of Hawthorn.

"I have declined to comply with your request that I should record my time in a book in the presence of the City Treasurer and leave such with him. You are not my master to direct how, when and in what manner I am to carry out my duties as the Government Municipal Auditor." Wilson, however, wasn't reluctant to remind others of the need for punctuality and advised umpires Crapp, Hood and Carter complaints had been received that they had started their matches "after the time allotted for commencement and that the half-time interval has been unduly prolonged".

Essendon and Geelong were the two leading teams and by the end of the first round Geelong held a slender lead on the ladder. Geelong had opened the season sluggishly losing the first three matches, put down to the fact that "training and practice have to now been only perfunctorily attended". That may have been part of the cause, but the absence of heroic ruckman Henry Young was a bigger factor. When he returned he headed a powerful ruck that included Joe and James McShane, Jack Parkin and rover Ted Rankin. The Pivotonians ran up 11 wins in succession before stumbling against Essendon in a match that gave the Dons the flag.

The four top teams at the end of the home and away season were Essendon, Geelong, Collingwood and Melbourne and, in the first round of finals matches, Essendon defeated Geelong and Collingwood defeated Melbourne. Even at this stage it appeared Essendon would become the first VFL premier. When Essendon defeated Collingwood by 40 points in the second round, only freak results in the final round could deny the red and black the

The raffish Edgar Croft has a unique place in the League's history. He kicked the only goal for Essendon against Melbourne in the match that decided the 1897 premiership. This picture was taken on Croft's honeymoon in 1900.

flag. Essendon then made sure of the premiership by defeating Melbourne by the only goal of the match in the third round. If Melbourne had defeated Essendon, a "grand final" between Essendon and Geelong would have been played the next week. The Essendon-Melbourne match was played in front of just 3800 fans at the Lake Oval. Neither side managed a goal in the first half and there seemed no breaking of the deadlock until just before three-quarter time when a shot by Essendon's "Tracker" Forbes fell short and the ball was marked close to goal by teammate Edgar Croft, who converted for the only goal of the match. As *The Herald-Standard* of September 4 reported: "Forbes took a shot, but kicked badly. Croft snapped it up and put on a goal, which had been fought for hard and long."

Oddly enough it was the second time he had been Essendon's sole goalkicker. Earlier in the year he kicked the only major in a score of 1.13 to 2.3. Before that he had kicked six points straight.

1907 Geelong
players Alf Gough,
Bill Eason, Henry
Young and Ted
Rankin in the
oufits of their era.

One of the earliest photographs of League football - Essendon versus Collingwood at East Melbourne, August 20, 1898.

The inaugural VFL season gave no indication that the new body would become the most powerful in the nation. The VFL competed fiercely for public acceptance in this first year and the VFA more than held its own, despite the body blow of losing most of its powerful clubs. However, the VFL at least was up and running and, as it was to prove in later years, there was no stopping once it gained momentum.

POOR OLD ST KILDA

St Kilda won its place in the VFL in 1897 mainly because of its superb ground, the Junction Oval. The St Kilda club itself had little else to offer. Its on-field performances were far from glorious and there were many who believed the club would struggle to stay competitive in the League.

St Kilda had never been a strong club and had been forced to amalgamate with other clubs early in its existence. In fact St Kilda had merged with the Prahran club in 1888, only for Prahran to reform several years later. St Kilda had finished ninth of 13 clubs in the 1896 VFA competition and was expected to finish at the bottom of the new competition.

These fears were justified and the Saints collected the first VFL wooden spoon, failing to win a match in 1897. St Kilda's misery continued the following year and by the end of the third VFL season and the nineteenth century it had yet to break through for a League victory. Indeed, in one match in 1899 St Kilda was on the receiving end of a terrible hiding from Geelong. The Pivotonians amassed the huge score of 23.14 (162) to St Kilda's solitary behind - still the lowest score in League history.

St Kilda opened the 1900 season more in hope than anticipation in a match against Melbourne, which had finished sixth the previous season. Even the most optimistic of St Kilda fans had little hope of success, despite a vigorous recruiting campaign over the previous few months.

To the amazement of all, St Kilda raced to a huge lead in the first quarter. Melbourne hit back hard and trailed by just one point with only seconds to play. The bell rang to signal the match, but Melbourne's Wardill raced in to kick a behind to level scores. The behind was allowed to stand and the match was declared a draw.

St Kilda, heartbroken at being deprived of its first VFL victory, immediately lodged a protest which was heard by the VFL the following Friday night. The match was awarded to the Saints on protest and *The Australasian* newspaper declared: "No further question could be raised by cavilling critics concerning their (St Kilda's) right to representation on the League".

St Kilda not only had won a match, but finally had won its right·to play at the highest level. But it took St Kilda another 66 years to win its first VFL premiership. Incidentally, St Kilda's 1897-1900 drought ran to 48 games which is still a VFL record. The second longest sequence is North's 35 losses between 1933 and 1935. St Kilda went 32 games without a win but with one draw from 1947-48. South Melbourne (now the Sydney Swans) went 29 games without a win in 1972-73.

St Kilda, which was formed in 1873, had trouble creating its own identity in its early years. The club originally wore red and white uniforms, but later adopted the now familiar red, white and black. However, World War I forced St Kilda into a change of colors yet again as Germany's national colors were red, white and black. St Kilda opted to play in the Belgian colors of red, black and yellow and maintained this uniform until 1922 when it reverted to red, white and black.

The only other club to have changed colors during its VFL career has been Fitzroy, which at various times has worn maroon and gold, maroon and navy blue, maroon, blue and white, and maroon, blue and gold. Melbourne switched to a lighter shade of blue for color television in 1975, but reverted to navy blue in 1987. Most other clubs have had design alterations.

When Richmond entered the VFL in 1908 its guernsey design was black and yellow stripes (although in its VFA days Richmond wore black, yellow and blue). Richmond switched to a black guernsey with a yellow band in 1911 and adopted its present design of black with a yellow sash in 1914. North Melbourne has had many variations on its

royal blue and white and Hawthorn wore a brown guernsey with a gold vee until 1950. It also briefly wore a gold guernsey with a brown vee.

Chapter Three

1898-1908

Amateur but popular

The Victorian football public had to make some tough choices after the formation of the VFL for the 1897 season. Would they stay with the old VFA, or flock to the new competition?

Naturally, fans followed their clubs regardless of which competition these clubs were involved in, but minor competitions also had tremendous support. In fact, *The Australasian* newspaper set the example for most newspapers of the time by refusing to acknowledge one competition superior to the other and, in fact, many junior clubs had as many supporters as VFL or VFA clubs. This was especially true in the country and football clubs in the Ballarat and Bendigo areas had huge followings. There were even moves to introduce clubs from these areas to either the VFL or the VFA. There also were suggestions the VFA and the VFL forget their differences and combine for a promotion-relegation system. However, the wounds of 1897 proved impossible to heal and the two bodies settled down to a war of attrition that lasted for decades.

The VFL won its battle to wrest the best grounds from the VFA and attendances climbed in the 1898 season, only to fall short of expectations during the finals series. That, however, was the VFL's fault for devising a finals system which not only was confusing to the public, but also had little relation to the home and away season of 14 rounds. The League decided that after that series the competition would be divided into two sections of four teams each for two separate series of round robin matches. The winners of these two series then would play off in the grand final, with the proviso that if the team on top of the ladder at the end of the home and away season failed to finish on top of its section it would be given another chance. And that was what happened!

Essendon finished on top of the ladder, but Fitzroy and Collingwood headed the section play-offs. Collingwood and Fitzroy then played a semi-final, with Essendon to play the winner in the grand final. Fitzroy defeated Collingwood by 11 points and then defeated Essendon by 15 points in what really was the first VFL grand final. The match, played at the Junction Oval, attracted just over 16,000 fans, a reflection on the poor program designed to determine the season's premier club.

The VFL also had to contend with a bitter dispute over the actual grand final venue, although this fierce debate eventually led to the thorough planning of finals matches and the selection of appropriate finals venues. It was left to the Essendon and Fitzroy delegates to choose the match venue, with Essendon nominating South Melbourne's Lake Oval and Fitzroy wanting the match played at the Junction Oval. Essendon bitterly opposed Fitzroy's choice and at first refused to take part in the match, adding considerably to public confusion.

Essendon claimed, justifiably, that the Junction Oval was unsuitable for a grand final as the ground had been top-dressed in preparation for the cricket

Fitzroy's 1898 flag side.

season. The League was asked to intervene and Essendon's protest was dismissed. The final went ahead only after the Essendon players met on the eve of the match and decided to compete to maintain faith with the paying public.

The Leader newspaper had this to say about the VFL's great grand final fiasco: "The objection of Essendon to play the deciding match against Fitzroy on the St Kilda ground can have caused very little surprise . . . it is worse than folly to ask two crack teams to play off for the premiership on a turf that has been recently top-dressed, and which has been surrounded by one of those abominations 'an asphalt cycling track' which may be useful enough in keeping down the cycle-riding population, but which will never be favoured as a means of decimating the ranks of footballers".

Essendon was quite right in its protestations; the ground was not up to scratch, but its poor condition - the newly-laid soil was blown in all directions by strong winds - had little effect on the match.

Essendon, then known as the Same Old, had lost its crown to Fitzroy.

Fitzroy's success marked an amazing recovery as the club had been riddled with dissension at the start of the 1898 season, perhaps due to the committee's edict that players had to attend at least two training sessions a week and exercise in the gymnasium. This "radical" concept worked and as Fitzroy gathered strength in the latter part of the season, others fell by the wayside.

One team to fall out of contention was Geelong which suffered the huge double blow of losing its star ruckman Henry Young with a broken leg and star rover Teddy Rankin with typhoid. The Pivotonians still made the four, but were not the power of the previous year. Essendon's quest for a second premiership hit a snag when champion forward Albert Thurgood was prevented from rejoining the club. Thurgood had been in Western Australia for a few years and when he returned to Victoria in June, 1898, red and black fans rubbed their hands with glee. But the League refused to grant him a permit. At first no reason was given, but then it was decreed he would have to meet the normal 12-week residential rule applying to interstate players.

Increasing numbers of fans paid their sixpence to watch League games and the game continued to prosper. Umpires were, as ever, under scrutiny, but some writers found matters to praise. Field umpire McCoy was commended for varying the throw-in...there were no boundary umpires at this stage.

The dispute over the 1898 grand final showed the importance attached to home ground advantage and even at this stage Collingwood held one of the biggest ascendancies. 'Markwell' in *The Australasian* put it down to "tufts" and wrote: "...the tufty nature of Victoria Park makes drop kicking practically impossible. I know that in the matter of tufts the ground is vastly improved upon what it was a year or two ago". He said Collingwood players stuck to punt kicks while visitors wasted their time with dropkicks on the uneven surface.

During 1898 a deputation called on the League to push for University's inclusion, but they would have to wait another decade for their chance. Meanwhile, the VFL was refining its rules. When the first League season was played in 1897, there were 20 men to a team. In 1899 this was reduced to 18 which, of course, remains to this day. The VFA retained the 20-man rule for the time being and in 1900 introduced the Essendon A club to its competition. It was a blatant attempt to scuttle support for the VFL. Essendon Town (later known as Essendon A) wore the same red and black colors of the Essendon VFL club and, ironically, played its matches at the Essendon Recreation Reserve (Windy Hill). The Essendon VFL club played its home games at East Melbourne and did not shift to Windy Hill until 1921. The formation of the new VFA club was only partially successful and the Dreadnoughts or As (for Association) survived only until 1921.

The League had other problems, none the least

The 1898 grand final between Fitzroy and Essendon at the recently top-dressed St Kilda ground. The patchy condition of the Oval almost caused the cancellation of the match.

being the search for a successful means of determining the premiership. Although there was vigorous objection to the clumsy scheme introduced in 1898, it was decided to use the same system in 1899. This time the top club, Fitzroy, won its divisional series and played South Melbourne in the grand final. It was a foregone conclusion and only 4823 people watched the grand final at the Junction Oval. Fitzroy won by just one point in appallingly muddy conditions.

There was a widespread and cynical belief that the League had only let the game go ahead because the muddy ground would give South a better chance to win and thus set up another game (and financial windfall) as Fitzroy had the right of challenge. Certainly money was a big component in the VFL's thinking as St Kilda Cricket Club wanted only 10 per cent of the takings compared with East Melbourne's demand of one-third. The best location, the MCG, was again unavailable as it had been top-dressed immediately after the home and away matches.

The opening round of 1900 provided little guide to what lay ahead with premiers Fitzroy tripping up on the "tufts" of Victoria Park and Melbourne suffering the shame of a defeat at the hands of St Kilda which had not won a game in three years of League competition. Fitzroy's loss was only a temporary aberration, but Melbourne's path to September was tortuous. By the end of the home and away matches Melbourne lay in sixth place, or third last, yet the team hit its straps in the sectional play-offs and proved the folly of the finals system by reaching the grand final against Fitzroy.

> " . . . the tufty nature of Victoria Park makes drop kicking practically impossible."

The Maroons were so confident of notching a hat-trick of flags they had carriages bearing the signs "Fitzroy- Premiers 1900" waiting to whisk them away to a celebration dance, but Melbourne had other ideas and withstood a storming finish to win by four points before a crowd of 20,181 people. It was the biggest attendance at a football match for a decade.

For all its inconsistency Melbourne had plenty of talent in its ranks and its ruck of George Moodie, Vic Cumberland and Fred McGinis was one of the best following divisions of all time. Rover McGinis had often been dogged by illness and injury, but at his top was the best footballer in Australia. He was best afield in the grand final and was rated the footballer of the year by experts. Tragically his career would be cut short by an eye injury within a year of his premiership triumph. Most people of his era who were still around by the time of Bunton and Nash in the 1930s, thought that McGinis was the greatest of all time. One teammate, Jack Leith said: "He was the daddy of them all. When we were being pressed, Fred would save us by his back play, when we needed goals he notched them, when a rover or follower was required Fred filled the breech, if the centre was weak he strengthened it. And didn't he win a match for us when he was on the wing?" His greatest asset was his perfect passing to position.

A lesser light in the premiership win was winger Corrie Gardner who four years later earned the unusual distinction of being Australia's sole representative at the 1904 Olympics in St Louis.

One of the highlights early in the season was the comeback of the legendary Albert Thurgood who had spent most of the previous five years in the West then encountered clearance hurdles on his return to Victoria. Thurgood had played one game in 1899, then was slipped back into Essendon's side for the third round match against Collingwood. He responded with a dazzling burst of four goals in the third quarter and six for the day. In measuring the quality of the performance it is worth noting that an eight goal score for a team was generally enough to win a game Thurgood booted 25 goals for the season and headed the goalkicking.

Thurgood only played a handful of games in the first months of the 1901 season, but was devastating when he returned just before the finals. Heading a potent attack alongside Fred Hiskins, Thurgood played one of his greatest games in the semi and kicked five of Essendon's six goals and shepherded for Larkin to score the other. Just for good measure he played at centre half-back when Essendon kicked against the wind! Strangely Collingwood's out of form centre half-back Jack Monohan was omitted from the grand final side even though he had previously been able to hold Thurgood. Monohan was a champion player, and the decision would be a point of discussion for years afterwards as the Magpies were comprehensively beaten in the grand final. The crowd of 30,000 at the grand final topped off another year of financial success for the VFL, but writers were already warning of the dire threat of 'under the table' payments and professionalism.

There were still alarmingly amateurish happenings in League games and none was more embarrassing than the fiasco in a Collingwood-Fitzroy game when the bell rang after only 20 minutes of play in the last quarter. Fitzroy was attacking strongly and looked about to make a breakthrough, but Collingwood scraped home. The Maroons protested, to no avail. It was Fitzroy that broke the famous "Collingwood System". The Magpies had left opposition in their wake as they embarked on revolutionary preparation that even included the use of blackboards before games to arrange set-plays! Fitzroy countered it by advising every player to pick up one man and stick like glue. It sounds fairly basic today, but in those times it was a new concept. They especially countered Collingwood's Teddy Rowell, a long kicking centre half forward who had wrought havoc in the past. At that stage the main goalkicker was usually played at centre half-forward and it wasn't until Dick Lee established himself at Collingwood that the full-forward became the focus.

Football flourished in the earliest years of the twentieth century and it soon became obvious that the code was becoming far too big to be localised. There was an obvious need for a national body. VFL clubs, despite being fiercely parochial, recognised this and representative matches were played in country areas, with Ballarat a popular venue.

The VFL also decided to play a match in Sydney in an effort to halt the march of rugby. Fitzroy and Collingwood were despatched to Sydney and played in front of more than 15,000 fans at Moore Park on May 23, 1903. Fitzroy defeated the Magpies by 17 points and the game raised 600 pounds for the newly founded New South Wales Australian Football League. It was touted in press advertising as the "Great Exhibition Football match between the Victorian Football League teams Collingwood and Fitzroy under Australasian Rules. As played through Victoria, South Australia, Western Australia, the South and Western Districts of New South Wales, and recently established in South Africa."

Readers were told the game would probably attract 20,000 to 30,000 spectators if played in Victoria, and was "Fast, brilliant, scientific and exciting". The success of the match prompted the League to schedule a game between Geelong and Carlton in Sydney three months later. Geelong won by 10

points, but Victorian parochialism again raised its head and the League abandoned its brief flirtation with promotional matches in "heathen" areas.

The promotion of the game therefore was left to the Australian Football Council, which was formed in 1905 to oversee the game's development. This was done at the instigation of the VFL and delegates from all over Australia and even from New Zealand helped form the body now known as the National Australian Football Council. Meanwhile, the VFL was ever aware of its rivalry with the VFA and in 1902 adopted what was known as the Argus finals system in an attempt to generate greater public enthusiasm in the fight for the premiership. *The Argus* newspaper argued, with considerable justification, that the divisional system was far too clumsy and proposed that the VFL organise a simple play-off system at the end of the home and away season.

> **The crowd of 30,000 at the grand final topped off another year of financial success for the VFL.**

It was finally agreed that the first and third teams would play off, with the second and fourth teams also playing off. The two winners then would play a grand final. The idea proved a sensational success and a then phenomenal attendance of 35,502 watched Collingwood and Essendon in the first grand final to be played at the Melbourne Cricket Ground.

Essendon, the reigning premier, had been expected to do well in the grand final. The Dons had won six matches in succession and *The Argus* commented they had been "in splendid form". Collingwood defeated Essendon by 33 points to the surprise of few Magpies fans. After all, Collingwood had been Essendon's conqueror seven weeks earlier. The Magpies were definitely the team to beat in 1902. They only went down twice in the home and away games before a shock loss to Fitzroy in the semifinal, but recovered to win their first flag. During the season Collingwood had travelled to Tasmania and to relieve the boredom against a local side had toyed with a style of stab-kicking and short passing that bewildered the islanders.

Chief practitioner of what would become known as "the system" was champion rover Dick Condon and when the Magpies disembarked at their next League engagement they decided to try the method at the top level even though many players were still feeling the effects of a rough trip across Bass Strait. It was a dazzling success and Geelong was the first of many sides to be ploughed under in ruthless fashion.

Money was looming larger and larger in the minds of football people and whispers grew to a crescendo when Collingwood star Teddy Rowell was accused of having played "stiff" against Fitzroy.

The allegations that Rowell had accepted money to play poorly were eventually quashed, but the trauma knocked Collingwood off balance for several weeks. At one stage the disheartened player resigned from the club, but returned when his reputation was cleared. Another unsavoury affair took place in the members' reserve at Carlton where umpire Crapp was kicked as he left the field, but the Blues had reason for a brighter outlook as the club had its best VFL season thanks to the coaching of Jack Worrall.

The football world was stunned when Essendon's champion Albert Thurgood was suspended in a controversial tribunal hearing that found him guilty of striking two St Kilda players. His teammates were so outraged they threatened to pull out of League representative sides in protest, but Thurgood eventually calmed them down. He was suspended on the Friday night before a vital game against Fitzroy and before charging into battle Essendon players gave him three cheers. Enforcement of rules was somewhat lax in those days and many people smelt a rat when reports listed a "Goodthur" as playing a key role in defence during Essendon's victory. However subsequent research has indicated that it may have been another player who took the field under that name.

The Dons had bigger problems at the start of 1903 when they lost a large slab of experience with the retirement of Thurgood, and the departure to Western Australia of Fred Hiskins and Hugh Gavin. Hiskins left under a cloud as there were "questions over his loyalty" according to one newspaper, but he would return to the club three years later.

As the Essendon run of success came to an end, Carlton was on the way up. The Blues kicked off the 1903 season by rolling defending premiers Collingwood and went on to reach the finals. Only late season injuries caused the Blues to falter and lose the semi-final to Collingwood. They weren't even fazed when they had to postpone a match at Geelong because of a railway strike. Despite all his footballing powers, Jack Worrall could not arrange a last minute boat trip and the game was postponed until later in the season when it was played in Sydney as a follow-up to the earlier game between Collingwood and Fitzroy. In the last game before the finals Carlton was cheered onto the field by their rivals St Kilda who well knew how hard it was to get off the bottom of the ladder.

But the Saints, for a long time the competition's "ugly duckling", were another team to show how the competition had evened up. Bolstered by the addition of Tasmanian rover Victor Barwick and ex-Melbourne ruckman Vic Cumberland, the Saints had a purple patch early in June when they rolled Melbourne, South and Geelong in the space of only seven days. The magnitude of the improvement could be measured by the fact that prior to June St Kilda's yield from six and a bit seasons and 102 games had been two wins and a draw!

Even though there were veiled comments that Collingwood, among others, was paying its players, the approach of players was hardly professional. Thus it was reported that Melbourne had to find a substitute for winger Corrie Gardiner "who was away on holidays".

Victorian pride had been pricked by three con-

The packed crowd at the 1903 grand final.

secutive losses to South Australia and state selectors chose what was described as the strongest state team for years. The only point of contention was the omission of Fitzroy's Chris Kiernan "but he has played rather indifferently at times", said *The Australasian's* Markwell. Kiernan's time at Fitzroy was studded with major controversy despite the fact that he was a gifted player in wet or dry conditions.

Early in his career Kiernan was reminded by one writer that "tripping is no part of the stock-in-trade of an accomplished footballer". Fitzroy sacked him in 1904 and there was a wide held belief that his dismissal was due to his lack of effort in a crucial game. The league rejected his applications for a clearance to Collingwood and South in what virtually amounted to a lifetime ban. He made a brief reappearance for Fitzroy in 1911, but by then his best football was well behind him.

The Vics slaughtered the South Australians by nine goals thanks largely to the Collingwood quartet of Dick Condon, Jack Monahan, Charlie Pannam

and Ted Rowell. Collingwood's clashes with Fitzroy were the meeting of two distinct styles and the Maroons applied close checking tactics to try to stifle Collingwood's short-passing game. In one match Tammy Beauchamp, one of Fitzroy's best players, was assigned the job of quelling Ted Rowell, but writers scoffed at the approach saying that his "day was practically wasted in unsuccessful efforts to hamper the play of Rowell". Taggers were obviously not an idea with great appeal and would have to wait several decades for acceptance.

On a hot gusty afternoon Collingwood staved off Fitzroy in a classic battle for the flag. After his side had two successive misses Fitzroy's Percy Trotter found his captain Gerald Brosnan with a pass as the bell rang. Brosnan coolly lined up for goal, but his shot was just wide and Collingwood took the flag by two points. Collingwood defender Bill Proudfoot maintained in later years that the shot was so close he had heard the lace of the ball clip the post!

The Magpies lost Rowell and McCormack to

Western Australia at the start of 1904, but regained their former champion "Charger" Hailwood. The traffic of players to and from the West was hectic and indicative of the increasing spectre of professionalism. Players standing out of the game for a year had been able to win automatic clearances prior to 1904, but the League's permit rules were changed so they had to stand out for a minimum of three years.

It was a sufficient deterrent to be "a clean knockout to the migratory merchants" according to one writer. The same scribe was aghast when he reported that he had heard of a leading VFA player who had hawked his services around several clubs "for a stipulated amount per week". He may have been referring to Bill Monagle, the Port Melbourne star who was denied a permit to play for South Melbourne.

The introduction of boundary umpires was hailed as a boon to the game and was seen as a step forward. From the first round of 1904 the pace of VFL football quickened. Promoting the game in Sydney continued to be one of the League's aims, but Essendon felt the backlash after its visit to the harbor city for a game with Melbourne which drew a crowd of only 6000. The Dons' torrid sea trip back to Melbourne took a couple of days longer than expected and by the last term of the following match against Fitzroy they were virtually at a standstill. The League was criticised for maintaining its "hopeless crusade against rugby".

Fitzroy, seasoned in handling the pressure of grand finals, ran over the top of a Carlton side appearing in its first play-off. The Maroons were fast, brilliant and well-manned all over the field and had the ability to produce something out of the ordinary at the right time in big games. Such an effort was the performance of full-back Fred Fontaine in the 1904 grand final when he grabbed the ball in the teeth of goal, ran to the centre and passed to Trot-

> **Promoting the game in Sydney continued to be one of the League's aims, but it was criticised for maintaining its "hopeless crusade against rugby".**

ter, who slammed on a vital goal. From that moment the result was never in doubt. Redoubtable captain Gerald Brosnan headed a magnificent ruck that was at the core of the team's success. The club recovered from a mid-season flat spot to storm home to a second successive flag in 1905 and Fitzroy established itself as the dominant force in League football as its membership boomed to 2650.

There was added satisfaction in having scored victory over arch rival Collingwood in the grand final and the head-on clashes between the neighbouring suburbs were the highpoints of the season. Bitterness between the two was said to be more prevalent between the supporters than among the players, and Fitzroy was accustomed to being pelted with bluestone whenever leaving the Collingwood area after a match. The Maroons devised a way of ensuring safe passage in their horse-drawn carriages as a Collingwood player would accompany them on the running board to deter home fans from attacking.

Despite that there were still times when violence boiled over on the ground and in one match police had to intervene in an on-field dust-up. The League protested vehemently against this disturbing trend.

Meanwhile the Sydney thrust continued to falter as Fitzroy and South played a demonstration game which was a flop. The holiday nature of the trip had ramifications later when South sacked one of its players, Jack "Paddy" Hassett, for his behavior. Hassett, a state representative a year earlier, was left in limbo until Geelong picked him up in early 1907.

Committee upheavals were not all that common in the early days, but prior to 1905 there were shock waves at VFL and VFA clubs. Richmond's committee was dumped after its part in the 1904 VFA grand final fiasco (Richmond had forfeited the 1904 grand final because it refused to accept the umpire appointed to the game), and St Kilda jettisoned its executive for squandering finances. This was the start of many years of off-field brawling for the Saints, and like most of the other ensuing administrative

Jubilation at the 1903 grand final between Collingwood and Fitzroy. The Magpies won by two points.

ructions, it had little effect on lifting the team's performance.

One heartening aspect for St Kilda came late in the 1905 season when it introduced an outsized lad from Benalla. Dave McNamara had originally been approached by South Melbourne, but the Swans told him that they would not be changing their side in the run-up to the finals. St Kilda's former rover "Curly" Jones convinced McNamara there was more future at St Kilda and he was whisked into the senior team without even a practice run. At six foot four inches, McNamara was a giant in this era, and the Saints could not find a pair of knickers big enough to fit him.

The lofty country lad in the painfully tight pants was met with derision when he won his first possession and placing it on the mound for a place kick, shot at goal from 65 yards out. It was suggested that he return to the bush to dig his rabbit burrows, but when he unleashed a mighty kick the hecklers were silenced forever. It was the first of four matchwinning goals for the day and of many that McNamara would kick during the next two decades. Ironically the first side to suffer at his hands was South Melbourne, the club which had fobbed him off.

Some things in football were no different to to-

day and a squabble between the rival leagues meant there was no interstate fixture against South Australia, which instead decided to play against a VFA side. The League sent a team to Ballarat, but the selection of that side was clouded when Collingwood refused to submit a list of suitable players due to a dispute with the permit committee.

Clubs increased the turnover of personnel in the quest for success and nowhere was this more evident than at Essendon where eight new players made their debuts in the opening round of 1906. League clubs turned their recruiting attentions towards the VFA and South netted crack Williamstown sharpshooter Len "Mother" Mortimer and Richmond's rover Charlie Ricketts. Even the VFA's best umpire, Allen, the man who had been at the centre of the 1904 finals fiasco, crossed to the League.

Bolstered by its recruits, South looked strong in the early part of the year, but Carlton was the club that set the pace. The Blues had a gifted attack which included Frank "Silver" Caine, George Topping, and the veteran Mick Grace. The Blues had talent to burn and its centre-line of George Bruce, Rod McGregor and Ted Kennedy was said to be the greatest of all time.

The wily Grace became the first man to kick 50 goals in a VFL season and helped the Blues triumph over his old club Fitzroy in the grand final. He was at the forefront of a deadly attack which kicked 15.4 to Fitzroy's 6.9. The last eight Carlton goals came without a miss.

This first Carlton flag was a tribute to coach Jack Worrall who had an uncanny eye for discovering footy talent. One of the most famous stories concerned the signing of Dave Gillespie. Gillespie was a local boy who often scouted the outer for the ball at training. One night he jumped the fence and kicked the ball back to a forward practising his goalkicking. Worrall immediately told him to go inside and get a uniform and Gillespie became a fine player. Worrall was similarly blunt in assessing Rod McGregor when he came to the club for a practice run.

"When do you get your clearance?" he asked McGregor in the rooms. Worrall introduced revolutionary training methods which made his men stretch for short, low stab passes. He would take the ruck aside and work with them individually and collectively in a manner which is parallel to the specialist training of today.

While Carlton prospered, all was not rosy at other clubs. Essendon and Collingwood kept their places in the 1906 four but only after surviving early season division. Dissent at Essendon centred on the return of champion forward Fred Hiskins after a three season absence, as he had been under suspicion of not giving his best when he had departed.

The Magpies' nest was also in a disturbed state as the committee believed some men were not trying their hardest under the captaincy of Alf "Rosie" Dummett, who had been a compromise choice in the first place. It was even suggested that some players were not passing to certain others because of the dissatisfaction, but the trouble subsided when Dummett stood down and Arthur Leach was appointed in his place.

Relations between the VFL and the South Australians were still strained and when the Croweaters came to Melbourne for a clash with the VFA, the League rescheduled games to divert the crowds. The scheme worked but resulted in a barrage of criticism for the VFL's action, and there was a touch of irony a year later when the League put back a round of matches because it did not wish to detract from the attendance at the visiting Canadian lacrosse team's game! On the same day a VFL team journeyed to South Australia as the two warring leagues had kissed and made up.

League matches were starting to draw huge crowds and 32,000 people saw a vital clash between South and Carlton. A lift in prices was said to have dampened enthusiasm for the finals, but it wasn't just the fans who turned their backs. Collingwood's Herbert Pears was unavailable for selection in the semi-final as he had left for the shearing season in Queensland! The VFA started to hit back in 1907 and the free-spending Essendon Town lured Fitzroy star Percy Trotter away from the VFL. He was the first of many players to make the crossing.

Meanwhile Carlton did not have long to bask in the glory of its premiership success. Barely two hours after the flag had been unfurled the Blues trudged off Princes Park after being thrashed by St Kilda. The Saints had recruited strongly and trained as never before in a bid to finally make an improvement. The nomadic Vic Cumberland was back in the colors and he resumed his old partnership with star rover Vic Barwick. St Kilda had brilliant recruits in West Australian Bert Renfrey and Ballarat forward George Morrisey as well as the serviceable Charlie Clymo, who achieved greater fame in 1931 when he led Geelong to a flag in his one and only year of VFL coaching.

The Saints stormed to the top of the ladder with an unprecedented six wins in a row, and captured public imagination so much that for the Geelong game there were two extra trains arranged.

Collingwood and South battle out the 1907 second semi at the MCG.

But then it all went awry for St Kilda. The side was more suited to dry conditions and undoubtedly the onset of wet weather played a part, but there were other factors in the demise. A letter written by Bert Renfrey and published in a Perth newspaper shed light on the inside story. "The fault with us," wrote the much travelled half-back, "is that every man thinks he is a champion and reckons when he gets the ball he can beat everything near him. There is too much individual play. You would think teams here would have a lot of system, but St Kilda don't have as much as we did at West Perth."

St Kilda's winning run ended in a savage game against South before the biggest crowd ever seen at the Junction. Markwell in *The Australasian* wrote: "A gladiatorial display in ancient times usually worked spectators into a savage frenzy, and it seemed to me that a heavy percentage of last week's crowd had their uncivilised instincts similarly influenced". The bruising encounter stirred up such controversy that before the next game St Kilda's Jack Wells, at his committee's instigation, visited the Carlton rooms and it was decided the game would be played as it should be.

It was a rough season and the league was frequently criticised for burying its head in the sand. Late in August 1907, the VFL went to the other extreme and handed down stiff penalties after a Melbourne-Essendon game described as disgraceful. Melbourne's Hunt was rubbed out until the following June and Stevenson of Essendon until July. Even then the League was castigated for getting the wrong players.

The League also laid charges after a South and Carlton game. It was reported that Carlton's delegate had told South officials after the match that he had no complaints, but then Carlton's committee "acting under the sting of defeat" laid complaints against Franks and Gent of South Melbourne. South responded by tabling charges against Gotz, Marchbank and Elliott of Carlton. The League heard the charges from 8pm till midnight on Thursday then from 8 pm till 5 am the following night. Gotz was cleared, Elliott suspended for the rest of the season and Franks and Marchbank until the end of June 1908. Gent copped a life penalty for a striking charge and Markwell noted it in a matter-of-fact tone, adding that he and Franks had "been punished not for

The 1908 "Carnival" Teams

NEW ZEALAND

• *(All black with gold fern leaf on breast)*

Wright, Dempster, Fisher, Ross, Porter, Smith, West, Paul, Ward, Bonas, Patrick, Furness, McGrath, Abfalter, Fletcher, Marshall, Lording, Breese, George, Gillett, Monteith, Darby, Swann, Wickens, Elvidge.

NEW SOUTH WALES

• *(Royal blue with red waratah on breast, white shorts and royal blue socks)*

Thomas, Welch, Mansfield, McConchie, Robertson, Vanmam, Murray, Delaney, Dartnell, O'Leary, Shipton, Carrick, Renfrey, Scott, Millhouse, Meadows, Hunter, Conlon, Gluyas, Rahilly, Greere, Haines, Watson, O'Keefe.

SOUTH AUSTRALIA

• *(Brown with turquoise blue cuffs, armbands and socks, white shorts)*

Gwynne, Bahr, Chamberlain, Townsend, Bennett, Stoddart, Le Mesurier, McKenzie, Ewers, Hyman, Hewett, Tredrea, Wallace, Alcock, Dickson, Mack, Beere, Woollard, Leahy, Tierney, Johns, Geddes .

WESTERN AUSTRALIA

• *(Dark green with gold swan on breast, white shorts, green socks with white top)*

Crase, Everett, Dunn, Edwards, Doig, Gravenhall, Jeffrey, McNamara, Sharp, Ord, Swetnam, Thompson, Cook, Weatherall, Matson, O'Dea Robinson, Renwick, Polglase, Smith, Truscott, Trewhella, C. Tyson, G. Tyson.

QUEENSLAND

• *(Maroon with white Q on breast, white shorts, maroon socks with white tops)*

Lorondes, Greenwood, O'Dwyer, Kier, Atkinson, McKellar, Coates, Hicks, Hay, Morris, Miller, McGregor, Parker, Pagett, Heidmen, Mcdonald, McCormack, Holten, Kelly, Hopkins, Watts, Parkin, McMaster.

TASMANIA

• *(Green, with rose and primrose braces, map of Tasmania on breast with football in centre. Green socks, white shorts)*

Bailey, Tynan, Ride, Badcock, Orwood, Carter, Burrell, Ritter, Searle, Thompson, Bridges, Arnold, Ward, Russell, Trotter, Little, Woolley, Lee, Valentine, McLeod, Abel, Webb, Mahoney, Forster, Tucker, Gardner, Webster, Pannam.

VICTORIA

• *(Dark blue with white vee. Dark blue socks, white shorts)*

H. Kelly, W. Payne, G. Johnson, G. Bruce, R. McGregor (Carlton); R. Nash, W. Lee (Collingwood); W. Busbridge, P. Shea (Essendon); B. Bailes, H. Milne (Fitzroy); H. Young (captain) (Geelong); H. Purse (VC), A. Pearce (Melbourne); W. Luff (Richmond); A. Franks, A. Woods (South); D. McNamara, H. Lever, H. Cumberland, W. Stewart (St Kilda) and T. Ogilvie (University).

Footy's first great festival - the teams for the 1908 Carnival.
Full page feature in *The Leader*, August 22, 1908

offences in the recent match so much as for previous misdeeds".

St Kilda recovered from its slump to earn a finals berth, but was bundled out by Carlton in the semi. The Blues won a titanic struggle with South in the grand final. South came from behind and the result was still in the balance in the last, desperate minutes, but Carlton hung on to win by five points. The men rated the best two players in the competition, Carlton's "Mallee" Johnson and South's Hugh Callan, staged a magnificent battle in the ruck.

The VFL desperately wanted to expand and it was even suggested in 1906 that the League would admit not one, not two, but four clubs to its fold. Nothing eventuated until the end of 1907 when it was announced that University would be admitted. This news raised more than a few eyebrows as *The Argus* had suggested during the season that North Melbourne was the club most likely to be admitted. Another VFA club, the now-defunct West Melbourne, was also keen to gain League status, as was Richmond. University's admittance alone would have meant a bye, so the League invited Richmond to join, therefore depriving the VFA of yet another plum venue.

The choice of University as a League club was strange as the club's players had to be matriculants or holders of university degrees. As such, it was regarded as something of an elitist club. Understandably, these restrictions hampered the club and it lasted just seven seasons in the VFL, with World War I leading to its demise. University, known as the Students, wore black guernseys with a blue vee and shared Essendon's East Melbourne ground from 1908-10 and then played its home matches at the MCG. University played a total of 126 matches for 27 wins and two draws; it defeated every other club at least once, except Collingwood.

The Melbourne University Magazine of 1907 had this to say about the admittance of 'Varsity to the VFL: "At a general meeting of the Football Club (University), a resolution was unanimously passed that application be sought to the Football League of Victoria. This action excited much interest in football circles."

After several meetings the League unanimously invited to admit University into its ranks. To make the number of clubs even, the League admitted Richmond.

The Association disapproved of the action of Richmond in applying, saying it was also a sign of weakness on the part of the League to admit University . . . "The 'Varsity oval will not be ready for next season's League matches, and the use of one of the League's grounds will be secured. Several old University men playing in League football will be included in the 'Varsity team next season. Now that University sport is on a sound footing, it will be interesting to watch the football club's career in the first grade. The earnest support of all University men is required, as it will be a a hard struggle for a year or two."

In fact, University's seven VFL seasons were all hard, although the club won eight of its 18 matches in 1908 to finish a highly creditable sixth. Its players included Edward Cordner (father of Melbourne's famous Cordner brothers), Albert Hartkopf, Chris and Tom Fogarty and Mark Gardner.

The 1908 Melbourne University Magazine had this to say about its team's first season at VFL level: "The season that has just ended has been one of the greatest import in University sport. The entrance of the University into the first grade of football was watched with keen interest, and their success in their first year has been the subject of much congratulation. Taking the season right through, the team is to be heartily congratulated on their success, in their first essay in League football. We are looking forward to next season with interest. Ogilvie was selected to play with the Victorian Team in the Inter-

> Victorian Premier Thomas Bent described the carnival as one of the "great highlights in the history of Australian sport".

state matches, and there was great surprise when Seward was not selected."

Richmond, which eventually thrived in its new environment to became one of the power clubs of the competition, struggled in its first year of VFL and won only six of its 18 matches to finish second last, ahead of Geelong. Carlton won the first VFL premiership in a 10-team competition by defeating Essendon by nine points in the grand final at the MCG in front of a record 50,261 fans. It was Carlton's third successive premiership.

"PAST & PRESENT CHAMPIONS."

(6) C. FORBES, 1888-1902.
ESSENDON FOOTBALL CLUB.

Essendon stalwart "Tracker" Forbes.

The Carlton annual report of 1908 trumpeted: "The players merited unstinted praise for their season's work - all self was eliminated and every man played for his side. They were the best of comrades on and off the field, and their year's record was a triumph of sustained brilliance and consistency. They were in many tight corners, but with the one exception against Essendon, in the mud, emerged triumphant. In the opinion of many experts, no finer team ever stepped on to a football field."

The 1908 season was momentous , not only for Carlton and the VFL, but also for Australian football. The Australian Football Council, founded in 1905, organised the first "carnival", which was held in Melbourne during the season. All states, and New Zealand, were represented. It was the only time New Zealand was to compete in a carnival and the Kiwis, in their black guernseys with gold fern leaf motif, were far from disgraced and a bemused MCG crowd watched them perform a haka in front of the members' grandstand at the start of the carnival. In fact, New Zealand won two if its four matches and could have been an important link in the creation of Australian football as an international code had it not

been for World War I.

The carnival was won by Victoria, which won its three matches. Victorian Premier Thomas Bent described the carnival as one of the "great highlights in the history of Australian sport".

Skippered by Henry Young, the Victorian team was a magnificent side that bristled with talent. Young played with a broken finger and confided to friends that he would have played with a broken neck rather than miss the chance of leading the greatest side Victoria ever fielded. The young University rover Ogilvie was almost knocked over by the force of the hitouts directed to him by Young and fellow ruckman "Mallee" Johnson. Young had to advise him where to stand at ball-ups and from then on the combination worked more smoothly.

The carnival celebrating the jubilee year of Australian football was voted an overwhelming success and AFC delegates voted to play another carnival in Adelaide in 1911, which was won by a brilliant South Australian combination. South Australia defeated Victoria by 43 points - its first win over the big white vee for nine years.

CARDBOARD HEROES

Footballers were worshipped even in the earliest days of the VFL and the mere glimpse of a football hero sent fans into paroxysms of delight.

In those days footballers would have been lucky to train twice a week, with few fans at training to watch the stars. There were relatively few photographs of the stars in newspapers, but every sports fan would have been able to recognise the game's

F. JINKS   L. BECK   A. LAING   F. CAINE   C. HAMMOND

Carlton guns Fred Jinks, Les Beck, Alex Lang, "Silver" Caine and Charlie Hammond.

leading lights. Cigarette cards, most of them elaborately produced, were enormously popular and helped many players reach "star" status.

Star players before World War I included Carlton's Jack and Vin Gardiner, Alan (Essendon) and Vic (South Melbourne) Belcher, St Kilda's Dave McNamara and Vic Cumberland, Essendon's Hugh Gavin and Charles "Tracker" Forbes, Fitzroy's Jim Freake, Collingwood's Dick Lee and Carlton's Billy Dick, just to mention a few.

Then, as now, it was every small boy's ambition to one day play at League level. It was a competition for the elite, although the VFA was still regarded by many to be as strong as the VFL. A young Billy Dick was invited to train with Carlton in 1908, but was told by supporters that he would not get a game at the premiership club. Dick therefore played with Fitzroy before transferring to Carlton in 1911 and then leading the Blues to their 1914 premiership triumph. Dick, who also captained Victoria in 1914, only left Fitzroy because of internal problems at the Brunswick Street club at the end of the 1910 season. He went on to become a tremendous favourite with Carlton fans.

Carlton's Gardiner brothers were destined to play for the Blues as their father, Jack Snr MLA, had been club captain during Carlton's early years. Vin, however, started his League career with Melbourne and played two games before shifting to Carlton in 1907 for a long and distinguished career of 157 games. Vin, despite being short and lightly-built, played as a key forward and actually topped the VFL goalkicking with 46 goals in 1911. Brother Jack started his career with Carlton, but switched to Melbourne after a short stint in Tasmania.

The Belcher brothers were regarded as two of the greatest players of their era. Alan started his career with Collingwood and played four games for the Magpies before transferring to Essendon in 1906. A big man, he had a tremendous temperament and always set a fine example for Essendon in the ruck. He was Essendon captain in 1910 and again from 1912-15. Brother Vic played a then record 226 games for South Melbourne and also was a tower of strength in the ruck or in a key position. He has the distinction of being the only player in the club's history to have played in two VFL premiership sides with the red and white as he was a member of the 1909 and 1918 premiership sides. He was club captain from 1913-16 and again in 1920.

Charles "Tracker" Forbes played in Essendon's inaugural VFL side, which defeated Geelong by 23 points at the old Corio Oval. Forbes at that stage was a long-established Essendon favourite. He had joined the red and black from local club North Park and was voted champion of the colony in 1891. A great high mark, Forbes played 54 VFL games for Essendon, but his best years were in the VFA.

His strength was high marking and he was one of the men who brought this feature to the game. As a youth he had been a Melbourne fan and was on his way there for a trial when the gatekeeper refused to let him into the ground, whereupon Essendon snapped him up.

Melbourne lived to regret the attendant's move as in future years Forbes played some magnificent games against them. His kind hearted nature off the field was legendary and when he was working in a factory where other workers were being retrenched he volunteered to leave to keep a married man in a job. On the field he once became so irritated by St Kilda rover "Curly" Jones that he deposited the diminutive Saint on a seat outside the fence! Although he was 32-years-old when the VFL formed he was still a power and marked, kicked and ran better than most youngsters. He lifted himself for the 1897 finals and showed his best form of the year to be instrumental in the Dons' first flag.

Teammate Hugh Gavin played his first game for Essendon against Carlton during the 1897 season and went on to play 108 games with the club. He was regarded as possibly the best defender of his era and as almost unbeatable at centre half-back. Gavin abandoned his VFL career at one stage to play for West Australian club Boulder, but returned to Essendon in 1904 before accepting the position as coach of VFA club Essendon Town.

St Kilda might have had a miserable start in the VFL, but it had several of its greatest players. Vic Cumberland was regarded as the best ruckman in the VFL. A football nomad, Cumberland played with several clubs, including Melbourne and Sturt. His career was severely interrupted by World War I, and

he played his last VFL game with St Kilda at the age of 43 in 1920. He remains as the oldest footballer ever to have played League football. A poet of the time wrote of Cumberland, who won a Magarey Medal with Sturt and was wounded three times in World War I:

"His height is just on five foot ten, His weight is thirteen stone, And on every football field, A champion he is known.

"The finest player of them all, We've seen what he can do. He's the greatest champion on the ball, St Kilda ever knew.

"When from the ruck he brings it out, Or taps it with his hand, You'll hear the familiar shout Of 'Good Boy Cumberland'."

Cumberland had two great teammates in David McNamara, possibly the greatest kicker of a football the game has seen, and the brilliant Victor Barwick, a Tasmanian who was regarded as the best rover of his era. Barwick played 104 games for the Saints from 1903-09 and in 1913.

Fitzroy's Jim Freake, along with Collingwood's Dick Lee, was one of the VFL's first goalkicking stars. Freake, who was small and lightly-framed, used guile to score his goals and his speed made him a difficult player to counter. He shared the 1915 VFL goalkicking honors with Lee, both players scoring 66 (then a League record) for the season. Ironically, Freake had wanted to play for Collingwood, but Lee's presence at Victoria Park thwarted those ambitions. He won the VFL goalkicking in 1913 with 56 goals, but Lee topped the table no less than 10 times (including twice as joint-winner). Freake kicked 442 goals in a 174-game career with Fitzroy and once kicked 10 goals in a match. Lee had an even better record as he kicked a massive 707 goals from 230 games and once kicked 11 goals in a match.

Albert Franks is a name that means nothing to the present generation of fans, and it could be said that he was not even one of the dominant players of his era.

> Then, as now, it was every small boy's ambition to one day play at League level. It was a competition for the elite.

Yet his was a turbulent career that would make him one of the game's great characters if he played today. A wild, woolly and frequently spiteful ruckman who also had a great deal of talent, he had a career spiced with controversy after coming from West Australia.

Some idea of his toughness can be gained from the time that he was working on a rabbit fence in outback WA and received the call to play for North Fremantle. He hit the trail on foot, lost it in the bush and ran out of damper. For the last 40 miles he was given food by farm hands and after walking 100 miles caught a train on Friday night which arrived at Fremantle at 11.45 am the next day. At 2.45 he was in the dressing rooms and despite his feet being covered in blisters was one of the best afield!

He had impressed Melbourne observers with his play for the visiting 1904 WA state side at full-back and was strong in the air as well as being a fine drop kick from the ruck. He had great endurance, but there was a darker side to his game and one writer of the time said: "He frequently resorted to unsportsmanlike and unwarranted tactics." In 1907 Carlton's committee reported him for striking their players during a particularly savage game just before the finals. He was suspended until the following June which prevented him from locking horns with the Blues in the grand final.

Some satisfaction was gained in 1909 when he and Vic Belcher controlled the ruck duels to give South a flag win over the Blues. After a tribunal hearing that involved his team-mate Casey in June 1910, Franks was accused of insulting and assaulting umpire Tulloch outside the building. He was found guilty of abusing the umpire, but the assault charge could not be proven. The League stood him down indefinitely and refused to lift the embargo in 1911. He returned in the first game of 1912 and at one stage looked like retaliating, but controlled himself

> In 1888, Worrall decided to temporarily concentrate on his cricket career so he could tour England with the Australian team. He played 11 Tests for Australia.

and one writer said he had "stopped getting cross at trifles".

In all he played 99 games and kicked 64 goals for South from 1906 to 1913. After that he transferred to North Melbourne in the VFA, but his fire showed no signs of dimming and he was one of the culprits in a notoriously vicious exhibition match against St Kilda in 1915.

JOHN WORRALL, THE FIRST COACH

It generally is conceded that when former Fitzroy footballer and Australian Test cricketer John Worrall was appointed secretary of Carlton in 1902 he became the first officially-appointed League coach.

Before Worrall's appointment, club captains assumed the role of the planning and execution of training sessions, devising match tactics (if any) and generally guiding the team through a match.

Worrall started his football career with South Ballarat, a strong provincial club. Even then he had tremendous ambition and, after impressing Fitzroy in a match against the Maroons in 1884, he was invited to shift to Melbourne to play for Fitzroy. Fitzroy secretary C.S. Cook knew that several other Melbourne clubs were chasing the brilliant defender, but was able to find Worrall employment at *The Age*. Worrall accepted the position and later became one of Australia's most prominent sports journalists.

Worrall, who had tremendous eyesight, combined football, cricket and journalism successfully until 1888 when he decided to temporarily concentrate on his cricket career so he could tour England with the Australian team. He played 11 Tests for Australia and in one match for the Carlton Cricket Club against University in 1896 he scored a then Australian record of 417 not out. Worrall was Fitzroy Football Club captain from 1886-7 and was reappointed to the position on his return from the cricket tour of England.

He was named champion of the colony of Victoria in 1887 and 1890 and was praised as one of the greatest exponents of long-distant kicking in the game. He played mainly on the half-back flank early in his career, but excelled as a rover with Fitzroy. It was suggested that he was the best rover of the pre-VFL era and undoubtedly was one of the game's biggest stars in an era of stars. Worrall was troubled by injuries late in his football career, resigned as Fitzroy's captain in 1892 and played his last match against Essendon on September 17, 1892.

The Carlton club, which had had a dismal season in 1901, appointed Worrall secretary-manager for 1902. He took on the role on one condition. "I must have sole power in putting players on and off the training list," he demanded. Worrall, a man of strong character and fiercely independent, involved himself in all club activities and assumed the role of what we know to be club coach. He recruited extensively, planned and supervised training and spoke to players about tactics before games.

When Worrall was appointed he made it clear he wanted full authority to guide the team as he saw fit. He also told the Carlton committee the club desperately needed new players. Worrall scoured the land for talent and even went to the trouble of seeking footballers who would suit his "game plan". He wanted a long-kicking, high-marking side capable of crushing the opposition. He was years ahead of his time.

Carlton virtually had a new team in 1902, but Worrall took some time to get his message across to the players. This did not deter Worrall, who had told the Carlton committee that he was unable to produce miracles. Discipline was paramount and Worrall shocked his players when he told them: "Boys, booze and football do not mix. You have to cut back on one or the other. Players who prefer beer to eucalyptus will be struck off the list". Carlton finished sixth in 1902, but climbed to third in 1903. Carlton was on its way, but the previously patient committee "sacked" Worrall before the start of 1904 despite the relative success the previous season.

Worrall's problems had nothing to do with on-field performances and in fact, he was sacked because of his unusual accounting methods. As club secretary, Worrall had banked gate receipts from matches against South Melbourne, Collingwood and Melbourne into his own account and then had written appropriate cheques to Carlton. There was nothing illegal or dishonest in what Worrall had done, but the Carlton committee voted 16-7 to dispense with his services. This, naturally, led to tremendous internal strife at Carlton and the players even rallied behind him at the club's annual meeting. Members also were furious and, with the support of the players, ran a ticket against the committee. They were successful and Worrall was reappointed. And just as well, as Worrall led Carlton to the 1904 grand final (losing by 24 points to Fitzroy) and taking the Blues to their first VFL premiership two years later.

Carlton won three successive premierships under Worrall and from 1906-8, the Blues were regarded as almost invincible. Carlton's discipline was the envy of all rival clubs, although most Carlton players felt Worrall was over-enthusiastic in his demands for fitness. A contemporary said of

Jack Worrall in his playing days with Fitzroy.

Carlton defeated South Melbourne by five points in the 1907 grand final and a Melbourne City Council councillor wrote the following poem in honor of the Blues' 1907 premiership side:

This great year of football is ended,
And old Carlton is still to the fore;
For our champions have nobly defended
Their title as Premiers once more.
Flynn and Elliott are both grand commanders,
They played for old Carlton rare games;
Both Elliott and Marchbank, 'spite slanders,
Bear still to all sportmen fair names .
"Mallee" Johnson played football the fairest,
The champion this year he has been;
For his play all round was the rarest,
His marking the grandest e'er seen.
Bruce and Kennedy's smart play will ever
Round football memories cling,
For their dash through the season so clever
Made them champions this year on the wing.
"Wee" McGregor was 'great' all season,
In the centre no one could oppose;
But Renfry's sad rush was the reason
Why he lost the last match by a 'nose'.
"Hacken" Clark, Payne and Beck are terrors,
They played back with great heart and soul;
With Gillespie right back made no errors,
But nobly defended their goal.
Mick Grace, our goal star last year,
Retired ere the season was o'er;

When the League hit old Carlton severe,
Mick returned and kicked goals as of yore .
Silver Caine's great punt took some stopping.
And Kelly, the star of the West,
With Harris and game little Topping,
Make a quartette that rank with the best
Jinks and Lang on the ball were splendid,
And both snapped smart goals as well;
Gotz and Hammond most ably defended,
And their dash in the ruck did tell .
Little Ingleman we greet with pleasure
For his roving, his pluck and pace;
He proved to old Carlton a treasure,
For he took "Wee" McGregor's great place .
When misfortune overtook so gravely Eli Elliott,
and Marchbank as well,
The great breach was filled so bravely
By Jim Kennedy, young Williams and Snell.
When Vin Gardiner plays like his father,
Who oft captained the Old Blues in the past,
In those days of great players - rather,
His fame, like Jack Gardiner's, will last
Three cheers for our champions tonight, boys,
The old Carlton team so dear;
Three cheers for the flag blue and white, boys,
Which waves for our Premiers this year.

Worrall after the 1907 premiership triumph: "To Mr John Worrall, more than any other man, is due the present eminence of the Dark Blues".

That great surge of enthusiasm carried into the 1908 season when the Blues won 19 of its 20 matches and defeated Essendon by nine points in the grand final. *The Age* had this to say about the Carlton triumph of l908: "The football season terminated on Saturday, when on the Melbourne Cricket Ground, Carlton de-feated Essendon by nine points - 5.5. to 3.8 - and won the League premiership for the third consecutive year. The match attracted an immense gathering of specta-tors, 49,371 persons passing through the turnstiles, and the gate receipts amounting to 1789 pounds, which eclipsed all previous records.

"On Saturday all the stands were densely packed, and the ground presented a splendid appearance. On two occasions part of the railing surrounding the

Carlton in 1903 at the start of Worrall's coaching career. Worrall is in the middle of the top row. Note the sheep in the background.

playing enclosure succumbed to the pressure of the crowd. Spectators were perched in the branches in the elms on the railway side of the ground, and numbers of people who had paid for admission to the big stand, being unable to obtain sitting accommodation under cover, sought and found it on the roof...

"The victory of the Carlton club for the third consecutive season roused intense enthusiasm, and as the players were leaving the ground several of them were seized and carried on the shoulders of their delighted supporters.

"Thus the season ended, and while Carlton deserve to be congratulated on their third successive attainment of the premiership honours - achieved by amazing retention of form and discipline - Essendon may certainly be complimented quite as deservedly on coming up from the bottom of last year's list to fight out the finish with the famous Old Blues.

"How much longer are they going to hold it, I wonder? asked one of the occupants of a crowded tram returning to the city, and there was evidence of keen knowledge of what's what in his friend's reply -'until Jack Worrall pegs out'."

That spectator was wrong, but how was he to know that trouble was looming for Jack Worrall. The great man might have taken Carlton to an unprecedented position of power, but there was a rising undercurrent of discontent among the players, many of the same men who had supported Worrall just a few years earlier. Worrall's discipline was fierce - possibly too fierce for the period of semi-professionalism - and players were becoming discontented.

Matters came to a head when Norman "Hackenschmidt" Clarke was dropped from the team after a row over expenses. Many Carlton players heard a rumor that Clarke would not be reinstated during the season and they called for Worrall's dismissal. As *The Australasian* wrote of the row: "Rumour was busy late in the week concerning the continuance of trouble in the ranks of Carlton. It was generally believed that certain prominent players were holding out for more liberal expenses and that the committee would not increase allowances beyond what it knew to be legitimate".

Worrall even stated it was no longer a pleasure to coach the side and tendered his resignation at a

Rucking legends Henry Young (Geelong) and Vic Cumberland (St Kilda) soar for the ball at Corio Oval.

committee meeting on July 19, 1909. The committee rejected the resignation, but Worrall said: "For the sake of the club and for peace and quietness, I consider it best to resign from the position and thus remove any unpleasantness". Worrall's resignation was then accepted and Fred "Pompey" Elliott was appointed playing coach. Worrall's era at Carlton had ended, but that was not the last of the drama as the Worrall row had angered the press and Carlton members. A reform group, backed by the players, was swept into power and Worrall lost any hope of returning to Carlton, which had to wait until 1914 for its next premiership . Worrall, the first VFL club coach, took over as coach of Essendon in 1911 and took the club to the 1911-12 flags. He died in 1937.

Chapter Four

1909-1918
Moral dilemmas

Australian football covered the broadest spectrum of society in the early twentieth century. It certainly was the people's game, but it was also popular with the merchant and professional classes. The University club had its fans and Essendon was regarded as something of an "Old Boys Club". However, a listing of occupations for the Carlton and Essendon sides of 1909 makes interesting reading.

The Essendon occupations were: L. Armstrong (manufacturer), C. Beckley (bank clerk), A. Belcher (general carrier), L. Bowe (cyanide worker), W. Busbridge (railway employee), E. Cameron (clerk), W. Davies (fitter), A. Daykin (miner), H. Farnsworth (plumber), W. Griffith (hide salesman), W. Harrison (mason), M. Londerigan (packer), J. Martin (lumber hand), F. Parkinson (railway employee), J. Prout (mechanical student), G. Ryan (salesman), P. Shea (commercial traveller), D. Smith (sports store proprietor), W. Sewart (commercial traveller) and F. Whelpton (school teacher).

The Carlton counterparts were: J. Bacquie (tea grader), L. Beck (shipping clerk), G. Bruce (estate agent), F. Caine (licenced victualler), N. Clark (tea grader), F. Elliott (slater), A. Ford (tea grader), D. Gillespie (zoologist), M. Gotz (tea grader), C. Hammond (paper ruler), R. Harris (clerk), F. Jinks (assistant curator), G. Johnson (police constable), E. Kennedy (dentist), H. Kelly (tea grader), A. Lang (contractor), R. McGregor (school teacher), J. Marchbank (mill owner), W. Payne (tea grader), L.

The men of the 'Varsity in 1909 - a year after their admission to the VFL.

Topping (tea grader).

It is interesting to note that seven of the Carlton players were employed as tea graders. It therefore is reasonable to assume that some Carlton official or influential supporter was a tea merchant. Even in those early days of the VFL it was common for clubs to find employment for players. In fact, it often was far easier to find a job if you had a football background.

The same lists, in a newspaper of the time, give the height and weight of each player and there was only one player in the Essendon squad who stood six feet or more. That was G.J.F. Parkinson, who stood exactly six feet. Carlton had three six-footers - Les Beck, Frank Caine and Jim Marchbank. Beck, at 6 feet 1 inch, was the tallest player on the Carlton list and played either in the ruck or in a key position.

Speed was considered more important than height and besides, there were few giants around. A man six feet tall was regarded as being almost over-sized and extremely tall players were rare. The average height of the Essendon squad was five feet eight and a half inches and the average height of the Carlton squad was five feet nine and a quarter. The smallest player was Carlton's George Topping, who was just 5 feet 5 inches and weighed only 9 stone 9 lb. But that did not stop him being Carlton's leading goalkicker in 1909.

Carlton's all-conquering side struck an unexpected snag in its first outing for 1909 when the VFL fledgling University caused a huge boilover.

The Blues were wracked by internal dissent at the start of the season and players were said to be dissatisfied with their "allowances" and the rigorous training methods of John Worrall. Half a dozen players refused to take the field at South Melbourne and were told that unless they appeared against Collingwood a week later they would be banished for-ever. All returned except star backman Norman "Hackenschmidt" Clarke whose "absence was unaccounted for".

It all became too much for Worrall who resigned after only a handful of games and paved the way for captain Fred Elliott to take over as coach. Carlton was imme-diately transformed al-though unrest would resur-face later. The team won six games in a row to catapult to second place. St Kilda had internal troubles too, although in the case of the seasiders there would be no wonder recovery. So desperate were the Saints that they used champion half-back Billy "Ginger" Stewart against Geelong despite the fact he had been suspended in a Bendigo League match a week earlier. Stewart starred in a one point win but

Welles Eicke who made his debut in 1909 for St Kilda at the age of just 15.

Geelong was quick to protest. St Kilda knew even before the game that Geelong would protest but was aware that without Stewart it didn't have a chance.

Within weeks of the protest match Stewart left St Kilda never to return. He headed to VFA side Prahran as St Kilda was said to have "undergone severe disciplinary measures".

It was reported that every disturbing element had been ejected from the team and that even included champion ruckman/forward Dave McNamara who packed his bags and crossed to Essendon Town. With a team of youngsters St Kilda plummeted back to the cellar. In the endless turnover of young locals one boy from the local state school was unearthed. Welles Eicke was thrown into battle at the tender age of 15 and went on to become one of the VFL's great defenders over a long career.

Another team which had trouble keeping pace with the pack was Geelong and it was reported that only a few of its players could reach train-ing before dark whereas at other grounds there were 20 or more players on the field by 5 pm. "Until Geelong can do the same they must continue to hold a poor posi-tion among their competitors," wrote Markwell.

Severe wet weather hit Melbourne in mid-winter and only exacerbated tempers. It was suggested that baseball matches held before games should be abandoned to reduce the wear and tear on grounds.

A sensational tribunal hearing in July involved police and a police court law-yer. The policeman gave evidence that led to the dismissal of a striking charge against Carlton's Jack Bacquie and the police court lawyer defended Richmond players Ted Ohlsen, Tom Heaney and Bill Burns. The highly qualified advocate did well to get

Carlton's dream of a fourth consecutive flag ends at the hands of South Melbourne in the 1909 grand final.

only four weeks apiece for Heaney and Ohlsen, but the tribunal didn't mess about with Burns and outed him for life on a kicking charge. Later the charge was commuted and he returned to play again in 1912.

South topped the ladder after the home and away games and entered the finals captained by the "downiest" skipper in the VFL - Charlie Ricketts. Carlton, with magnificent pace and skill, was the tallest and heaviest team in the competition and had too much brawn in the final for South which went down by 22 points. South had the right of challenge, but entered the grand final without Jim Caldwell (suspended) and Bill Dolphin and Dick Casey who were both injured.

Carlton benefited by the return of Clarke from injury, but lost Bacquie during the grand final with an ankle injury. South had learned valuable lessons from the final and entered the last quarter leading by a goal. In an engrossing quarter of football the red and whites had to withstand a constant bom-

bardment from a Carlton side chasing an unprecedented fourth flag in a row. Thunderous cheering and stomping of feet greeted every wave of Carlton attack, but South hung on to win its first flag by two points. The win was a triumph for the generalship of Ricketts. "Sonna" Thomas was a magnificent half-back and Bert Franks was invincible on the ball. For the Blues no-one battled harder than Alex "Bongo" Lang who had to shoulder the roving duties after Bacquie's departure.

Before the ball was bounced for the start of the 1910 season Carlton endured yet another upheaval with a reform group taking control of the club. Champion players Fred Jinks, Charlie Hammond and "Mallee" Johnson left and headed to VFA side North Melbourne and other stars Harvey Kelly, Ted Kennedy and Les Beck also quit. Such was the depth of talent at the club that Carlton's performance hardly suffered at all and no-one could get near the Blues in the early weeks of the season.

The roughness and ferocity of league football was

growing worse and a disgraceful series of incidents in round four brought matters to a head. "Nearly every game played last Saturday was distinguished with undue roughness," wrote Markwell in *The Australasian*.

In the match between Carlton and South, South's Streckfuss was knocked out cold a few minutes before the end of the game, and at Collingwood the Magpie skipper George Angus was said to have "lay on the slab, more dead than alive" after the match in which he had been frequently hit and then accidentally elbowed across the heart. At St Kilda field umpire Hastings was set upon when a bad decision let Melbourne off the hook to win by three points.

In response to public outcry the Premier and the Chief Commissioner of Police announced they would act against rough players and one who faced the courts was Streckfuss, the man KO'd in the Carlton and South game, but who was said to have instigated the trouble.

Meanwhile the League disqualified Carlton's George Topping for the rest of 1910 and all of 1911 (the equivalent of a 35 week suspension) over his part in the incident and South's Dick Casey was sidelined for the rest of 1910. Ironically, Casey had only stayed in the game as a player because his pre-season application to become an umpire had been knocked back!

The sensations continued after Casey's hearing when his teammate Albert Franks abused the umpire and was called back to face a charge of using insulting language. Franks was stood down - "at the League's pleasure" for an indefinite period. The ban was not lifted until the start of 1912 by which time he had cooled his heels for 36 games.

In the weeks after the tribunal hearings there was a general improvement in player behavior, but all the while there was an undercurrent of disquiet about betting on big games and under-the-table professionalism. Trouble of another sort flared over the fence at

> In response to public outcry the Premier and the Chief Commissioner of Police announced that they would act against rough play.

East Melbourne when Fitzroy fans pelted the umpire with stones during the game against University. The Fitzroy larrikins even hung onto the ball when it went over the fence in the last term - and knocked it about themselves, then it was deliberately kicked over the back fence onto the railway lines.

The VFA approached the league to seek a meeting on professionalism, and veteran administrator Con Hickey suggested a plan of dividing the metropolitan area into 16 zones from which the clubs could recruit players.

One of the biggest stirs in football history forced officials into confronting the professionalism issue. On the morning of the Carlton-South semi-final the Blues committee decided to remove three players' names from the team list. Alex Lang, Douglas Fraser, and Doug Gillespie were alleged to have received money to play "dead" against South. Spectators soon got wind of the story and South met with an icy reception even though it was later proved that no-one from the club had been involved. The Swans won easily.

A detailed inquiry by the VFL cleared Gillespie of guilt and he was back in the team for the next final, but Lang and Fraser were suspended for five years. Lang actually returned to the field for the Blues in 1916. Rumors whirled around the football scene with sums of 100 pounds and 60 pounds being mentioned. Umpire Jack Elder said he was questioned about the performances of certain players and while saying that umpires did not have time to assess players he admitted some players seemed to be "below form".

The atmosphere surrounding the League finals was distinctly unpleasant and the situation erupted in the grand final between Collingwood and Carlton which proved to be one of the roughest games ever with tripping, fighting, elbowing and kicking from the start. Umpire Elder wrote in later years that he sensed a feeling of "sullen hostility" in the rooms before the game.

In the middle of the last quarter a wild fight broke out in front of the old Harrison stand and several players were floored. Umpire Elder was powerless to stop the fight and instead of blowing the whistle he merely bounced the ball and signalled play on. Twenty five years later, Elder reflected: "By this time a wave of barrackers were being driven back across the green by police. The whistle and the bounce did the trick. Suddenly players remembered that there was a ball to be chased. The sparring and the grumbling and the swinging rights and lefts stopped like magic. I feel certain that if I failed to get the game going again that day the crowd would have swarmed onto the ground and the rival camps of barrackers would have been at each other's throats."

As a result of the melee Carlton's Sheehan and Collingwood's Shorten were suspended for all of 1911 and half of 1912 and Blue Jack Bacquie and his Collingwood opposite number Tommy Baxter were outed for the whole of 1911.

Collingwood pulled a swift trick when one of its players Daykin stated to the League that it was he, not Baxter, who had been responsible. Despite the fact that umpire Elder said he knew them apart, and the fact that Daykin's hair was red and Baxter's black, the League quashed Baxter's sentence on appeal.

Despite the fisticuffs Collingwood held firm to take out its third flag. Dick Lee, the first in a dynasty of great Magpie full-forwards, kicked four of his side's nine goals and was best afield.

A landmark decision came early in 1911 when the League sanctioned the payment of players. Seventy players had met in February, 1911, to discuss VFL proposals to tighten payments and scribes who were against professionalism warned of dire consequences. It was even suggested that the genuinely amateur clubs Melbourne and University would be forced out of the competition.

Football was not destroyed and some people even went as far as suggesting there would be more pressure on players to perform. Clubs also ruled they would not pay players under suspension which should have been more of a deterrent to rough play.

In the opening weeks there was less of the rough play that had plagued the competition in the preceding years. Essendon had secured John Worrall as coach and the ex-Carlton wizard transformed the team's performance. The red and blacks had stars such as Alan Belcher, Fred Baring and Len Bowe, but the side was notable for its evenness. The Dons showed their quality early on when they handed out a huge hiding to the previous year's premier, Collingwood. Essendon kicked 12 goals straight and won by 85 points.

> **A landmark decision came early in 1911 when the League sanctioned the payment of players.**

Worrall's team had a hiccup when its fiery ruckman Jim Martin was disqualified for the rest of the year on a striking charge and was then summoned while he was watching the Essendon-Carlton game to appear in court on assault charges relating to the same incident. He was found guilty, but then had the conviction overturned on appeal. The VFL took no notice and refused to re-open the case.

Martin wasn't the only man hauled into court over an on-field incident. Carlton's Martin Gotz flattened University's Vic Trood in the last five minutes of the match. University issued a summons against Gotz for assault and told Carlton that it would not play the Blues again unless "certain players were left out". Gotz was fined 10 pounds or two months in jail, but the finding, like that against Martin, was quashed on appeal.

One of the year's more bizarre features was a players' strike at St Kilda. When Melbourne entered the field on time for a game against the Saints the opposition did not appear. The crowd wondered what was happening and so did the Melbourne players. Eventually, St Kilda straggled onto the field, and it was soon pitifully evident that something had gone wrong in the dressing rooms. The committee had decided to recall 10 passes entitling the holders to enter the dressing rooms.

Collingwood heroes
Bob Nash, Arthur
Leach and Ted
Rowell.

According to secretary Stoddart, young Eicke and old-time champion Joe Hogan were affected, as were two generous supporters of the club. The other holders of the passes were not put out by this Committee ruling, but on the morning of the Melbourne match a newspaper had reported that Harry Lever had said he would refuse to strip against Melbourne, and that the other players would also consider their positions.

Before the game started Lever approached the committee and asked it what it was going to do. Blandly, the committee replied, "about what?" The players said they would not play unless Eicke's and Hogan's passes were returned to them. The committee replied that St Kilda would forfeit the match

and the players would be reported to the League. The players took the field - but after the match the wordy warfare flared again.

The players asked the committee to reconsider its decision and with no change the players met, then told the committee they would not play. The committee went one stage further and interviewed all the players separately. All except three players stood by their teammates. The upshot was the committee took the unprecedented action of asking the players to hand in their uniforms. Other matters aside from the passes were also aired with the players complaining they had not been well looked after in the way of smoke nights.

St Kilda, as a suburb, was rent with the dispute. There were calls for the Mayor to intervene and on training night, 62 juniors volunteered to play with the side. The club didn't even have enough training guernseys for all the newcomers. A team of juniors took the field against Carlton, with the result that St Kilda was beaten by 19 goals.

One player who did catch the eye in this game was a youngster from Middle Park. His name was Roy Cazaly.

University was another club which had a disappointing season and its troubles continued when the Uni hierarchy refused to let the club develop a league class facility in the grounds. In the end University's home games were transferred from East Melbourne to the MCG.

With the meticulous Worrall calling the shots and the shrewd captaincy of Dave Smith leading the way, Essendon stormed into the finals determined to advance further than the five fourth placings that had been the red and blacks' lot in the previous seven years. Worrall and Smith ordered all players to wear sleeves in the wet grand final to assist in marking, whereas seven Collingwood players were sleeveless. At half time Essendon players had longer stops put in their boots. But a far bigger issue than sleeves or stops was said to have influenced the result.

Collingwood went down by a goal and there were

widespread allegations that one of its stars, Tom Baxter, had played "dead" in the big game. Two kicks into the man on the mark late in the game were cited as evidence, but as Collingwood historian Richard Stremski points out, Baxter was one of the main players getting the ball forward, and he also kicked the Magpies' only goal in the final term. An injury to star forward Dick Lee early in the game had resulted in Lee being placed in defence and Baxter assuming an even more important attacking role. Baxter asked the Collingwood committee to have an inquiry into the charges and he was exonerated. All the same, Collingwood cleared him to St Kilda the next season.

Numbering of players was introduced in the 1911 second semi-final, although it had been first used in the Collingwood-Fitzroy game in Sydney in 1903. The numbers used in the 1911 finals were found to be too small. Carlton wore small white numbers and Collingwood small black numbers which were hard to distinguish and Essendon's red numbers could hardly be made out at all. For 1912 the League decided to use big white numbers for Carlton, Essendon, Richmond, University, Fitzroy, Melbourne and St Kilda, black numbers for Geelong and Collingwood and red for South Melbourne.

Players' names were displayed next to their numbers on big scoreboards at either end of the ground. First man on the ground was Essendon's number 13 - captain Dave Smith - and the first goal was kicked 13 seconds after the start by Carlton number 13 Vin Gardiner.

The League had extended the power of making reports to boundary umpires in 1911, but this did not have immediate results as the boundary umpires usually appeared only as witnesses in cases brought by the field umpire. It was announced at the end of 1911 that stewards would be introduced. The stewards would be paid 30 shillings an afternoon to stand between the boundary line and the fence with the purpose of detecting behind-the-play incidents.

Blue boys Norman Clarke, Fred Jinks and Rod McGregor.

An early season sensation surrounded the efforts of former Carlton star Harvey Kelly's efforts to join South Melbourne. Kelly had been in Tasmania three years and when he tried to return to South Melbourne the League ruled he was still a Carlton player and the Blues refused a clearance.

Essendon went into the 1912 season without its captain Dave Smith who was part of the Australian cricket team touring England. Alan Belcher took over the captaincy. The name of Essendon loomed large in both major competitions and the Essendon Association team set the pace. In one amazing effort Dave McNamara kicked 18 goals for the VFA team which must have been an acute embarrassment to the St Kilda committeemen who had eased him out of the club.

Essendon won the League premiership after a somewhat patchy season in yet another triumph for coach Worrall. "Follower" wrote: "Worrall has, in the most practical manner earned the reputation of being a veritable wizard of the football world. He had been equally successful as a cricket coach and as a practical teacher of two games his equal could not be found in Australia."

Essendon even withstood its share of adversity through the loss of champion Bill Busbridge who was forced out by a knee injury. Newspapers had voted him the best player in Victoria in 1908 and 1909 and he was renowned for his gentlemanly conduct. Once he had refused to tackle a hobbling Fitzroy opponent in a gesture that would be treated with scorn today.

Another mid-year upset would have reminded Worrall of his last days at Carlton. Star defender Billy Griffith stood out of the team for three months after failing to get a pay rise.

Essendon's meeting with South in the semi-final saw the rare occurrence of brothers captaining opposing sides. Alan Belcher led the Dons and Vic Belcher stood in as skipper in the absence of Charlie Ricketts. Essendon won this and the grand final two weeks later which was an amazing turnabout as South and Carlton had fought out the honors for top place in the closing part of the season. Carlton's committee stunned the football world when it suspended champion centreman Rod McGregor for 12 months. McGregor had refused an order by captain Jack Wells to move from centre to the half-forward line in the final against Essendon.

The biggest upset to the established order was Collingwood's failure to make the finals for the first time in League history. The Magpies fought back in 1913, but on their way back up they passed a declining Essendon. The Dons lost a number of key

> Numbering of players was introduced in the 1911 second semi-final, although it had been first used in the Collingwood-Fitzroy game in Sydney in 1903.

players and struggled throughout the year.

Another club with a change of fortune was St Kilda which had shown signs of recovery in 1912. The return of the dynamic ruckman Vic Cumberland was the prelude to an ambitious plan to regain former champion Dave McNamara from the VFA. McNamara was in his prime as a player and St Kilda fans were overjoyed when he was cleared by his VFA club. For some unaccountable reason the VFA refused to ratify the clearance and it may have had something to do with the "huge" sums of money that were said to be involved.

One story suggested that McNamara was to be paid nine pounds a week to play for the Saints. "That sum would approximate about 180 pounds for the season which is altogether absurd," trumpeted one critic. On hearing that McNamara had been offered a hotel as part of the deal, one St Kilda player was reported as saying "If he gets a hotel then I will want Luna Park". McNamara told the VFA that he had put 1300 pounds towards a hotel business in the area and he hoped trade would benefit by him playing for the local side. The VFA wouldn't budge despite the threat of legal action and McNamara had to sit out the season.

The League and Association introduced independent tribunals in this year as a further effort to stamp out rough play. There was disquiet over the role of stewards and it was suggested umpires were content to umpire the game and leave the reporting of players to the officials on the other side of the boundary line.

Fitzroy set the pace in 1913 winning 16 games and losing only two. Earlier in the year the club had endured the sorrow of its five premiership pennants being destroyed by a fire . Fitzroy had a deadly attack with coach Percy Parratt and leading goalkicker Jimmy Freake, and a perfect blend of pace and strength.

Fitzroy looked set to contest the premiership from the middle of the season, but the other place was up for grabs. The cinderella side St Kilda earned a finals place thanks to a heartstopping finish over Carlton in which star centreman Billy Schmidt kicked a huge drop-kick goal after marking as the final bell sounded.

St Kilda rolled the more fancied South in the semi, but few people gave the seasiders a chance against Fitzroy in the final. Yet the free-flowing Saints turned the predictions on their head in a dazzling performance with stars such as Gordon Dangerfield and Vic Cumberland showing the way.

Fitzroy, by finishing on top, had the right of challenge and the rematch captured public imagination as never before. The crowd of 59,479 surpassed the previous year's mark by 5000 and set a record for any sporting event in Australia. For the first three quarters the crowd was disappointed as the plucky, tenacious Fitzroy applied the squeeze to the more brilliant Saints who seemed overawed at chasing their first flag. By the time St Kilda kicked its first goal to wild cheering almost three quarters had passed and Fitzroy held a 25 point lead.

Maroons' barrackers even broke into a victory song, but suddenly the Saints mounted a comeback - and commenced piling up points "to the most prolonged cheering that has ever been heard on the Melbourne ground".

Within minutes St Kilda slammed on four goals and drew to within one point as pandemonium broke loose. St Kilda blew its chance when Baird tried to handpass to Morrisey instead of taking a shot at goal which, if successful, would have given St Kilda the lead and possibly the flag. Years later Baird wrote that he had handpassed because of a pre-game instruction to play through Morrisey. Morrisey had called for the ball, but instead of running right into goal, merely kicked from the spot. Fitzroy whisked the ball away and kicked a steadying goal. Another opportunity was lost when ruckman Bill Woodcock was crashed to the ground after taking a mark. The ball was bounced because he could not take his kick

- it would be many years before the rule was changed. The Saints' chance was lost and the club would have to wait 53 years to win a flag.

When the 1914 VFL season started the prospect of war in Europe was only a matter of discussion in bars and at dinner tables. When war finally was declared on August 4, 1914, the *Sydney Morning Herald* cried: "It will be our (Australia's) baptism of fire". Crowds celebrated the announcement and young men rushed to enlist, convinced the war would last only weeks, or months at the most.

The announcement of war at first had little effect on the VFL competition. After all, the 1914 season was nearing its climax and it was only a matter of weeks to the grand final. However, the 1914 grand final between Carlton and South Melbourne attracted only 30,000 fans, well down on the previous year's attendance of almost 60,000. Some extreme groups already were urging the abandonment of all sport, although this cry did not reach a crescendo until the following year.

The VFL grand final might have been important, but the war raging in Europe, naturally, attracted all the headlines. The Battle of the Marne was being fought and many peripheral football fans believed it wrong to watch a football match when the mother country was bleeding to death on the battlefields of France and Belgium. Sadly, two of the South Melbourne grand final players of that year - Sloss and Freeman - were killed in the war.

The debate as to whether sport should be played even on an amateur basis raged throughout the nation. The Sydney rugby union competition was abandoned and the rugby league competition in Brisbane was abandoned, not to resume until 1929. One newspaper editorial complained that 25,000 sports fans attended a race meeting while on the other side of the world Australians were fighting for the Empire. The VFL met half-way through 1915 to decide

> **"It will be our (Australia's) baptism of fire." Crowds celebrated the announcement and young men rushed to enlist, convinced the war would last only weeks, or months at the most.**

whether to continue in the face of mounting losses, dwindling attendances and the fury of many Victorians who believed it to be morally wrong to be playing football while other young men were dying. The League delegates (two from each club) voted 12-8 against the motion of abandoning the competition for the season. The motion did not get a three-quarters majority and the season continued. The six clubs which voted for the season to continue might have had cause for regret as attendances continued to dwindle and some clubs ran up huge debts trying to stay competitive.

Late in 1915 there was a sensational game at the MCG between South and Melbourne in which South's George Payne was flattened by Melbourne's Incigneri. "As often happens when a player is temporarily disabled a couple of supporters jumped the fence to go to his assistance," wrote one reporter, "to my mind it was their intention to render first aid to Payne, and he needed it. However , it afforded the chance for undesirables to get in some disagreeable work."

Reports on the number of "undesirables' ranged from "hundreds" to 2000. It stopped the game and South barrackers swarmed towards Incigneri who was hustled off the field by teammates. In a 15 minute battle Melbourne's Jack George felled a barracker "like a log" and rover Jack Bacquie who was sidelined with injury could be seen swapping punches with two soldiers. The game eventually started up again, minus Incigneri, and the Southerners won by seven points. Incigneri was considered lucky to get only an eight week suspension.

Only 20,953 fans watched the 1915 grand final

Collingwood trojan Danny Minogue. In the latter part of his career he guided Richmond to its first flag.

between Fitzroy and Carlton. this was the lowest attendance at a VFL grand final since 1900. Carlton defeated Collingwood by 33 points, but the Magpies had had trouble fielding a full-strength side because of the war. Besides, two of their players - Rowan (later killed in the war) and Seddon - had been on an army route march earlier in the day.

Carlton can consider itself lucky to have won the 1915 premiership, and not only for overcoming a sluggish third quarter in which Collingwood outscored the Blues by 11 points. Only two Victorian football competitions were completed that year - the VFL and the Victorian Junior Association. Newspaper editorials of the time roundly criticised the VFL for pressing ahead and there were genuine fears there would be no competition at all in 1916.

The situation was so worrying the Australian National Football Council (renamed from the Australian Football Council) asked the NSW Rugby League to consider the amalgamation of the two football codes. The original suggestion was for rugby league to abandon its scrums and to have a throw-in from the boundary lines. In return, the Australian code was willing to accept the idea of a cross-bar. Surprisingly, eight of the 10 VFL clubs agreed to the proposals, but Carlton and Richmond fought a rear-guard action to kill the idea. Australian football lost what might have been its last chance to gain international status.

Football's cause was not helped by a charity match between St Kilda and VFA side North Melbourne in August 1915. North, the VFA's champion side, bolstered its stocks by adding three stars from other Association clubs, saying that its list had been depleted by enlistments and sickness. The game raised 254 pounds for Lady Stanley's Fund for Wounded Soldiers, but that was the only saving grace. From the first bounce it was a vicious encounter with snide punches being thrown by both teams. North won by 26 points, but the game soured relations between the two main football bodies.

Meanwhile, University was disbanded over the summer of 1915-6 and five other clubs - Melbourne, Geelong, Essendon, South Melbourne and St Kilda - were unable to field teams. Enlistments had taken their toll and only Carlton, Collingwood, Fitzroy and Richmond competed in the 1916 season. Even then, these clubs had trouble selecting sides as players drifted in and out of clubs owing to enlistments, leave or other military reasons. The four competing clubs asked their footballers to play as amateurs and only out of pocket expenses were paid.

This code of amateurism was widely highlighted in newspapers to reduce criticism. Even so, the four-team competition attracted little public interest. In fact, many sports fans regarded the competition as ridiculous. The four teams played each other four times and, to make the season even more farcical, there was a final four. Carlton topped the ladder with 10 wins and two losses, Collingwood won six of its games and drew another, Richmond had five wins and seven losses and Fitzroy struggled to win two games and draw a match against Collingwood. The farce became even more ridiculous over the following month when all clubs were involved in the finals and Fitzroy landed the premiership, after what had been an utterly miserable home and away season for the Maroons.

Collingwood's Jim Jackson who later became Hawthorn's first VFL skipper.

Fitzroy had been instrumental in the 1916 VFL season going ahead, despite enormous opposition. Matches were played only on the condition that 10 per cent of all gate takings and 50 per cent of all finals gatetakings would be paid towards war funds. This still did not satisfy some critics and *The Age* commented: "No man eligible for service should be allowed to wear a stocking, or to be a partner in the applause that comes from victory". *The Age*'s disapproval of football during the war years seemed to be echoed by the miserable attendance at the 1916 grand final, with only 20,953 fans at the MCG to see Fitzroy play Carlton. Fitzroy, wooden-spooner of the home and away season, defeated the Blues by 29 points to win a premiership in most unusual fashion.

Geelong and South Melbourne returned to the competition in 1917, but this only fuelled controversy over the playing of football during a war that was proving very costly in terms of young Australian lives. Average attendances at VFL home and away games fell to between 5000 and 7000 and even the finals failed to attract large numbers of fans. The conscription issue had divided the nation's thoughts and the VFL tried to improve its image by allowing recruiting officers to address the crowds before matches. Form was impossible to assess because of the varied availability of players. However, it was generally conceded that Carlton would be the team to defeat for the premiership.

The Blues made the finals without difficulty, but succumbed to Fitzroy in the first semi-final. This prompted *The Australasian* to note: "Carlton, as in the previous year, played their worst, just when a spe-

Collingwood's champion goalkicker Dickie Lee soars for a classic mark. The picture was taken by Albert Sutcliffe with a tripod camera and a shutter release.

cial effort was required. Judging by the last two years' displays the side has evidently lost the secret of being cherry-ripe in the finals. Carlton, while still a good strong and capable body of men, at no time looked a premier team. Combined with their strength - which they can always use to best advantage - they have hitherto maintained the necessary pace, but this season this fine asset was found wanting. Many of their cracks had appreciably slowed down."

Fitzroy, which was accused of playing men fit enough to have been in France, clashed with Collingwood in the 1917 grand final. Again, the grand final attendance was disappointing and only 28,385 fans watched the match. Collingwood, possibly inspired by a message of goodwill from teammate "Doc" Seddon in France, defeated the Maroons by 35 points. The match, according to *The Australasian*, had been uninspiring and was well over before half-time. In fact, many fans drifted from the MCG well before the final bell to give newspapers yet another chance to trumpet anti-football sentiments.

Essendon and St Kilda returned to the competition in 1918 to considerably boost VFL stocks. This meant only Melbourne was missing from the competition, although Essendon rejoined in unusual circumstances. The Essendon Football Club committee had no intention of accepting an invitation to join the 1918 season, but changed its mind on the suggestion of the Essendon Cricket Club, which desperately needed football funds to survive. Essendon, with most of its best players on active service, was unable to find a strong side, but it managed three victories.

All VFL clubs struggled financially and Carlton even wobbled on the edge of bankruptcy despite reasonable on-field success. Players were scarce, but the newspapers of the time finally admitted the playing of football was perhaps good for morale.

It certainly was good for South Melbourne's morale as the red and white won its second VFL premiership in 1918. The Southerners defeated Collingwood by five points in the grand final, which attracted a crowd of 39,168. The end of the war was just around the corner, but no-one in the grand final crowd that day could have guessed that.

The war ended at 11 am on November 11, 1918. The world was left to count its dead. About 416,000 Australians - 13 per cent of the male population - had enlisted during the war. Approximately 330,000 of them embarked for overseas service and about 63,000 died on active service, with another 152,000 wounded or regarded as casualties. Australia had been badly scarred. Little wonder the population wanted to forget the war years. Little wonder football boomed after the war.

OVER THE SEA AND FAR AWAY

The notion of spreading the gospel of Australian Rules is nothing new. Exhibition matches held in the United Kingdom and the USA in the late

1980s were only the latest in a long line of expansionary moves that were mooted as far back as last century.

New Zealand teams first played the game in 1875 and at one stage there were more Aussie Rules teams than rugby union teams playing in the South Island. The Kiwis sent a side to the first Australian Football Carnival in 1908 and the game prospered until World War I. After that, lack of organisation caused a decline although there is still a small competition running in Auckland.

In 1874 one of the game's founders, Tom Wills, tried to convince friends in Cambridgeshire, Nottingham and Yorkshire to take up the game and he even embarked upon the huge task of taking a Geelong team to England to promote the game. These elaborate plans were shelved when Wills was waylaid by the illness that eventually killed him at a young age. Later H.C.A. Harrison visited England and had similar ideas of organising a touring party, but squabbling interstate organisations back in Australia snuffed out the idea.

Australian troops serving in South Africa in the Boer War played the game and a local competition continued to function for several years after hostilities had finished. There was even talk of sending two VFL teams there as late as 1913, but World War I ended plans for that coming to fruition.

The Great War also put a halt to the entrepreneurial plans of Jim Smith, a former St Kilda captain who was a character in his own right. Smith had been a sturdy ruckman for the Saints and was the club's first player to reach 100 VFL games. He took a brief turn at field umpiring, but then decided to resume playing football. Not noted for his flamboyancy on the field, Smith showed considerable flair on the other side of the fence when he announced detailed plans to send a representative team overseas in 1914. The outbreak of war crushed the idea, but football was played in London after all.

A match of great historical importance was

Stills from rare news film of the London game in 1916.

played on October 28, 1916, at the Queen's Club Ground, West Kensington, not far from The Oval where the Foster's Cup would be contested later in the century. The match between the Third Australian Division and the Combined Training Groups attracted a crowd of 3000 people who were said to have been "aroused to a high pitch of enthusiasm".

A former Victorian marathon runner, Sinton Hewitt, umpired the game and there were plenty of VFL stars among the servicemen that took part. These included Bruce Sloss (South Melbourne), Harold Moyes (Melbourne and St Kilda), Carl Willis (South Melbourne), Percy Jory (St Kilda), Jack Brake and Leo Little (Melbourne and University), Dan Minogue (Collingwood and Richmond) Hugh James (Richmond), Billy Orchard (Geelong), Bill Sewart (Essendon), Jack Cooper and Percy Trotter (Fitzroy) and Charlie Lilley (Melbourne).

The Third Division won 6-16 to 4-12. There was a sad note to the game as two of the stars - Bruce Sloss and Jack Cooper - were later killed in France. Sloss had been a player who looked capable of becoming a champion in his short time at South and Cooper had skippered Fitzroy as well as being part of the 1913 flag side.

Considerable interest in Australian Rules had been shown in America at the very highest level. President Theodore Roosevelt had sent for inquiries about the game after the brutality in gridiron matches caused a number of deaths of players, and American sailors who had visited with the US fleet in 1908 were so impressed by the game that they organised matches upon their return home.

From the end of World War I there is little evidence of attempts to take the game overseas until the late 1960s when Harry Beitzel organised the "Galahs" tours to Ireland and the US. Because of Gaelic football's similarity to Australian Rules it was possible to intermesh the two codes, but attempts to play regular games petered out after a couple of years.

In the mid 1980s international games were revived with Australian teams touring Ireland and the Irish travelling here. As with previous attempts the tours have run in fits and starts and the continuity of international competition has not been built to this day.

Chapter Five

1919-1929
Rough and ready

Of course, it took many years for the world to return to normality after the carnage of the 1914-18 conflict, but everyone wanted to forget the war and what better way to do this than to indulge in sport?

The VFL welcomed the return of Melbourne to the competition and nine clubs played off for the 1919 premiership. The demise of University left a gap in ranks to be filled at a later stage. A bye system was introduced but it was far from satisfactory and even during the 1919 season there were suggestions around the VFL delegates' table that a 10th club was needed to balance the competition. The VFA sensed it was in danger of losing at least another club to the League and made moves of its own. The Association ended an agreement with the League to recognise each others' clearances and a state of war developed between the two senior football bodies.

Meanwhile, the 1919 competition was an uneven affair, with Melbourne failing to win a game in its return and reigning premier South Melbourne and Collingwood dominated the home and away season. However, Richmond defeated South in the finals and eventually won the right to play Collingwood in the grand final. It was Richmond's first grand final appearance in the VFL and although it had the sympathy of most fans, Collingwood won the big match by 25 points in front of more than 45,000 people.

Richmond recorded an amazing turnaround in a mid-season game against Essendon. They trailed by 35 points at three quarter time and looked thoroughly beaten. An 8.7 to nil last quarter transformed the game after Richmond had struggled all day with its famous ruck of Barney Herbert, Dave Moffatt and Clarrie Hall being eclipsed by the opposition. The controversial Moffatt, whose shepherding tactics in the ruck cause plenty of comment, was one of the leading lights in the charge during the last half hour.

It was hoped that the introduction of the District Football Scheme would reduce the money troubles that had pervaded the game and it was likely to assist clubs such as Richmond, Collingwood, Fitzroy and South Melbourne which were in industrial suburbs. It reduced the ability of Melbourne and Essendon to offer inducements to players from any point of the compass. On another front the ever active Jack Worrall called for a review of starting times. The nominated time was 2.40 with 10 minutes grace, but Worrall said games rarely started before 3 pm. This meant that games in June and July were finishing at 5.30 and in near darkness. "Watching unrecognised shadowy forms running to and fro in the mist chasing a ball that cannot be seen anyway is scurvy treatment for the ardent followers of the sport."

The end could not come soon enough for St Kilda in their game against South. The Southerners booted 17.4 in the last quarter (still a record for any League quarter) and Harold Robertson established a new individual record of 14 goals.

The famous Boromeo mark in 1920. It was said that Boromeo was still on the way up when the camera's shutter clicked.

Cumberland held his own as a ruckman in an year when ruck duels were the subject of much debate. The tactic of shepherding in ruck duels was an eyesore and Worrall wrote of Richmond's Dave Moffatt: "He was at his old game. While the ball was out of bounds, and frequently more than 20 yards away, Moffatt worried and harried Baring beyond measure...only once during the day was Moffatt penalised for undue interference."

Richmond also had problems over its brilliant recruit George Ogilvie. When completing his registration form Ogilvie had stated that he had been on active service for "about three years". When it turned out to be a period of two years nine months his permit was withdrawn on the eve of the finals and he was ruled an Essendon player. Ogilvie was no ordinary footballer and the experienced Jack Worrall had described his debut as the best he had ever seen.

The Tigers didn't allow the Ogilvie drama to throw them out of step. Richmond had its revenge on Collingwood - and its first VFL flag - in 1920. Richmond's captain was Dan Minogue, a wise old footballer and masterful leader who later became a well-known football media personality. On the day of the grand final Minogue left his sick-bed to lead the side. A few days earlier he had gone home to Bendigo for a few days' rest and a rumor reached Melbourne that he had actually died!

Richmond, which had entered the competition only in 1908, celebrated its first premiership triumph with a dinner at Phair's Hotel (no longer in existence) and players paraded through the streets of Richmond before being introduced to fans at the old Tivoli Theatre in Bourke Street.

One of Victoria's most famous grounds was closed in October 1921. The East Melbourne ground in Jolimont had been the home for Essendon Football Club since 1882, but now the government took over the area to extend its railyards - (in the 1990s it was sold to developers for residential purposes). VFA club North Melbourne suddenly announced

With so many of Australia's soldiers returning home after the war there was a short-lived suggestion they should form a League team of their own, but the idea did not take off. One soldier who resumed his place because of turmoil at his old club was Vic Cumberland - at 43 the oldest man ever to play League football. He returned to his club when St Kilda was wracked with problems that were extreme even for the Saints. Champion half-back Welles Eicke refused to play in the same side as centreman Bill Schmidt and Eicke strode away to take up a place in junior ranks.

in mid-1921 that it would disband and amalgamate with Essendon in the hope the Dons would shift their home games to Arden Street when they moved out of East Melbourne. The government put a stop to that by saying the Arden Street reserve could only be used by North Melbourne residents.

Most erratic team in the competition was St Kilda which could only manage a score of 0.18 against Fitzroy then a few weeks later knocked off Geelong when the Pivotonians were making a run for the finals.

Richmond won the flag again in 1921 and the celebrations that year were no less spectacular than they had been in 1920. The Tigers had a great side led by ex-Magpie Danny Minogue. Left footer George Bayliss was a stylish full-forward and at the opposite end of the field there was Vic Thorp, one of the best full-backs of all times. In a finals match between Carlton and Richmond players left the field at half-time unaware of what lay in store. "When we left the ground it was hard and dry," recalled Richmond's Hughie James, "during the half-time break a storm broke and when we came out there was six inches of hail on the ground. The match should have been callled off at that stage, but on it went. Before ten minutes we were playing in slush."

Richmond beat Carlton in the grand final, but had to fight all the way. The Blues had experienced great tragedy during the year when brilliant rover Lyle Downs had collapsed at training and died of a heart seizure within five minutes.

Meanwhile movement in players between the VFL and VFA increased after the 1918 decision not to renew the clearance agreement between the two bodies and top players began to make the most of their monetary value. Essendon returned to a position of power in 1922 under captain-coach Syd Barker, but it was Fitzroy which secured the flag. Big, strong and mean, the Fitzroy team muscled its way to the flag with a finals win over Essendon then two titanic struggles to secure the honors over Collingwood. Barrell-

chested 15 stoners called the tune in 1922 and the crowds delighted in the sight of them clashing hip to hip and shoulder to shoulder. It should not be thought that the Fitzroy combination lacked ability and men like Percy Parratt, Gordon Rattray, Jimmy Freake and Len Wigraft were all stars in their own right. Years later Wigraft outlined the approach of that Maroon team. "If a man was coming with the ball you had to meet him and knock him down. I don't mean that we were doing the wrong thing, but as I say, we had big strong players."

Two heroes of the game were the veteran forwards Freake and Parratt who were recalled for one last hurrah. Freake said later: "I think my confidence came from being the petted kid of the club. Only a splinter weighing 10.3 and standing 5'7", the big fellows in the team never failed to deal with any opponent who used weight on me excessively". Of Parratt he said: "I always had two definite chances to my opponent's one when leading out to Parratt. He kicked the ball at a height that did not allow the man behind a chance, and it went to a position that gave me the lead. If I failed to take the pass I almost invariably was pushed and got the free kick."

Fitzroy was condemned for its tactics in the semi-final against Geelong the following year when it set out on a premeditated plan to neutralise Geelong's star forward Lloyd Hagger. *The Argus* writer was appalled at the way one of the Fitzroy half-backs deliberately stomped on Hagger's feet behind play. It was a time when malice permeated the game both on and off the ground. Hooliganism among crowds, abuse of umpires and the throwing of missiles became big problems. League umpires complained of menaces and threatening letters and asked the VFL to ensure their safety in getting home from grounds.

Old neighbours and foes St Kilda and South Melbourne met in a last round showdown for a place in the 1923 finals. Nobody was quite sure how many people were at the Albert Park ground that day as the gates were closed when the ground was bursting at the seams. The official estimate was 49,000 people - Roy Cazaly was even told there were 70,000 ! - but the truth was that fans even perched on top of the grandstands and in trees surrounding the oval.

Cazaly visited the ground on the Sunday after the match and saw the fence had been broken in at least a dozen places. Cazaly and rover Mark Tandy went into the game carrying injuries, but they played magnificently and led South to victory and a finals berth. Cazaly ran himself to a standstill against his old club. He didn't forget young Colin Watson who he nurtured as a young player. Watson was told to mind Cazaly at one stage and when he wondered aloud whether he would be able to do it, Cazaly offered him words of encouragement. "If you don't Colin, I'll give you something to go on with."

Geelong's finals campaign ran off the rails when it dropped skipper Bert Rankin from the first semi-final team. Cliff Rankin was made captain, but refused to play because of the club's treatment of his brother. Not surprisingly Geelong lost.

Essendon employed their famous Mosquito Fleet in these years. Charlie Hardy, Jack Garden, Vince Irwin, Rowley Watt, Frank Maher, Harry Sullivan and George Shorten each weighed less than 10 stone, but all had lightning pace and perfect delivery.

Nevertheless it was thought the bigger, stronger Fitzroy side would beat them in the grand final as they had twice done during the year, especially in the wet conditions. Essendon pulled a surprise by including George Rawle in its finals team. A former VFA star with North Melbourne, Rawle was the coach of Essendon's seconds and he jumped at the idea when star rover Charlie Hardy suggested that he could help counter Fitzroy's ruck. The game was postponed due to heavy rain and it finally took place on October 20 - the latest finish in League history. The day of the actual 1923 grand final was a warm, spring afternoon and Essendon outpaced and out-

> The government put a stop to that by saying that the Arden Street reserve could only be used by North Melbourne residents.

witted their heavier opponents

The season of 1924 was studded with spiteful football, in-fighting and numerous injuries. One of the more unusual incidents came when St Kilda's Welles Eicke asked for a count to be applied to the Carlton team which he claimed had 19 men on the field. The umpire counted 18 and legend grew that one St Kilda player had quipped: "You didn't count yourself!"

In old age Eicke revealed that he had called for the count because one of his players was abusing the umpire. When the umpire turned around, the player yelled that St Kilda was playing 19 Carlton players, including this 'so and so'. "I had to act quickly . The St Kilda player seemed certain to be reported for using abusive language. As a desperate gamble I turned to the umpire and said 'yes that's right, line them up and count them'. By this time the St Kilda player's language had become a secondary matter.

Later in the 1924 season Eicke was the centre of controversy when he staggered out of a pack with a double fracture of the skull. A sharp elbow to the face was the cause and South's Mark Tandy was accused, but the League found it had occurred in the general run of play and was accidental.

After a finals confrontation between Essendon and Fitzroy there was a big agenda for the tribunal. One Fitzroy player took a swing at Essendon's Tom Fitzmaurice as they left the hearing. He was called back before the tribunal and told any similar repeat would see him suspended for life.

Many disgruntled fans believed Collingwood had been throwing the ball for years, but the Magpies were aggrieved when umpire Alex McKinnon penalised the team repeatedly. As a result there was a clearer definition of handball, emphasising that the ball had to be held in one hand and clearly punched with the other.

Typical of a bizarre year was the action of Ernie Copeland, the Collingwood secretary who was the

Collingwood versus
Carlton 1923.

VFL's delegate to the Australian Football Council. The Council voted on a proposal to introduce a rule that awarded a free-kick whenever the ball went out of bounds. The VFL had voted against it, but for reasons known only to himself, Copeland voted in favor of it! It proved an unsatisfactory rule and later was dropped because players would shepherd the ball out of bounds in order to get a free kick.

Incredibly, the VFL changed its successful finals format in 1924 by reverting to the old round-robin series between the top four teams. It proved to be a major error of judgement, although it really turned out to be a blessing in disguise. The VFL in 1924 played six finals matches, with no grand final. Essendon won its first two finals matches, against Fitzroy and South Melbourne, and then only had to go through the formalities against Richmond in the fifth match of the series to win the premiership. Essendon already had a huge percentage margin in the round-robin series and although Richmond defeated it by 20 points, the flag was Essendon's on percentage, even though another finals match was being played that day between South Melbourne and Fitzroy.

There was considerable feeling between Essendon and Fitzroy and when they met in August, captain-coach Barker told his team: "I intend to bowl over my opponent in the first couple of minutes and I expect you to do the same. Then maybe they will cut out the rough stuff and play football." It was a bitterly cold day and Barker gave his ruckmen a few nips of whisky to warm them for the battle ahead.

The Essendon-Richmond match, played at the Lake Oval, attracted just 25,000 fans. "Old Boy" wrote in *The Argus*: "It was an inglorious ending to an unsatisfactory season". He said the Essendon room hardly seemed jubilant. "There was none of that hilarious applause and speech making and uproarious cheering, and though they felt that they

> Many disgruntled fans believed Collingwood had been throwing the ball for years...as a result there was a clearer definition of handball.

were the best side on the whole year, they were not quite sure that had a grand final been necessary they would have done any better when they met Richmond again."

Essendon was not a happy combination. Before the last final it was known on the Friday night that Jack Garden was unfit to play, yet the club did not name his replacement. The experienced Charlie Hardy, the first emergency, had not played much football during the year, and it was said there had been forces at work to keep him out of the team.

In true understatement "Old Boy" wrote: "It was evident that all was not harmony. In the dressing room at South Melbourne there were blows struck, and after the team had dined at Carlton's and had returned to their quarters at Essendon there was further trouble. There were some arguments, and again fists were flying."

However, the season was far from over as VFA premier club Footscray was poised for a challenge match against the VFL premier club. Essendon was reluctant to play this match, largely because of internal squabbling and also because it felt it had nothing to gain and plenty to lose by facing a challenge from the premier club of what was regarded as the lesser competition.

The match had been arranged by singing legend Dame Nellie Melba to aid the Limbless Soldiers' Fund and she simply would not take "no" for an answer. Essendon finally was convinced to take part in the match, which was played at the MCG on October 4. Football fans licked their collective lips in anticipation and the attendance of 46,000 justified Dame Nellie's persistence.

Essendon was in total disarray from the in-club fighting of the previous week. It had been suggested that some players believed there had been little effort by others in the match against Richmond. It was a matter of pride, but that was the least of the allegations after the match against Footscray, which defeated the VFL club by 28 points. It was an amaz-

INCIDENTS IN THE INTERSTATE FOOTBALL MATCH BETWEEN VICTORIA AND SOUTH AUSTRALIA, PLAYED ON THE M.C.C. GROUND; WON BY VICTORIA The captains are shown in the centre, above V. Richardson (S.A.), below P. O'Brien (V.). The game was witnessed by 44,642 persons.

State Football at the MCG. Insets feature South Australian skipper - the famous Victor Richardson, and Victoria's leader Paddy O'Brien.

ing result and there were immediate charges that some Essendon players had "laid down" and allowed Footscray to win what it considered to be a match vital to its future. After all, Footscray even then was pressing for inclusion in the VFL as the 10th club.

Allegations of bribery flew thick and fast and although nothing was ever proved Essendon took many years to recover from the ignominy of defeat and its aftermath. In fact, champion defender Tom Fitzmaurice refused to continue his career with Essendon and crossed to Geelong the next year. Meanwhile, Footscray had won an important battle in its bid for VFL status.

There had been rumours throughout the 1924 season that the League would introduce a 10th club to eliminate byes. VFA and junior clubs had been

lobbying for at least three years to win this highly-prized status. The VFL decided at its delegates' meeting on July 3, 1924, it would settle the issue once and for all.

Victorian football fans fully expected to awake the next morning to the news of the 10th club. Instead, the sports pages of newspapers were full of reports about an incident in a Geelong-South Melbourne match of the previous Saturday. Geelong had protested over the result of the match and the vital decision on the 10th club was postponed.

And what was that earth-shattering protest about? Geelong claimed it had lost the match because a South player named Hando had shaken a goalpost when Geelong's Pink had taken a shot for goal. The ball hit the post for a behind and the

Neighbors South Melbourne and St Kilda met in the final home and away round of 1923 with a place in the finals at stake. A huge crowd estimated at over 50,000 crammed into the Albert Park ground.

Southerners had scraped home.

The VFL dismissed the appeal, but left the larger and far more important decision on the 10th club unresolved. The football world was kept waiting. A large number of junior clubs were waiting on this decision, with Footscray just one of the interested parties. Other VFA clubs in North Melbourne, Hawthorn and Prahran were interested in joining the VFL, along with the Public Service Football Club. Other VFA clubs in Brighton and Brunswick had written letters of interest to the VFL. The Footscray City Council wrote to the League that Footscray had a "first class ground and a first class team" and the Hawthorn City Council sang its team's praises.

The VFL still refused to make a quick decision and the football public grew weary of waiting as postponement followed postponement. The issue was not resolved until early in 1925 and by then it was generally considered the VFL could not make a decision in time for the new season.

However, the League made its decision on January 9, 1925, and that decision stunned the football world for two reasons. Firstly, the League decided to admit not one new club, but three. Secondly, there was a surprise choice in the three admissions. Letters from the Caulfield and Hawthorn City Councils were discussed and there was an immediate recommendation that the Footscray, Hawthorn and Prahran clubs be admitted.

Had the matter rested there, football history would have been altogether different as North Melbourne would have been destined to play at VFA level rather than seek its fame on a higher stage. The meeting went into camera and Prahran's name was replaced by North Melbourne's. The VFL therefore had a 12-team competition for the 1925 season. The VFA reacted by admitting Coburg to its ranks that year and Camberwell and Preston the next.

The first six-match round was played on May 2, 1925, with tremendous interest in how the newcomers would fare. Footscray was expected to do well, with North a traditionally powerful VFA club. But Hawthorn? It was a club rich on promise, but poor in tradition and results. However, it had an excellent ground and even made the proud boast that its railway wing had seating for opposition fans. In those days only the MCG provided such luxurious facilities for rival supporters.

In the opening round, Footscray was drawn to play Fitzroy at the Brunswick Street Oval, North Melbourne was scheduled to play Geelong at the old Corio Oval and Hawthorn drew a home match against Richmond. North had the most auspicious start in defeating Geelong by eight points, with Fitzroy defeating Footscray by nine points. Richmond thrashed Hawthorn by 39 points to again raise the suggestion that Hawthorn could consider itself lucky to be a VFL club.

Goal square action in the 1929 Grand Final. From left Fincher (Richmond), Ron Baggott (No. 14) Richmond, Henry Wescott (Collingwood), Syd Coventry (Collingwood), George Clayden (Collingwood), Charlie Dibbs (Collingwood), Albert Collier (Collingwood) and Maurie Hunter (Richmond).

Hawthorn, however, did not see it that way and although the Mayblooms (as they were known, after the hawthorn bush) won three matches in 1925, it took many, many years for the club to find credibility at the highest level. Hawthorn defended itself from the outset although it admitted in its annual report of 1925 that it was the "baby" of all senior clubs. After all, the report presented on February 15 "under League auspices" was only the club's 12th annual report.

The report stated: "Your committee right from the start recognised that it was going to be a stern battle, and that it would take some time for our young club to hold its own with the best-organised and wealthiest clubs, not only of Victoria, but of Australia and, without any flourish of trumpets, set out in a steady, but sure, manner to prove to the football world that the confidence of the Governing Body had not been misplaced. The flat rate system of payment was adopted and the policy of building

up the side with young players decided upon. Although we were awarded the wooden-spoon, your committee is satisfied that it went on the right lines and has now the nucleus of a young team, which is going to make a name for itself in "big" football much earlier than many enthusiasts predicted - notwithstanding our position on the premiership list, our players right to the conclusion of the season displayed truly wonderful enthusiasm and attended most regularly to training."

Hawthorn started its VFL career wearing rose-tinted glasses and was not to know that it would take 36 years to win a VFL premiership. However, by the end of the 1980s Hawthorn was established as the power team of the competition and the most successful club of the modern era. Interestingly, Hawthorn's total income for the 1925 season was just 2599 pounds (about $5200). Donations amounted to just over 249 pounds and funds from membership sales totalled 579 pounds. Expenditure matched income, with player payments totalling a meagre 1261 pounds. Incidentally, Hawthorn's wins in 1925 were at the expense of Footscray (14 points in the fifth round on May 30), St Kilda (three points in round 13) and North Melbourne (25 points in the 17th round). Hawthorn's biggest defeat was at the hands of Fitzroy, by 84 points on July 11. Incredibly, that is still a record Fitzroy margin over Hawthorn.

> Just for something different, players reported a boundary umpire in the Richmond-Essendon game.

Just for something different, players reported a boundary umpire in the Richmond-Essendon game. Richmond's Jim Smith infringed the rules when he grabbed George Shorten of Essendon. As Shorten took the free kick, boundary umpire Campton called out: "Go Tich, you have them beaten, keep going". The League took no action against Campton.

St Kilda protested against the registration of Melbourne's Gerald Donnelly in an attempt to reverse the result of their match against the Fuschias. Donnelly showed better sportsmanship than the Saints when he held back in contests against Colin Watson who was still recovering from a broken jaw. St Kilda's protest was turned down, but Donnelly's permit was withdrawn and it was ruled that he was tied to North Melbourne.

As the deadline for issuing permits had passed, he had to sit out the rest of the season. It was a big loss for Melbourne as Donnelly had made the state side.

Geelong showed they could score freely or adapt to rougher situations where necessary. The Geelong-North clash on August 2 was described as the most vicious league match for 20 years. Six players were reported on 17 charges and after one incident a piece of concrete was hurled over the fence and struck Geelong's strongman Arthur Coghlan on the knee. North Melbourne's Rutley was suspended for life on kicking charges. Geelong's Sid Hall did not hold back when giving his evidence and said: "The ball was sent on and Rutley ran up and kicked me. I was sore

for two days". Rutley's suspension was lifted in 1930 and he played four more games. Geelong's Arthur Coghlan and Stan Thomas were both disqualified until the end of the following season and the suspensions remained in place despite a protest meeting called by the local MHR.

A couple of weeks earlier Geelong had piled on 11.4 in the opening quarter against South. As if to prove that the previous year's defeat of Essendon by Footscray was completely out of context, Essendon thrashed the VFL newcomers by 48 points in their first clash in 1925 in round three. Essendon finished the home and away season in second position behind Geelong, which had suffered only two defeats from 17 matches.

Geelong, naturally, was the premiership favourite and duly landed the pennant - the club's first at VFL level - by defeating Collingwood by 10 points in the grand final in front of a record crowd of 64,288. The city of Geelong went wild with delight and more than 5000 fans flocked into the streets around the Geelong Town Hall to welcome their heroes. Geelong had lost to Melbourne by 15 points in the second semi-final, but as minor premiers had the right to play the winner of the Collingwood-Melbourne preliminary final for the flag.

Collingwood defeated Melbourne by 37 points in that match and Geelong found form just in time to land the big one. They were a superbly even team, strong and purposeful and were well led by Cliff Rankin.

Brownlow Medallist for 1925 was St Kilda's Colin Watson who shocked his club by heading back to the bush. Over the next few years the attempts to woo him back would occupy the news columns and at one stage the VFL suspended the entire Ballarat League for letting him play for Maryborough without a clearance. It would be several years before he made a belated return to the Saints.

North, Footscray and Hawthorn filled the bottom three positions in 1925, but had performed better than many critics had expected with 12 victories between them. All three clubs expected to climb the ladder quite dramatically over the next few years, but found the going rough in 1926. In fact, North did not record a win for the season and finished in bottom position three games adrift of Hawthorn; Footscray finished 10th with four victories.

North at times wished it had never entered the VFL and there were suggestions the League newcomer would struggle to maintain its new-found status as a senior club. North even admitted to the League it was struggling to make ends meet and in 1926 the match committee voted to stop match payments to suspended players.

Then, in 1928, North ran a special drive for funds by selling life memberships at 10 pounds a head. By 1931 North was asking the League to give it an advance on its finals dividend. The League agreed, but ordered North to keep its books in balance in future.

Collingwood, Geelong and Melbourne dominated the 1926 season, with Melbourne defeating the Magpies by a whopping 57 points in the grand final. The Fuschias led by only nine points at three-quarter time, but made certain of the premiership with a seven-goal burst in the third quarter. Melbourne had toughened up its approach and matched muscle with Collingwood. Led by captain-coach Bert Chadwick, Melbourne had lifted from the depths. He had a core of up and coming players when he took over the coaching role and added stars like Bob Johnson, Ivor Warne-Smith and Colin Deane.

A week earlier Melbourne's star centreman Bob Corbett had been knocked out in the preliminary final against Essendon. Corbett was KO'd just before half-time, but returned in the closing minutes of a tight game with his head swathed in bandages. Melbourne's doctor had left him to recuperate in the rooms and Corbett fell asleep. When he woke, Corbett made his way unnoticed from the dressing room and his presence spurred the team to a win.

Melbourne, surprisingly, slipped down the ladder in 1927 and missed the finals (finishing fifth). The real surprise at the start of the season was the devastating form of North Melbourne, which had its first victory for two seasons when it defeated Fitzroy by four points in the opening round. North went on to win its next two matches and the football world simply could not believe that one of the "baby clubs" of the League actually was on top of the ladder. North's bubble soon burst as it lost its remaining 15 matches to finish second last, ahead of the hapless Hawthorn (one win).

St Kilda, like North, experienced financial difficulties and the club was split by a faction fight over a 500 pound debt. Players went unpaid for several weeks, but the Saints still managed to finish seventh with eight wins.

One of the greatest solo performances of all time was played out at Victoria Park in June. Carlton's Alec Duncan had a purple patch. He took mark after mark "above the eager, outstretched fingers of friend and foe alike, like some huge vulture swooping on its prey". Even that sober journal, *The Age* said that Duncan took his 33rd mark for the day five minutes before the end. Duncan's form was sometimes erratic, but on this day he made such an impact that it came to be known as "Duncan's Match".

Collingwood, the premiership favorite, played Richmond in appalling conditions in the grand final. Rain started falling the day before the match and continued to tumble from the start of play. The MCG was a quagmire and Collingwood slithered to a 12-point win in what is still the lowest scoring grand final in League history. The Magpies managed 2.13 (25) to Richmond 1.7 (13). There were just two goalkickers in the match, with Gordon "Nuts" Coventry kicking Collingwood's two goals and Jack Fincher kicking Richmond's solitary goal - in the last quarter.

> **The VFL suspended the entire Ballarat League for letting him (1925 Brownlow Medallist, Colin Watson) play for Maryborough without a clearance.**

Collingwood's victory was the start of the greatest premiership run in VFL history and the Magpies by 1930 were known as "the invincibles". It was said that Collingwood was a team without weaknesses and, with stars on every line.

Footscray managed to climb to seventh position in 1928, and in the process won itself a new nickname. Footscray had been known as the Tricolors because of the club's blue, white and red guernseys. However, a fan took a bulldog onto the ground during a match in 1928 and the nickname of the Bulldogs stuck. Footscray certainly played like bulldogs in 1928 and became the first of the new clubs to prove itself at the higher level.

Carlton great Horrie Clover.

In the scramble for a place in the four there was a sensational finish to the Round 17 match between St Kilda and Melbourne at the Junction. Play continued after the final bell rang and St Kilda's Bert Smedley booted a goal. After a conference between timekeepers and goal umpires the score was allowed to stand and St Kilda won by a point. The St Kilda timekeeper said he rang the bell for at least 12 seconds before the field umpire signalled the game was over. It sparked an unsuccessful protest from Melbourne and prompted calls for better methods of signalling the end to games. Essendon installed an electric siren in 1933 but several years would pass before others followed suit.

Meanwhile, the VFL concerned itself with the highly controversial issue of reserve players. Some clubs agitated for a reserve player to be allowed, but the League steadfastly refused to budge and even refused to allocate umpires for Public Schools matches after the schools introduced the reserve system for injured players.

The League did not move on the issue until it allowed the introduction of a nineteenth man in 1930.

Collingwood drew with Melbourne in the second semi-final and then defeated the Redlegs by four points in the replay before facing Richmond in the 1928 grand final. Collingwood had been defeated only three times during the home and away season and was hell-bent on successive premierships. The Collingwood brains-trust therefore went to extraordinary lengths to match Richmond's strengths in the big one.

Collingwood deliberately countered Richmond's high-marking strength and decided to put as much physical pressure as possible on its rivals. The tactics succeeded and Collingwood swept to a 33-point victory.

Money was becoming a more pernicious influence in the game as St Kilda's captain Bill Cubbins found out a couple of nights before his team's appearance in the 1929 first semi when two burly men arrived on his doorstep and offered him a bribe of 30 pounds to ensure that St Kilda lost the game.

Collingwood was at the height of its glory and the 1929 season was the greatest in the club's history. The Magpies went through the home and away season undefeated and kicked a then record 2058 points in the process. It had the competition's leading goalkicker in Gordon Coventry and the season's Brownlow medallist in Albert "Leeter" Collier. Coventry had the League goalkicking award to himself from early in the season and finished with 124 goals. His nearest rival, Carlton's Harry "Soapy" Vallence, managed just 64 goals. Collingwood therefore marched into the finals with tremendous expectation of matching Carlton's hat-trick record. The Blues had won the flag in successive years from 1906-

8 and Collingwood dearly wanted not only to equal the record but smash it.

The Magpies therefore were shocked to their back teeth when Richmond swept the black and white aside with almost ridiculous ease in the second semi to win by 62 points. It was one of the great upsets in League history and Collingwood did not take kindly to the humiliation. It went into the grand final against Richmond desperate for revenge. Collingwood, despite the drubbing in the second semi-final, was still rated a good chance of winning the flag and one anonymous football follower obviously agreed as he sent 11 death threat letters to Magpie players before the match. The Collingwood committee withheld the letters until after the match, which Collingwood won by 29 points. Collingwood had equalled Carlton's record and immediately set its sights on breaking it.

There seemed to be omens at work for the Magpies in a game against South late in the season when it seemed their winning run may have been about to end. A real magpie landed on the field and after hopping around for a few seconds it flew through the goalposts. The football team then followed suit by slamming on the goals. Secretary Copeland merely remarked: "That's one of the tricks we use when things are going wrong". Indeed, there were complaints that Collingwood's dominance was robbing the game of interest.

Following the VFA's introduction of a reserve system in 1929, new VFL secretary Mr Like McBrien managed to convince the VFL to follow suit and a 19th man was allowed from the opening round of 1930. It was actually argued this would help Collingwood remain the power team of the competition as the Magpies had far more depth than other clubs. Collingwood had the good fortune to be supported by one of the wealthiest men in Victoria, controversial businessman and sportsman John Wren. At the end of the 1920s it seemed nothing could silence the roar of the Collingwood machine.

Stan Judkins. This photograph was taken on top of the *Herald-Sun* building

THE GREAT CHAMPIONSHIP SWINDLE

It was meant to be the big decider between the top sides from each of the main competitions.

In the end it provided two hours of football that had the stench of corruption. Essendon, the VFL premier, had nothing to gain by taking on VFA top side Footscray. The Dons were reluctant at first, but the structure of the VFL's finals system meant that there was a spare weekend because the result had been finalised early.

The proceeds went to the Dame Nellie Melba Limbless Soldiers Appeal and pressure to 'do the right thing' weighed heavily on Essendon. It was hard to avoid the perception that Essendon saw the whole exercise as drudgery. Their opponents on the other hand, saw it as the best way to showcase their right to join the League. Essendon was a team that bristled with talent. Its famed Mosquito Fleet had brought all opposition undone and it was hard to see how a team from a lesser competition could come anywhere near them. That opinion was strengthened when Essendon rattled on the first two goals. They peppered the goals while Footscray could only once force the ball into attack for a behind.

Essendon eased back in the second term and some of its players started to sense something was wrong. They held a slight one point lead at half-time and as he left the field, champion defender Tom Fitzmaurice was asked "Where is the smell coming from?" He replied that it was coming from out Footscray way. After half-time Essendon sunk further into the mire as Footscray worked together like a well-oiled machine and displayed slick handball and system that was irresistible.

Fitzmaurice said by three quarter-time he knew there was no chance of saving Essendon's honor. "It was evident to me that some of our players were not doing their best and at three quarter time some of us held an indignation meeting on the ground and decided it was useless 'busting our boilers' when teammates were letting us down." As Fitzmaurice pointed out it was incomprehensible that a League team could kick only 1.11 in the last three quarters against opposition that was not in its class. By the end of the game the scoreboard showed Footscray as victors by 9.10 to 4.12.

Sections of the crowd hooted Essendon as they left the field and in the rooms Fitzmaurice criticised a teammate about letting the side down. The reply he received was "What are you squealing about? You could have been in the cut-up." Fitzmaurice told officials that he was disgusted and would never play for Essendon again. Another star, Charlie Hardy, supported Fitzmaurice's version of events when they were aired in a newspaper 10 years after the event: "One of our players created a scene in the rooms.

T. FITZMAURICE, NTH. MELBOURNE.

Tom Fitzmaurice, who walked out on Essendon after the 1924 sham and later blew the whistle on the affair.

He said he had been offered 20 pounds that morning to 'run a bye'. 'I wouldn't take my pals on as did some chaps in the side. What did some of them get when I was offered 20 pounds?"

Hardy said there had been some strange happenings at Essendon in 1923 and 1924 and there was a clique of dodgy types within the club.

Under the round robin finals system that was used in 1924 there was a chance for a grand final if Essendon was beaten by a large amount in the last game of the series. "It was only direct action in the third quarter by a couple of players who refused to 'stay put' that enabled us to prevent Richmond winning by a margin large enough to entitle them to another game."

Hardy was sceptical of the value of the VFL versus VFA concept and he heard rumors during the week that made him even more concerned. Once the game was under way his worst suspicions were confirmed when he led to position and a usually accurate teammate sprayed a pass over his head. At one stage the Essendon captain moved Hardy away from the attacking wing and replaced him with a lesser player.

At the last change when players stood around in whispering groups Hardy knew the cause was lost. "My greatest regret is that I did not walk off the ground during that term."

Alex Eason of Footscray sternly attacked the notion that Essendon lay down. He said they beat Essendon by handball. "We know that they slacked off at training. We had four scouts watching them. They showed small respect for our gang. We were just a bunch of saps playing a league premiership team." Eason said the problem lay more within the Essendon team itself and all over the field the Essendon players were having verbal shots at each other.

Hardy said plenty had been written in subsequent years about Footscray's "great" form. "This is nothing short of an insult to the common sense of those who know the facts."

THE BROWNLOW MEDAL

The very mention of the word "Brownlow" strikes a chord with League footballers. Winning the Brownlow Medal is regarded as the greatest individual honor in the game, although not even those fortunate enough to be recipients of this award know the background of the man who gave the medal its name.

Charles Brownlow was one of the game's greatest early administrators, but also was a top-line footballer and a man absolutely devoted to the spread of the Australian code.

Brownlow was born of English parents in Geelong in 1861 and, as Australian football was being developed in that era, he became involved in the game from an early age. However, his parents objected to him playing in the rough and tumble matches, even though he was regarded as one of the best footballers in the Geelong area.

Young Brownlow played for North Geelong under the name of "Charles Green" and did so well that he was invited to play with Geelong in 1880. By this time his parents reluctantly accepted that Charles was in love with football and there was no stopping him.

He became Geelong captain in 1883 and was rated one of the champion footballers of the colony. Brownlow gave the Geelong club its early direction and character and in 1885 became its secretary.

This proved a blessing for Australian football as Brownlow not only devoted himself to Geelong's cause, but also spent countless hours planning the progress of the code. He even found time to coach

Brownlow Men. 1. Syd Coventry 2. Ivor Warne-Smith 3. Albert Collier 4. "Carji" Greeves 5. Colin Watson.

his beloved Geelong and organise interstate matches. He combined secretarial duties with playing performances up to 1892 and just a few years later played a vital role in the establishment of the VFL.

Brownlow was undoubtedly one of the backroom engineers in the breakaway from the VFA in late 1896 and instructed the Geelong VFA delegate on how to handle delicate manoeuvring in the formation of the League in 1897.

Brownlow became Geelong's delegate to the League and held that position for 21 years, during which time he advocated some critical innovations, including the introduction of boundary umpires and the numbering of players. He also became vice-president of the League, as well as chairman of the Umpires and Permits Committee.

Few men served the League better than Brownlow and when he died in 1924, the football world mourned his passing.

The League decided later that year to strike a medal to perpetuate Brownlow's memory and the Brownlow medal for the competition's "Fairest and Best" player in each season had its debut at the end of the 1924 season. Fittingly, the first Brownlow was won by a Geelong player, Edward "Carji" Greeves, who polled the most best-on-ground votes from umpires that season.

The VFL Permit Committee meeting on February 29, 1924, resolved: "To perpetuate the memory of the late Charles Brownlow and his many years of most valuable service to the Australian game as player, club secretary, delegate and vice-president of the League, and president of the Australian national Football Council, a gold enamel medal shall be presented annually to the best and fairest player in premiership matches each season - the medal to be called the Brownlow Medal. The field umpire of each match shall post weekly by first post after the match his idea as to the fairest and best player in the match umpired by him. Such votes to be forwarded to the secretary of the League in a sealed addressed and stamped envelope marked "Brownlow Medal".

The League retained the best-on-ground voting until the 1931 season when it was decided to cast votes on a three-two-one basis. Then, with the introduction of the two-umpire system, both umpires cast votes for the 1976-77 seasons. However, since then both field umpires in a match have conferred to cast one set of votes.

In the earliest years of the medal, winners were notified by telegram or by mail. The public soon let it be known that it regarded the winning of the medal as a significant achievement and the direct broadcasting of voting from Harrison House became popular. Then, in 1970, the VFL arranged a live telecast of the voting from a function room in East Mel-

bourne. Now, the telecast of the Brownlow Medal is regarded as one of the highlights of the football year.

In 1989 the VFL decided to award "retrospective" Brownlow Medals to those who previously missed out on countbacks. This added Footscray's Alan Hopkins, Collingwood's Harry Collier, Hawthorn's Col Austen, St Kilda's Verdun Howell and North Melbourne's Noel Teasdale to the prestigious list of Brownlow medallists

Chapter Six

1930-1939
The golden era

The Great Depression cast a blanket of gloom over Australia in the 1930s and sport was the one part of life that provided hope and escape.

Jack Dyer was just one of hundreds of young footballers who strove for a place in VFL teams at the start of the 1930s. They started by seeing the progress to the top level of football as the natural step from junior ranks, but before long it came to have more material significance as the only means of putting food on the family table.

"She was very tough to break into sides those days," recalled Dyer before reciting the back, half-back and centre lines that Richmond would field each game. "That was the side they would pick every week." The reserves played on alternate grounds to the senior team and Jack remembers with a chuckle: "We would rush back from the seconds and ask if anyone was injured in the firsts!"

Competition for places in senior teams was fierce and injuries were dreaded as they could drastically reduce a family's income.

The League, at this stage in its history, was worried about what it considered to be "excessive amounts" being offered to players and in March 1930 introduced the Coulter Law, named after Melbourne delegate Gordon Coulter, which restricted player payments to three pounds a match. But because the depression had hit hard, it also was decided that a player who was out of work could be paid an extra three pounds. Most clubs struggled to find the bare minimum payments.

Within a month of the Coulter Law being passed the League flexed its muscles. The brilliant Albury youngster Haydn Bunton had been chased by Carlton and Fitzroy in a bidding war. After a long discussion it was decided to refuse his permit and that he could not play with any league team or in any competition affiliated with the League. There was doubt over whether he could even play with his old club in the Ovens and Murray league. The Association clubs "ever ready to take advantage of any League difficulty", expressed interest in Bunton, but the Northcote and Oakleigh clubs risked disqualification by the Australian National Council if they played Bunton.

Despite this show of cheek by the VFA, the Association tried to build closer relations later in the year, with talk of amalgamation and the proposal of a charity match between representative VFL and VFA sides.

Coaches were critical of the new holding the ball rule which required a player to punch or kick the ball as soon as he was held. Collingwood's Jock McHale said unless the VFL re-introduced the flick pass the VFA would replace the league in the public's favor. South Melbourne players adapted to the holding the ball rule in the opening round by soccering the ball instead of picking it up. The holding the ball rule was repealed two months into the season.

Some familiar themes emerged and while *The Argus* chief writer was impressed with the Carlton team he was scathing in his comments on the Princes Park press box - "the shed which serves as a press box is a disgrace to the ground. It is uncomfortable and insanitary, and should be condemned by health authorities."

Forwards prospered and the brilliant Gordon Coventry's 118 goals headed the table ahead of new boys Bill Mohr (St Kilda) and George Margitich (Melbourne). Margitich from South Australia, booted 11 goals against Essendon and Mohr kicked 10 goals out of his team's 14 against a strong Collingwood defence. Collingwood, as expected, dominated the home and away season and headed the ladder on percentage from Carlton. Collingwood's percentage was 69.2 to Carlton's 70.6. In those days, a club's percentage was determined by multiplying the points against by 100 and dividing this figure with the points scored. This meant the club with the lower figure would be placed higher on the ladder.

Central to the Collingwood success was bulky full-forward Gordon "Nuts" Coventry. In 1929 he broke the long-established record by an individual in a game when he bagged 16 against Hawthorn, thus surpassing Harold Robertson's 14. In 1930 Coventry went one better with 17 against Fitzroy. The tally could have been larger as Collingwood fed the champ in the final quarter. Two Fitzroy men tried to hold Coventry down while Magpie teammate Bill Libbis, with ball in hand, tried to pass to him. The umpire whistled the free to Coventry as Libbis popped it through for a goal. Rather than penalise the side by giving Coventry the free, the umpire signalled all clear for the goal to Libbis.

On a less happy note was the reaction of North captain-coach Johnny Lewis at the end of a tough afternoon against Hawthorn. Resenting the treatment he was getting, Lewis moved towards the crowd and had to be restrained by a cordon of officials.

Collingwood defeated Richmond by three points in the second semi-final and then went down by 26 points to Geelong. Collingwood, as minor premier, had the right to challenge Geelong for the premiership and the grand final was played on October 11. Collingwood made no mistake this time, although Geelong led by 15 points at half-time. An eight-goal burst in the third quarter helped the Magpies to a 30-point victory. Their quest for a fourth successive premiership had been achieved.

Collingwood's 1930 triumph resulted in considerable acrimony as some clubs felt the challenge system in the finals had been unfair to Geelong. After all, Geelong had defeated Collingwood fair and square in the finals only to lose the flag through a challenge. The VFL therefore decided to alter its finals system yet again in 1931 and the Page (named after football official Percy Page) system was introduced. Under this system, the teams finishing third and fourth played each other in the first semi-final in the first week of the finals. The teams finishing first and second then played off in the second semi-final the following week. Then, the winner of the first semi-final played the loser of the second semi-final in the preliminary final for the right to challenge the winner of the second semi in the grand final. It was agreed that this system would be fair to all clubs in the top four, and the system operated until the introduction of the final five in 1972.

Collingwood's grip on the premiership was loosened in 1931, but not by the finals system devised by Mr Page, who at that time was chairman of the Permit Committee. Collingwood simply had glutted itself on success and lacked the desperate drive for more premierships. In fact, Collingwood barely made the finals in 1931 and pipped the fast-rising young Footscray club for fourth position only on percentage. Footscray probably would have been a worthier finalist as Carlton defeated Collingwood by an incredible 88 points in the first semi-final.

> Coaches were critical of the new holding the ball rule which required a player to punch or kick the ball as soon as he was held.

The men from the western suburbs were led by the tough, experienced ex-Saint Bill Cubbins. In a vital game Cubbins' opponent Harry "Soapy" Vallence lined up for goal with the chance of giving his side a one point victory. "You won't get this one Harry," said Cubbins calmly and the Blues champ slewed the kick.

Richmond broke new ground by booting a league record score of 30.19(199) against the hapless North, but even in the joy of a runaway win the Tigers remembered the purse strings and a 17-year-old kid was left on the bench all afternoon so the club could save money on his match fee. Jack Dyer would subsequently become the club's greatest name in a career that would extend to almost two decades. "I never found out until years later that it was because they were trying to save money. The 30 bob was nice, but the three quid would have been better."

He would endure another full day on the bench later that year as Richmond saved another 30 bob. Another recruit in the Richmond team had a good run that day against North. Doug Strang kicked 14.2 for the Tigers. It may have been a temporary setback for Dyer, but for North it was yet another chapter in a sorry log of failure. By the halfway mark of its seventh season North had only 11 wins from 116 games and there were calls by the press for help. Its local territory was occupied by factories and non-English speaking immigrants and North wanted Essendon to relinquish part of the zone. The Dons were less than sympathetic.

The long-running wounds caused by the VFA-VFL split finally showed signs of healing after more than 30 years. A charity match between the two bodies was arranged for June and there was even talk that they may amalgamate. The atmosphere was so cordial that the two bodies sat down for a conference in May 1933 to discuss a two division competition, but the gulf between the two was too large and the idea fizzled. In the 1931 on-field meeting the League side wore its traditional Big V, while the VFA wore

Richmond defender Basil McCormack gets his kick despite strong pressure from the South opposition. The Tiger backline was the basis of the side's success in the 1930s.

Williamstown colors - gold with a blue sash. Sadly this spirit of co-operation was soured by the weather and the pocket in front of the MCG members' stand was inches deep in water at the start of the game. The VFL won the match after a scare early on.

There was bitterness between two old VFA clubs trying to make their mark at league level. Hawthorn accused the Footscray timekeeper of ringing the final bell six seconds early in a tight game. Hawthorn's star Ted Pool had the ball and the umpire was moving a player back onto the mark when the bell sounded. Hawthorn argued it should have been time-off and the time clock should not have started again until the umpire blew the whistle to let Poole take the kick. The VFL dismissed the protest.

A great deal of debate centred on the very fabric of the game and much of it focussed on the boundary line rule in which free kicks went against the team that kicked the ball last before it crossed the line. Scores ballooned as a result of the law. It was said that it had been introduced at the 1924 national conference when the Victorian delegate who was supposed to vote against it, changed his mind at the last minute. Early in 1931 there was a move at the League table to change back to the old rule with some delegates suggesting the old rule kept the play nearer the boundary line where spectators could get a better view.

The fans seemed happy enough with what they were seeing and were prepared to tolerate being packed into grounds like sardines. In May 1931 a clash at Punt Road between Richmond and Collingwood drew more than 40,000 people and as a section of the crowd swayed dangerously the fence gave away and people spilled onto the field. Police rushed to the scene and several people were hurt.

The Minister for Lands declared that it was a disgrace, but he offered little in the way of a solution. The Richmond Football Club said it had approached its landlord, the cricket club with suggestions on how to alleviate the problem and had even offered its players to provide free labor to remove the adjoining tennis court and create more space. The cricket club flatly rejected all suggestions for change and like many other football clubs around town Richmond simmered with anger at the cricketing attitude.

The Tigers were smiling, however, over their four point victory against Collingwood - the team that had so often made them play second fiddle in recent times. The resolute Richmond defence led by Martin Bolger withstood a fierce onslaught in the final term.

All through 1931 there was confrontation between football and cricket clubs over revenue. The football clubs were tired of being treated like second-class citizens when they were attracting crowds and money far in excess of what cricket did. Cricket club members were being admitted free to the football and the football clubs demanded a financial return. The Minister for Lands decreed that cricket clubs should pay an annual sum to football clubs based on 20 pounds for each 100 cricket club members, but the VFL was still unhappy with the situation and even secured options on the Motordrome (later Olympic Park) and Exhibition grounds just in case the ground dispute worsened.

As in any era there were always radical suggestions to change the game. One of those was a move to standardise ground sizes, but it soon faded.

In this environment of free-flowing football Geelong flourished. The club struck the right blend with experienced campaigners like Arthur Rayson and Arthur Coghlan heading a band of interstate recruits and youngsters. Full-forward George Moloney, Tommy Quinn, Len Metherell and Bob Troughton were instant successes. Moloney, who had starred for Western Australia in the 1930 interstate carnival, quickly achieved hero status as a prolific goalkicker. Geelong revelled in the wet conditions that prevailed for most of the season and finished the season on top of the ladder with 15 wins, defeating Richmond by 20 points in the grand final. There was consternation when it was suggested that Moloney wanted to head home, but he stayed and would boot 109 goals the following year.

The 1932 season saw the rise of South Melbourne to a position of strength. The Bloods, as they were known, had finished seventh in 1931, but under the presidency of grocery king Mr Archie Croft embarked on the most ambitious recruiting drive imaginable. South combed the country for players and landed a large number of interstate stars, including 1926 Sandover medallist Johnny Leonard (Subiaco), Linton "Blue" Richards (East Fremantle), Gilbert Beard, Ossie Bertram and Tasmanian cricket

> The VFL therefore decided to alter its finals system yet again in 1931 and the Page system was introduced.

These days players occasionally reach for the oxygen, but in this 1932 match South's Peter Reville opted for a smoke at three quarter time. Champion full-forward Bob Pratt looks over his shoulder.

and football champion Laurie Nash, not to mention a Mitcham youngster named Bob Pratt, who had made his debut in 1930 but did not start to make his presence felt until 1932.

One important pick-up was Jack Bissett, discarded by Richmond after a disappointing 1931 final. The Tigers acted hastily as it was revealed that Geelong had instructed the burly "Bull" Coghlan to nullify Bissett and not worry about getting kicks himself.

The red and whites won the first 10 games on the trot and stirred the imagination of the football public. Croft was able to supply a rare commodity in these depressed times - employment - but it wasn't all smooth sailing and when some of his player/em-

ployees refused to join a union there was talk of an industrial dispute. Ultimate success was but a season away for South as under captain-coach Leonard the club rose to fourth position.

Controversy over Haydn Bunton continued to rage with the revelation that he had been paid two pounds a week by Fitzroy throughout the 1930 season when he was forced to stand out of football. Meanwhile there was another push to change the out-of-bounds rule, but it remained in force.

The League's lease on the Motordrome came in handy in unforeseen circumstances when Melbourne could not play its early home games on the MCG which had been re-surfaced after athletics event, the National Games, in preparation for the coming English cricket tour of 1932-33. There was background talk of a tour to the United States to promote the game, and inaugural Brownlow medallist "Carji" Greeves said that Aussie Rules would be an assured success. He was well placed to make a judgement as he had spent the 1928 season as kicking coach at the University of Southern California.

St Kilda had a long record of upheaval, but the club's fireworks hit new heights in the middle of 1932 after coach Charlie Hardy was dumped and open war erupted. A "citizens' committee", headed by the St Kilda mayor, called a public protest meeting to complain about the way the club was run. The reform group ran a plebiscite asking "Has the present committee your confidence?" and was stunned to hear the result was 492 "No" and 136 "Yes". The discontent was reflected in the team's erratic performance.

Collingwood defeated South in the first semifinal, but the Southerners not only were on their way, but also were becoming known as the Swans. It is generally believed that the club gained its nickname because its old Lake Oval was only yards from the Albert Park Lake, home of many swans. However, *The Sporting Globe* in 1932 suggested there were so many West Australians playing with South that

Carlton's "Mocha" Johnson introduces the State Governor to his team at Princes Park.

the club should be known as the Swans; the name stuck, although for many years old diehards preferred the old nickname of the Bloods or the Blood-stained Angels. There was a move in the 1950s to change the club's nickname from the Swans to the Bloodhounds, but club members were horrified at the suggestion.

Meanwhile, Richmond played Carlton in the 1932 grand final, with the Tigers squeaking home by just nine points. It was a classic grand final, with high-marking a feature of the match. Richmond had a team of champions and would remain a League power for several years to come, the Tigers' clashes with South over the next few years the talking point of football.

The League, forever attempting to improve its competition, changed the percentage system in 1933 and adopted the method that is still in use. A club's points for were multiplied by 100 and then divided by the points against.

The out of bounds rule continued to cause discussion and experts warned rucks and rovers to be well up with the play to be ready for the rare throw ins. Free kicks went against the last player who had kicked the ball, but throw-ins still occurred when the ball bounced off a player's hands or off any part of the body above the knee.

One team that revelled in the open style of play was Fitzroy. The dynamic Haydn Bunton was at the core of a team that also relied heavily on full forward Jack Moriarty. Three victories in the first three weeks was a great start to 1933, but there were doubts over whether the team had enough depth beyond its stars Bunton, Moriarty and "Chicken" Smallhorn the man who would win the 1933 Brownlow Medal. The shadow of investigation of Haydn Bunton also hung over the team, but once that was resolved they had a good season. A fortnight before the finals Fitzroy was third on the ladder, but then missed the finals by dropping the last two games. It was the closest the Maroons would come to a finals berth in the early 1930s despite fielding sides that included three Brownlow Medallists.

Troubled St Kilda hit the headlines for the right reasons when they fought out a torrid encounter with North Melbourne in which they finished with just 15 fit men. The situation was so bad that Stuart King ran down the field in the last quarter and there was no player to pass to. The Saints' committee honored the team's heroic victory by striking a medal featuring the shield that was subsequently incorporated in the guernsey.

A wonderful match between South Melbourne and Richmond ended dramatically. Umpire Jack McMurray gave a free kick against the Richmond full back Maurie Sheahan when the Tiger took 28 seconds to set up the ball for a place-kick into play after a point. Ivor Warne-Smith wrote: "Whether the decision was right or wrong according to the rule has caused considerable dissension. Even if 'time-off' were signalled before Sheahan made his kick and was not blown again, if in the opinion of the umpire the player was wasting time 'or loitering with intent' to waste time, he was quite within his rights to give a free kick." Critics of the umpire argued that as the watches had been stopped Sheahan could take as long as he liked. From that free kick Bob Pratt calmly booted a goal, but South went down by five points.

Richmond finished the 1933 season on top of the ladder two games clear of South, which had started the season indifferently. In fact, South had won only four of its first nine games and was eighth at the half-way mark. South's "Foreign Legion" then found devastating form and won the double chance ahead of Carlton on percentage.

The Swans had more than their share of luck in finishing second as a match against Collingwood towards the end of the season should have been drawn. Scores were level when timekeepers rang the bell. However the umpire did not hear the bell and South's Terry Brain kicked a goal from a mark to give his side a six-point victory. It proved to be a critical goal as South would have finished the season third without it. South made the most of its good fortune by defeating Richmond by 18 points in the second semi-final for entry to the grand final. Richmond then defeated Geelong by nine points in the preliminary final and League fans anxiously waited for another classic grand final.

Naturally, South's big trump was Pratt, who had been in superb form for the entire season. Yet Pratt managed just three goals in a low-scoring match. The Swans won by 42 points and restricted Richmond to four goals.

At the National Football carnival late in the season there was a flirtation with the idea of merging Australian Rules and Rugby league. A secret trial game was held, but the players found the rules too hard to absorb.

South started the 1934 season as overwhelming premiership favorite and while it was known as the team of champions this may have been the reason why the red and white did not win more premierships in that era. The Bloods always seemed to have difficulty utilising their individual greatness for the benefit of the team as a whole. However, South did have to contend with some bad luck in that era, and particularly in 1935 when Pratt missed the grand final against Collingwood after being knocked down by a truck and injured on the eve of the big match.

South exploded from the blocks in 1934 and Pratt was nothing less than sensational as he rewrote the League's goalkicking records. South kicked huge tallies in its opening games and by the end of the third round, Pratt already had amassed 33 goals, including 15 against Essendon. South's opening round win over Collingwood was particularly significant as it was the first time the club had kicked 100 points or more against the Magpies.

There was a clear gap between the top five teams and the rest in 1934 and the competition between the leaders was often ferocious. Victoria Park was the scene of one of the most savage games of the era when Carlton and Collingwood locked horns in July. "Charging, tripping and unfair play marked every minute of the third quarter of the Collingwood-Carlton match," wrote *The Sporting Globe's* J.M Rohan. The flashpoint came when Collingwood's Syd Coventry was felled by Gordon Mackie and had to leave the field. Coventry's opponent, Carlton's "Mocha" Johnson was later reported on a charge of kicking another Magpie player Jack Ross - "I got off. I actually kicked Jack Knight!" chuckled the veteran in later years.

Blues Maskell and Mackie also went into the umpire's notebook after the Collingwood game. Police had to separate players in the brawl and Carlton later lodged a complaint about the umpires, saying one of their men had been singled out by the umpires from the start of the game and there had been "many and various instances of failure to enforce the laws of the game". A couple of weeks later Carlton announced that the team would not take the field in any game in which Scott was umpire. In late 1934, Johnson was reported in the finals and copped a 10 week suspension.

There were calls for a greater police presence when a goal umpire was stoned by an unruly Fitzroy crowd. Footscray coach Bill Cubbins was the butt of an attack of a different nature when he resigned saying there had been an organised campaign within the club to oust him. At Fitzroy there was trouble too, and coach Jack Cashman resigned just two games into the season because he felt a section of club members were against him. Cashman was promptly snapped up by Carlton and played good football for the Blues as a centre half-forward.

The game retained its magnetic appeal to the public with crowds averaging 100,000 a week - 10 per cent of Melbourne's population. One of the reasons was the prevalence of brilliant full-forwards. Gordon Coventry became the first man to kick 1000

> At the National Football carnival late in the season there was a flirtation with the idea of merging Australian Rules and Rugby league.

career goals and Bob Pratt scaled new goalkicking heights. When he had joined South, Pratt had been advised jokingly by veteran Joe Scanlan: "Now Bob, what we require of a full-forward is a couple of hundred goals a season, so hop in and do your best". History does not record Scanlan's reaction when Pratt bagged 150 (in 21 games) for the 1934 season to become the highest season scorer of all time.

By season's end, South had kicked 20 goals or more in matches no less than eight times - a phenomenal achievement in that era. Yet South also dropped matches it should have won comfortably and wound up in third position, with Richmond and Geelong filling the top two places. South defeated Collingwood in the first semi-final and then brushed Geelong aside in the preliminary final for the right to play Richmond again in the big one.

sHowever, Richmond breezed home by 39 points and Pratt, who was regarded as the key to his club's chances, was restricted to two goals. The Tiger side was a robust, hard-bumping unit chock full of some of the club's all-time greats such as Percy Bentley, Alan Geddes, Jack Dyer, Gordon Strang, Ray Martin, Basil McCormack, Maurie Sheahan and Jack Titus. It was Titus who stole the limelight from Pratt in the grand final with six clever goals.

Pratt had to pull out of the Victorian side that played South Australia late in the year, but a South Melbourne teammate who was a late inclusion more than filled the bill. Laurie Nash went to full-forward at quarter time, after Bill Mohr was injured, and went on a rampage kicking 18 goals. Nash's astounding display was only watched by 17,800 people and the critics of state football queried its worth.

The 1935 VFL season saw a novelty that eventually would become a regular feature of the competition - a night exhibition match was played between South Melbourne and Richmond at Olympic Park. The Tigers had touted a possible full-time move there after continuing disputes with the Richmond Cricket Club over the Punt Road ground. Indeed, the game was played because Richmond could not use their home ground for a practice match. This, however, was not THE first night match as there had been several of attempts to make night football a regular feature of the season. In fact, the first recorded night match in Australian football was in 1879 between Collingwood Artillery and East Melbourne at the MCG. The standard of lighting in the 1930s was nowhere near good enough for regular night matches and, besides, the League had more pressing concerns.

For example, in 1935 it was still debating the merits or otherwise of the Coulter Law. The League debated a motion to scrap the law in 1935, but football's controversial financial restraints remained intact, much to the anguish of several of the wealthier clubs.

The free scoring continued unabated and Essendon forward pocket Ted Freyer started the ball rolling for 1935 with 12 goals on the opening day - an individual record for the first round. Not every side joined the scoring spree and there were proposals to ditch the hapless cellar-dwellers North Melbourne and Hawthorn. It was a real struggle for the Shinboners (North Melbourne) and lack of revenue cause the club to drop its match fees to 30 shillings a week. All but one player accepted the cuts.

Despite the effects of depression, football retained its magnetic attraction for the Melbourne population and arch rivals Fitzroy and Collingwood drew a Monday holiday crowd of 35,000 people to their clash at the Brunswick Street Oval. They turned on a fitting spectacle and a new star was born. In just his second game the 18-year-old Albury youngster "Dinny" Ryan booted five goals on Collingwood hero Jack Regan, but it was another Ryan, Collingwood's Allan, who sent a drop-kick through the uprights after receiving a free on the siren. The mighty kick tied the scores.

Young Clen Denning showed that ex-VFA players were worth recruiting. He made a dazzling start

to his VFL career with four goals in the first half-hour for Carlton. He finished with six for the day.

Collingwood was still undefeated by late June, but Carlton ended the run and South repeated the dose a couple of weeks later. These three teams dominated the competition and Richmond had slipped since its premiership. Multi-club coach Dan Minogue had turned the Saints into a powerful unit and they made a strong push for the four. In the end Richmond held fourth spot. The showdown for the flag was fought out between South and Collingwood.

Old-time South fans still get misty-eyed when they think of how Pratt was injured in a bizarre match eve accident when he was struck by a brick truck whilst getting off a tram on the Thursday before the big game. In the book, 'Bloodstained Angels' Pratt said: "I didn't see him until he practically hit me. I just jumped to get out of the way, but it caught my leg, tore the leg out of my trousers, the heel off my shoe and threw me over the bonnet."

South replaced Pratt with Herbie Matthews and reshuffled its forward line in an attempt to cover the loss of its champion goalkicker. Collingwood also went into the game below full strength, but it coped better than South. Pratt had kicked 103 goals for the season, including six in the second semi-final, and his loss to the Southerners was inestimable. Collingwood took full advantage of the situation and although South led by 15 points at the first change, Collingwood won by 20 points for its first flag since 1930. Young centre half forward Phonse Kyne and midfielder Marcus Whelan were the Magpies' best, but it was the small man brigade which won the day. Fighting spirit and teamwork won out over brilliant individualism and pace. Collingwood's hard bumping took its toll and South looked lost after captain Jack Bissett left the field with concussion.

Collingwood's domination continued the next

The game retained its magnetic appeal to the public with crowds averaging 100,000 a week - 10 per cent of Melbourne's population.

season, which was one of the most controversial in League history. In fact, the very foundations of the League were challenged by a dispute over whether clubs had the legal right to charge admission at grounds on Crown land. Matches at Richmond's Punt Road ground were gatecrashed for two separate matches early in the season and the matter was even taken to court. However, Richmond and the Melbourne City Council fought a rearguard defence of the pay system and the Lands Department eventually ruled that League clubs could charge for admission to matches played on Crown land.

According to the group opposing the charges, the Punt Road ground formed part of the Yarra Park, which was reserved from sale for use as a public place in 1873. The complicated dispute at one stage threatened the financial viability of several clubs and the League was obviously relieved to see the dispute ended in its favor.

Meanwhile, League president Dr W.C. McClelland looked forward to the start of the 1936 season when he wrote in *The Age*: "On every hand the happiest anticipations of the League football season on which we are about to enter are to be found. Everywhere there is unprecedented interest, sales of membership tickets have been well up to the usual volume, and the attendances at the preliminary trials have far exceeded the expectations of everyone.

"In common with the thousands of enthusiasts who are to attend the opening of the Victorian Football League season tomorrow, I hope to see the Australian game played at its best during this season. I am certain that the clubs low on the list last season are going to strive gallantly to climb to greater heights and that this year's competition is bound to be one of the most entertaining for years. To the young man about to enter the game I would say: 'Always uphold the glorious spirit and traditions of this wonderful national sport. Play with manliness, self-reliance, chivalry, unselfishness and courageousness and success must be yours.'"

The 1936 season opened on April 30 in fine, warm weather. The six matches attracted 115,000 fans and *The Age's* 'Forward' had this to say in his summary of the opening: "Indicative of the amazing popularity of the Australian football game in Melbourne is the fact that 115,000 spectators - more than one-tenth of the population of Melbourne and suburbs - attended the opening matches of the Victorian Football League on Saturday afternoon.

"Played in glorious sunshine, the games revealed a particularly high standard for an opening day. With conditions ideal for the forwards, tall totals of 24.19, 20.24, 17.15 and 17.4 and the like were registered. By far the outstanding game was that staged at Richmond, where the greatly improved St Kilda side was defeated by a point after a hair-raising finish. Carlton nearly kicked a club record against Fitzroy; Geelong piled up 20.24 to 10.9 against Footscray; South Melbourne proved far too experienced for Melbourne; Essendon carried too many big guns for North Melbourne, and Collingwood scored 15.14 to 12.11 against Hawthorn."

South appeared to attract most of the controversy of 1936, with star forwards Pratt and Nash always in the news. Pratt decided in mid-season that he wanted to leave the club, a prospect that filled supporters with dread. He had seen the money thrown at interstate recruits and felt that as a local recruit he had been taken for granted. Another factor was ongoing trouble with the ankle that had been injured in his pre-grand final accident in 1935.

The matter was resolved and *The Age* commented under the heading of 'R.Pratt's Return to Form': "South Melbourne officials and supporters were delighted with the welcome return to form by Bob Pratt, the champion full-forward. Though closely watched on Saturday, his amazing leaps, quick thinking and clever leading out saw him at his best and when he kicked his first point, encouraging cheers came from all around the ground. He was accorded a splendid ovation on leaving the arena at the interval and at the close of the game. As the result of the publicity last week, Pratt is to have an interview with a likely employer today."

Pratt, in returning to the fold, had kicked 4.7 in a win over Geelong. Nash was voted best on the ground but later in the season crashed heavily into the picket fence in a match against Carlton at the Lake Oval. At first it was feared that Nash had fractured his skull, but he climbed to his feet and continued playing; the fence was smashed. Nash was also involved in an incident in a mid-week match and the repercussions could have been serious for the Southerners. Nash was enticed to play for the Southern Suburbs' Police against Russell Street in a Wednesday match at the Lake Oval and was reported for 'unseemly behaviour'. Any suspension could have affected the Southerners' premiership prospects, but the Police Tribunal decided that it had been a case of mistaken identity.

South finished the home and away season on top of the ladder with just three defeats, one game clear of bitter rival Collingwood, with Carlton and Melbourne in third and fourth. It had been a fine effort by Melbourne, whose players mid-season had been promised pay bonuses for victories. *The Age* reported one player as saying that if the bonuses continued, the players would be able to retire. Melbourne also awarded a bunch of orchids to the wife or girlfriend of the club's best player each week. The enticements might have been unusual, but Melbourne made the finals for the first time since 1923.

Melbourne defeated Carlton in the first semifinal, but then had to contend with the powerful Southerners in the preliminary final. Collingwood had defeated South by 13 points in the second semifinal, but South was still rated an excellent chance of taking the flag, especially as Collingwood was without champion goalkicker Gordon Coventry, who had been suspended for eight weeks after an incident involving Richmond's Joe Murdoch. Collingwood fans were outraged and protested to

Spectacular Carlton defender Jim Park launches himself for a mark over Melbourne's "Tarzan" Glass.

the League about the Tribunal decision. Coventry had never been reported and Magpie fans - and Coventry himself insisted the penalty was far too severe, especially as the Magpie star was the retaliator in the incident.

Coventry had gone into the game suffering boils on the neck and Collingwood's defence was he had hit back after being hit repeatedly in that area. In old age he admitted that was not the entire story. "It wasn't that at all. I copped a beautiful uppercut and lost my temper and let go one in reply. Even if the story about the boils had been correct I should not have punched up. If a player is silly enough to play with boils in a vulnerable spot he deserves all he gets."

When Collingwood named its side for the following week, for a match against Fitzroy, *The Age* wrote: "Without Coventry on the field tomorrow Collingwood will not look like a Collingwood side. For 17 years the popular and unassuming full-forward has taken his place in the team with a regularity unrivalled by any player in the game, and all true lovers of the sport regret that his long and honourable career has been marred by suspension."

South defeated Melbourne by 26 points in the preliminary final and was confident of defeating the Magpies in the grand final. However, Collingwood defeated South by 11 points to record its second successive premiership. For South, it was the end of an era and the red and white has played in only one grand final (1945) since its great run of four in a row (for just one premiership) from 1933-36.

If the 1936 season had a well-attended start, League officials must been delighted with the response to the opening of 1937. *The Age* reported 120,000 fans had attended the six opening matches. The shock result of the round was Carlton's 70-point victory over South at the Lake Oval. *The Age* even ran a cartoon depicting a South supporter threatening to throw himself into the Albert Park Lake. It was the start of a decline for the Southerners, who finished the season a dismal ninth.

Geelong got to within 15 points of Collingwood at Victoria Park and there was immediate speculation that there was to be a new order at the top of the League ladder. Geelong's form of the first round continued through the season and the Cats finished on top of the ladder with 15 wins, ahead of Melbourne on percentage, with Collingwood third and Richmond fourth.

The season was marred by a number of brutal incidents and in one match between Carlton and Geelong a spectator jumped the fence to remonstrate with umpire Blackburn. Fans were angered by the "deliberate stopping" tactics of some clubs. Star players were belted into submission and there was so much public resentment *The Age* launched a campaign against what it saw as "The Stopping of Champions". The League, it seemed, was under pressure from all sections of the community and even saw itself embroiled in an argument with parliamentarians over a decision to increase the cost of admittance to finals matches. The League, arguing that many clubs were struggling to make ends meet, increased charges from one shilling to one shilling and sixpence.

This sparked a savage response from Mr Barry (Labor, Carlton), who told the Legislative Assembly that the League seemed more interested in acquiring property than meeting the sports needs of the community. Mr Barry was referring to the League's decision in 1930 to acquire a property at 31 Spring Street for 21,200 pounds ($42,400). This building became known as Harrison House and served as the League's headquarters until the shift to Jolimont in 1971.

Meanwhile, the League's decision to increase admittance prices to the finals proved a financial bonanza as gates totalled 14,586 pounds. The grand final between Geelong and Collingwood attracted a record 88,540 fans who paid a record 5960 pounds.

Collingwood won the right to challenge Geelong in the grand final by defeating Richmond in the first semi-final and then Melbourne by 55 points in the preliminary final. Collingwood was on a roll and as Geelong had struggled to defeat Melbourne by only 12 points in the second semi-final, Collingwood was considered an excellent chance of winning its third successive grand final. Collingwood led at the first two breaks, but Geelong managed to draw level by three-quarter time in what was later declared a "classic" grand final. Geelong, through brilliant high-

> It was a game free of spite, in contrast to many matches during the season.

marking and precision teamwork, raced to a big lead in the final quarter and eventually won by 32 points. It was the swansong for Gordon Coventry whose 306 game career had netted a record 1299 goals.

The League was delighted not only with the huge attendance, but also with the manner in which the grand final had been played. It was a game free of spite, in contrast to many matches during the season.

The changing order in 1937 promised to extend to 1938, especially as Hawthorn had recorded a club record of seven wins in 1937 to finish a creditable eighth. There was tremendous optimism at Hawthorn, as the club was building a new grandstand that would be completed before the end of the 1938 season. *The Age* tipped before the start of the season that Hawthorn would be one of the teams to watch in 1938 and said under the heading "New Era For Hawthorn - Previous Worries Disappear: Never since the club attained promotion to League ranks has a season opened so auspiciously for Hawthorn. Activities restricted by lack of finance, successive committees have striven valiantly against almost overwhelming odds to justify the club's membership of the VFL, confident that eventually Hawthorn would rank, not as the Cinderella of the League, but as one of its leaders."

That prediction was about 30 years premature, especially as Hawthorn suffered a slide in 1938 and finished in 11th position with just four wins. It finished above only South Melbourne, whose fall from power was complete with only two wins for the season. South had suffered badly from the absence of star full-forward Pratt with a broken foot.

Hawthorn's new stand was opened late in the season and was expected to cater for the home membership for decades to come. The stand is still a proud part of the Glenferrie Oval, but who was to know in 1938 that Hawthorn would shift to Princes Park for its home matches from 1974. The Glenferrie Oval was the first municipally controlled sports ground

in Victoria when, in 1905, local state member Sir George Swinburne sponsored the Municipal Grounds Act giving local councils the power to control sports grounds. The Hawthorn council was the first to exercise the new powers and facilities for football, cricket, bowls, tennis, swimming and other sports were established at or near the Glenferrie Oval. The Glenferrie Oval stand, opened in 1938 at a cost of about 17,000 pounds, was considered the best in Melbourne at the time.

Most disturbing story for 1938 concerned the offer of 50 pounds to Richmond's Jack Titus to "play dead" against South Melbourne. The man offering the bribe said he represented the promoters of a football betting card. Titus told his committee and played brilliantly to kick five goals.

> **Most disturbing story for 1938 concerned the offer of 50 pounds to Richmond's Jack Titus to "play dead" against South Melbourne.**

It was one of VFL's newer clubs which attracted the sustained interest of football fans in 1938. Footscray, which had won just four games in 1937 to finish eleventh, recorded 13 victories in 1938 to become the first of the new clubs to make the finals. The Bulldogs actually finished third, behind Carlton and Geelong and one game ahead of fourth-placed Collingwood. It had been an amazing transformation, brought about by plenty of hard work and a deliberate policy of fostering local juniors. Footscray, under coach Joe Kelly, did not necessarily have the playing talent of other top sides, but played through the 1938 season with wonderful commitment and teamwork.

Footscray in fact could have won the double chance by finishing second but suffered an inexplicable loss to St Kilda late in the season and lost the double chance to Geelong on percentage. Footscray completed its home and away season by defeating North Melbourne at the Western Oval and then prepared to make history for its first semi-final against Collingwood.

However, the Bulldogs were no match for the experienced Magpies, who won by 41 points in a canter. Carlton, under former South Melbourne star Brighton Diggins, then defeated Geelong by 32 points in the second semi-final to emerge as raging premiership favorite. Collingwood defeated Geelong by 37 points in the preliminary final which meant a Carlton-Collingwood grand final. The League could not contain its glee as these clubs had been traditional rivals for decades.

The grand final attracted a phenomenal attendance of 96,834, which was easily a League and Australian record. The fans were not disappointed as Carlton won an enthralling match by 15 points, thanks largely to Collingwood's foolishness in playing injured skipper Albert Collier, who had a knee problem. Coach Diggins instructed his Carlton players not to bump Collier as this might have meant him being taken from the ground and replaced by nineteenth man Jack Carmody. Collier had no influence on the match and Carlton secured its first premiership since 1915.

A story relating to the 1938 grand final illustrates the "take no prisoners" attitude that has prevailed between Carlton and Collingwood. Diggins worked for the brewery where Collingwood coach Jock McHale was the foreman. On the morning of the grand final McHale rostered Diggins to be on duty. The Collingwood players who were brewery employees were given the morning off!

There was a turnaround in the traffic between the VFL and other competitions which was in sharp contrast to the early 1930s when the League clubs had bled interstate and VFA clubs. In 1938 two of the VFL's most talented players, Haydn Bunton and Carlton's Keith Shea, were lured to West Australian club Subiaco along with Geelong's Les Hardiman. Another high profile star, Laurie Nash, moved to VFA club Camberwell without a clearance and VFL-VFA relations took a dive just when they had seemed to be on the improve.

A mustachioed poppinjay named Adolf Hitler had dominated the world's political stage throughout the 1930s, and although it seemed another world war was inevitable, few Australians took heed of the warnings and preferred the claim by British Prime Minister Neville Chamberlain of 'peace in our time'. When the 12 VFL clubs lined up for the opening round of the 1939 season on April 15, no-one was to know that Australia would be at war by season's end.

The only 'war' that concerned football fans early in 1939 was the one waged by the daily newspapers and the football public against the VFL over the League's decision to increase admission to the outer areas - by twopence! League secretary Like McBrien defended the League's decision by arguing: "All money derived in the way of profit from the grounds should be expended on them".

Fans at the six grounds on opening day protested against the new admittance charges and the extra twopence must have had some effect on the relatively disappointing total attendance of 104,000. The weather was fine and warm, but the largest attendance was at the Carlton-South Melbourne match at Princes Park - just 21,000 fans. Only 13,000 fans watched the North Melbourne-Fitzroy match at Arden Street. *The Age* reported that "indignation was forgotten as soon as the thrilling play commenced".

The surprise of the first round was St Kilda's mammoth 61-point win over Hawthorn at the Junction Oval. The Saints, under former Carlton rover Ansell Clarke, seemed destined for a big season. Their good work did not end there as St Kilda eventually made the finals for the first time since 1929.

Clarke had left Carlton before the start of the 1938 season and therefore missed out on the Blues' premiership triumph of that year. However, he was quick to make his presence felt at St Kilda, which at last had the nucleus of a good side with Roy "Man Mountain" Fountain, Sam Snell, Alan Killigrew (later a legendary coaching figure with St Kilda and North Melbourne), Reg Garvin, Bill Mohr and others.

Two of Victoria's most talented footballers - Keith Shea and Haydn Bunton on their return from the 1937 Carnival in Perth. After years of raids by Victorian clubs the West Australians hit back and made huge bids for Shea and Bunton. Both moved across the Nullarbor in 1938.

The other shock of the opening round was a horrific injury to Footscray defender and Australian boxing champion Ambrose Palmer in the match against Essendon at the Western Oval. Palmer was accidentally sandwiched between two Essendon players and had his jaw and skull fractured in several places. The Essendon club doctor treated him in the Footscray rooms before he was rushed to the Alfred Hospital where he lay on a hospital bed in agony for three hours before being transferred to a private hospital. Palmer's injury was symbolic of the Bulldogs' season as Footscray slumped from fourth in 1938 to 11 in 1939.

Most of the world was girding itself for war and Australian Prime Minister Bob Menzies could see the conflict coming. However, it did not stop him seeing his beloved Carlton in action and he made an unexpected visit to Geelong's old Corio Oval to watch the Blues. Geelong officials entertained the Prime Minister in their rooms at half-time and Mr Menzies even suggested that "paying his two bob at the gate" proved to be one way of finding relief from political pressure. Unfortunately for the Prime Minister, Geelong ruined his day by defeating Carlton by 13 points.

Neither side was to make the finals in 1939, with Melbourne making a surge with St Kilda to the top of the ladder. Hawthorn even climbed into the top four by the end of the fifth round (with three wins, a draw and a loss), but managed only two more wins for the season.

St Kilda always managed to stay in or close to the top four, but stumbled badly late in the season against Collingwood at Victoria Park. St Kilda's dreams of playing in the finals therefore seemed in ashes until Richmond thrashed Carlton in the mud at Punt Road

Brighton Diggins and Jim Francis lead Carlton into battle for the 1938 grand final.

in the second last round. As St Kilda had defeated Geelong at the Corio Oval that day, everything hinged on the final round when Carlton had to defeat a vastly-improved Essendon at Princes Park and pray that bottom side South Melbourne could upset St Kilda at the Junction Oval. Carlton did not put a foot wrong in defeating Essendon by 55 points, but the Saints had little trouble with the Swans and won by 27 points to march into the finals.

There was some doubt about whether the first semi-final between St Kilda and Richmond would be played on schedule as the final round of the season had been played in heavy hail and the MCG was waterlogged just days before the big match (round 17 had been postponed due to wet weather). However, drying winds enabled the League to decide that the match could go ahead on schedule.

In normal circumstances, St Kilda's climb to power would have ensured a bumper attendance for the first semi-final. However, war had been declared just before the finals and many sports fans could find

little interest in football. There was talk that St Kilda might change their colors from the red, white and black of enemy Germany as they had in World War I, but they opted to stick with their traditional guernsey.

The match attracted just 51,411 fans, more than 16,000 down on the 1938 first semi-final. St Kilda, also known as "The Seasiders", were confident of victory and would not hear of defeat. How right they were - St Kilda won by 30 points to advance to the preliminary final. Melbourne defeated Collingwood by 14 points in the second semi-final and St Kilda therefore had to face the Magpies for the right to challenge Melbourne for the flag.

St Kilda's dreams were shattered by Magpie full-forward Ron Todd, who kicked 11 goals in his side's 29-point victory. *The Age* reported: Realising it was to be a KO decision for the losers, the Magpies, speedy and purposeful, made the most of their chances from the outset".

Melbourne had defeated Collingwood by 88 points earlier in the season and obviously was a red-hot favorite for the flag. And Melbourne never looked like letting the outsider snatch victory. Melbourne won by 53 points, even though Collingwood held a four-goal lead early in the match. Collingwood was outmarked all over the field and there were no complaints from the Magpie camp after the match. Melbourne had been the dominant side throughout the season and deserved its premiership - the last played in normal circumstances until 1945.

The big news of the season had been the suggested return to Victorian football of triple Brownlow medallist Haydn Bunton, who had been starring for Subiaco in Western Australia. It had even been suggested the champion rover had been offered a job, a big football salary and a car to return to Victorian football. Nothing came of the offers. And, to prove that nothing is new in football, interstate squabbling reached a peak in 1939 when Western Australian clubs complained that Victorian clubs had used an interstate match in Perth as an excuse to "pirate" players from the West.

Western Australian Football League secretary Mr Bill Orr said after WA had defeated Victoria by 12 points: "Any visit of a Victorian team to Western Australia is always looked forward to with keen anticipation. It is realised in the West that Victorian football is on a very high plane, with players expert in every department of the game, and that there is much to be learned from watching them. But it is to be regretted that any official accompanying the party, and whose expenses are paid for by the Victorian Football League, should utilise this opportunity to pirate players - The naked and unashamed methods of some officials were positively crude."

The most disquieting incident of the season was a vicious brawl at Windy Hill during an Essendon-North Melbourne match, with five young North supporters arrested. The brawl was watched by more than 1000 fans and police had to control other brawls as spectators left the ground. Meanwhile, visiting American university lecturer (in dentistry) Dr Robert Strang, of California, suggested to the League that grounds be marked off in 10-yard areas so that fans could recognise and applaud exceptionally good kicks. That idea was not to be adopted for almost 50 years when the League decided to introduce the 50-metre arc in front of goals at both ends.

Australia's attention was focussed on the outbreak of War in Europe. It was the end of a golden era for football which had seen some of the great teams and players of all time strut their stuff on the Melbourne sporting stage.

Ups and Downs

Tommy Downs was a footballer who evoked great love and loyalty from his own Carlton fans, but was reviled by opposition barrackers.

The Blues saw him as a brilliant little goer (he was just over five feet tall) and a man who stood up for his rights when bullied. Opposition fans saw him in a far different light. They thought he was an opportunist whose conduct on the football field knew no bounds.

Downs was regarded highly enough to be made the stand-in captain for a game early in 1931, but his season ran off the rails late in July when he was reported by a goal umpire for allegedly kicking Richmond's skipper Maurie Hunter during the third quarter. *The Sporting Globe* writer sprang to his defence: "This season he has been battered from pillar to post, but he has taken it all like a Britisher. His object has been the ball. Unfortunately for Tommy, his style of play is so robust that where he is on the field there is usually a fierce scrimmage."

Downs was no stranger to the tribunal. He had been suspended for 12 weeks in 1928 and for 18 in 1930.

The VFL was merciless in its treatment of Downs this time and suspended him until the end of 1932. Downs' initial reaction was that he would never play football again. It amounted to a 28 match disqualification and Carlton fans were indignant. On the Sunday after Downs was rubbed out a crowd of 2,000 people flocked to a protest meeting at Prince's Park where it was said that Downs had been unfairly treated by opponents in virtually every game and had taken what came his way without retaliation.

Some fans believed Carlton had not done enough to help Downs and the more radical ones even suggested that Carlton should not play its remaining games for 1931.

A second protest meeting in mid-August demanded that the VFL should re-hear the case. One spokesman said goal umpire Nicholson was the only person of the 28,000 at the game who had seen the alleged incident. Carlton's captain Ray Brew, a solicitor, said it was a travesty that Downs had been disqualified on evidence that would never be accepted in a court of law.

Downs wrote in his submission for a re-hearing:

"Kicking an opponent, to me appears to be cowardly in the extreme, and whatever my offences in the past have been, and I have expiated them, I had never been charged or even cautioned for kicking".

The VFL remained unmoved by the heat of the debate and the suspension remained in place. Downs served his time then returned for a final season with the Blues in 1933. Carlton supporter Robert Menzies QC advised the Blues there was no avenue of appeal and Carlton had to accept the decision. Carlton raised 74 pounds for their rover.

Two decades later the controversy entered the public spotlight again. Richmond's Jack Rourke admitted it had been his boot that had connected with Maurie Hunter and a photograph was produced which proved the story. Even his detractors had to admit that Tommy Downs had been telling the truth.

> The very mention of his name brings a tear to the eye of all who saw his grace and elegance on a football field.

HEROES OF THE GOLDEN AGE

Every football era has produced its champions, but the era of eras for champions was between the two world wars.

It was the golden age of football when Victorian fans sweated on every deed, every movement, every word from one of hundreds of football heroes. The greats of this era would have been champions in any era and their names are still spoken with the greatest reverence.

Fitzroy's legendary Haydn Bunton is still regarded as the greatest player the game has seen, but what about such champion forwards as South Melbourne's Bob Pratt and Laurie Nash, or Collingwood's Gordon "Nuts" Coventry, or his brother Syd? Then there was Richmond's Jack "Captain Blood" Dyer, St Kilda's Colin Watson, Melbourne's Ivor Warne-Smith (the first dual Brownlow medallist), Essendon's fabulous triple Brownlow medallist Dick Reynolds, Footscray's Alan Hopkins, Geelong's Edward "Carji" Greeves, Collingwood's Albert and Harry Collier and Jack Regan, Richmond's Stan Judkins and many, many more. These were glittering years.

A framed color photograph of the late Haydn Bunton holds pride of place in the Fitzroy Football Club offices. Little wonder! The very mention of his name brings a tear to the eye of all who saw his grace and elegance on a football field. To be rated the greatest player the game has seen is a tribute of the highest order. Some football fans and critics would argue with the selection of Bunton for that honor, but few would doubt that he would be in the top three or five.

Bunton's great rival in his VFL days was Essendon's "King Richard" Reynolds, also a freakish rover who joined the Windy Hill club in 1933 and also went on to win three Brownlow Medals. But whereas Bunton was a feted footballer even before his League debut, Reynolds was an unknown from Essendon District League club Woodlands. The skinny rover was just 16 years of age when he trotted into the Essendon Recreation Reserve for the first time. No-one at Essendon could have known the immense influence he would have at Windy Hill. Besides, Reynolds had been raised a Carlton supporter. Reynolds, writing in *The Argus* of September 23, 1950, told of how his family, especially his father, had played a vital part in the development of his football career:

"While my Dad was alive he never allowed anyone else to touch my boots. Week after week he used to clean them and check the stops. He knew that balance was my greatest asset. and I never lost a stop while Dad took care of my boots. He did more than that. He was on night shift when I first started with Essendon, and he used to give up his sleep in the afternoons so that he could pick me up in the truck and run me across from my work to the ground.

"He and my mother both kept a pretty strict

watch on my diet. They made me eat plenty of fresh food. It's largely due to them that I don't drink or smoke. My parents used to say that I'd been a football crank ever since I was a little boy. They told me that when I was very young I used to take a football to bed with me. What really started me on a football career was the trip I had to Perth in 1929 with the Victorian State Schools' team. We didn't do very well, but it made me more determined to become a good player."

Reynolds neglected to mention that he went to train with Carlton as a schoolboy, but was rejected on two counts. Firstly he was too young and, more importantly, he did not live in Carlton's zone. He was residentially tied to Essendon and trialled with that club in a practice match on a wing. He thrashed his opponent and found himself on a wing in his first senior match, against Footscray in 1933. It did not take him long to assume the role of first rover, a position he made his own over a then record VFL career of 320 senior games.

Reynolds rewrote the Essendon record book. He was club captain from 1939 to his retirement in 1950 and was coach from 1939 to 1960. During his 12-year reign as captain-coach, he took Essendon to four premierships and, under his guidance, Essendon played off in an incredible 11 grand finals. Little wonder Essendon fans knew him as "King Richard".

Bunton and Reynolds were the great rovers of the era, but the 1930s also saw the dominance of champion forwards. South Melbourne, whose golden age coincided with the pre-war era, had two of the very finest in Pratt and Nash. Pratt, recruited from Mitcham, became one of the greatest full-forwards the game has seen, while Tasmanian Nash was a truly superb centre half-forward with the ability to play at the other end of the ground if necessary. In fact, in one interstate match for Victoria Nash was shifted to centre half-forward after half-time and kicked 18 goals, a remarkable achievement at any level of football.

Pratt possibly was the first of football's great aerialists and would propel himself at the ball from behind a pack and hover in the air as he plucked the ball to the delight of his army of fans. Pratt, shorter than most full-forwards but with tremendously strong hands, was part of an extensive recruiting drive by South Melbourne club president and grocery tycoon Archie Croft. The stocky Pratt rewarded the Southerners' fight for his signature with a string of impressive seasons. In 1933 he kicked 109 goals and played in the club's premiership side. In 1934 he kicked a VFL record of 150 goals, a feat equalled by Hawthorn's Peter Hudson in 1971.

When Pratt kicked six goals in South's 1935 second semi-final win over Collingwood he took his season's tally to 103. Everyone expected him to kick at least four or five goals in the grand final to help South to another premiership triumph. However, Pratt was knocked down by a truck on the eve of the grand final and South was unable to clinch the premiership without him. Pratt amassed 678 goals with South to the end of the 1939 season when he decided to try his luck at VFA club Coburg, with which he kicked 182 goals in the 1941 season. Pratt returned to South for one more game in 1946, but soon realised that it was time to quit. His son, Bob Jnr, made his debut against Richmond at the Punt Road Oval in 1959 and sent Swan fans wild with delight when he kicked a goal from full-forward early in the match.

Dick Reynolds - hero to a generation of Essendon fans.

Old-time South fans claim that if Pratt didn't stitch up the opposition, Nash would. Nash was a sports prodigy and almost every VFL club tried to lure him from Tasmania. South won the race for his signature and he shifted to Melbourne to become a sensation in two sports. Not only did he play in South's 1933 premiership side in his first year of League football, but he later played Test cricket for Australia. Nash played at centre half-back in the 1933 South premiership side, but always seemed to play his best football on the forward line.

A man of unswerving confidence in his own ability, he always referred to himself as "the greatest", but always in the nicest possible way. And there are many who would say he was the greatest! Nash played just 99 senior games for South, his VFL career interrupted by a stint with VFA club Camberwell, which offered him a huge pay rise to switch clubs. That was in 1938, but Nash returned to South for the 1945 season. Nash, who coached the Swans in 1953, was fanatical in his support of his VFL club and was shattered when South shifted north to become the Sydney Swans in 1982.

Two other great forwards of the era played for Collingwood. Gordon "Nuts" Coventry still holds the League overall goalkicking record of 1299, kicked in 306 games between 1920 and 1937, and he was succeeded in front of goal at Victoria Park by the brilliant Ron Todd. Gordon and brother Syd were idolised by Collingwood fans, and for good reason. They were both champions and had black and white blood flowing through their veins. "Nuts" Coventry was the butt of many a snide joke when he was recruited from Diamond Creek in 1920.

He was big, slow and, according to the critics of the time, awkward. However, legendary Collingwood coach Jock McHale saw something in the youngster and tried him on the forward line with only modest success in his first couple of season at League level. McHale persisted and was rewarded with consistency in goalkicking rarely seen at any level of foot-

ball, let alone at League level. Coventry became a goalkicking machine and his talents were feared by all rival clubs.

"Nuts" Coventry once kicked 17 goals in a match against Fitzroy - a League record until Melbourne's Fred Fanning kicked 18 goals in a match against St Kilda - and in another match against Hawthorn he kicked 16 goals. Naturally, he played a huge part in Collingwood's record achievement of four successive premierships from 1927-30. He also played in Collingwood's 1935 premiership side. He retired at the end of 1937 after having topped the goalkicking list in his final year. Brother Syd was Collingwood's captain from 1927-34 and the name of Coventry is one of the most revered at Victoria Park.

"Nuts" Coventry retired at the age of 36 knowing the Magpies had a more than adequate replacement standing in the wings. A skinny youngster named Ron Todd had kicked those four goals as a stand-in in the 1936 premiership triumph and on Coventry's retirement became the focal point of Collingwood's attack. Collingwood had recruited Todd from Victorian Railways and he played mainly on the half-forward line until "Nuts" called it a day. When shifted to full-forward, Todd proved as brilliant at kicking goals at his predecessor. A high-flier like South's Pratt, Todd was a tremendous crowd-pleaser and was poised to match the exploits of the greatest of League full-forwards. After all, he kicked 120 goals in 1938 and 121 in 1939 to top the League goalkicking both times. However, VFA club Williamstown made him an almost unbelievable offer to switch clubs for the 1940 season and he signed with the Seagulls.

He crossed to Williamstown without a clearance and copped a five-year suspension from League football for his trouble. Todd proved a huge drawcard in the VFA and did not let anyone down. He kicked 188 goals in the 1945 season, a senior Australian football record he still holds. Todd played just 83 games with the Magpies and old-time Collingwood fans still wonder what might have been if he had not been lured to the rival VFA.

Another Collingwood hero of the era was dashing full-back Jack Regan, still known as "the prince of full-backs". Regan had the most difficult task in football during that golden era - minding the likes of Pratt, St Kilda's Bill Mohr, Richmond's Jack "Skinny" Titus and company.

Collingwood recruited the straight-backed Regan from Northcote as a forward, but soon discovered that his poise under pressure best suited him in defence. Besides, as former Collingwood captain Lou Richards recalls, Regan had the misfortune to cost Collingwood a vital match early in his League career. As Richards tells the tale, Regan had a shot for goal after the final siren in a match against Fitzroy at the Brunswick Street Oval. Collingwood trailed by four points and needed a goal for victory. Regan's shot went wide and the Magpies lost, much to the anguish of coach McHale. Regan, ever so politely, walked over to McHale in the dressing rooms after the match to apologise. McHale, twisting his hat in anguish, did not even bother to look up as he told the youngster: "Go throw yourself in the Yarra".

Instead, McHale threw Regan into defence and his duels with the great forwards of the time were star attractions. He often outmarked the star full-forwards and then would use his dash to tear downfield to create scoring chances for Collingwood. In this respect he was years ahead of his time and Collingwood fans roared with delight when he took off on one of his runs. Regan eventually played 193 games with Collingwood, his career interrupted by World War II. He started with Collingwood in 1930 and retired in 1946. He later served the club for many years as assistant secretary and secretary, and heaven help anyone who criticised his beloved Magpies within earshot.

Of course, the great character of the pre-war era was the infamous Jack "Captain Blood" Dyer, who started with the Tigers in 1931 and played until 1949

for 310 senior games. Dyer was a Richmond boy through and through, even though he spent his earliest years at Yarra Junction. He attended the St Ignatius school in Richmond and remains to this day its most famous former student. When Dyer went to Richmond in 1931 as a 17-year-old, he was in awe of the great Tiger players of the time. He was not to know that he would become the greatest of them all and his swashbuckling style - and that was how he got his nickname - would become synonymous with Richmond.

Dyer was a hard-hitting ruckman greatly feared by the opposition because of his no-nonsense, straight-ahead style. He was the typical "protector" and it just did not pay to get in his way. Dyer was Richmond captain-coach from 1941-9 and was non-playing coach until 1952. He led the Tigers to the 1943 premiership and although he was regarded as one of the truly great players of the war and immediate post-war periods, his contribution to football before the war earns him a place alongside the greatest of this era. Former champion Melbourne forward and legendary coach Norm Smith once wrote of one of his tangles with Dyer: "There was a floating sensation of unreality as I crashed face first into the turf. A yellow light flashed across my eyes. No human could hit that hard, but then I often have wondered if Jack Dyer was human."

One of Dyer's teammates at Richmond was Jack "Skinny" Titus, whose nickname was well-deserved. In fact, Titus looked more like the pull-through for a rifle than a champion League forward. Titus might have been little more than meat and bones, but he proved more than a handful for most full-backs in the 1930s. Richmond recruited Titus from Castlemaine when he was just 15 years of age. He made his senior debut in 1926 and went on to play 294 games, 204 of them in succession - still a League record.

He topped Richmond's goalkicking every year from 1934-42 and kicked exactly 100 goals in the

1940 season. He played in Richmond's 1932 (as a half-forward) and 1934 (as full-forward) premiership sides, but missed glory with the 1943 premiership Tigers because of an injured ankle. Titus retired at the end of 1943, but later played in the VFA with Coburg. However, he was not lost to Richmond as he served the club for more than 30 years as a selector and/or committeeman. He was even coach for a brief period in 1965 when the great Len Smith died suddenly. Titus himself died in 1978.

Richmond's only Brownlow medallist of the pre-war era was dazzling winger Stan Judkins, whose son Noel later became Essendon's recruiting manager. Judkins, Collingwood's Harry Collier and Footscray's Alan Hokins tied for the Brownlow in 1930, with the medal awarded to Judkins on a countback. In those days, only the best player on the ground polled a vote. The three players collected four votes each that year, but as Judkins had played fewer games during the season (12, to Collier's 18 and Hopkins' 15) he was awarded the medal. This created such an uproar that voting was changed the following year and field umpires awarded votes on a three-two-one basis. Richmond recruited Judkins from VFA club Northcote and he made his senior debut in the 1928 grand final against Collingwood. He had a relatively brief VFL career and retired in 1933 with 133 senior games to his credit.

Hopkins and Collier finally had their 1930 brilliance rewarded when the VFL decided to award retrospective Brownlows in 1989. It was voted to scrap countback decisions and to award Brownlows to all those who had tied in earlier counts. For Hopkins, it meant the end of all talk that he had been most unfortunate in failing to win a Brownlow. He had suffered the heartbreak of being runner-up twice (apart from the original 1930 count) and was fourth in 1933.

Hopkins was probably Footscray's greatest pre-war player and was always destined to play for the Bulldogs. His father Con had been a star player with the club in its VFA days and Alan was already an established player when it was admitted to the League in 1925. He was the club's first League superstar and was idolised by Footscray fans because of his dazzling skills across the centreline. Known affectionately as "Banana Legs" because of his bandy appearance, Hopkins proved that appearances certainly could be deceptive and was the mainstay of the Footscray club in its early years of League competition. Hopkins played 153 VFL games with the Bulldogs to his retirement in 1934 but, of course, had two seasons with the club in its VFA days.

Harry Collier was overjoyed with the announcement in 1989 that he would receive a Brownlow Medal. Losing on a countback to Judkins in 1930 had upset him for more than half a century. The chirpy Collier therefore completed a rare family double as his brother Albert had won the 1929 Brownlow. Collingwood recruited the Collier brothers from Ivanhoe and they proved to be tremendous acquisitions, with Albert playing mainly in defence and Harry excelling as a rover. Albert Collier was Collingwood's first Brownlow medallist, landing football's most coveted individual award five years after its inception.

The first winner was Geelong's Edward "Carji" Greeves, a champion with tremendous natural ability. Most football fans did not even know his Christian name, but knew him simply as "Carji", a nickname he picked up as a baby, after a celebrated circus star of the time. Greeves was a schoolboy champion, at football and on the track, with Geelong College. He was so brilliant that Geelong tried to lure him to League football during his final year at school. The headmaster refused Greeves permission to play for Geelong and he had to wait until 1923 to make his debut. The classy centreman was a star from the first day he played League football and was idolised by every Geelong supporter. He was an excellent mark, a strong ground player and excelled in his kicking. In fact, he was such a good kick that he was offered the position of specialist kicking coach at the University of California. Greeves accepted the position and was lost to League football for a year. Greeves, who was runner-up in three Brownlow counts, played 137 games for Geelong to his retirement in 1933. He died in 1963.

The second Brownlow medallist, in 1925, was St Kilda's Colin Watson, a nomad who had several stints with the Saints. Watson started his football career with South Warrnambool and did so well that he was invited to play with VFA club Port Melbourne. He was lured to St Kilda in 1920, but stayed only four games before returning to the country for another two years.

St Kilda shifted heaven and earth to get him to return and the club's efforts were rewarded with a string of brilliant performances on the wing in 1924. The following year, playing in the centre, he polled nine best on the ground votes from 15 matches to easily win the Brownlow. However, there was no fanfare for his achievement and he did not even know he had won the Brownlow until he received a telephone call when he was dancing at a popular Melbourne nightspot. Watson went to VFL headquarters several weeks later and a clerk had to search through drawers before presenting the St Kilda champion with football's most treasured possession.

Watson, who never really settled into city life, applied for a clearance to Stawell in 1926 and was forced to stand out of football when the Saints blocked the move. He then became captain-coach of Maryborough in 1927, without a clearance. The League reacted by disqualifying him, the ban not lifted until 1930 when he returned to South Warrnambool. Watson returned to St Kilda in 1933 and was club captain-coach the following year. He retired from League football for good after one game of the 1935 season and, naturally, returned to the country.

One of his great teammates was champion full-forward Bill Mohr, whose exploits would have given

him greater prominence had he not played in the same era as Pratt and "Nuts" Coventry. St Kilda recruited Mohr from Wagga and early in his career used him in defence. However, his brilliant leading soon had him switched to the forward line where he became one of the game's finest players. In one game against Collingwood in 1931, Mohr kicked 11 goals. At the other end of the ground, Coventry also kicked 11. It was one of the most amazing goal duels seen in any League match. Mohr's contribution helped the Saints to a 14-point victory over the Magpies and *The Sun* newspaper later lavished praise on the two champion full-forwards. The headlines read: "Forwards 11 Each". Mohr became the first St Kilda player to head the League goalkicking when he booted 101 goals in the 1936 season.

The other truly great forward of the era was Carlton's Harry "Soapy" Vallence, who won his nickname through being "a slippery customer". Carlton recruited Vallence from Bacchus Marsh in 1926 and he played 204 games for the Blues for 722 goals. A strong mark and a long kick, Vallence was equally at home at centre half-forward or at full-forward. He left Carlton at the end of the 1938 season to pursue a coaching career and in 1946 played his last 'senior' game as captain-coach of now-defunct VFA club Brighton. In that last match, Vallence kicked 11 goals, 10 of them straight before he missed and kicked a behind. He played in minor competitions around Melbourne until he was well into his 50s.

Melbourne's Ivor Warne-Smith had the distinction of being the first dual Brownlow medallist, winning in 1926 and 1928. Good football judges at that time considered him unlucky not to have added to his collection. Melbourne recruited Warne-Smith from Wesley College in 1919, but he played only a handful of games for the Fuschias (as they were known) before he shifted to Tasmania to run an apple orchard. He won several best and fairest awards in Tasmania, prompting Richmond to woo him back from the Apple Isle. However, Melbourne refused to clear him and he resumed his League career in 1925 as a 27-year-old.

The brilliant utility, who was superbly balanced and could kick with either foot, soon showed that he should never have been lost to League football and became one of Melbourne's greatest players. He was appointed Melbourne captain-coach in 1928 and retired as a player after the 1931 season, only to make a brief comeback the following year. Warne-Smith was Melbourne chairman of selectors from 1949 until his death in 1960.

Of course, there were many other fine players of this era, but these were the superstars of the golden age of football and their names will be remembered for as long as the game is played.

HAYDN BUNTON - SHOULD HE HAVE WON FOUR BROWNLOWS?

To win three Brownlow Medals in seven seasons is a feat that gives some idea of Haydn Bunton's greatness.

Add to that the statistic of three Sandover Medals in Western Australia and you can build a perception of the man's mastery of the game of Australian Rules. It is a record that is unsurpassed in itself, but Bunton could easily have won a fourth Brownlow to place him on a pedestal distinct from all others.

It was a tale related by Bunton's son - Haydn Junior and repeated by others who knew him well. The definitive confirmation comes in a 1946 article in *The Sporting Globe* in which Bunton looked back on his career.

"An injudicious remark to an umpire - which I don't remember having made - might have cost me the 1934 Brownlow Medal. The last home and away game of the season was against Essendon and if I felt I had played the game of my life, I did that day. On the Monday the papers gave me a great boost and I thought I was Christmas. When the Brownlow votes were opened, however I learned that I had not received a vote for that match. Some time later, a Fitzroy official was informed that I had disqualified myself by making a remark which the umpire considered was a canvas for the top vote."

Bunton was alleged to have said "Well, that's the best I have ever turned in", but he could not remember doing so.

Essendon's Anderson scored the three Brownlow votes followed by Fitzroy's Dawson and Smallhorn. *The Argus* nominated Bunton as Fitzroy's best, mentioned Dawson as fourth best and did not even list Smallhorn. *The Sun* said Bunton was best afield and Smallhorn was little inferior. Anderson was rated Essendon's second best.

In a touch of irony, Bunton's opponent Dick Reynolds did well until he injured a shoulder. Reynolds pipped Bunton by one vote in the Brownlow.

Haydn Bunton was a controversial figure even before he played a League game.

The boy from Albury was such a brilliant young footballer that 11 League clubs beat a path to his door. Older brother Cleaver said in 1995 that North Melbourne was the only club that did not chase him. Carlton and Fitzroy led the charge, but hit a snag in the form of young Haydn's mother who did not want him to go to the city. Eventually she agreed to him going to Melbourne only if he could get a transfer in his employment.

Carlton was informed and within days the Buntons received a telegram saying that his work transfer had been granted - "come to Melbourne at once".

Cleaver Bunton recalled: "The telegram was bogus. New Zealand Loan (his employer) had not even been in touch with its Melbourne office". The Bunton family was furious when they realised that Carlton had sent the telegram as a lure.

By the start of 1931 the VFL had agreed to grant Bunton a permit. *The Sporting Globe's* W.S Sharland, one of Bunton's most ardent supporters, received a swag of letters when Bunton made a slow start to his career. But by September he could smile in satisfaction when the youngster won the Brownlow Medal. "The accusation that he was an umpire's pet was silly and the result of envy."

In April 1932 the Bunton affair raised its head yet again in football circles as there were revelations the Fitzroy star had been paid two pounds a week during 1930 while he was forced to stand out of football. In addition to the two pounds he was paid another one pound 10 shillings plus 40 pounds for medical expenses due to an injury he sustained playing in a country match against the advice of club officials. The revelations came from former Fitzroy secretary Tom Coles.

Bunton was appointed captain in 1932, but after three games he resigned. He said he had come to the conclusion he could serve the team better as a player without the responsibilities of captaincy. The season had started in a blaze of glory for Fitzroy with a win over Carlton and best on ground status for their 20-year-old skipper. He told *The Sporting Globe*: "The job of leading a side does not worry me at all, for I know that I have the backing of the players. I feel however that I am too much in the game to be worrying much about what the other fellows are doing".

Fitzroy started the 1933 season brilliantly, but the spectre of the Bunton payment drama loomed again. Two long sittings by the investigation committee and 72 pages of evidence was a fair indication of the VFL's hand-wringing. It was a ticklish situation for the VFL as it was well-known that all clubs transgressed the Coulter Law which restricted

The debonair Haydn Bunton. Was he the greatest?

payments, but because the VFL had no access to club payment records there was no way it could enforce the rule.

The matter of Bunton's payments flared into an issue in 1933 because Fitzroy's former secretary Tom Coles reacted after Bunton said that no payments had been made to him. Ironically the case could not be heard under the Coulter Law provisions because no complaint had been lodged by another club. Coles, in what seemed to be a vindictive action, had been the complainant. The Permit Committee found Bunton guilty, but the VFL gave him only a severe reprimand as he had previously. Bunton told the hearing he had received money from supporters of Fitzroy in 1930, but not from club officials. "It was made clear to me by the president and secretary of the club that as the money was not coming from the club I was not breaking the Coulter Law."

The waters became muddied when Bunton was asked who had handed him the money. "The two pounds a week was paid by a cricket club official and the 30 shillings was paid by Mr Coles." When he was hospitalised after injury Bunton was visited by a club official. "I found 30 pounds under the pillow after he left," said Bunton.

Respected writer "Jumbo" Sharland wrote: "There has never been a footballer like this Albury boy for all round accomplishment and his wonderful stamina makes him most dangerous. Apparently there is no limit to his capacity. He is a ruckman-rover - an ubiquitous player who is always doing something brilliantly".

There was some quibble over his kicking and it was the reason Gordon Coventry left him out of his top five players of all time. Coventry wrote: "Bunton failed dismally in that important phase of football - passing. He attempted to do too much. Bunton won plaudits from the crowd for his brilliance, but key position men in his side could be heard lamenting. He often disorganised his team through individualism".

Gordon Rattray a former Fitzroy captain said early in Bunton's career that if there was a weakness in Bunton's game it was his kicking. But by 1935 Rattray reckoned he had improved it. "Until this season I could never recall having seen him drop kick a ball either in passing or to a teammate or in shooting for goal. That he himself must have known it was evident on Saturday. I was particularly pleased to see him concentrate on stab-kicking." Rattray labelled Bunton "uncanny".

"The main reason is his astounding balance. How rarely is Bunton seen off his feet. He possesses that invaluable knack of converting a solid bump into an added momentum to his pace. I have seen him stumble, yet with his head almost touching the ground recover himself in a manner that I consider definitely uncanny . His stamina is also astounding. He could, I am sure, rove for all four quarters in the fastest of games. His long strides are deceptive, for he is fast yet does not really appear to be so. He is ultra scientific as a footballer . He wastes no energy in futile bumps and does not waste a yard of ground. He is undoubtedly the finest exponent of handball I have ever seen and always uses it to advantage.

"I would prefer if possible to see him being able to kick with both feet, but he is clever enough to be very rarely caught in a position where his left foot is vital. He always resorts to his wonderful hand-passing or cleverly feints and eludes the opposition so that one realises, with a little surprise at first that he is not an 'either foot' artist."

Chapter Seven

1940-1945

And back to war

It was obvious that the war would have a serious effect on all football and not just at VFL level. Young Australians rushed to enlist and many junior clubs were forced to disband or stand down for several years.

However, Prime Minister Bob Menzies declared sport should continue to be played to maintain morale and, with that in mind, the League started its 1940 season with a full 12-club competition, even if a number of star players were unavailable because of military service.

Footballers helped the war effort by agreeing to take a 50 per cent pay cut, from 3 pounds to 30 shillings, and then taking part in a war-effort lightning premiership late in the season. Football was not to get back to normal for another six dark years.

The 1940 season opened on April 27 in brilliant sunshine in front of just over 100,000 fans. The big sensation of the opening round was Hawthorn's huge 72-point win over North Melbourne to put the Hawks on top of the League ladder for the first time in the club's history. Rover Alec Albiston became the first Hawthorn player to kick 10 goals in a match as the Mayblooms impressed enormously with their teamwork and cohesion. Football fans were still talking about it when the first season's bombshell was dropped.

St Kilda captain-coach Ansell Clarke, who had done so well to take the Saints to third position in 1939, announced his retirement as a player after just one round of the 1940 season. Clarke told the club's committee that he wanted to "make way for youth". He had played 25 games with St Kilda after earlier spending nine years (145 games) with Carlton. In his letter to the match committee he wrote: "I feel that I could carry on this season but after watching the form of many promising young players on our list I consider that it will be in the best interests of the club to direct all my energies to coaching these boys".

One of "these boys" was a Brighton youngster named Keith Miller, who later won enormous acclaim as an Australian Test cricketer and footballer of some note. St Kilda signed Miller during the 1940 season after he had restricted the great Bob Pratt to just one goal in a match against Coburg.

Clarke was not the only coach to make a big decision that year as Geelong's Reg Hickey decided after five rounds he could not accept the club's decision that he become a non-playing coach. Hickey's coaching position went to Les Laver, who had coached the reserves to 12 successive finals series. Hickey eventually returned as Geelong coach in 1950 and took the Cats to the 1952 premiership.

The other early season shocks were the cancellation of the planned Hobart Carnival because of the war and the suggestion of a promotion-relegation system between the VFL and the rival association. This caused a great stir and Camberwell (VFA) president Dr F. Harnett was quoted as saying: "If there is to be unified control, there should be equality for all. We (the VFA) are not a junior body and we are not to be treated like one." The promotion-relegation proposal was dropped forthwith.

Enlistments continued to bite into club playing resources and by June all Melbourne newspapers had reported a steady stream of League footballers swapping club colors for khaki. North Melbourne's captain-coach joined the AIF and was replaced by R.J. "Jimmy" Adamson, who had been North's captain in 1938. Adamson must have relished the responsibility as he won North's best and fairest in 1940. Fitzroy and Carlton players, among others, contributed to the war effort by purchasing war certificates with their football earnings.

Patriotism was paramount and players had no objection to taking part in a special lightning premiership at the MCG on August 3. This lightning premiership was played in front of 30,407 fans, with the gate takings of almost 3000 pounds going to the war effort. The series was played on a complicated knock-out basis, with Richmond and North clashing in one semi-final and St Kilda and Carlton on the other.

Richmond defeated North by 16 points in their mini-match, with St Kilda defeating Carlton by two points to set the scene for a replay between Richmond and St Kilda of the 1939 first semi-final. St Kilda repeated its big win over the Tigers in that match by thrashing Richmond by 24 points to annex the lightning premiership.

St Kilda, however, had no chance of making the

A.LA FONTAINE

Brilliant Melbourne skipper Allan La Fontaine who led the Demons to three flags.

finals and finished the season in 11th position. The big improver had been Footscray, which made a gallant bid to play in the finals for the second time in the club's history. Footscray was scheduled to play Geelong at the Corio Oval in the second last round and, with both teams in the fight with Carlton for fourth position, it was to be a do-or-die effort.

Footscray coach Norm Ware told his players at training on the Thursday night before the match: "We can beat Geelong at Geelong, Darwin, or anywhere else". He was wrong. Geelong defeated Footscray by five points to clinch a place in the finals. Footscray had to settle for sixth, just behind Carlton.

The four comprised, in order, Melbourne, Richmond, Essendon and Geelong, with Melbourne the raging premiership favorite under coach Frank "Checker" Hughes, who had coached the Tigers to the 1932 flag. Essendon knocked Geelong out in the first semi-final and Richmond then marched into the grand final by pipping Melbourne by six points in the second semi-final. Melbourne won a second crack at Richmond by defeating Essendon by five points in the preliminary final.

Melbourne made nonsense of its poor second semi-final form by defeating Richmond by 39 points in the grand final. Hughes sportingly went into the Richmond rooms after the match and declared that part of his heart was still with Richmond and added he had been happier the previous season when Melbourne had defeated Collingwood in the grand final.

The 1941 season started with the war taking more and more men from the home front. The first League captain to enlist was North's Len Thomas who patriotically told a reporter: "Well, a man just can't be out of a thing like this". Sadly Len Thomas was killed at the front, leaving a wife and two young children.

There was a surreal flavor to it all when *The Sporting Globe* published a picture of Melbourne's Harold Ball and Fitzroy's "Chicken" Smallhorn shaking hands before a services football game in Malaya where they were on duty. Ball had asked whether someone back home could donate footballs to the cause and the story suggested a Melbourne supporter could keep Ball in touch so he would retain his form for the day he returned "to Melbourne's lair". Like Len Thomas, Ball would make the supreme sacrifice. Smallhorn, the 1933 Brownlow Medallist, would spend much of the war in a P.O.W. camp.

A number of League footballers were in the military camp for the start of the new season and had to get special leave to play football. The Southern Command headquarters announced that special leave had been approved for all selected players. The first round, played on April 26, attracted just 87,000 fans - down almost 20,000 on the previous season. Footscray topped the ladder after the six games by defeating Hawthorn by 41 points in a relatively tight round.

Geelong abandoned its old Corio Oval headquarters in favor of the new Kardinia Park, which remains Geelong's home.

Football might have been seen in some quarters as counter-productive to the war effort, but it certainly took minds off the dark events in Europe and Asia. However, the football world was shocked in August that year when news was released of the death in action of talented and popular Melbourne rover Ron Barassi. *The Age* reported that when the Melbourne players were told of Barassi's death at Tobruk, "everyone in the rooms at the MCG was silent". Barassi left behind a widow and two children, one of whom became even more famous than his father. Ron Barassi Jnr carried his father's name with great pride and dig-

Norm Smith is remembered for his coaching achievements, but he was a fine player who could have won a Brownlow if the medal had not been suspended during World War II.

nity during a playing career with Melbourne and Carlton and a coaching career with Carlton, North Melbourne, Carlton and Sydney.

Meanwhile Carlton, Melbourne, Richmond and Essendon comprised the final four and the League decided to increase finals prices from one and sixpence to two shillings. This resulted in a financial bonanza as the finals netted a record 21,748 pounds. The price hike was vital to the survival of several clubs as the war had hit attendances during the season and coffers were empty.

The VFA had money to spend and enticed two champion forwards to switch competitions without getting clearances. Ron Todd went to Williamstown and Bob Pratt lined up at Coburg.

Captain Blood

THEY call him Captain Blood, not because he is a pirate but because this captain-coach of the "Tigers," the Richmond Australian Rules team, is a bone-shaking, body-bruising, ruthless footballer.

His name is Jack Dyer. He stands 6.3 and weighs 14 stone. He's a hero in Richmond, but the "bad man" of the game to supporters of other clubs.

On Saturdays he preaches and practises the gospel of vigor. He has instilled the same idea into his team-mates. On the field he is the ruthless, relentless, cold-blooded win-at-any-spoken, personable, children-loving giant whose time is always at the disposal of charitable bodies and who is always ready to teach the kids how to play football.

Jack was once a policeman. Now he's got a milk bar, confectionery and smallgoods shop in Richmond. Kids comes from miles around just to buy their ice-cream from Jack.

Dyer has played with Richmond since 1931. He has become almost a legendary figure because of his vigorous strength and still undimmed brilliance. He's always been a dominant figure, and in earlier days was the fastest big man playing football.

Bump them hard and often, and then bump them again" has been his philosophy. He's practised it himself. He's taught it to his colleagues. And so the "Tigers" are one of the hardest-hitting sides in the game. And Jack

SPORTING LIFE, September, 1948

Face Light

Captain Blood prepares to punch the footy ...but Jack Dyer's opponents were more worried about their own safety when in the path of the Richmond champ.

Essendon defeated Richmond in the first semi-final and then Carlton by 25 points in the preliminary final for the right to challenge Melbourne in the grand final. Melbourne was always the hot favorite after winning the two previous grand finals and easily disposing of Carlton in the second semi-final. And that was the way it worked out in the grand final, with Melbourne defeating the Dons by 29 points with a blend of ruck power and confident, flowing football.

The VFA had abandoned its competition in 1941 and for a time it was thought the League would follow suit. Some clubs struggled to find enough players to field full teams and even powerful Melbourne indicated during the season that it might have to forfeit matches or even pull out of the competition. This never eventuated, but players were hard to come by and gaps were filled from week to week.

Melbourne, of course, dearly wanted to equal Collingwood's record of four premierships in a row, but was never in a position to seriously challenge this mark and finished the 1942 season in eighth position. Geelong, however, missed the 1942-43 seasons because of war-time travel restrictions and a number of its players headed to rival clubs. These included star full-forward Lindsay White, who switched to South Melbourne and topped the League goalkicking for the Swans with 80 goals in 1942.

To make matters even more difficult for the League, the MCG, the Lake Oval, the Junction Oval and the Western Oval were taken over by the military and Prahran's Toorak Park and the Yarraville Oval were used as alternative League venues. Fans were still drawn to the League matches, but they also supported numerous service games and it was not uncommon for League footballers to represent clubs on Saturdays and their service during the week.

There was even a patriotic game between Richmond and Fitzroy at the Punt Road Oval on May 2, with funds going to the war effort. More than 15,000 fans watched the game, which raised more than 700 pounds. The match was watched by several high-ranking American officers, who later suggested the game had the potential to interest America's vast number of sports fans. Brigadier-General Morhouse, who represented General MacArthur at the match, described the match as the fastest game of football he had seen. There were suggestions of an America versus Australia service game, one half of Australian football and one half of American football.

Meanwhile, the opening round of the 1942 season attracted just 44,000 people - a clear indication fans had other thoughts, even allowing for the bye created by the absence of Geelong. Richmond made an amazing start to the year, kicking 99 goals in the first four weeks made up of 30, 19, 25 and 25.

The game was hit hard by the war in the Pacific and the absence of star players weakened teams. No club was ever sure it would have a full side and selection was frequently made just before the game was due to start.

Essendon, Richmond, South Melbourne and Footscray filled the top four positions, in that order. For Footscray, it was another attempt to get past the first semi-final, but the Bulldogs failed again, this time by 27 points, although South could not get past Essendon in the preliminary final.

It was an Essendon-Richmond grand final, with Essendon trying to reverse the 22-point second semi-final defeated inflicted by the Tigers. Richmond, naturally, was the hot favorite, but could not contend with Essendon's determination in a fierce and sometimes fiery match in front of 49,000 fans. Six players were reported in the game, but Essendon was able to withstand the pressure and captain-coach Dick Reynolds was chaired off after a magnificent individual game. Essendon won by 53 points to make a mockery of its second semi-final disaster. Six players were reported, but the resulting suspension for Richmond's George Smeaton meant little as he served it while overseas with the AIF.

Geelong was still missing from the competition in 1943, as interest began to dwindle. Newspapers gave less and less space to football which again failed to attract the interest of the pre-war years. St Kilda, as the bottom club after 11 rounds, dropped out of the competition. The voting for the Brownlow Medal was abandoned after round 11 and was not resumed until 1946.

Only 16 rounds were played and Richmond, Essendon, Fitzroy and Carlton filled the top four, with the Blues squeezing into the finals only on percentage ahead of Hawthorn, which had yet to play in a League finals series. Under coach Roy Cazaly the Hawthorn side had its best season. Both Carlton and Hawthorn finished the season with 40 premiership points, but Carlton had a percentage of 125 to Hawthorn's 103. Hawthorn would have made the finals had it defeated North in the second last round,

SUPPORTERS behind the northern goal. Essendon led by 33 points.   EXPRESSIONS OF DISGUST at a decision of the umpire.

Essendon's full forward, marks. The Carlton player is d, who was later hurt.   ALAN HIRD (ESSENDON) FLIES HIGH TO KNOCK THE BALL AWAY FROM THE WAITING GROUP.   UP TO IT: "Micky" Crisp (left) and J. Wrout (both Carlton) blanket an Essendon player as W. Buttsworth waits for the ball to come down.

The 1941 preliminary final between Essendon and Carlton.

but failed by just one point after being held goalless in the first half.

Carlton did not press home its lucky break as Fitzroy defeated the Blues by 51 points in a lop-sided first semi-final. The following week, Essendon defeated Richmond by 27 points. Richmond bounced back from that setback by defeating Fitzroy by 25 points in a preliminary final for a second successive crack at Essendon in the grand final.

Richmond made no mistake this time, although the winning margin was just five points - the closest grand final for 22 years. Jack Dyer recalled in later years that centreman Bernie Waldron had played a mighty last quarter which was a direct result of the needling he had been given in the press by one leading reporter. Dyer used the criticism as a spur for Waldron and it worked to perfection.

A pre-game drama had centred on Tiger Jack Broadstock who had been discharged from the army but had not registered for the militia and therefore been arrested. An army officer who was a Richmond fan let Broadstock stay in the custody of Dyer who was a policeman and Broadstock was thereby able to play in the big match.

Football started to get back to some semblance of normality in 1944 with the easing of transport regulations enabling the return of Geelong to the League competition and the Junction Oval and the Western Oval were back in the hands of St Kilda and Footscray respectively. The return to a full-strength competition was reflected in the increase in attendances - from 138,000 in 1943 to 225,000 for home and away matches.

Strangest finish to a game for the year was in the Essendon-Fitzroy clash. Essendon's Noel Smith marked in the last minute of the game and goaled from the angle, but the umpire disallowed the score because he had run around the mark. His second kick only managed a behind, which left the scores tied.

The season was sensational for several reasons, none the least being a remarkable finish to the Carlton-Footscray match at Princes Park. The Bulldogs were 17 points down with only seven minutes to play, but pulled level with the Blues with seconds left on the clock. Footscray's Harry Hickey had a 50-yard shot on the ball, but the ball was stopped by Carlton's Bob Chitty, only to bounce off his shoulder and through for a Footscray behind. Footscray won by that single point. It proved absolutely critical in the determination of the final four as Footscray finished the season fourth, one game ahead of Carlton, which had a far better percentage.

Carlton still had a great chance to make the finals with just a couple of rounds to play and a ground record of 38,222 fans watched the Richmond-Carlton march at the Punt Road Oval on August 19. Football was on the way back and the Tiger's 18-point win over the Blues helped Footscray into the finals. But again the Bulldogs failed to clear the

> There was even a patriotic game between Richmond and Fitzroy at the Punt Road Oval...The match was watched by several high-ranking American officers, who later suggested the game had the potential to interest America's vast number of sports fans.

first hurdle as Essendon defeated them by 49 points in the first semi-final.

Richmond suffered the double blow of a second semi-final loss to Fitzroy and the suspension of brilliant centreman Jack Broadstock. Tiger players were so incensed they held a meeting and asked the club to consider forfeiting the final against Essendon unless Broadstock's case was reviewed. In the end it was changed to a strong plea for the creation of an appeal board, and the Tigers won a second chance at the Maroons by defeating Essendon by 21 points in the preliminary final.

With the MCG still unavailable, the grand final was scheduled to be played at the Junction Oval on September 30. Proof that football again was the dominant thread in the life of Victorian sports fans was the 43,000 attendance, a remarkable figures considering the match was played in a blustery and searing north wind and there was a tram and bus strike. Thousands jammed Flinders Street station from 1pm and queues at booking windows were more than 100 yards long.

Fitzroy was always going to win the big one as it had introduced the concept of spying on the opposition and had a man watching rival clubs train and in action the week before facing the Maroons. Fitzroy's homework, now a vital part of the match build-up, helped the club to a 15-point grand final win over the Tigers. Maroons' skipper Fred Hughson recalled in later years that Dyer had told him Richmond could not counter big Fitzroy ruckman Bert Clay who constantly put the ball into the hands of Alan Ruthven. Hughson said: "Bert rucked all day and when the bell went he just collapsed. The trainers had to carry him off the ground."

Fitzroy players were feted - it had been 22 years between premierships for the Maroons. However, many club supporters and even some members of the training staff had to walk back to the Brunswick Street Oval for the celebrations. No-one really minded that minor discomfort.

Football attendances rocketed in 1945 as Melbourne realised the war was about to end. Players were more freely available and there was far more consistent form in the competition. Fans devoured the football action and could not wait for the finals that year, as South Melbourne, Collingwood, North Melbourne and Carlton filled the top positions.

South was plunged into controversy when skipper Herb Matthews was suspended for a week by the club for having refused to play against St Kilda. He had objected to the fact he had been moved from his normal centre position to the half-forward flank.

Carlton had its revenge on Footscray by pipping the Bulldogs for fourth position, with North making its finals debut. The Shinboners had created a club record by winning 13 of their 20 games including six wins in a row at the end. Expectations were high at Arden Street, but Carlton defeated North by 26 points in the first semi-final. South marched into the grand final by defeating Collingwood by 11 points in the second semi-final, which meant a Carlton-Collingwood preliminary final.

And that match gave a clue to what would occur in the grand final. Carlton and Collingwood tore into each other with rare ferocity and in one of the fiercest finals of them all, Carlton won by 10 points. It was to be a South-Carlton grand final, and there was considerable bad blood between the two clubs. As all finals matches that year were played at Princes Park, it was argued Carlton had been given an easy ride into the grand final because of its home ground advantage.

An incredible 62,986 fans squeezed into the ground expecting fireworks. And they got it, from the start to finish, in a match still described as the Bloodbath.

What started the greatest running brawl in the history of League football is still a matter for debate, but Carlton captain Bob Chitty was certainly in the thick of the action right from the start. Chitty, one of the toughest men ever to play the game, was in-

Bob Chitty sports a badly cut eye. The Carlton tough man was in the thick of the action in the wild 1945 "Bloodbath" grand final.

volved in an incident with South youngster Ron Clegg (who later won a Brownlow Medal), the young Swan left to count the stars. South retaliated by flattening Carlton players and Blues youngster Ken Hands (later to coach the club) was knocked unconscious in an incident which sparked a near riot. Hands was left with a broken nose, two missing teeth and a split mouth. He remembered coach Percy Bentley yelling at him to stay on the ground as the 19th man was already on the field. "We heard it was gambling," said Hands, "South had been offered big money by a big punter."

Umpires worked overtime separating players who seemed intent on killing each other. Police had to quell fights in the crowd and one fan even raced on the ground and shaped up to players.

Umpire Frank Spokes had a tangible reminder of the tension of the grand final and the marathon tribunal hearing that followed it. "I didn't have a grey hair in my head until then. But when I looked in the mirror next morning I saw a line of grey above my ears extending back from the temples. The worry and the pressure of giving evidence for almost four hours had sent me grey overnight."

Spokes said he almost lost his voice shouting to the players to calm down. The League branded the match a disgrace and "a blot on the game". Carlton had the last laugh as it won the match by 28 points. Carlton, less talented than South, had muscled its way to a premiership. The League Tribunal later heard charges against nine players.

South winger Ted Whitfield was disqualified for 12 months for a number of offences, including attempting to strike umpire Stokes and trying to conceal his number (he turned his guernsey inside out).

South defender Jack "Basher" Williams was disqualified for 12 matches after being found guilty on several counts.

Carlton skipper Chitty was suspended for eight matches being found guilty of elbowing South's Billy Williams.

South ruckman Don Grossman was disqualified for eight matches for striking Carlton's Jim Mooring.

South full-back Jim Cleary (known as Gentleman Jim) was disqualified for eight matches after being found guilty of striking Carlton's Hands. Carlton ruckman Ron Savage was disqualified for eight matches after being found guilty of striking Grossman.

South skipper Herb Matthews was reprimanded for throwing the ball away and charges against Hands and South's Keith Smith were dismissed.

World War II had seen less bloody battles and it was appropriate the war years ended with the greatest football bloodbath of them all.

The Sporting Globe annual of 1946 listed the following League players who had made the supreme sacrifice in World War II: Carlton - J. Park and W. Atkinson; Collingwood - N. Oliver and N. Le Brun; Essendon - J. Keddie, G. Goldin and E. Regan; Geelong - J. Knight, C. Helmer, J. Lynch and R. Lancaster; Hawthorn - R. Pirrie, G. Young, J. Drake and M. Wheeler; Melbourne - S. Anderson, J. Atkins, H. Ball, R. Barassi, N. Ellis, J. Fraser and K. Truscott; Richmond - F. Stamford, A. Jennings and W. Cosgrove; St Kilda - S. King, W. Hudson, H. Comte, R. Flegg and B. Shields; South Melbourne - G. Sawley, A. Pearsall and J. Wade; North Melbourne - M. Shapir, S. Mutimer, E. Egan and L. Thomas (who had also been captain-coach of Hawthorn and North Melbourne).

MAKER OF DEMONS

"CHECKER" Hughes was the man who literally turned Melbourne Football Club into Demons.

When he crossed to Melbourne from Richmond, the first thing Hughes did was to dump the nickname "Fuschias" and replace it with the more daunting Demons. That wasn't all he dumped. At the end of 1933 he gave 13 players their marching orders and Melbourne was on the way up the ladder.

In 1936 and 1937 the Demons came third and after missing the finals in 1938, hit the heights in 1939 for the first of three successive flags. Hughes knew how to handle footballers and was also a fine strategist as he showed in the 1940 grand final. He told noted writer Hugh Buggy that during the week before the grand final he had brought together six players to discuss negating the vigorous Jack Dyer. "All six said that they would take on the job of checking Dyer, but I turned to Jack O'Keefe and told him he was the man I wanted. I told him I remembered seeing him play for a VFA team against the VFL team a year or so before and was impressed with the way he handled Dyer."

"Checker" Hughes
- architect of
Melbourne's first
great era.

Hughes told O'Keefe to follow Dyer wherever he went. "I had noticed that Dyer was never as effective against a player who stood shoulder to shoulder with him." It is history that O'Keefe did the job and helped win the flag for Melbourne.

Hughes assembled a fine array of footballing talent headed by the dazzling Alan La Fontaine, high marking Jack Mueller and brilliant forwards Norm Smith and Ron Baggott. Percy Beames, a fine rover in that Melbourne side and later a respected commentator on the game, said he never saw La Fontaine beaten in the centre. "Sometimes they would break even with him, but he was never beaten."

Mueller achieved greatness despite the horrific setback of losing parts of two fingers which had been severed above the knuckle in an industrial accident. He was the first man to wear a glove in League football. "I only wore the glove for about two months until the skin healed," recalled Mueller.

Mueller never lost faith that he would be able to resume his career. Not only did he resume, he went on to become one of Melbourne's all time greats in a career that spanned 16 seasons. Despite the hand injury he built a reputation as one of the best marks in the League. A big, powerful man, he took delight in calling the shots on the football field, so much so that opponents like Jack Dyer would remember his "supercillious sneer" after kicking a goal.

Mueller admits he liked to get the psychological ascendancy in any battle. In nearly all instances he would remain impervious to whatever was thrown at him, but history shows his temper would flare on occasions. One notable case was early in World War II when a barracker next to the race screamed "You German bastard, why don't you join the army" and Mueller shoved the wire fence into his face. As it turned out Mueller eventually served in the locally based forces. Full service was ruled out because of his damaged right hand.

He could play in any key position and in the middle of his career was a ruckman. History shows that he was named as full-back in the 1939 flag side, but that move lasted only five minutes. "They started me against Ron Todd because we had a kid in the side who they wanted to settle down before going to full-back." That move was part of coach Checker Hughes' strategy. Hughes would chide Mueller that he had inherited the worst characterictics of his Irish and German background. Mueller thought the world of the old coach and reveals he was ahead of his time in some ways. "Before the 1940 grand final he refused to name the side in position. The League and the papers were furious," chuckled Mueller.

Mueller's teammate Percy Beames said Hughes was a great psychologist. "He'd get the best out of players by knowing each one. He would say to me that I was getting a bath from my opponent and that would rouse me, whereas he would use something else with other players. Ray Wartman was a winger who liked to kick a goal and I remember "Checker" would tell him to go down to the park on a Saturday and kick a few goals to get it out of his system."

Beames said Melbourne's strength was its ability to play in the positional style of the time. "You couldn't go and pinch kicks from the opposite side of the ground." He recalls that one of his opponents of the time - Keith Stackpole - was once dropped from the Collingwood team after kicking five goals from the half-forward flank. Magpie coach Jock McHale told him it was because he had not stuck to his position. That was the style of the time and Melbourne played it best of all.

The call to arms in 1940 hit a chord at Melbourne, as you would expect from a club with such strong establishment ties. Beames agrees that Melbourne possibly suffered more than others in terms of enlistments and casualties. "It was the nature of the club. Some of them wanted to enlist because of the glamor of it and we lost several who joined the air force. It took a long time to regroup. Often we didn't know until the start of a game who was going to play."

The Demons may have won more than three flags on the trot if not for the war. Percy Beames believes they could have taken as many as five in a row. "We were at our zenith and we had a couple of younger players like Harold Ball who were coming on. He was not as big physically, but ability wise he was like Wayne Carey today." Beames' assessment is borne out by Ball's amazing effort in the 1940 second semi-final when he gave a sensational display of marking in sodden conditions. One report credited him with 15 marks in the final term. Ball, along with three other premiership players - Ron Barassi, Syd Anderson and "Bluey" Truscott - died on active service. The premature end to their young lives far outweighed the footballing sadness of a great team being prevented from setting new highs in the game.

Chapter Eight

1946-1950
A gigantic industry

In 1946, VFL secretary Like McBrien described football as a "gigantic industry". He stated the 12 League clubs distributed more than 50,000 pounds in fielding sides each winter week. He even produced figures stating that more than 53,000 footballs were bought and used in competition each week and that an average uniform cost two pounds. He argued that football kept many clothing workers, bootmakers and others occupied in hard times. But in 1946 the estimated total player payments amounted to no more than 27,000 pounds.

Despite McBrien's words and figures, football was still almost an amateur code. The Coulter Law governing match payments was still in force and players generally trained only twice a week, on Tuesday and Thursday nights. Training started about six weeks before the first round of matches and there were no inter-club practice matches. The "March" champions, as they were known, paraded their talents in intra-club practice matches as selectors decided whether to place these newcomers on senior lists. Recruiting from country areas was fierce as there was no zoning and many a country youngster ended up at a League club because his mother had been given a box of chocolates (with a five pound note tucked under the wrapper), by a recruiting officer.

Football fans in 1946 were wanting to forget the war , but not even public enthusiasm could restore normality to League football. Melbourne, which had played its home matches at Richmond during the war, finally returned to the MCG late in the season, but South still had to play its games at the Junction Oval and did not return to the Lake Oval until 1947.

South as expected because of the loss of several players through suspension after the 1945 grand final, slipped badly in 1946 and finished seventh. Melbourne, which had a disappointing 1945 season, promised a bright new future by defeating Hawthorn at the MCG on August 17 in the first match on the hallowed turf since 1941 and it helped secure fourth position on the ladder, two games clear of Richmond. The Tigers had missed an opportunity to reach the finals when they had lost in a chaotic finish against Footscray. Jack Dyer ran into an open goal and the ball burst as he kicked it and slewed away for a point. In later years the yarn was embellished to the point where it was said that the cover went through the goal and the bladder went through for a behind!

The four comprised Essendon, Collingwood, Footscray and Melbourne and, again, Footscray could not get past the first semi. Melbourne then defeated Collingwood in the preliminary final to challenge Essendon for the flag.

Essendon played with force, weight and pace in the right places and was beginning to develop the streamlined system that would make it a formidable power for six years. Big marking and long kicking

> **Football fans in 1946 were wanting to forget the war , but not even public enthusiasm could restore normality to League football.**

Carlton's durable full-back Ollie Grieve punches clear of North spearhead Jock Spencer.

were the central themes in Essendon's game under coach Dick Reynolds, but it was the fleet of small men that would break the back of opposition sides in coming years. The Dons had a few hiccups along the way, losing to Geelong at a stage when the struggling Cats only had one win on the board, and being forced to a thrilling draw with Collingwood in the second semi. The Magpies lacked the ruck power and weight to match more physically powerful sides, but were still a gallant team.

Melbourne matched it with Essendon in the high scoring first half of the grand final, but then the Dons turned up the heat and incinerated the opposition with an 11-goal burst in 20 minutes. Gordon "Whopper" Lane was invincible at centre half-forward and youngster Bob McClure dominated the ruck in only his eighth senior game, giving an armchair ride to the small brigade headed by Bill Hutchison.

Essendon played jet-age football and set the standard for others to reach. The Bombers kept at the forefront by continuously introducing new young stars. Flamboyant Aboriginal Norm McDonald was one of the new boys blended into the side in 1947 and the speed which once produced a second placing in the Stawell Gift launched many attacks from half-back.

Essendon didn't have things its own way all the time and in one memorable afternoon at Arden Street the lowly North Melbourne came back from 44 points down at three quarter to steal the match. The brilliant Les Foote inspired the Northerners with a stunning individual performance.

As the pace of the game quickened even more, there was a corresponding decline in kicking standards and in the first four rounds 10 teams kicked more than 20 behinds in a game. One man who found no trouble hitting the target later in the year was burly Demon forward Fred Fanning who followed up a 10-goal effort with a record breaking 18 goals from 19 shots. This surpassed Gordon Coventry's record of 17 in a match and fans wondered whether someone would break the 20-goal barrier, but to this day the record stands - despite the later emergence of the great John Coleman.

Collingwood slipped out of the finals race in a dramatic manner late in the season when it lost a crucial game to Essendon which kicked two goals in time-on. The sealer came from "Bluey" McLure who had been forced to the forward pocket by injury.

Carlton started the year with the surprise announcement that Ern Henfry would captain the club. Henfry was a West Australian who had made the state side against Victoria at the age of 17 just before the war, but then played little football apart from a couple of games with the Blues while on leave from the RAAF. Henfry stood out of football for 12 months waiting for a clearance which was eventually granted by the Australian National Football League. He proved to be an inspired choice and as well as being a cool, clever centreman he was one of the best leaders in the club's history.

He was at his peak in Carlton's stirring grand final showdown with Essendon. Six times he launched attacks only to see five of them turned out. Yet with 44 seconds left to play, the sixth thrust got the ball forward for Ken Hands to pass to rover Fred Stafford whose left foot snap from 20 yards gave the Blues a one point victory. Carlton had the most successful season in its history with membership rising to a League record of 11,213 and brilliant centre half-back Bert Deacon winning the Brownlow.

The excruciating pain of losing a grand final by the barest margin did not knock Essendon off course and while the erratic Carlton dipped to sixth place the Bombers lost only two home and away games in 1948. One unexpected obstacle along the way was a coal strike which restricted train services and threatened the immediate playing future of young ruckman Percy Bushby who travelled from Stawell each week. Entering the finals on a 12-game winning run, Essendon was a raging favorite to take the flag, but nothing in this spectacular final series was predictable.

The first semi-final was turned on its head when Collingwood's star centreman Bill Twomey limped to the forward pocket with a foot injury after asking to be replaced and proceeded to kick eight goals in 50 minutes to overwhelm Footscray. Twomey had struggled for form in the lead-up to the finals and his performance left many Collingwood people open-mouthed.

Melbourne looked like paddock footballers losing to Essendon in the second semi but sprung a selection bombshell by recalling veteran Jack Mueller. Mueller had spent the year captain-coaching the reserves and the old champ responded by kicking eight goals and coupled with the six kicked by his old mate Norm Smith the effort powered Melbourne to a big win. A week later Mueller booted another six to help Melbourne win the flag. At 33 years of age he had kicked 20 goals in three finals. It was a graphic display of his big-match temperament.

Joy for the Blues as captain Ern Henfry is chaired from the ground after the 1947 grand final. Carlton players from left are Jack Conley, Jim Clark, Ern Henfry, Ray Garby, Ken Baxter, Bert Bailey and Fred Stafford - the man who scored the winning goal with just seconds to play.

"I never worried about big games or finals. I know some blokes did, but I would get down to the MCG in the morning, watch some of the baseball (played as a curtain-raiser in those days) and then have a rub down. Sometimes I would even fall asleep on the rub-down table."

The Demons pulled another rabbit out of the hat by naming amateur star Denis Cordner in the grand final side despite the fact he had only played one senior game five years earlier.

Essendon had squandered the previous year's flag with wayward kicking and the same pattern began to unfold from the earliest stages of the 1948 play-off. By half time the red and black scoreline read 2.15 and the inaccuracy continued to the bitter end with four shots not even registering a score in the vital last quarter. Reynolds left the inaccurate Bill Brittingham at full-forward and responded to criticism after the game by saying that he didn't like to hurt people's feelings. Melbourne coach "Checker" Hughes was far more ruthless and his side's attack had more of a plan built around Mueller and Smith than did Essendon which had a crowded attack throughout the day.

With scores level (Essendon 7.27 to Melbourne's 10.9) Norm Smith grabbed the ball at a throw-in near goal, but teammate Don Cordner knocked it out of his hand and before Smith could regain the ball it was spirited away by Essendon defender Cec Ruddell. As the siren sounded Ruddell smiled to Bill Hutchison and said: "Isn't this good, we'll get another 10 quid for playing next week!"

His teammates did not share Ruddell's enthusiasm the following Saturday and could not thwart the Demons' momentum to succumb by 39 points in the replay.

Essendon had lost one grand final and drawn another in the previous two years, but all thoughts of gloom were dispelled in the opening round of 1949 when a young full-forward from Hastings made the most electrifying debut in VFL history.

John Coleman had not been overly impressive in practice games in 1947 and 1948 and almost crossed to Richmond, but his five goal first quarter entrance to League footy left no one in doubt the game had a new champion. He kicked 12 for the day and would go on to become the first man to reach 100 goals in his opening season.

It would have seemed a side which had missed two flags through poor kicking would have been unbeatable with the inclusion of a champion spearhead, but at first everything went askew as the Bombers lost six out of eight matches and slumped to eighth midway through the year.

A crowd of 46,000 squeezed into Punt Road to watch Carlton beat Richmond on the King's Birthday. Health Commission offi-

On a magic day in 1947 Fred Fanning wrote his name indelibly in the record books when he kicked 18 goals from 19 shots in a game for Melbourne and thus created a record for an individual in a VFL game.

cials tried to let some of the crowd out, but the plan backfired when more people stormed through the gates. Part of the fence around the oval collapsed and people spilled onto the field.

Big improver for 1949 was North Melbourne which had been on the upswing since the end of World War II when Bob McCaskill took over as coach. McCaskill instilled greater discipline at the club and guided it into the finals for the first time in 1945. By 1949 Wally Carter was at the helm and he was an astute leader with a sharp eye for potential. He had the gifted Les Foote as captain: a footballing wizard whose handling skills were unrivalled. Foote would weave his way through a pack and leave the opposition looking like fools and his creative use of handball was ahead of its time.

North also had a backline with the reputation of being the most ferocious and uncompromising in the League. Full-back Jock McCorkell was one of the League's best, and flankers Ted Jarrard and Les Reeves were feared throughout the competition. In front of goal the team had Jock Spencer, a talented spearhead. North topped the ladder at the end of the home and away round for the first time, but could not counter Carlton's talented goal-to-goal line and lost the second semi-final.

Pitted against the revitalised Essendon which had won its past nine games, North fought bravely in the preliminary final. A tight game swung Essendon's way after Spencer was penalised for taking a mark over McClure when Umpire McMurray ruled he had interfered with the Bomber big man. North players were dumbfounded, but Essendon, seasoned in handling finals pressure, kept its cool and goals by Ted Leehane and Dick

Reynolds ended North's dream. This was achieved despite a minimal contribution by Coleman who was held to three goals by McCorkell.

Coleman was back on top in the grand final and Essendon was so far ahead of Carlton by the last term that 19th man Gordon Lane could chip the ball away from goal to get Coleman within one goal of the century. Coach Reynolds ensured the fairy-tale ending when he hit Coleman on the chest with a pass. Essendon won by a thumping 73 points and Coleman could not get out of the dressing rooms for an hour after the game as he was besieged by ecstatic fans.

Coleman was that rare individual with the ability to draw spectators through the gate, but there was plenty more talent in the 1950 Essendon side which was the most accomplished and best balanced team since the war. It would rank as one of the all-time great teams with brilliance on every line. McClure was a dominant ruckman who had aggressive backing from Bob Syme and "Chooka" May and this was the perfect foundation for an outstanding batch of small men headed by Bill Hutchison and the lightning fast Ron McEwin. Essendon lost only one game all year to surpass the club's previous best effort of 1911 when it suffered only two defeats.

At the other end of the ladder Hawthorn hit rock bottom with not a single win during 1950. A young ruckman in his first VFL season achieved the personal honor of winning the club best and fairest, but the winless year would remain burnt into his psyche. John Kennedy tasted football's down side at the start of a football involvement that would span four decades and reach dizzy heights of success as a coach.

One of the earliest memories for the young Kennedy, then just about to make his debut, was the sad sight of the two Hawthorn greats in tears as they departed the Glenferrie Oval. Col Austen had lost the 1949 Brownlow on countback (it was later awarded retrospectively) and over summer he was plunged into a swirling controversy that would see

him make a sad and jagged departure from Hawthorn. His friend Alec Albiston, Hawthorn's captain-coach, had agreed to relinquish the coaching role, but was told he would retain the captaincy. The committee then went back on its word and replaced Albiston with Kevin Curran. It was too much for the loyal and highly principled Austen and he told Hawthorn he would leave the club unless the situation was rectified. The committee then sacked Austen and Albiston on the eve of the 1950 season.

A club noted for its smoothness of administration also became embroiled in a pre-season flare-up. Collingwood's legendary coach Jock McHale announced his retirement. Leading officials had promised the job to reserves coach Bervyn Woods a couple of years earlier, but in the meantime the team's captain, Phonse Kyne, had emerged as a serious contender. When the committee invited applications for a non-playing coach it was thought that Kyne, still a player, would be blocked.

> Health Commission officials tried to let some of the crowd out, but the plan backfired when more people stormed through the gates.

A savage committee battle spilled over to include players and members who at the club's final practice match surrounded the committee box and hurled abuse. There was almost a punch-up between two committeemen, and it was all too much for Woods who handed in his resignation after an appointment which had lasted a mere five days. Appointing Kyne as coach did not save the committee's hide and it was thrown out by a reform group soon after. Collingwood finished seventh, one win and percentage out of the four. There were few rays of hope in a frustrating year for the Magpies although Bill Twomey's 11.9 solo effort against Footscray did bring a smile to Collingwood faces.

While Collingwood endured the agonies of revolution, St Kilda started with five wins in a row and dreamt of glory. A crowd of 46,973 crammed into the Junction Oval to watch the Saints roll Carlton.

John Coleman exploded onto the VFL scene in 1949 with a 12-goal debut. Here he marks against Fitzroy.

It was the biggest attendance ever recorded at the ground, including finals. St Kilda's great strength was a star-studded goal-to-goal line which comprised Bruce Phillips, Keith Drinan, Harold Bray, Jack McDonald and Peter Bennett. All played state football at various stages and Bray went desperately close to victory in three Brownlow Medal counts. Sadly, it all fell apart when the rising Geelong handed out a drubbing and several key men were injured. The Saints fell away to finish a distant ninth.

Ironically St Kilda pulled off an upset win against the Cats in the return game just before the finals, but Geelong was still able to grab fourth spot and achieve a landmark on the trail that had started from scratch when the team resumed competition in 1944 and won only a single game. In 1950 the Cats overcame Melbourne in the semi, but were rolled by North in the preliminary final. Geelong was a young side, but brimming with talent and every step of its progress had been carefully planned by coach Reg Hickey.

If any team could seriously hope to challenge Essendon for the 1950 flag then it had to be North Melbourne which had inflicted the Dons' only loss during the year. North pushed hard all day in the second semi and Essendon only scraped in by three points. After a misdirected handpass of the greasy ball from full-back Jock McCorkell was grabbed by Coleman, it was relayed to rover Ron McEwin for a goal.

This was the first year the club was known as the Kangaroos; it had previously travelled under the uninviting nickname "The Shinboners". North, which outslogged Geelong in the preliminary final, had tremendous support as it chased the club's first flag, but from the moment Coleman sent through a long, bouncing goal the Roos knew it would be an uphill battle. Despite a seven-goal opening quarter, Essendon had still not shaken North by the last change and the blue and whites threw everything into the final half hour. The effects of three hard matches in a row combined with Essendon's class were too much in the end and the Bombers racked up their 14th consecutive win to take out the flag by 38 points.

Coleman scored a modest four goals, but he was still the top scorer for the match despite the close attentions of North's defence. His rival Jock McCorkell paid tribute to Coleman in later years, admitting the North defence had used niggling tactics. "If a player has spirit he reacts. Coleman did. He absorbed a lot of punishment . . . Although he came back hard he always took it well." McCorkell also recalled an incident when Pat Kelly's boot connected with the Essendon champ.

"Why did you do that?" protested Coleman as he prepared to punch the notoriously tough Kelly.

"Sorry, John it was an accident," replied Kelly and Coleman said: "That's okay" and got on with the game.

The Bombers' second successive flag capped a five-year reign of dominance in which the club could have easily won the title every year. In 105 games between 1946 and 1950 Essendon was successful 83 times and drew twice. Captain-coach Reynolds retired as a player to concentrate on his coaching role. The club had great depth which was shown by its flags in the reserve and under-19 grades and there was no reason for Reynolds to be concerned for its future. With Coleman leading the way, it seemed there were plenty more flags for the taking.

POST-WAR HEROES

World War II had severely disrupted football and it took several years for fans to adapt to a new era, to new heroes.

Some clubs even had to get used to losing star players. Some retired from senior football to accept lucrative coaching positions in the country, others failed to settle down after the war and some swapped clubs. For example, star full-forward Lindsay White returned to Geelong after playing with South Melbourne during the war years. White had topped Geelong's goalkicking with 66 goals in 1941, but Geelong did not compete in the VFL from 1942-43. White therefore spent a brief period with South and topped the League goalkicking in 1942 with 80 goals. He was just as prolific in his second spell with Geelong and topped the Cats' goalkicking from 1947-49 before his retirement in 1950.

His replacement in front of goals was an extremely talented footballer named George Goninon, who would have won even greater acclaim if his achievements had not been eclipsed by a footballer many still believe to have been the greatest full-forward of all - the legendary John Coleman.

Football in the post-war years was looking for a new hero, a successor to the Bob Pratts and Gordon Coventrys of the 1930s. Melbourne's Fred Fanning might have kicked 18 goals in one match, against St Kilda in 1947, but he never kicked the "ton" of goals in a season. White was brilliant, but not in the same

John Coleman had magnetism like no other. Here he is besieged by young fans.

class as Pratt or Coventry. The football public liked nothing better than a man who could kick goals, and no-one kicked them better than Coleman although it took Essendon more than two years to acknowledge the man's extraordinary talent. In fact, Essendon almost lost his services to Richmond in what would have been the greatest recruiting blunder in football history.

Coleman started his football career in the Essendon District League, but did not start to make a name for himself until his family shifted to the seaside town of Hastings. However, Essendon already was well aware of his talents and invited him to train with the club before the start of the 1947 season. Coleman played in intra-club practice matches and made no impression. He was allowed to return to Hastings where he kicked 136 goals for the season. Rival League clubs were starting to take notice of the spring-heeled youngster from the Mornington Peninsula. Essendon invited him back for the 1948 practice matches and he again failed to impress. It was back to Hastings for Coleman and this time he kicked 160 goals for the season.

Essendon simply could not ignore him a third time, especially as Coleman was ready to talk terms with Richmond, even though he had signed with Essendon. It was third time lucky for Coleman, but especially for Essendon, before the start of the 1949 season. Coleman clicked in the practice matches and was named at full-forward for the first round, against Hawthorn at Windy Hill.

Essendon had gone down to Melbourne in the grand final replay the previous year and its lack of a quality full-forward had cost it dearly. In fact, there are many old-time Bomber fans who suggest that if Essendon had recruited Coleman a year earlier the club would have won the 1948 flag.

Coleman's debut in 1949 was nothing less than astounding. He kicked 12 goals to equal the opening round record set by another Dons' player, Ted Freyer, in 1935. It was one of the most sensational debuts in League history and the Saturday evening newspapers raved about Coleman's performance in the 63-point Essendon victory. But Coleman, like Freyer in 1935, failed to go on with the job the next week. Freyer kicked his 12 opening round goals against Melbourne, but managed only four the next week against St Kilda and finished the season with just 34 goals. Coleman, in the second round of 1949, kicked only three goals against North Melbourne and some foolish critics suggested his opening round burst had been a freak.

Coleman proved them wrong time and time again and kicked exactly 100 goals in that 1949 debut season to become the only footballer in League history to kick a "ton" in his first season. More importantly, Coleman helped Essendon land the 1949 premiership. He kicked six goals in the Dons' grand final triumph over Carlton. His sixth goal of the

> Football in the post-war years was looking for a new hero, a successor to the Bob Pratts and Gordon Coventrys of the 1930s.

match, and his 100th of the season, came just before the final siren in front of more than 90,000 fans.

Coleman captured the public's imagination with his acrobatic high-flying, his raw courage and his unerring accuracy. Give Coleman even half a chance and he would kick a goal. He became the target of physical abuse and rival clubs used every tactic, foul and fair, in an attempt to stop the Essendon match-winner. He was virtually unstoppable and a rival full-back would congratulate himself if he had limited Coleman to four or five goals. Coleman kicked 120 goals in 1950 and again played a vital part in an Essendon premiership triumph. He kicked four goals in the grand final win over North Melbourne and seemed set to add to his, and Essendon's, premiership record the following year.

However, Coleman was involved in one of football's most famous incidents in the final home and away round of 1951. Essendon was playing Carlton at Windy Hill when Coleman tangled with Carlton defender Harry Caspar. Coleman was reported for allegedly striking Caspar and was in serious danger of missing the finals series. Coleman had never been suspended and it was generally held that he had acted in retaliation. Coleman therefore was not prepared for the tribunal decision on the eve of the finals. He was suspended for four games. Coleman, in tears, had to be helped from Harrison House.

Essendon's premiership hopes tumbled and the Dons went down to Geelong by 11 points in the grand final. There now seems little doubt Essendon would have won that grand final if the great Coleman had played.

Coleman kicked 103 goals in 1952, but Essendon failed to flatter and finished a dismal eighth. Coleman then kicked 97 goals the following year and probably would have kicked a "ton" if Footscray had not defeated the Bombers in the first semi-final. Coleman, the idol of thousands of Essendon fans, was not to know that he had played his last finals match.

Coleman started the 1954 season with 10 goals against Hawthorn and in the seventh round against Fitzroy kicked 14 goals - his highest League total. It was Coleman's last full match.

The following week, against North Melbourne at Windy Hill, he started the match as if he was desperate to break that week-old record. He had already kicked five goals when he flew high for a mark and landed awkwardly. Essendon fans watched in horror as Coleman writhed in agony. They knew instantly their hero had been seriously injured. Coleman had dislocated a knee so badly that he was never able to play football again.

It has been suggested that modern surgery techniques would have salvaged Coleman's career, but in 1954 there was no alternative to retirement - at 25 years of age. Coleman had kicked 42 goals to that stage of the season and seemed destined to kick another "ton". His injury was one of football's greatest tragedies and the football world mourned his absence from the Essendon team.

The Melbourne *Herald's* Alf Brown, considered the doyen of football writers, considered Coleman the finest player he had seen. He wrote this of the great Essendon champion: "He had all football's gifts. He was courageous, a long straight kick, he had a shrewd football brain and, above all, he was a spectacular, thrilling mark. Coleman, flying high above a pack provided football's finest spectacle. He was a match-winner - the player every coach and selection committee spent hours worrying about."

Coleman might have played his last game in 1954, but he was not lost to Essendon in particular or football in general. Essendon, realising the value of his shrewd football brain, appointed Coleman coach in 1961 and he took the Bombers to the 1962 and 1965 premierships before stepping down in 1967.

Coleman had served Essendon mightily, on and off the field, and deserved a long and happy retirement from the game he graced with such distinction. However, tragedy continued to stalk him and

he died of a heart attack at just 44 years of age in 1973 after collapsing at his Dromana hotel. Football had lost one of its greatest identities. John Coleman, many would argue, was the greatest player of all, and he played in an era in which it was difficult to stand out above a plethora of champions.

Geelong's Goninon had been a teammate of Coleman's at Windy Hill. Goninon had started his League career with the Dons in 1948, a year ahead of Coleman, and although he kicked seven goals in his two matches that year, was unable to get a game ahead of Coleman in 1949 and left for Geelong after seven games in the black and red. He went on to top Geelong's goalkicking from 1950-53 and even headed the League goalkicking with 86 goals in 1951. He also tasted premiership success with Geelong that year, thanks largely to Coleman's suspension.

However, there also were great defenders, although Coleman had by far the better of his duels with full-backs possibly with the exception of Fitzroy's Vic Chanter. The most elegant defender of the era was Carlton's Bert Deacon, who epitomised the image of the modest champion. Carlton recruited Deacon from VFA club Preston and he made his debut with the Blues in 1942 after he originally had signed with Richmond. Deacon won the Brownlow Medal in 1947 and went on to play 106 senior games with the Blues. He later served the club as secretary from 1970 to his untimely death in 1973. Deacon, a member of Carlton's 1945 and 1947 premiership sides, played alongside other such great Carlton players as Jack "Chooka" Howell, Ollie Grieve, Ken Hands and Ern Henfry.

Richmond missed out on the services of Coleman and Deacon, but the Tigers had two great Brownlow medallists of the era in Bill Morris (1948) and Roy

> **They knew instantly that their hero had been seriously injured. Coleman had dislocated a knee so badly that he was never able to play football again.**

Lou Richards - the nuggety Collingwood rover who never conceded an inch to the opposition.

Wright eventually played 194 games for the Tigers and later became a highly-respected and popular television commentator.

Of course, the other great star of the immediate post-war era was the inimitable Lou Richards, a Collingwood captain in the club's finest tradition. Richards is better known to younger football followers as a multi-media personality, probably the greatest the game has produced - and his on-field achievements tend to have been overlooked in recent years. Richards was born to be a Collingwood champion. His uncle, Alby Pannam, was a star rover with the Magpies and Richards' great ambition as a student at Collingwood Tech. was to emulate Uncle Alby. Richards broke into the Collingwood team in 1941 and captained the Magpies from 1952-55.

The pinnacle of his career was leading Collingwood to the 1953 premiership. Richards played 250 games for the Magpies to his retirement during the 1955 season and always will be remembered as a cheeky, never-say-die rover with considerable skill.

Wright (1952 and 1954). Richmond first spotted Morris during a services game at the Punt Road Oval in 1942, but the gangling ruckman was tied to Melbourne as he had played a game with that club's reserves. Richmond, undeterred, arranged for a player swap and Morris went on to win three Tiger best and fairests. He died, aged just 38, in 1960. Morris had played 145 senior games for Richmond and passed on the great Richmond ruck tradition to another pale-faced big-man in Wright, who was the post-war era's first dual Brownlow medallist and a footballer of outstanding sportsmanship.

Wright was a most unlikely footballer as he had spent part of his youth in splints because of rheumatic fever. Indeed, football at any level seemed only a dream for Wright until he tried out with suburban club North Kew in 1945. His form was so impressive that Richmond invited him down to training at Punt Road Oval and he made his senior debut in 1946. Yet, ironically, Wright had to wait for Morris to cross to VFA club Box Hill in 1952 before he could establish himself as Richmond's number one ruckman.

Chapter Nine

1951-1954

Geelong's flyer, Footscray's first

By 1951 the restrictions of war-time had eased and Australia was returning to normal. The motor car and the Sunday drive were becoming a larger part of Australian culture. A federal government announcement that one quarter of Australia's petrol needs would be handled by a new refinery at Geelong was a boost to the Corio Bay community. The five million pound Shell refinery was a panacea for employment, but the form of the local footy team put the spring into the step of the locals.

Geelong had blistering pace in every position, but it wasn't just tearaway recklessness and was intelligently directed and systematic. The Cats were quick thinkers as well and exploited the open spaces by driving the ball to where one of their speedsters could reach it first. Centre half-forward Fred Flanagan was a focal point and beside him on a flank was the "Geelong Flyer" Bob Davis who could drop kick 60-yard goals on the run. He was capable of shredding an opposition defence in the space of a few minutes and he delighted in creating havoc.

By a quirk of fate Geelong had picked up a quality full-forward in George Goninon from Essendon. Goninon had been left out in the cold when Coleman arrived at Windy Hill, and Geelong was only too happy to pick up the shrewd spearhead whose deadly drop-punts bagged eight goals in his second game for the Cats. The only problem at first was getting him from Melbourne in time for train-

ing and the Geelong secretary appealed in the local paper for someone to give him a lift.

The biggest sensation of the year was the suspension of the great John Coleman on the eve of the finals. Essendon had overcome an early season slump to storm into the finals with 11 wins straight, but in the last home and away game Coleman was booked for striking Essendon backman Harry Caspar. Before the hearing an Essendon committeeman was said to have offered Caspar 50 pounds to say what he had done to the star full-forward, but despite his pleas that it was a matter of retaliation Coleman was rubbed out for four weeks and Essendon's hopes plummeted as he left Harrison House in tears.

Without Coleman the Dons scraped home against Footscray in the first semi-final, and watched from the stands as Geelong dismembered Collingwood a week later. Coleman's previous understudy George Goninon booted 11 goals for the Cats to set up the 82-point slaughter.

Essendon edged out Collingwood by two points a week later, but despite the booming confidence of Geelong the Dons were not about to meekly surrender their place at the top of League affairs. In a surprise move Dick Reynolds came out of retirement to take his place on the reserve bench for the grand final. For a while it seemed that his introduction into the game would alter the course of proceedings as Essendon narrowed a 27-point leeway to nine

"Chooka" Howell shepherds perfectly to clear a path for teammmate Jack Spencer with the ball. Essendon's Alan Thaw tries to get through.

points, but this was Geelong's year and the Cats kicked again to run out winners.

Cats back pocket Bernie Smith won the Brownlow and the eagle-eyed Goninon topped the goalkicking with 86. Coleman had 75 on the board before his tribunal encounter.

The League changed the Coulter Law to increase player payments from four pounds to five pounds per game, but there were still interstate clubs willing to pay more for players. Tasmanian clubs chasing Carlton's Jack "Chooka" Howell angered the Blues and the state ruckman stood out of football for a year before returning to the fold. It was even reported another club had offered to set him up in a 1000 pound business.

Geelong continued to set the pace in 1952 and many of its methods revolutionised the game. Hickey used the half-back line as a springboard for attacks rather than a defensive unit and Russell Middlemiss, John Hyde and Geoff Williams constantly swooped on the ball and sent long driving kicks downfield. Hickey was a man capable of keeping the diverse temperaments through the club under tight rein and he certainly had the results on the field. The locals flocked to Kardinia Park and the clash with Carlton late in the season drew a record 49,107 people to the Cats' home ground. Part of the attraction that day was the fact Carlton was playing for a place in the finals, but the Blues were overwhelmed by Geelong and only kept fourth place because of results elsewhere.

During the year the League tried one of its more unusual experiments by playing an entire round of football at various centres across Australia. One hiccup occurred in Brisbane where the Geelong and Essendon game had to be postponed until the following Monday because of torrential rain. Eventually it was played under lights in front of a crowd of 28,000 and Coleman turned on a champagne display to kick 13 goals. Fitzroy defeated Melbourne in Hobart, South Melbourne defeated North Melbourne in Albury, Carlton thrashed Hawthorn in Euroa and Collingwood defeated Richmond in Sydney. The Sydney match attracted 25,000 fans even though conditions were appalling and a rugby league match just a couple of hundred yards away attracted just 11,000 fans. *The League Record* enthused: "Crowd enthusiasm proves that our grand winter sport is without peer as an entertainment medium. Given a fine day there is little doubt 60,000 would have packed the SCG to see the match. The fact that so many stood in torrential rain is proof of this."

The 1952 first semi-final was a stunning affair which ended with Fitzroy getting past the post thanks to a last-minute point by Alan Ruthven. During the game Carlton's high-flyer Keith Warburton crashed spectacularly and after the game collapsed at a club dance. "I looked down and saw this big lump and it was my stomach that had burst." He had ruptured a bowel and burst an intestine. Public interest was so great that photographers had to be ejected from the hospital. "They told me later that the shock of the flashbulbs could have killed me," said Warburton who was close to death for several days, but pulled through in the end.

Geelong stormed into the finals as red-hot favorite for the flag and was virtually untroubled in accounting for Collingwood in the second semi-final and then repeating the dose two weeks later. Geelong had even more poise than the previous year and the only threat to it was over-confidence. Nothing typified the Geelong style in the 1952 grand final win better than the 100-yard dash around the wing by Bob Davis which started deep in the backline and ended with him handpassing to Bert Worner for a goal. With the momentum everything fell into place for the Cats and no sooner had veteran ruckman Tom Morrow hung up his boots at the end of 1951, than he was replaced by the highly promising Norm Sharp.

After losing the Brisbane match against Essendon in 1952 Geelong had set out on a mighty winning run. The Cats won the next two games after the Essendon debacle then tied with the Dons at Windy Hill. When they romped home over

Collingwood to take the flag it was their ninth win in succession and the juggernaut charged on unchecked in 1953.

Geelong needed to beat North to surpass Collingwood's record winning sequence of 23 but was hit by an attack of the wobbles. With three minutes left the Cats trailed by seven points, but Hovey goaled to level the scores, then 30 seconds before the bell George Swarbrick marked and kicked the decisive point. The Cats stretched their winning run to 23 before playing host to Collingwood. For most of the game Geelong cruised and Magpie skipper Lou Richards recalled later that his team was just about exhausted by three-quarter-time even though the black and whites led by 11 points.

"We were still resting when the umpire blew the whistle as a signal he was ready to start the quarter. They were on their feet and looked smugly confident that the game was theirs for the taking."

Collingwood threw everything at the home side and in the end won by 16 points. Richards said Geelong was stunned after the game and the usually convivial treatment of visitors was decidedly cold. The result would have more significance than just ending Geelong's winning streak as it gave Collingwood a vital psychological edge for future meetings in the finals.

The 1953 season featured some extremely wet days, but none was worse than that which greeted Footscray and Fitzroy on May 23. One side of the Western Oval between the half-forward lines was under water and the combination of atrocious conditions and an unrelenting Bulldog defence kept Fitzroy totally scoreless for most of the day. Ten minutes before the end Fitzroy's Brownlow medallist Alan Ruthven took a wild kick at the ball in mid air and it rolled through for a goal. St Kilda's one point

The League changed the Coulter Law to increase player payments from four pounds to five pounds per game, but there were still interstate clubs willing to pay more for players.

Brilliant Magpie Bill Twomey relished the finals atmosphere at the MCG. Here he rises above Geelong's Norm Sharp for a fine mark.

Collingwood players had decided among themselves that whenever they grabbed a player they would hurl him to the ground in a bid to wear down the Geelong side and Richards informed rival skipper Fred Flanagan as they tossed the coin that anyone coming near a Collingwood player would have his head kicked over the grandstand. Star Geelong ruckman Bill McMaster was flattened by a crushing Pat Twomey bump and players flew in from all directions. Collingwood was using the oldest ruse in the book and Geelong fell for it.

There was also some science in Collingwood's approach as coach Kyne placed speedster Terry Waites at centre half-forward on Geelong's John Hyde. Hyde went into the game carrying a leg injury and it was exploited by Waite's pace. Collingwood was determined no player who went to ground would stay there and even battled on despite several cases of cramp. Even captain Richards was not immune from criticism and wrote: "In the last five minutes I went down with cramp myself and Bob Rose rushed up to me and said "Get up you weak bastard, you're letting the side down".

The Magpies kept up the momentum into the 1954 season as Geelong had done 12 months earlier, and by a stroke of irony it was the Cats who ended the winning streak. Essendon suffered a crushing blow when champion full-forward John Coleman dislocated his right knee in round eight. His career was over at 25 just when he was at his peak. Only a week earlier he had booted a club record 14 goals against Fitzroy. Essendon won the game against North Melbourne when Coleman was injured and at first it seemed the Bombers would be able to go some of the way towards covering the star's absence. That proved an illusion although Essendon was still highly competitive in one of the tightest seasons of all time. The Dons were only one and a half wins behind second-placed Footscray, but finished sixth.

Big improver of 1954 was Melbourne which had finished second last a year earlier. The Demons

score of 1899 thus remained as the all-time lowest score in League football. On the same day Geelong's Goninon booted 11 goals out of 15, but by the end of the year he would find himself languishing in the seconds.

Goninon's fall from grace was symptomatic of Geelong's suddenly exposed vulnerability, but the Cats still topped the ladder and entered the finals as favorites. Collingwood had other ideas and served up a vigorous approach in the second semi-final. To their credit Geelong's players did not shirk an issue, but still went down by five goals. The Cats earned another crack at Collingwood by disposing of Footscray.

pumped a succession of youngsters into the side and typical of their faith was tall 18-year-old Bob Johnson who made an immediate impression and was included in the team for the finals series.

North attempted to win a clearance for Essendon's Bill Hutchison as captain-coach, but in the end the brilliant rover remained at his old club, and Jock McCorkell took on the North coaching role. Another ex-North man Les Foote was appointed captain-coach at St Kilda after a two-season stint coaching bush team Berrigan. Foote proved he was no has been by winning the Saints' best and fairest award, and when he coached the Saints to a first-round win over Footscray his side was hailed as a premiership chance. In the end, though, roles of the two teams were reversed with St Kilda finishing on the bottom of the ladder. Foote upset his old club when he induced North ruckman Col Thornton to train at St Kilda without permission and the Roos threatened to report St Kilda to the VFL.

Collingwood's flag win of the previous year resulted in the sale of a club record 10,700 tickets and the Magpies announced a plan to spend 100,000 pounds on improving facilities for spectators providing they received a longer lease on the Victoria Park ground. At the same time Richmond expressed concern at the proposed widening of Punt Road which threatened to make their oval unusable within 10 years.

Relations were strained between Victoria and South Australia as the Croweaters were furious that two of their best players were being chased by League clubs. When things eventually settled down Jim Deane was cleared from South Adelaide to Richmond and Clayton "Candles" Thompson went to Hawthorn. One man heading the other way was Essendon ruckman "Chooka" May who was cleared to South Australian team Sturt after standing out for a season.

While eight teams scrapped for three places in the finals, Geelong sat on top of the ladder one and

The drains at the Western Oval were blocked after a downpour and the ground resembled a lake in this 1953 match. In impossible conditions Footscray won easily as Fitzroy could not score anything until a lucky goal late in the day.

a half games clear, then as proof of the unpredictability of the season was bundled out of contention with two losses. The Cats full-forward George Goninon had walked out earlier in the year.

History was made on grand final day when Footscray won its first flag by doubling Melbourne's score. Footscray was not as nervous as North had been in chasing a first flag several years before, and it was the younger, inexperienced Demons who made the mistakes. Footscray had a magnificent goal-to-goal line which consisted of full-back Herb Henderson, centre half-back Ted Whitten, centreman Don Ross, centre half-forward Peter Box and full-forward Jack Collins. Collins, the leading VFL goalkicker for the year, equalled the grand final record of seven goals.

The fanatical Bulldogs, led by the inspiring Charlie Sutton, would not be denied and Melbourne never looked a chance after the Dogs rammed on six goals to one in the opening half hour. Sutton says his team believed they played for more than just a football club. "We were there to represent the people of Footscray," he said. "People in Footscray were

The goal umpire positions himself perfectly as Collingwood's
Mick Twomey and South's Jack Hudson lunge over the goal-line.

hungry for victory." No man personified that spirit
more than Sutton. He bowled over Ron Barassi, John
Beckwith and Geoff Collins to set the tone early on.

There were plenty of lessons for Melbourne and
its coach Norm Smith would use them with devastating effect. Melbourne's pain of 1954 would be
overcome by an era of unprecedented dominance.

STARTING THEM YOUNG -
THE BOOM BABIES

Tim Watson wouldn't have been able to start his
career in 1977 if today's draft rules had been in place.

At the tender age of 15 years he would have been
under the minimum age limit for a country player to
be drafted. Maybe the draft system will change in
the future, but it seems highly unlikely that we will
see any more players added to the elite half dozen
youngsters who played League football at the age of
15. Watson said several years ago that he thought it
was still physically possible in the modern era for a
15-year-old to play senior football. "It is quite possible that someone could progress quickly enough to
make it."

Watson did concede that at a solid 13 and a half
stone he was "fairly big" at the age of 15, but he
doesn't think a slender build should prevent a youngster from joining the fray at top level. "In today's
football there's a lot of running. Look at someone
like Gavin Wanganeen. He's lightly framed but
doesn't have any problems because of his skills."

Watson saw only one possible drawback to starting
at such a young age as 15. "I think the only problem
about starting so young is that you may be burnt out at
an earlier age" he said, but that thought was not even
in his mind when he first took the field for the Bombers half a lifetime ago. "I didn't worry about that at the
time because it was that far ahead. I had a year off when
I was 25 or 26 when I injured a knee and in a way that
may have been a blessing in   disguise."

The big League was a long way from his child-
hood days at Dimboola when young Tim spent hours
kicking a footy with his young mates. In those days
he sported the number 9 Dimboola guernsey as a
show of his respect for the local full-forward and captain-coach. That Dimboola hero lived in the same
street as the Watson family and young Tim went to
school with his kids. His name was Keith Bromage
and although neither of them knew it at the time,
Watson would later join him as one of the elite band
of League "superkids".

When it is considered that of 10,000 men who
have played League football there have been only
six who have played as 15-year-olds, it is quite amazing that two of them once lived in the same country
street! "I didn't realise when I was a kid that he
(Keith Bromage) had started when he was only 15,
and I only found that out later when I first played,"
said Watson.

The youngest VFL player was in fact Bromage
(born November 8, 1937), a tender 15 years and 287
days when he started out for Collingwood on August 22, 1953.

Bromage answered quickly when asked at what
age Watson showed the talents that would equip him

for league football - "About seven years old! Even then he could kick 20 or 30 yards and hit you straight on the chest." Bromage is full of admiration for the kid down the road who became one of the game's superstars, but Bromage himself has a unique niche in the annals of League football. His story is a fascinating one although he admits to some embarrassment when friends constantly introduce him as "the youngest bloke ever". Bromage went straight from Collingwood Tech to Victoria Park. His play for a Victorian schoolboys' side in Perth prompted a phone call from famous Collingwood secretary Gordon Carlyon and like any young local boy he was thrilled to the back teeth to receive an invitation to join the Magpies.

By the final week prior to the 1953 season he was playing in the senior practice match. He showed enough to be selected in the reserves for the first two games but hardly had a sniff of the football. "They dropped me to the under-19s...it was the only game I ever played in the thirds... and I never got a kick! Somehow I was back in the seconds a week later." The selectors must have known something because Bromage's play started to blossom. He kicked six goals then eight in successive weeks, both against regular senior full-backs who had been lowered to the early games.

"I never had an idea that I would be picked in the seniors, but then the coach Phonse Kyne pulled me aside at training on Thursday night and said "We might give you a go tonight". I went to the pictures with a mate that night and by the time we came home there were photographers everywhere because I had made the side." It is often said that players introduced to the top level too early are not ready physically and are prone to injury. Bromage was 11 stone 6 pounds when first chosen and sees some validity in the argument.

"It may have been the case. I had all the weight in the legs and not much in the upper body. Maybe you are not developed enough at that age. On the other hand I had played most of the season in the reserves so I had a pretty good grounding. It wasn't as if I was rushed into it like some people think."

He revealed for the first time that he could have easily missed his history-making day because of a dose of the flu. In a natural reaction Bromage kept it quiet from those in charge at Collingwood. "I shouldn't have played, but when you're a kid you never know if you'll get a second chance." He knew that there had only been a handfull of 15-year-olds in League ranks, but was unaware that he was the youngest of the batch. "There was a suggestion that I was the youngest, but no-one was quite sure. It was mainly that I was the youngest ever at Collingwood."

Over the years there have been misconceptions about the youngest boy ever to play VFL football and as records are scanty prior to World War II the facts remained unchallenged for years. It was a common belief that Richmond's Mick Maguire was the youngest ever, but a search of the dusty tomes at the Births and Deaths office showed this to be wrong and that Bromage was the youngest.

In all he played 28 games and kicked 29 goals for the Magpies from 1953 to 1956 then shifted to Fitzroy at the start of 1958. He played 41 times and booted 48 goals for the Lions up to 1961 then left the VFL scene after nine seasons at the ripe old age of 24.

Just behind Bromage in the youth stakes, but miles ahead in terms of footballing profile, was Albert Collier - another Collingwood player. Collier (born July 9, 1909) lined up at full-forward for the black and whites in the opening round of 1925. Collier was 15 years and 299 days and had a nervous start. In that first year he played only four games, but he blossomed when placed in defence. His style was to take finger-tip marks and bolt away, meeting any opposition with a crunching hip and shoulder. As a

> **Tim Watson wouldn't have been able to start his career in 1977 if today's draft rules had been in place.**

centre half-back or ruckman he was a dynamo and many who saw him regard him as Collingwood's greatest player of this or any other era. He won the Brownlow Medal in 1929, the same year as Collingwood won the third of four successive flags. The origins of his nickname "Leeter" were obscure even to him although it was believed to have started out as "Leader".

The Depression and lack of job opportunities led to him accepting a lucrative coaching position with Tasmanian team Cananore after the Magpies had won the 1930 flag. Collier was just 21 and in his prime, yet had lost none of his brilliance when he returned to Collingwood in 1933 and went on to play in the 1935 and 1936 flags. In all he played 205 games and kicked 54 goals for Collingwood from 1925 to 1930 and 1933 to 1939. He also played 12 games for Fitzroy in 1941 to 1942. He died in 1988.

The wise heads said for years the pace and strength required in modern football would preclude any more under-16 players from breaking through, but Tim Watson (born July 13 1961) proved them wrong on May 14, 1977, when he debuted for Essendon at the age of 15 years and 305 days.

Legend has it that St Kilda had wanted Welles Eicke to play senior football when he was still 13, but his parents refused permission. Eicke (born September 27, 1893) was 15 years and 315 days when he made his debut for St Kilda on August 7, 1909. He started as a

Keith Bromage. At 15 years and 287 days old, he was the youngest player ever to appear in a senior game.

forward pocket, but within a couple of years he established himself as a centre half-back of the highest order. Lightly built, he had the knack of being able to hang in the air for marks with an apparent "second spring" and was regarded as the best mark in the competition for his inches. He was a frequent Victorian representative, captained and coached St Kilda and was universally regarded as a champion.

Like Albert Collier, he was outspoken off the field and often clashed with committees. He was at the centre of several off-field flare-ups over a long career and once caused a stir as captain when he stopped a game for a count of the opposition. Eicke admitted years later that he had called for the count to calm down one of his own players who had been sniping at the umpire.

Eicke played for St Kilda from 1909 to 1924 then was appointed as North's first coach in the club's VFL debut year in 1925. He played there again in the early part of 1926 and then returned to St Kilda. In all he played 197 games for the Saints and 21 for North.

Mick Maguire (born June 6, 1894) played his first game for Richmond on April 30, 1910. A forward, he played 39 games for the Tigers from 1910 to 1912 and kicked 62 goals. He crossed Yarra Park in mid-1912 to play 19 games and kick 23 goals for Melbourne until 1914. After the war he re-appeared at Collingwood for nine games and 10 goals in 1918. Maguire was a clever rover and forward who had a tendency to run too far with the ball, but he could usually get out of trouble thanks to his great pace. He was a champion amateur boxer and was a handy rower. Later in life he became a succcessful publican in Melbourne then Brisbane. He died in London in 1950.

"Oldest" of the 15-year-olds was Len Fitzgerald (born May 7, 1929) who was 16 days short of his 16th birthday when he lined up for Collingwood on April 21, 1945. He was a half-forward with strength, great ball-distribution and uncanny position sense, but was lost to Collingwood in his prime when a Sturt supporter offered him a job early in 1950. This was in the midst of an upheaval at Collingwood and it was said that John Wren had promised a political ally in South Australia that he would push the clearance through. A bargain was struck when Fitzgerald returned to the Magpies for the last four games of 1950 on the condition that he would be cleared the next year. He duly went to Sturt and won the Magarey Medal in 1952, 1954 and 1959. He was selected in the All Australian side after the 1953 carnival. His Collingwood career encompassed 96 games and 49 goals from 1945 to 1950.

There were a number of different versions of who was the youngest player of all time, until the Births and Deaths office provided the definitive answer and Bromage admitted relief. "I remember seeing Welles Eicke and Mick Maguire listed in the Miller's Guide at one stage, but I'm glad it was sorted out. I try to steer away from too much discussion on it."

His career at Collingwood took a nosedive in 1956 when he injured a knee at training, and had to have a cartilage removed. When he returned he hurt the knee again and doctors said his career was over. He had every intention of retiring until a couple of years later when he was cajoled into doing the pre-season at Fitzroy. The atmosphere was different to Collingwood and before long he had been cajoled into picking up the threads of his career with the Maroons. He stayed there until 1961 when at the ripe old age of 24 (with a nine season career behind

him) he headed to Canberra to coach Manuka.

As an afterthought he mentions what may be a record just as unique as the one he is most known for, but much harder to check.

"I'm probably the only bloke who kicked a goal with his first and his last kick in League football. As for the possibility of seeing another 15-year-old (even allowing for rule changes) Bromage said he was sceptical.

"I don't think we'll see it. Everyone is bigger and stronger these days."

BULLDOG BITE

Charlie Sutton was a hard man who knew what was required in finals matches.

"Shop early to avoid the rush," was the metaphor he emphasised to remind his players to hit first and hit hard. Ron Barassi was one opponent who found out early in the 1954 grand final that the gnarled old Footscray veteran meant business.

"I wanted all the other players to stand up and be counted. It (the Barassi clash) was a fair bump, I thought, but he got a free."

Charlie could see his 1954 Footscray side was on the verge of a premiership six days before it happened. "They scintillated," was Sutton's recollection of the Sunday morning session before 15,000 people leading up to the big match. It was a carnival atmosphere as Western Oval was the scene of the finish for the Warrnambool to Melbourne cycling race and the finely tuned footballers responded well to the big crowd - "they were ball-hungry and very keen to win". The instincts of the tough old captain-coach were spot on. His beloved Bulldogs romped away from Melbourne for a 51 point victory.

Footscray beat Geelong comfortably in the second semi-final and went into the play-off as favorites. "I had to keep their feet on the ground. That was our third time in the finals in four years and we had only ever got as far as the first semi before 1953," remembered Sutton. That victory was a turning point even

Footscray's Charlie Sutton gets his kick in despite the attention of Essendon's Bob Syme.

though the Dogs succumbed to Geelong in the preliminary final. "It was a big breakthrough," said Sutton, "and was one of the things that stood us in good stead for the following year. Every final is more intense and for a side to go in first up it is very hard."

As a coach, Sutton said it was important to maintain the same routine and approach. On every street corner of Footscray there was someone willing to offer advice.

But the Bulldogs were a team on a mission and a six goal opening quarter put Footscray down for the count. "We had the undisputed best backline in the League," said Sutton of the defensive six - Wally

Donald, Herb Henderson, Dave Bryden, Alan Martin, Ted Whitten and Jim Gallagher.

The first flag for the Western suburbs was an intoxicating event. When Footscray rolled Collingwood in the opening round of 1955 it looked like there would be no stopping the Dogs, but it wasn't long before the alarm bells started to ring for Sutton. "I could see the complacency coming in and it went right through the suburb."

Footscray took a long time to get back onto the rails and by then the late run for the 1955 finals was a belated one. The Bulldogs missed a finals place on percentage.

Chapter Ten

1955-1959

Demon domination

*A*ustralia's image as the lucky country was established in the 1950s. "Riding on the sheep's back" was a phrase which summed up the growing prosperity of the nation.

The volatility of the Petrov affair continued to cause political ripples in Canberra, but Australian society was settling into a conservative state of well-being. Competition in League football had experienced its share of instability in 1954 with one of the closest seasons on record, but 1955 would set the scene for an established order which would vary little in the latter half of the decade.

Heading that new order would be the Melbourne Football Club which was about to surpass its efforts of the previous golden era of 1939 to 1941. The Demons had returned to power briefly immediately after the war, but slid dramatically to earn a wooden spoon in 1951 and a second last placing two years later.

An influx of youth had turned the club's fortunes around and resulted in a leap from eleventh to second in 1954, but even the amazing talents of coach Norm Smith could not prepare the young side for the new experience of a grand final and the Demons had gone down to Footscray. Captain Geoff Collins retired after that game and two other veterans Lance Arnold and Ken Albiston moved on. By the time the Demons took the field for the 1955 grand final new men such as Peter Marquis, Ian Ridley and Trevor Johnson had won their spurs and it was part

of Smith's planned evolution of a new footballing dynasty that more youth would be blended into the team.

At the core of Melbourne's success was Smith. One of his players, Don Williams, summed it up in later years when he said that Smith had a cruel tongue. "But after deflating you, almost crushing you, he would pick you up and explain the reasons for his tirade. Even after the most devastating Smith tonguelashing you would somehow leave his presence feeling happy and keen to do better."

Melbourne sounded a warning to the rest of the competition by winning the first 10 games of 1955. A trademark of the Demons' teams in this era was the uncanny ability to pluck a game out of the fire when all seemed lost. To a large extent this was due to the superb level of fitness created by Norm Smith, but the knack also demonstrated the qualities of determination and confidence in the team. Against South early in 1955, the Demons needed five goals with only 10 minutes to play. With skipper Noel McMahen playing do-or-die football in defence and Denis Cordner taking every knockout, Melbourne stormed forward in wave after wave and got home by a point. A similar performance overwhelmed Richmond on the Queen's Birthday.

South had no trouble in beating a woeful St Kilda, 25.16 to 4.8. Critics slammed the uninterested Saints who had a miserable year. When they finally won a game against North Melbourne there were even veiled suggestions that a couple of North players had been paid to perform below their best. It was the only win for the Saints who finished with a dismal percentage of 45.4.

Collingwood halted Melbourne's run at Victoria Park after a dour struggle dominated by defences. The Magpie small men Bob Rose, Thorold Merrett and Des Healey gave Melbourne plenty of headaches and set up the win. Geelong sowed further seeds of doubt on Melbourne's invincibility by knocking the Demons off two weeks later. Strangely enough the move of skipper Bob Davis to the unaccustomed role of centre half-back helped achieve the win for the Cats.

Geelong and Collingwood were Melbourne's main threats while Essendon managed to scrape into the four by a slender 0.6 per cent ahead of Footscray. The Demons dispelled the doubts over their ability by notching up a gritty win over Collingwood in the second semi-final. Collingwood, as game as ever, was outgunned in the grand final rematch as the effect of three tough games and a number of injuries took its toll.

Former Melbourne star Percy Beames, writing in *The Age*, said Melbourne's approach had been the same one used successfully against Collingwood since 1937 and had been laid down by former coach Checker Hughes who said: "Use strength, take advantage of high marking ability, develop the long game and don't be taken in by Collingwood's handball. Once Collingwood starts handball meet the player with shirtfront football." Noel McMahen gave a perfect illustration of the point when he dealt out a full-blooded bump to Collingwood champion Bobby Rose early in the day. Rose had the chance to dispose of the ball a second before impact, but preferred to take on his opponent.

The two men had often tangled before and jousted again late in the day. Rose had been under strict instructions to keep clear of trouble as he had

> An influx of youth had turned the club's fortunes around and resulted in a leap from eleventh to second in 1954.

missed the last five games of the year through injury. One head-on clash from the 1955 grand final was talked about for years afterwards. Melbourne nineteenth man Frank "Bluey" Adams charged onto the field and collided with star Magpie winger Des Healey. Both men lay on the ground, out cold, and Collingwood fans bayed for Adams' blood. Healey's nose was broken and his face bruised. It was also the end of his career.

The pace of football was increasing all the time and coaches wanted to have a more direct method of distributing instructions. Runners were introduced in August 1955.

No-one could catch Melbourne which opened 1956 with 10 wins on the trot. The club had enormous depth of playing talent and men who could not get a senior game with the Demons would have walked into most other teams. About the only problem for Norm Smith was the forward set-up and he adapted the team's game to score goals through rovers and ruckmen. In this regard "Big Bob" Johnson was used in tandem with the decoy full-forward Athol Webb. The fast-leading Webb would move downfield and open up the attack as passes were speared towards the waiting Johnson in the square.

One club which underwent a drastic overhaul in personnel was St Kilda. Under firebrand coach Alan Killigrew, the Saints savagely cut their list and included 10 new faces in the team for the first round. One of Killigrew's biggest coups was the signing of lightly built Stratford full-forward Bill Young who was an immediate success and headed the VFL goalkicking with 56. Killigrew injected a new brand of fanaticism that had been sorely lacking at the club for years and the team showed great tenacity, even though it only won four games and drew another. In years to come 1956 would be seen as the turning point in the club's history.

The League, as always, tried to come up with ideas to spread the game's appeal. Several years earlier a night match had been played between Richmond and Essendon at the Showgrounds at the end of the season. This experiment eventually led to the development of night football on a regular basis and a post-season night series was arranged for the 1956 season at the South Melbourne ground.

The first game between South and St Kilda was a wild affair which resulted in three players and a trainer being reported. The final between South Melbourne and Carlton attracted more than 30,000 people to the Lake Oval with the home team defeating the Blues in a memorable match.

The night series initially was enormously popular and big attendances promised a financial bonanza for the league. However, the matches attracted unruly elements and within a few years only the semis and final attracted the crowds and in 1971 the competition was held for the last time until resurrected in something like its current format in 1977.

Melbourne's semi-final win over Collingwood was the third success over the Magpies for the year. Melbourne's ability to get the quick breakaway from the packs was too much for the Magpies to handle and the story was no different in the grand final. A rampaging Demon side crushed Collingwood by 12 goals and credit went to the selectors who had stuck with players who had performed indifferently in the home and away matches. They stuck to the plan of using Webb in attack and he responded with five goals. Courageous centreman Ken Melville was another who rewarded the selectors' faith. An all-time record crowd of 115,802 crammed into the MCG which had been refurbished for the coming Olympics.

The introduction of television in 1957 breathed more life into football although the League initially had problems determining the extent to which the cameras could take the games into the family home. Matches were televised live from three-quarter-time and at one stage all three stations of the time covered League matches and had panel shows. It was overkill and the League later disallowed the "live"

Collingwood usually ended up on the losing end of their clashes with Melbourne and that did not sit well with the Magpies. When Collingwood lost narrowly at Victoria Park late in 1956, umpire Allan Nash needed a police escort as he left the field.

last quarter telecasts. The first announcers were Ian Johnson (GTV 9), Ken Dakin (ABV 2) and Tony Charlton (HSV 7).

Melbourne's rule over the footballing roost was not as pronounced in 1957 and the Demons had more than their share of narrow scrapes. Their defence, though, was as tight as ever and in one game tied down the Saints to a score of 1.5-11. That did not reflect the Saints' improvement as the club won eight games for the year in its new-look uniform featuring black sleeves and black backs.

The 1957 surprise packet was Hawthorn which had made steady progress since hitting rock bottom in a winless 1950. Coach Jack Hale had turned around an amateurish and lackadaisical attitude that had kept the club firmly rooted at the bottom of the ladder. He had a willing disciple in captain John Kennedy and the Hawks had recruited fine players such as John Peck, Graham Arthur and Brendan Edwards.

The Hawks were a fiery combination and steamrolled many teams to rise to top place in mid

Winning brew. Melbourne came up with the right recipe in an era of unparallelled success. From left Ron Barassi, Noel McMahen, Don Williams, coach Norm Smith, Geoff McGivern and Peter Marquis.

season. The highpoint was a courageous win over Melbourne at Glenferrie Oval when the rugged defence led by Len Crane and Roy Simmonds exposed the flaws in the Demons' attack. Hale's transformation of the Hawks was nothing short of amazing. He even made sectarianism, one of the club's biggest problems, work for him, by dividing training groups into good natured Protestant and Catholic squads. More importantly he taught the Hawks to hate defeat.

Collingwood had been the bridesmaid to Melbourne for the past two seasons, but just as the Demons seemed to be slipping back to the field, the Magpies also suffered from erratic form. The big two clubs played a draw at Victoria Park, but then Collingwood lost unexpectedly to Fitzroy.

It was certainly an action-packed year both on and off the field with Footscray pulling one of the biggest surprises by axing 1954 premiership coach Charlie Sutton. What made the move harder to un-

derstand was the fact that the Bulldogs were sitting in third place at the time. Sutton was replaced by his 23-year-old protege Ted Whitten and the Bulldogs lost the next four games to slip out of contention.

Crowds continued to grow and the VFL introduced reserved seating for the finals following its success at the Olympics. The finals contained a fair share of surprises and none was bigger than Essendon's upset of Melbourne in the second semifinal. The Demons had not lost a final for three years, and during that time they had thrashed Essendon three times on the MCG, but the Bombers turned on a nine-goal, second-quarter blitz.

Melbourne was made painfully aware it could not afford the luxury of using Bob Johnson in the forward pocket as Essendon tall men Geoff Leek and John Gill controlled the ruck duels. Even more galling for Melbourne was the ascendancy of ruck rovers Hugh Mitchell and Mal Pascoe over Ron Barassi.

The Demons returned to the winning circle with a big victory over Hawthorn in the preliminary final and set themselves for a rematch with Essendon. This time the Demons were not about to let the opposition get the upper hand and had a goal on the board within 16 seconds of the start. The second semi turnabout fired up Melbourne and Percy Beames wrote in *The Age*: "The defence never faltered, the centreline exceeded expectations, the rucks more than held their own, while the attack brought off feats that at times were positively brilliant".

Beames hailed this as the greatest of the three successive flags because the club had to reorganise after the losses of Noel McMahen, Ken Melville, Denis Cordner, Stuart Spencer and Geoff McGivern and then had to come back after the shock semifinal loss. Beames pondered whether teams that had missed their chance to knock off Melbourne in its "vulnerable" year would be able to topple the Demons in the foreseeable future.

The night series included all teams in a change of format as finalists joined the competition after bowing out of the day series. It was not a success due to various complications and two weeks after the grand final the last three matches were played in the space of five nights. A year later the series returned to its original format.

Melbourne gathered all of its might for 1958 and kicked clear of the field once again. Ron Barassi was back to top form and the Demons rediscovered the quality of being able to pluck games out of the fire from impossible situations.

The clashes with Collingwood captured the public's imagination and a record home and away crowd of 99,346 packed the MCG on the Queen's Birthday to see the home side snatch victory with a last quarter flurry, and Collingwood was left wondering just what it had to do to knock this side off its perch. Melbourne coach Norm Smith always held up the clashes as something special for his players and told

them that a footballer had not proved himself until he played Collingwood at Victoria Park. "If you could hold your head high after a match there, you were a man."

The Queen's Birthday game was the ninth time in a row that Collingwood had gone down to Melbourne and even Collingwood's skipper Murray Weideman admitted in later years that he didn't think his side would ever beat them. The belief was that they had champions on every line and in every position, and one of Weideman's contemporaries told Collingwood historian Richard Stremski in his book *Kill For Collingwood*: "They hit harder, they were bigger, they were stronger".

For all of that, things didn't always go Melbourne's way and the team lost for the first time in 1958 in a thriller at the Junction Oval against St Kilda. The Saints clung tenaciously to a one point lead in the final term and won largely because of the efforts of a crewcut country ruckman named Ray Barrett who had the call over "Big Bob" Johnson. Best afield in the Saints' biggest win for 10 years was dashing centre half-back Neil Roberts who was on his way to a Brownlow Medal. Roberts was acting captain after a tragic knee injury ended the career of the 1957 medallist Brian Gleeson. The Saints' match of the day clash with Melbourne had almost been shifted because of Health Department concerns over the ground, but in the end it went ahead as planned.

Club matches were put aside for 20 days as state teams gathered in Melbourne for the Centenary Carnival. Victoria's team bristled with talent and won the title. Best match of the series was between the Vics and Western Australia when the home side had to overcome the loss of John Dugdale and Jack Clarke with injuries in the second quarter. Bob Skilton had to stay on the field with a corked thigh,

> Crowds continued to grow and the VFL introduced reserved seating for the finals following its success at the Olympics.

but fellow rover Allen Aylett took up the challenge and kicked six goals in a great solo effort.

North Melbourne made the greatest resurrection in 1958, after starting in abysmal fashion with a 120-point loss at home against Fitzroy. By round 12 North was in the four and late in the year featured in a bizarre incident against Essendon when the team was lined up for a player count. North's Brian Martyn went down heavily in the centre and as he was being attended to, nineteenth man John Waddington ran on the arena. He was actually replacing Albert Mantello who had just left the field, but Essendon officials thought North had jumped the gun and captain Jack Clarke called on umpire Barbour to line up the Roos. Apparently the Essendon runner had noticed Martyn lying on the ground and alerted officials on the bench who promptly sent him back to tell Barbour. A boundary umpire was also heard to say that North had 19 men on the ground. After a five-minute delay the game started again and North ran out winners.

In a strange turnaround North met Fitzroy, the team that had thrashed the Roos in the opening game, in the first semi, and even more remarkably the Northerners won by four points. In the dying moments there was controversy when North's Allen Aylett flattened Fitzroy's Vin Williams and Williams shot a pass to teammate Alan Gale at centre half-forward. Umpire Barbour called the ball back and made Williams take the free again, but this time North spirited it away.

North had hopes of making the grand final when facing up to a Collingwood that had been lacerated by a brilliant Melbourne side in the second semi-final. Collingwood dumped four players and seemed to gain yards of pace to run out a comfortable 20-point winner. Next came the biggest challenge against a virtually unbackable Melbourne team steaming towards a fourth successive flag that would equal Collingwood's cherished record.

For the finals Collingwood had included the tall

Collingwood halted the Melbourne juggernaut in the 1958 Grand Final. Triumphant skipper Murray Weideman - a central figure in the controversial game, is surrounded by Ian Brewer, Thorold Merrett, Kevin Rose, Ken Bennett, Peter Lucas and Ray Gabelich.

Graeme Fellowes and another more combative ruckman, Barry "Hooker" Harrison. Newly appointed recruiting officer Jack Burns had to cajole the selection committee into the idea of using the fiercely determined Harrison, but it proved to be a master stroke in the grand final. Kyne told him to stick to the dynamic Barassi all day: "Let him know you are there all the time. Bump, push, shove, (and) harass him".

Harrison and skipper Murray Weideman were a fearsome pair, but in the opening quarter of the grand final there was no indication of what lay ahead as Melbourne skipped away to a three-goal break. At the first change Weideman said to Harrison: "Let's see who we can collect", and after a couple of bone-crushing incidents Melbourne's concentration was destroyed. The main targets were Barassi and the brilliant but volatile Laurie Mithen. The two Demons responded angrily and were involved in almost every flare-up. As the rest of the Melbourne players were drawn into the fights Collingwood settled down to play football. Two quick goals by Ken Bennett in the pouring rain put the Magpies two points clear at half-time. Coach Kyne said to his men: "Whatever you're doing, just keep doing it", and the Magpies stitched up the result with a five-goal to two-point third term.

Harrison recalled his instructions: "Mine was basically the original tagging role - just to stop Barassi getting kicks. What most people don't realise is that we tried it out for the first time in the Queen's Birthday game that year. By the grand final we really got onto the target." Funnily enough when Harrison was told to mind Barassi he had to be pointed in the right direction of football's biggest name. "I'd never met him and had just come out of the Navy." But in the grand final it was a case of no holds barred. "All the rules go out the window. Forget all the goody-goody stuff. You don't take any prisoners do you?"

Watertight defence by Harry Sullivan and Ron Reeves quelled any of Melbourne's hopes for a last quarter revival and Collingwood was able to pull off one of the most remarkable and heroic premiership wins of all time.

The Magpies were slow to start in 1959 and in the early stages of the season it was Carlton which set the pace. By late in the year Collingwood had regained some form and rolled the Blues in a torrid game. Carlton had more than its share of drama during the season and in the match against Fitzroy backman Bob Crowe injured his knee in the race as he was running onto the field. Crowe limped whenever the ball came his way and was soon forced off in an incident which highlighted the inflexibility of rules covering the 19th and 20th men.

Another unusual incident occurred in a Collingwood game when rover Ken Bennett played in the reserves then was told he would be senior 20th man after Ray Gabelich withdrew at the last minute with an injury. Bennett was not called upon until three-quarter time.

Most controversial late inclusion for the year was St Kilda's star full-back Verdun Howell who was originally unavailable for the Fitzroy game because he had to complete his military service training on the weekend. Howell went absent without leave from the nearby Albert Park barracks and ran onto the Junction Oval as part of the Saints' team.

The army threatened to take action against Howell, but nothing happened in the end. He was one of St Kilda's best and may have even gained Brownlow votes. At the end of the year he tied with South star Bob Skilton, but lost on a countback. Thirty years later he was awarded a retrospective medal, but it may never have happened had he not broken army rules.

Melbourne's clashes with Fitzroy in this era were like chess matches as brothers Norm and Len Smith pitted their wits. Melbourne's Laurie Mithen was

> The main targets were Barassi and the brilliant but volatile Laurie Mithen. The two Demons responded angrily and were involved in almost every flare-up.

swung to full-forward and kicked six goals in an effort which looked likely to win the first tussle between the two in 1959, but Len's Fitzroy got up by 13 points. When they met later in the year they tied.

Football was not always as scientific as the brand practised by the Smith brothers. South won a tight game when Max Oaten misunderstood a direction from the bench to shift to the half-forward line. Oaten went to the wrong flank and on the way took an "accidental" mark from which he kicked the decisive goal.

Carlton headed the League list half-way through the year, thanks to a powerful bigman brigade headed by Graham Donaldson, John Nicholls and Sergio Silvagni, but then everything ran off the rails when Donaldson was injured late in the year. The Blues went out of the finals with two losses including a humiliating effort against Melbourne in the second semi-final. Despite the September failure, Carlton had fought back remarkably after a preseason upheaval in which the committee had been dumped and Ken Hands had replaced Jim Francis as coach. The feud was so bitter that it left Francis and Hands as enemies. Francis had been Hands' best man and the two had helped build each other's houses.

The grand final was a showdown between Essendon and Melbourne with the Demons desperate to obliterate the memory of their 1958 loss to Collingwood. For three quarters Essendon took the game up to Melbourne, but was overwhelmed by strength and experience in the last half hour. Setting up the victory was Ron Barassi who avenged his failure in the 1958 grand final with a devastating performance. *The Age* reported: "Twice he pulled down typically strong and brilliant marks over the pack to kick goals then followed up by snapping a third - all in the space of seven minutes just before half-time".

> "Norman Smith is of middle class size, and is an unobtrusive personality. That nonchalant manner covers a great deal of cleverness, a quick-thinking football brain and a very cool head."

NORM SMITH: SUPER COACH

Mention the name of Norm Smith to the modern-day football fan and he will instantly acknowledge the man as perhaps the greatest coach of all time.

That may well be true, but his coaching excellence tends to mask the fact that Smith was also a magnificent footballer in his day, and could have won a Brownlow had it not been for the war years.

From his youth Norm and elder brother Len were taught the virtues of teamwork by their father playing for the Northcote-based club, Dennis. A natural sportsman who also played District cricket, Norm broke into the Melbourne side at the age of 19 in 1935. He admitted in later years that he entered the side in a humble frame of mind, and while confidence grew with experience he never lost the sense of being a unit in the team.

This early description of his play by a journalist gives an insight. "Norman Smith is of middle class size, and is an unobtrusive personality. He's redheaded, but a placid footballer. He neither bumps nor executes fancy turns, but strolls around the field in a quiet sort of way, and one does not notice him particularly. The ball comes near him and he picks it up, handballs it to someone nearby or stab-kicks neatly. That nonchalant manner covers a great deal of cleverness, a quick-thinking football brain and a very cool head."

The common word in all descriptions of Smith as a footballer was "unselfish" and his estimate of any player was the man's capacity for fitting into a team pattern. Coach "Checker" Hughes said of him: "He was a genius at handball. He flips the ball to the man running in and never forgets to block. The things he does amaze me. He is different from the others. He makes a team work around him. Others make the team work for them. He is a master at creating play."

Smith became a regular player in his second year

Master Coach. Norm Smith (centre) on the bench with the Melbourne brains trust from left "Checker" Hughes, Jim Cardwell and Ivor Warne-Smith.

at Melbourne and played on the half-forward line, feeding full-forward Ron Baggott. When Baggott was sidelined through injury for a month Smith was shifted to full-forward and there he stayed even when Baggott returned. He built a close understanding with Baggott who was centre half-forward, and often acted as a decoy to draw the opposing full-back out of goals then shot a lightning hand or foot pass to Baggott who could slam through a goal.

Smith and Baggott formed a lethal combination that was a nightmare to all opposition defences, and played a big part in Melbourne winning three flags on the trot from 1939 to 1941. Smith always regarded these sides as the greatest he had seen in the League and he was a big contributor to the success. He booted 80 goals in 1938, 54 in 1939 then steered through 86 in 1940 and was second on the goalkicking list. In the grand final he bagged seven great goals to equal the record. He headed the VFL goalkicking in 1941 with 89, but after that Mel-

bourne struggled as the club was one of the hardest hit by the war.

He was appointed skipper in 1945 and led a resurgence which landed the club in the grand final the following year, but the Demons were overwhelmed by a brilliant Essendon side. In 1948 Smith severely injured a thigh in a practice game and Don Cordner was made skipper. Smith's season was disrupted by injury, but in September he formed part of an amazing duet with Jack Mueller. Mueller, a champion player who at 34 had been coaching the seconds all year, was elevated after the Demons were walloped in the second semi by Essendon. The two veterans revived the "decoy" set-up which had been used by Smith and Baggott years earlier and scored 16 goals between them.

A week later the Demons tied the grand final with Essendon, and Mueller kicked six more goals while Smith was one of the best afield. Smith had the chance to win the match when he grabbed the ball from a boundary throw-in close to goal and a teammate tried to punch the ball over the goal line. An Essendon defender seized the ball and the game ended as a draw. In the replay Melbourne skipped away to a six-goal lead in the first term and never eased the pressure. Smith was best afield, closely followed by Mueller.

Melbourne's coach "Checker" Hughes retired after the triumph and Smith applied for the job, yet missed out on the casting vote of the committee chairman and the nod went to Allan La Fontaine.

Fitzroy snapped him up as captain-coach, but his playing days were limited. He added only 17 games and 26 goals in 1949-50 to his magnificent record at Melbourne of 210 games and 540 goals. He had won the Demons' best and fairest award in 1938 and 1944.

Smith coached the Lions for three years in which the club ran seventh once and fifth twice, but the football world regarded his stint there as the launching pad for a return to Melbourne and it came in 1952. He was given the job by only one vote and this may have contributed to an early tendency to try to please too many people at the club. He said in later years that in 1954 he decided to please only one person - himself. "If I failed, I'd fail on my own merits."

This determination combined with his own bluntness and fiery temperament led to conflict with members of the hierarchy, but they were soon silenced by the sheer weight of success. Melbourne made the 1954 grand final but was well beaten by Footscray. It was only a temporary setback and in 1955 the Demons began an amazing run with a flag win over Collingwood.

Aided by the great recruiting talents of secretary Jim Cardwell, Smith built an awesome team of depth and strength. Melbourne won five out of six flags from 1955 to 1960, only slipping up when Collingwood sucked the Demons into fighting in the

> "Desire is that cold fury burning inside a player that makes him want to beat the other fellow. Deep desire can be seen."

1958 grand final. That reverse was the greatest disappointment in Smith's coaching career, and ironically he had barracked for Collingwood as a youth. Smith recorded his greatest success as coach by navigating the Demons to the 1964 flag with a side that was only a shadow of the great teams of the late 1950s.

As a coach Smith was never satisfied and a hard taskmaster. He was intolerant of errors and demanded complete control. His former coach "Checker" Hughes sat on the bench with him for a while, but one day made the mistake of pressing a point too hard. "Get up in the grandstand where you belong, you old bastard," exploded Smith, and the aged Hughes hobbled away on a walking stick. Hughes did not return to the bench for a long time after that. Smith was stubborn and could be prickly to those he considered knew less about football.

In 1965 Melbourne began well with a succession of wins by small margins, but it all fell apart on the Queen's Birthday when the Demons were thrashed by St.Kilda. A month later Smith was sacked after the Demons continued to struggle. He had stood on some toes over the years and now the old resentments surfaced as his detractors dragged him down. Within four days he was reinstated, but the damage to Melbourne was irreparable and the club would not make the finals again for almost a quarter of a century.

Smith was a ruthless coach, but had always inspired loyalty and he was well aware of those people in the club who had orchestrated his downfall. It was a shabby way to treat a man who had guided the team into 11 successive finals series and been involved in 10 premierships as a coach or player.

There were petty suggestions at the time that Smith had eased Barassi out of the club a few months earlier in order to protect his own position as coach, but that was far from the truth, and when Barassi took up the offer to captain-coach Smith said: "I knew it was time for him look out for himself. He has come from nothing to the position he is in and he richly deserves it."

Any suggestion that Smith had caused Barassi's departure for his own gain was against the great reputation he had for helping friend and foe in the football world. Barassi retained his respect and admiration for Smith and when he heard that Smith had been sacked he roared into Jim Cardwell's house and reduced the famous secretary to tears for what he saw as treachery against the man who meant so much to him.

Heart problems led to his retirement at the end of 1967, but he could not stay away from the game and in 1969 took on the South Melbourne coaching job. He scored one of his greatest triumphs by squeezing every ounce out of a team with only a couple of stars and plenty of battlers. The Swans made the finals for the first time in 25 years thanks largely to Smith's tactical genius. He finished as South's coach in 1972 then was persuaded to help out his old pupil Ron Barassi at North Melbourne. It was to be only a brief resumption of one of football's great partnerships as Smith's health deteriorated. He died in July of that year.

Despite popular opinion Smith never saw himself as a great orator. He once said: "I'm no Bob Menzies, but I am surprised sometimes by the emotion I am capable of achieving. Players respond differently. Ron Barassi was a player who would look you directly in the eye and suddenly you would detect a wild look. You had got across - "the tiger was pacing in his cage!" Others involved with him say that Smith was too modest in his appraisal of his speaking abilities. He was fluent, colorful and forceful in his addresses to players and could inspire them to great heights.

Barassi, who had virtually been brought up as a son by Smith in his late teens, paid the final tribute to the man revered in football as "The Fox". "I had the privilege of seeing him at closer view than most. I owe a tremendous amount to him both on and off

the football field. He was a man of principle who wouldn't back away from any confrontation."

One of his players, Clyde Laidlaw, later served as assistant coach to Smith at South. Laidlaw still treasures notes on coaching that Smith prepared for him and other coaches at South Melbourne. They make fascinating reading and it was clear Smith had studied great motivators in sport and public life.

"He was a great admirer of Churchill," said Laidlaw and pointed to the quote that courage was not the absence of fear, but the mastery of it. The notes give an insight into Smith's coaching ethos.

On desire - "Desire is that cold fury burning inside a player that makes him want to beat the other fellow. Deep desire can be seen (Ron Barassi, Wes Hall, Carl Ditterich)."

On complacency - "After a long winning run you become the target for an ambush".

And finally on Melbourne's tradition - "Melbourne's winning tradition will not be entrusted to the timid or the weak".

MURRAY WEIDEMAN: THE ENFORCER

Murray Weideman's career inspired extreme reaction beyond the norm. After one game in 1959 there was even a bullet fired through his window after a particularly rough game and his tough, uncompromising tactics inflicted bruises on a succession of opponents.

It wasn't always that way, though. In 1952 he trained at Collingwood for the first time and wasn't considered good enough for the thirds. By the end of the next season he was a part, albeit as twentieth man, of the black and white combination that stormed to a flag.

Richmond's Des Rowe gave him a first game initiation that was typical of the feeling between the Tigers and Magpies when he sneered: "Collingwood must be going pretty bad to send kids like you onto the field".

Collingwood "Enforcer" Murray Weideman soars for a big mark against St Kilda in the opening round of 1962.

Weideman's junior years were spent in the Preston and District Junior Football Association, the same competition which also spawned Ron Barassi, later to become an arch-rival.

Weideman soon showed promise as a high-flying centre half-forward with a strong pair of hands. Just over six feet tall, he weighed only 12 and a half stone in the early years, but by the end of his career topped the 15 stone mark and had trouble keeping the poundage down. The more aggressive side of his game did not develop until hard men like Bob Rose retired and Weideman was elevated to the captaincy role. He built the image of an enforcer, but also had the reputation of "copping it sweet" when he was on the receiving end.

Magpie fans loved Weideman and regarded the handsome, well-groomed skipper as a buccaneer at the head of their troops. Married to a former Miss Victoria, he enjoyed the spotlight but one of his more outlandish moves stunned the Collingwood commit-

tee when he announced late in 1962 that he would join the professional wrestling ranks. The gimmicky, staged matches of the 1950s had been tremendously popular, but by 1962 the show was on the downturn and promoters wanted to cash in on Weideman's drawing power. He almost lost the captaincy over the issue, but in the end it all blew over. Weideman later said the only risk of injury was being thrown out of the ring. As long as you knew how to fall flat on the seats you would be okay!

Weideman's strong-arm approach angered more than opposition fans and with betting on football prevalent in the 1950s it was thought some of the threats made by phone or letter might have come from the underworld. A detective friend offered to maintain a constant guard on the house and when word passed around the Weidemans were left alone.

His most enduring mark on the football field was leading Collingwood to the 1958 flag as stand-in skipper for the injured Frank Tuck. Weideman and the lesser-known Barry "Hooker" Harrison took on the whole Melbourne side in the grand final and left the football part of the afternoon to their teammates. Demon skipper Ron Barassi took the bait and his team followed suit.

It would be wrong to think that physical application was the only side of Weideman's play. He won the Copeland Trophy as Collingwood's best and fairest player in 1957, 1961 and 1962 and played for his state five times. He kicked 162 goals in his 179 games from 1953 to 1963.

At the age of only 27 Weideman announced that he was quitting Collingwood to take up a country coaching post; 1963 had been an unhappy year for him and the club. The Magpies had finished well down the ladder and he had barely conversed with coach Phonse Kyne all year. He had also said on TV that he found some of the coach's moves bewildering. Kyne was replaced by Bob Rose and some cynics wondered whether part of Weideman's reason for leaving may have been the stricter training regimen under the new coach.

After coaching NSW country club Albury he moved to South Australia. In Adelaide he achieved good results with West Adelaide after going there in 1968 as a playing coach and proved the critics wrong who said he was too old.

His desire had always been to return to Collingwood as coach and after the 1974 season he was named in the position. Insiders saw it as a recognition by president Tom Sherrin of Weideman's help in the club's big bust-up 11 years earlier, but the position became complicated when Sherrin was voted out of the presidency soon after Weideman's appointment. Sherrin was replaced by Ern Clarke, a radical president with definite ideas on all aspects of the club's performance. Before long he and Weideman were at loggerheads and the animosity between the two men snowballed. Weideman guided the team to the elimination final in 1975, but there were already question marks over his coaching. It was written of him that he "won the love of the players, but not their respect".

For a variety of reasons matters went from bad to worse until they finally erupted in May 1976 when Weideman publicly announced that he could no longer work with Clarke. Things were papered over briefly but then Clarke resigned. Collingwood was a divided and unsettled club and it showed on the field when the Magpies finished last for the first time in their proud history. That was the end of Weideman's coaching career but the family name maintained a connection with the club through his son Mark who had a brief career at Victoria Park.

RON BARASSI: BORN TO WIN

Ron Barassi was the ultimate football personality. At the peak of his popularity Barassi was dubbed Mr Football by an adoring public, even though Footscray fans claimed the crown belonged to Ted Whitten.

Barassi in his prime.

He had the wits to make the most of his high profile and appeared in everything on television from a five-minute footy hints segment on the kids' show to regular spots on football panel shows. It was the beginning of a media involvement that continues three decades later.

"Tenacity" is the word most often used in describing Barassi's approach to football and he carried that over to life in general. His father, Ron senior, was killed at Tobruk in 1941 leaving behind his widow Elza and the five-year-old Ron. A George Washington-like story is told of how Barassi senior found his four-year-old son with axe in hand and a prized rose tree at his feet. With jaw jutting out characteristically even at this stage, the youngster stood his ground and took his punishment without a whimper.

The elder Barassi had played 55 games for the Demons and made his last appearance for the club as nineteenth man in the 1940 premiership side. A good rover who was just starting to develop, he had to contend with a talented band that included great rovers such as Percy Beames and Alby Rodda.

When Ron Barassi senior died, the Melbourne coterie pledged to look after the family's welfare.

Norm Smith, a champion player and friend of Ron's father, was one of those who had willingly signed the legal charter and he was to play a key role in influencing Barassi's future. Barassi had been cared for in Castlemaine by his grandparents while his mother eked out a living in Melbourne. She missed him so much that she sent for him to come to Melbourne. Later when she married again and moved to Tasmania she wanted him to come there.

That was when Norm Smith stepped in and offered to take him in. Smith was then Fitzroy's coach and had already spotted the boy's tremendous capability as a footballer, but he took the youngster to Melbourne when Barassi said he wanted to follow the path of his father. At home there was a fascinating clash of wills between the fiery red head Smith and the fiercely determined Barassi. They competed fiercely at everything from table tennis to cricket and the Barassi hatred of defeat often boiled to the surface. Smith conceded in later years that he might have been too hard on the teenager at times, but it was all part of the learning process.

Smith returned to Melbourne as coach, but that didn't give Barassi a free passage from the under-19s. Late in 1953 he finally broke into the seniors for a few games at full-forward and on the half-forward flank, but was quickly discarded. It seemed the Demons couldn't find him a niche until Smith decided that he would use him in the ruck with Don Cordner and rover Stuart Spencer. The chunky Barassi not only found his true place he actually created a new role: the ruck rover.

Barassi and a talented group of fellow under-19 graduates fuelled the Melbourne resurgence. The club had finished second last in 1953 and charged into the grand final a year later only to be humbled by Footscray. Smith and Barassi suffered the pain of that defeat and the next year Melbourne showed greater resolve in the start of a golden era. A solid win in the 1955 grand final was followed by a comprehensive success in 1956.

At the core of the success was Barassi and in 1957 he played a magnificent game, possibly his greatest grand final, to drive the Demons to victory. The run was broken in 1958 when Collingwood diverted Barassi's concentration and the rest of the Demons also lost their way.

From the outset Barassi was a natural leader and when he took the reins in 1960 it was a natural progression. The Demons won flags in 1959 and 1960 to cap an era of near absolute domination. Barassi won the club's best and fairest for the first time in 1961 - amazing in view of the fact that he had been the club's outstanding player for seven years - yet there were signs even in the early 1960s of the chronic groin problem that would plague his later playing years.

As a footballer he was not blessed with the natural skills, but he was totally team-oriented and had the knack of taking the desperate mark and playing on without any loss of momentum, a trait mandatory these days but rare in his era. He was a belligerent and explosive footballer who pushed himself to the point of exhaustion even though it was said that doctors thought he had a physical condition that made him prone to dislocations. Above all, he was an inspiration. Whenever Melbourne needed the extra lift it was the famous number 31 who produced that matchwinning goal or desperate charge through a pack.

A suspension on the eve of the 1963 finals cost Barassi a place in the finals and almost certainly put the Demons out of contention for the flag. A year later he was there on the winner's dais, admittedly after a game in which he had little influence. Not long after came the biggest bombshell in years when he signed to captain-coach Carlton. A few months

> As a footballer he was not blessed with the natural skills, but he was totally team-oriented.

earlier when the suggestion had first been made it was ridiculed by Melbourne officials.

He had long been touted as coaching material and immediately applied Melbourne methods. Carlton's fortunes started to turn and the club was in line for a finals berth in 1966 until Barassi was unloaded against South. He had momentarily relaxed after a mark and the impact not only dislocated his shoulder but also ripped the ligaments to put him out of action for eight weeks.

In 1967 he guided the Blues to the finals, but they had a disappointing campaign losing both matches. They made up for it the following year and despite the Blues' limitations Barassi guided the club to a flag. By 1970 Carlton had greater talent around the field and more flair. All that counted for nothing when the side trailed Collingwood by 44 points at half time. Barassi then pulled the master stroke of calling for all-out handball and the move turned the game. It also set the scene for a change in style that all clubs would pursue.

His authoritarian approach showed signs of tiredness with players beginning to question instructions. He retired from the coaching post at the end of 1971 saying: "I'm tired of football. I've had it up to the neck." Business commitments had been his main reason for quitting, but at only 35 years of age it was inevitable that he would not be out of the game for long. He maintained his media involvement and even pulled on the boots a few times for VFA club Port Melbourne in 1972.

North Melbourne, long the chopping block of the VFL, had embarked on a big-spending mission to lift off the bottom and a man with eight premierships (six as a player and two as a coach) was an obvious target as coach. A breakfast meeting with North chiefs Allen Aylett and Albert Mantello convinced Barassi to pick up the threads of his coaching career and he signed what was described as a gentleman's agreement on a serviette. With the aid of the 10-year rule he set about chasing the club's first flag.

His new club made the jump to just outside the five in 1973 and a year later the Roos made the grand final only to be overwhelmed by Richmond. The next year saw the Arden Street club's dreams come to fruition with the first-ever flag and two years later he brought another pennant home.

In the later years of his time at North the calls became louder from the Melbourne devotees and after he retired from the North job in 1980 it was inevitable that the Demons' favorite son would come home to the club he had left 16 years earlier.

But this time there would be no fairytale ending. Melbourne was sadly undermanned and even the magic of Barassi could not lift the club to its former glory. Early in the piece he admitted that he should have retained the playing services of former captain-coach Carl Ditterich and the Demons often seemed to lack muscle around the field.

Many optimists at the MCG had assumed that Melbourne's return to power under Barassi would happen as a matter of course. But it was a hard road to hoe for the coach so accustomed to success and high quality players. He had come from coaching a team of mature, experienced players to a club that fielded a swag of novices. His mere presence was tremendously daunting for some players and his incessant demands for perfection created a gulf at first. Gradually he modified his approach and adapted to the hitherto alien environment of a struggling club. He would later describe it as a salutary experience.

Barassi was vitally involved in the concept of recruiting Irish players and it was a scheme that produced Sean Wight and eventual Brownlow Medallist Jim Stynes. Ironically the Demons finally blossomed two seasons after he left, but even this barren chapter could not take the gloss off a magnificent career.

> "Despite his faults I believe that in the 10 senior games I played under Barassi, I learned more about football than I did from my other coaches in 10 years."

Barassi's decision to accept the Sydney Swans coaching job in 1993 surprised many people, but he had always espoused the value of the game going national and it was a case of putting his money where his mouth was. The Sydneysiders were at rock bottom when he took over, but by the time he left at the close of 1995 the team was a competitive unit.

Barassi's playing career spanned 16 years from 1953 to 1969, and included 203 games with Melbourne and an even 50 with Carlton. He wore the Big Vee on 19 occasions, played in six premierships with Melbourne and coached four flag sides. His coaching career encompassed 514 games.

Figures don't tell the true story of Barassi, a complex individual driven by a raging intensity that guaranteed success. Of all the thousands of opinions aired on Barassi perhaps the most telling came from Gary Baker, a veteran at Melbourne whom Barassi sacked from the senior list. Baker was bitter about being sacked but said: "Despite his faults I believe that in the 10 senior games I played under Barassi, I learned more about football than I did from my other coaches in 10 years".

Chapter Eleven

1960-1964
The pace of change

At the start of the 1960s the world was changing rapidly and would undergo even greater transformation in the decade ahead.

The Beatles were a pop group known only to the aficionadoes of Liverpool's Cavern Club and John Fitzgerald Kennedy was a hopeful candidate for the American Presidency. In Australia Robert Menzies led the Liberal Party into its second decade as the nation's government.

Just as the Liberals firmly controlled national destiny, so too did Melbourne Football Club hold sway on VFL playing fields. The Demons had dominated the competition for the last half of the 1950s, and had it not been for a hiccup in the 1958 grand final would have created a record for successive premierships. Melbourne had improved upon Geelong's style of breakneck pace and teamwork that had made the Cats the major power in the VFL. Melbourne's wily coach Norm Smith believed in the speed that characterised Geelong's play, but added a rugged element of power football that left all other teams in their wake.

The days of the mark and kick specialist had long gone and the new breed of footballers needed to have pace as well as marking and kicking ability. A new element "the ruck-rover" had been introduced in Melbourne sides in the bristling form of Ron Barassi, and the fast, hard-hitting powerhouse was emulated by other coaches who sought strong, mobile players who could play on the ball all day.

Other clubs tried to mould their team structure on Melbourne's but it wasn't easy to match them. The Demons had big-man strength spread evenly around the ground, and a blend of high-marking, physical power and pace that set the benchmark for the era. The Melbourne administration had fed coach Smith with a constant supply of quality recruits, and the team boasted stars on every line with players such as Ron Barassi, Bob Johnson, Laurie Mithen, Brian Dixon, Frank Adams, Clyde Laidlaw, Geoff Tunbridge, Ian Ridley and John Beckwith.

Collingwood had been the only club to break Melbourne's stranglehold on the top place, and although lacking the brilliance of their great sides of the past, the Magpies were a tough, dour combination who were never beaten. Their dogged, indomitable spirit typified the working class suburb they represented and the games with south-of-the-Yarra Melbourne represented a clash of classes as much as a confrontation of footballing styles. Melbourne-Collingwood games became the clashes of the year and drew huge crowds.

It wasn't long before fans had a taste of things to come in 1960 when the round of matches on April 23 was abandoned because of torrential downpours which flooded grounds. This was only the ninth time

> The days of the mark and kick specialist had long gone and the new breed of footballers needed to have pace as well as marking and kicking ability.

in history that a VFL round had been postponed. The VFL had already planned to play two games on Anzac Day for the first time, and the cancellation of the Saturday games helped to boost the crowds at the St Kilda-Melbourne and Fitzroy-Carlton games. The combined attendance of 68,000 was considered a satisfactory result.

> The VFL announced before the season that there would be no live telecasts of football in 1961.

Heavy rain throughout May produced quagmire conditions at all League grounds, and Victoria Park, never renowned for its capacity to cope with the rain, was the scene of Melbourne's most embarrassing performance for years. The Demons could only manage a paltry 2.7 to Collingwood's 7.13 which raised the old spectre of their vulnerability on heavy grounds against ferocious opposition. The Demons were said to have "run around in circles" in the face of the fierce-tackling home side which was inspired by centreman Bill Serong, who dispatched class opponents Laurie Mithen, Ron Barassi and Allan Rowarth during the afternoon.

Any thoughts that the Demons were on the downturn were quickly dispelled a few weeks later when they withstood a late challenge to beat Essendon, the boom team of the early part of the season. From that point the Demons kept their place on top of the ladder.

Fitzroy was a new force to emerge after a patchy start to the season. Under coach Len Smith, an innovative thinker and strategist ahead of his time, the Lions employed a game based on snappy movement of the ball by a band of clever little men, and strung together nine wins on end before the finals. Len Smith often lived in the shadow of his older brother Norm, but those who knew him and worked with him still speak reverently of his coaching skills.

Smith had nurtured many of the Fitzroy players in the under-19s before taking over the senior post in 1958, and he devised tactics to compensate for the team's lack of big men around the ground. The rugged "Butch" Gale and Ron Harvey were the only

big men of note in the Maroon colours, but players such as Wally Clark, Graham Campbell, Ray Slocum, and Ian Aston kept the ball moving at ground level. There was enough talent around the field with top-flighters like Owen Abrahams, Kevin Murray and Bob Henderson to ensure the Lions were a big hurdle for all sides.

By the end of the home and away series Fitzroy trailed Melbourne on percentage only and as the Demons had lost their last three games, Len Smith's team entered the finals full of confidence. Elder brother Norm Smith was ready and waiting for the Lions, however, and the reigning premiers crushed Fitzroy in the second semi-final. Fitzroy redeemed itself with a fighting display on the MCG bog against Collingwood in the preliminary final. Scores were level half-way through the final term, but in the end Fitzroy was pipped by five points and tumbled out of the finals race.

So it was down to Melbourne and Collingwood for the 1960 flag. Rain on Friday night and Saturday morning stirred memories of 1958, and Collingwood selectors showed their thinking when they promoted Barry Harrison - Melbourne's nemesis of that year - for the big game. But there were no trip-ups this time as Melbourne set the tone for the day by holding the Magpies scoreless in the first term and that was an indicator of the result. The hapless Magpies could only score two goals for the day and were comprehensively thrashed. If the Demons' power was beginning to wane then it certainly wasn't obvious on this wet final Saturday of the 1960 season. Five flags in six years spoke for itself. In that time Melbourne won 96 and tied two of its 120 games.

The established order of League supremacy was under threat from several clubs, and two which showed glimpses of future prosperity were Hawthorn and St Kilda - so often the chopping blocks of the competition. Under iron-fisted coach John Kennedy the Hawks had developed a fast play-on style that equipped them to win games on grounds other than their poky oval at Glenferrie. Hawthorn had been unlucky in several of its early games in 1960, but had finished the year with a full head of steam. Kennedy's team collected the scalps of grand finalists Melbourne and Collingwood during the season and had a chance of making the finals even in the last round, but missed on percentage. The win at Victoria Park was the club's first success there since joining the VFL 35 years earlier, and only a John Peck goal after the siren made the result different from the near misses of 1958 and 1959.

St Kilda finished in sixth place, but had been out of contention for a finals berth two weeks before the end of the season. The Saints had been revived under Allan Killigrew's coaching from 1956 to 1958, but under ex-Carlton man Jim Francis had held their position and not advanced during the next two years. The team had plenty of talent all over the field and Brownlow medallist Neil Roberts and the man who lost a medal on a countback, Verdun Howell, headed a defence that was as tight as a drum. Always a threat at the Junction Oval, the Saints had to progress to become a team which could take its share of points away from home.

They entered 1961 with a new, young coach. Allan Jeans had been a sturdy player until forced out by injury and had tasted coaching in the latter half of 1960 when he took over the Saints' reserves. On a narrow vote he was a shock choice as the senior coach, but time would prove it to be one of the wisest moves in the club's history.

Another new coach in 1961 was a man with a far more glittering playing record than Jeans. Famous full-forward John Coleman replaced the long-serving Dick Reynolds as Essendon's coach and it soon became obvious he intended to erase the Bombers' reputation for having ability and no vigor.

The VFL announced before the season that there would be no live telecasts of football in 1961. From 1957 to 1960 the final quarter of a selected match had been telecast each week, but the League had

Saint Ross Smith and Hawthorn opponent Charlie Abbott fly in the goalsquare before a packed Glenferrie grandstand.

become increasingly wary of the effects of TV. In the first year the VFL had sold the right to televise the last quarter for a mere 5850 pounds and in the first year attendances rose by 168,000. After that there were gradual falls culminating with an 88,000 drop in 1960, although the wet weather did not help.

The League expressed fears about decreasing numbers in junior and country football and cited the growing number of TV receivers as another concern. In the space of three years the number of TVs had increased from 91,000 to 384,000. For 1961 there would be no telecasts or replays, but the VFL seemed to be leaving the door open for negotiation on the replay aspect. Certainly the fact that attendances rose by 341,000 in 1961 killed any chance of

Hawk Morton Browne snaps for goal at the MCG in 1961. Browne was one of Kennedy's Commando Squad.

live telecasts being revived.

The status quo on the field remained in the early stages of 1961 and after seven rounds Melbourne sat atop the ladder. It was obviously going to be a tight, competitive season with Carlton, St Kilda, Footscray and Geelong showing improvement. Of the previous year's finalists Fitzroy had slipped and Collingwood was struggling.

Collingwood was always a tough nut to crack, but seemed to fall away after Hawthorn dished out a hiding at Glenferrie Oval. The Hawks were a ruthless combination and when they met Melbourne they dictated terms from the moment they flexed their muscles with three goals in the first seven minutes. Melbourne's famed last-minute surge never came and Hawthorn scored its third successive win over the Demons to place a wedge in the League leader's invincibility.

As Melbourne's form began to splutter and cough, Hawthorn's gathered momentum and the brown and golds took over top position at the start of August. Interest now centred on the battle for the last two finals places, and with one round to play St Kilda, Footscray, Geelong and Fitzroy had a chance. Footscray and Geelong met at Western Oval in a clash that would decide one spot, but the other place was not as clear-cut. Fitzroy had to beat South and hope for St Kilda to stumble against bottom side North. The Saints spent three quarters dithering and seemingly trying to throw away a finals chance. Only heroic efforts by Allan Morrow steadied the ship in the final term and ensured a five point win.

There were jubilant scenes as St Kilda fans celebrated the club's first entry into the finals for 22 years. It was a year of newcomers for the September series, and in the first semi-final clash between Footscray and St Kilda the only man on the field with finals experience was Bulldogs' captain-coach Ted Whitten. Hawthorn, like Footscray and St Kilda, had long been one of the League's ugly ducklings, and entered the finals with only six men who had appeared in the 1957 finals. Oddly enough, Melbourne, who had vast finals experience, needed a boost from youth and brought in first-gamer Mike Collins and Bruce Leslie for his fourth.

The Demons bounced away with four goals before Hawthorn had scored, but in a tough encounter the Hawks pegged them back and surged to a seven-point victory. The fierce match left the Demons jaded and they were bundled out of the finals by Whitten's enthusiastic young Bulldogs. Footscray, with only one flag in its history, now met a Hawthorn side chasing its first premiership.

A struggling first half by the Hawks saw them trail by eight points at the long break, but in the third term John Winneke gained the upper hand on Footscray Brownlow medallist John Schultz in the ruck duels and combined with several other moves this swung the match around. Within three minutes of the start of the third term Hawthorn hit the lead and from that point the result was never in doubt. Skipper Graham Arthur proudly hoisted the club's first premiership cup aloft after a 43-point victory, and a new football power had been born. Best afield was appropriately Brendan Edwards, a fitness fanatic whose endurance and stamina stood out even in a team dubbed Kennedy's Commandos.

The Hawks' sudden rise to prominence was followed by an equally startling tumble down the ladder. Footscray reversed the grand final result in the opening round of 1962 and that signalled the start of a horror stretch for the reigning premier that saw the club hurtle to ninth place, the biggest fall by a premiership team in VFL history.

Off the field the VFL made two moves of long-term importance. The first decision was to allow video-tape replays of matches which was a welcome relief after the "blackout" of 1961. Secondly the VFL bought 212 acres of land in the then outer suburb of Waverley, on which it was intended to build a new football-only stadium. The League had discussed the idea of having its own stadium for several years and in 1959 had given the go-ahead to the executive committee to find a suitable location.

Interstate recruits were nothing new to VFL football - South had experienced one of its greatest eras with a foreign legion side in the 1930s - but seldom had there been as much publicity as that given to two debutantes in 1962.

Graham "Polly" Farmer had been chased for many years by countless clubs who marvelled at his ruck dominance in interstate games for Western Australia, and Darrel Baldock's magical ball skills had given him similar legendary status in Tasmania. The lateness of their arrival - Farmer was 27 and Baldock 23 - raised doubts in the minds of critics, but both proved to be champions. Farmer's ruck work for Geelong and Baldock's forward line dominance for St Kilda were the driving forces behind those clubs' successes for the next six years.

Early in the season St Kilda looked to be the competition's big improver. The Saints had gone down narrowly in the 1961 first semi and had been boosted by the return of big full-forward Bill Stephenson, who had missed the last part of 1961 with a broken ankle. This was an era of low scoring, but when Stephenson began with tallies of five, three and seven goals in the opening three rounds there was talk of him reaching 100. He had five on the board by half-time in the match of the day against Essendon, but then Stephenson's and St Kilda's world collapsed. He fell awkwardly, twisting his knee and effectively ending the Saints' hopes for the year. Essendon, three goals down at the time, steadied and fought back to a four-point win.

> The VFL (in 1961) bought 212 acres of land in the then outer suburb of Waverley, on which it was intended to build a new football-only stadium.

Bombers coach John Coleman had suggested a flag was possible in his first year (1961) and many people wondered whether he was only 12 months early with the prediction. Essendon brimmed with skill, pace and experience and Coleman had instilled more fire into a side which had lacked it in the past. A strong ruck division headed by gentle giant Geoff Leek had all the ingredients for success. Hugh Mitchell had long been acknowledged as a master at the craft of ruck-roving and crumb gatherers Jack Clarke and John Birt were the best roving duet in the competition. The Bombers gained their drive from the half-backline of Alec Epis, Ian "Bluey" Shelton and Barry Davis and also had a fine centreline trio. Centre half-forward Ken Fraser was one of the best of that ilk in this era. The team dropped only two games all year to comfortably head the ladder after the home and away series.

Geelong, a team which had languished near the bottom a few years earlier, made up for the near-miss of 1961 and grabbed the double chance. The Cats had several players of exceptional skill such as goal to goal players Brownlow medallist Alistair

Lord, Doug Wade, Fred Wooller and Roy West as well as rover Billy Goggin, but there were "holes" on the flanks.

Injury-plagued Melbourne was shunted out of the finals in the first week by Carlton in a two-point cliffhanger. The Demons still had the core of a fine side, but had not won a final since the 1960 premiership triumph over Collingwood.

Essendon had far too much all-round strength for Geelong in the second semi-final and the Cats sorely missed Wade, their champion goalkicker and star recruit Farmer, who were both injured. Farmer was out for the year, but Wade was fighting to get fit. He missed the preliminary final against Carlton which ended in a chaotic draw after 1961 Brownlow Medallist John James had a chance to win the match with the final kick of the day. James had come off the bench and played an inspiring game, but his final 55-yard snap went out of bounds.

Wade returned for the preliminary final replay and was in the thick of the action with six goals out of Geelong's 10. It was another nailbiter and ended in controversy when umpire Irving disallowed a mark to Wade in the dying stages. The siren sounded seconds later with the Blues five points up.

Coleman was worried at the extended break given to his team by the drawn final and drew criticism when he held a full-scale match practice against Melbourne. Essendon had sat back for three weeks and watched Carlton slog out a succession of gruelling finals, but its peace of mind was jolted when star ruckman Geoff Leek injured his ankle in the last minute of the Thursday night training session. Carlton had tremendous ruck power in the form of John Nicholls, Sergio Silvagni, Maurie Sankey, Graham Donaldson and Ken Greenwood, and the absence of Leek would have given them a great chance. Leek finally took the field, and was able to contain the awesome might of Nicholls, thus set-

> By 1963 the game was beginning to change rapidly, not so much in style but more in terms of publicity and profile.

ting up the Essendon win. For Leek it was a fitting end to a career that had seemed destined for the scrapheap in his early days. A woeful kick in his youth he once suffered the indignity of being led from the field by the hand like a chastised schoolboy.

The Bombers looked as fresh as paint and skipped away to a 34 point lead by quarter time. Carlton fought hard, but to no avail and Essendon was untroubled in winning its eleventh pennant.

It was a triumph for Coleman who had made the transition from champion player to top-flight coach. He had a ruthless outlook and was not afraid to drag a player from the field in the first quarter if he was not performing. Brilliant and outspoken defender Alec Epis had challenged Coleman's authority early on and had been slammed. He had a fiery temper and had little time for interfering committeemen. Yet it was said that after achieving the premiership with Essendon he had wanted to quit, and had to be cajoled into continuing.

There was no such support for Bill Faul, the coach of South Melbourne who bitterly attacked the committee for replacing him with former Melbourne star Noel McMahen. Faul told the Swans' annual meeting: "South officials played a despicable trick on me - a bloke who had tried to do his best for the club. It is embarassing to be phoned by Press men and asked 'Did I know McMahen was replacing me?'" Faul said McMahen would go the same way if he did not get the committee's support, and he was right. Two years later McMahen got the chop.

By 1963 the game was beginning to change rapidly, not so much in style but more in terms of publicity and profile. Television had been the biggest influence, giving the sport unparalleled exposure, and a special half-page section of the magazine *Footy Fan* listing all football programs on radio and TV, gave an indication of the saturation coverage the game now generated.

Previews, reviews, inquests . . . the list went on. Match descriptions could be heard on radio stations

3AR, 3GL, 3KZ, 3XY, 3AW, 3UZ and 3DB. Channels Nine and Seven ran replays in prime Saturday evening time-slots, and *The Tony Charlton Football Show* (9) vied with *World of Sport* for the midday viewers every Sunday. Every type of manufacturer and business enterprise jumped on the football bandwagon as even staid banks wooed youngsters to save in moneyboxes recommended by Lou Richards or Ron Barassi. Club colours were splashed over everything from car cushions to umbrellas and the interest grew unabated.

Amid the razzamatazz of 1963 football lovers mourned the passing of two of the game's legendary figures, Roy Cazaly and "Carjie" Greeves. The shout of "Up there Cazaly" had become a catchcry for Australian troops in World War II and "Carji" Greeves had etched an indelible place in the game's history as the first Brownlow Medal winner.

The season itself was chock full of action from the outset and it soon became obvious that Hawthorn's 1962 fall from grace was an aberration. The Hawks were back as a power and the ruthless, force-the-ball-forward-at-any-cost approach left other sides in their wake. In classic confrontation to this was Geelong's fluent elegance, a long-kicking and high-marking game of style.

Hawthorn had shaken off the gloom of 1962 and even had a bit of luck on the Queen's Birthday when St Kilda star Darrel Baldock ran into an open goal and mistook the posts. Baldock slammed through a behind and St Kilda went down by four points. It hadn't all been gloom and doom for the Saints who had unearthed four star players in the opening round. Carl Ditterich, Ian Stewart, Bob Murray and Jim Wallis went on to be stars, although Wallis's career was tragically cut short by injury. St Kilda selectors had wanted to delay Ditterich's first game, but it was felt that Melbourne's rucks offered less of a hurdle than other sides so they took the risk on the 17-year-old and he responded with one of the most dazzling first games of all time.

Meanwhile Collingwood was licking its wounds after a summer of savage in-fighting over the club's presidency. The Magpies had missed the finals in 1961 and dumped a batch of players in 1962 without achieving a turnaround on the football field. Now the forces within the club looked to changes in the committee room and the showdown between Tom Sherrin and Jack Galbally contained elements of religion and class factionalism. After a very public display of mudslinging between the two rival groups, Sherrin was elected president, but the in-fighting had rocked the club and the Magpies finished a distant eighth on the ladder.

> **Channels Nine and Seven ran replays in prime Saturday evening time-slots.**

At the end of 1963 coach Phonse Kyne announced he would resign, and the committee chose former star Bob Rose to replace him. Rose had been sounded out by Richmond a month earlier for the Tigers' coaching position and had asked his old club whether it wanted him as coach.

Geelong was the 1963 pacesetter with a brilliant line-up that thrived on all-out attacking football. The Cats' pure style was suited to fine conditions, but they chafed under close-checking opposition in wet conditions. That recipe led to the biggest boilover in years when Fitzroy rolled them on the sodden Brunswick Street Oval. It was the Lions' only win for 1963 and they didn't have a single victory the following year. Geelong only scored three goals for the day and there was cruel irony for Lions' captain-coach Kevin Murray who was playing for the Victorian team in Adelaide.

The interstate clash produced plenty of drama in its own right when Victorian John Peck flattened local Brian Sawley with a right cross that would have done justice to Cassius Clay. Peck said he had reacted to Sawley kicking him when he was on the ground, but the SA tribunal found him guilty. Sentencing was the responsibility of the VFL tribunal and the Croweaters were furious when Peck was giving the relatively "light" sentence of two weeks.

Still the South Australians had enjoyed the satisfaction of beating the Vics on the MCG earlier in the year. They had not humbled the Big V on home turf since 1926 and Victorian coach Bob Davis bore the stigma for years after.

Competition for places in the final four narrowed to five teams, but the tightness between those contenders was extreme. Essendon had been clear leader for three quarters of the year, but went from first to fifth in the space of a three-week slump.

Even a win did not guarantee holding a place as St Kilda found when it rolled Geelong before a huge crowd at the Junction Oval. Essendon had built its percentage by a big win and sneaked back into the four.

Just before the finals there was a sensation when Melbourne skipper Ron Barassi was reported for striking Richmond's Roger Dean. Dean, a fine player for the Tigers, had the reputation of "staging" for free kicks and there was no doubt his theatrics had made the incident seem worse than it was. Melbourne tried unsuccessfully to use a Channel Nine video tape as evidence, but the tribunal wasn't having a bar of it and suspended the Melbourne skipper for four games, ruling him out of the finals series.

The last round of the year became a shootout with Essendon and St Kilda playing lower-order teams and Geelong needing

Hawthorn full-forward John Peck outbustles his North opponent.

to beat Hawthorn to grab the double chance. Mathematicians even calculated a set of scores which would require a play-off for fourth position. By three-quarter-time Geelong was well on top of Hawthorn and interest centred on the battle between St Kilda and Essendon for fourth place. St Kilda bolted away from North in the last quarter to record a huge win and take fourth place by a mere 2.6 per cent advantage. Bitter Essendon fans said North coach Killigrew had let his old side run away with the game, but that was hardly in the competitive nature of the fiery little coach. Still Essendon's hurt could be understood. The team had finished only half a win behind the top team, yet wouldn't play in the finals.

Geelong had benefited from the experience of the 1962 finals and fielded a side that was much stronger in several departments than the one which been unable to win a final 12 months earlier. For a start "Polly" Farmer was able to take his place in the line-up and full-forward Doug Wade was 100 per cent fit. Tough ex-West Australian John Watts added a touch of dash to the defence and half-backs Stewart Lord and Peter Walker had developed remarkably.

The Cats pulled away from Hawthorn in the second semi and bolted clear in the grand final two weeks later when the strain of three hard matches in a row was too much for even the super-fit Hawks. Melbourne, seemingly unable to take a trick in this year, had bowed out on the preliminary final after acting skipper Brian Dixon was a last-minute withdrawal and John Lord was injured in the opening minutes. Farmer had vindicated all of Geelong's efforts in winning his services from Western Australia and his football chemistry with rover Billy Goggin was one of the joys of the era.

Geelong did not rest on its laurels and the success of Farmer, and to a lesser extent Watts, prompted another recruiting raid across the Nullarbor. This time the Sandgropers manned the ramparts and refused to let the Cats bring home the brilliant Denis Marshall without a huge fight. Marshall, a fast, strong-kicking stylist fitted the Geelong mould perfectly. Claremont was rumored to want 4000 pounds for his clearance, but was said to have been talked down to 3000 pounds by an influential group of Geelong supporters. Even when the WA League agreed to his clearance, Marshall and Geelong had to face investigation under the farcical Coulter Law which outlawed excessive signing-on payments. The Cats started the year confidently without Marshall, and had to wait until the eighth round before it could unveil its prize recruit.

Marshall couldn't keep out of the headlines even when he finally made it onto the field. In his third game he was ironed out by a bump from North's Ken Dean who was later informed by a Geelong policeman that he would be charged. That was only the start of the action as a fight broke out in the players' race at the end of the game in which Geelong's Geoff Rosenow clashed with diminutive North coach Allan Killigrew. Killigrew ended up with a broken nose from the dust-up.

Killigrew's North side had made a move up the ladder early in the year and it looked like the Roos were about to bring their cellar-dwelling days to an end. But a thumping 108 point loss to Collingwood knocked the stuffing out of the Arden Street team. The Roos suffered a couple of serious injuries to key players during 1964. Vice-captain Noel Teasdale's skull was fractured in the second round and there was a fear his VFL career was over. Teasdale fought back and an unusual protective headband became his trademark in later years. Skipper Allen Aylett planned to retire at the end of the year and his plans

were advanced when he broke his arm in July.

Coaches were permitted to address players at quarter-time in 1964. Previously they had to remain off the arena as the teams changed ends. Still they came up with ingenious ways to gain the all-important edge on opponents, and St Kilda's Allan Jeans came up with the idea of equipping his runner with a "walkie talkie". Others showed interest in the new idea, but it was quickly outlawed by the VFL who feared the antennae could injure passing players.

Melbourne was still a strong combination even though there was a heavy reliance on workhorse ruckman Graham Wise. Norm Smith was accustomed to building a game plan without a leading ruckman and the Demons looked stronger with the improved form of skipper Ron Barassi who had conquered the groin problems which had plagued him. Melbourne's old foe Collingwood returned to prominence and a huge MCG crowd on the Queen's Birthday stirred memories of the great clashes of the 1950s.

There were plenty of tight finishes in a low-scoring season, and one of the thrillers was a draw between Essendon and Geelong. Bomber Ken Fraser kicked a point from 60 yards out at the 33-minute mark of the final term and was given the chance to take another kick, but he elected to let the score stand. The siren blew moments later.

The most dramatic and telling finish in the context of the premiership fight was in the second last round at Glenferrie. With only 90 seconds of play remaining, Melbourne star Hassa Mann threaded through an impossible goal from 30 yards out on the boundary line. The goal sealed Melbourne's finals spot and put Hawthorn out of contention.

On a heavy ground Melbourne slaughtered Collingwood in the second semi-final which gave the Demons breathing space to rest some injured players. It was Collingwood's first finals appearance for four years and it had been the club's longest absence from the finals apart from a five-year span during the depleted years of World War II.

Collingwood won a second crack at Melbourne with a battling four point win over Geelong. The Magpies would obviously be tougher in the grand final and they began strongly to lead by two points at half-time. In one of the truly memorable grand finals it seemed Collingwood would take the flag when the 17-stone Ray Gabelich unleashed a mighty charge downfield. After four wobbly bounces he slammed through a goal with only four minutes plus time-on left.

> Coaches were permitted to address players at quarter-time in 1964. Previously they had to remain off the arena as the teams changed ends.

The game still had a sting in its tail and Demon back-pocket Neil Crompton who had followed his rover downfield gathered the ball and popped through a goal. Melbourne won by four points with a side that still had liberal splashes of talent even though it might have lacked the all-round brilliance of it predecessors. The defence was skilled and tough and players such as Barassi, Bluey Adams, Brian Dixon, John Lord, Hassa Mann and Brian Roet were among the top flight.

As Barassi held the 1964 premiership cup aloft it seemed all was rosy in the Melbourne camp. There would have been howls of derision in the Smokers' stand for anyone who suggested that Barassi would never play for the Demons again, Norm Smith would be sacked within 12 months, and the famous red and blue colours would not be seen again in the finals for almost quarter of a century.

KENNEDY'S COMMANDOS

They were called "Kennedy's Commandos" - a tough fighting unit drilled to perfection by a tortuous fitness regimen.

This was the Hawthorn side of the early 1960s under its wily commander John Kennedy that shook off its loser's tag and rose to the top of the League ladder . . . the Cinderella story of football for a club which had been the surprise addition to League ranks in 1925 and had struggled near the foot of the ladder for more than three decades.

As a player John Kennedy had a total lack of style - he was an angular ruckman, all bony arms and elbows, but he was a tremendous team-man and great battler. He toiled for 165 games between 1950 and 1959 and four times earned selection in state sides. He won the first of four club best and fairests in his debut season.

Immediately after his retirement as a player he succeeded Jack Hale as coach. Hale was a fiery character who was blunt and dogmatic in his attitude to players and had learnt to be a winner during his playing days at Carlton. He was stunned to see the attitude at Hawthorn when he came to the club. At the first training session a player raced to the head trainer after the ball hit him on the top of the fingers! "I said to tell him that he either comes back out on the ground in four minutes or he can have a shower and not come back. He didn't come back!"

Hale instilled a fanatic approach in his players that John Kennedy was only too ready to nurture as the basis of the club's future. "They reckoned I was a tough coach, till they got Kennedy." Kennedy observed early in his playing career that Hawthorn needed "to turn nasty" if the club was to get off the bottom. "Our attitude was a bit social," he said in an interview on the Coodabeen Champions *Legends* tape.

Kennedy had been captain under Hale's coaching for five years before Hale's retirement and the two built a great understanding. They also introduced a jovial form of competitiveness that endured for years at Hawthorn. Hale knew that sectarianism, the antipathy between Protestants and Catholics, was rife in some clubs and he was determined it would not happen at Hawthorn. Whenever a new player arrived Hale would ask his religion. If it was Catholic he would say "He's one of your lot John", and point him in Kennedy's direction.

Hawthorn won most of its games on the cramped unusually-shaped Glenferrie ground by employing close-checking and bullocking tactics that bottled up opposing sides. High marking and long kicking teams found themselves frustrated by the swarming Hawks. Kennedy knew that the team needed a faster style that emphasised rapid movement of the ball if it was going to succeed on other grounds and more importantly, on the MCG during finals.

He also believed that peak physical fitness would wear down any form of op-

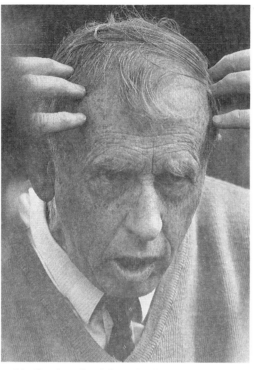

It's all up here. Coach Kennedy addresses his charges.

position in a tight finish and he embarked on a gruelling pre-season program the likes of which had never been seen in football. He thought the area of fitness was one which could be developed to give the Hawks an edge. Kennedy used the talents of one of his players - Brendan Edwards - a fitness expert who developed a circuit training scheme which the team would undertake on top of normal training sessions. Often the training sessions were tougher than actual matches. "I think that tough training made tough teams. I saw players get up from knocks that were really crunchers and get up and go on with it. When you take that out onto the field on Saturday it becomes very hard to beat."

Strangely enough the change in Hawthorn's style may have been partially responsible for the disastrous start to Kennedy's first season as coach. The Hawks lost three games at Glenferrie in the first five weeks which was contrary to the impregnable front they had always presented at home.

Kennedy wanted Melbourne's power style of

game combined with Collingwood's fighting spirit and by the end of 1960 the right amalgam was almost achieved. The Hawks just missed a finals spot and were considered "the side most likely" in 1961.

The cornerstone of the Hawthorn team under Kennedy was the defence which stood close to their opponents all day until the ball came within range and they went after it with everything they had. Full-back Les "Killer" Kaine and the dreaded half-back trio of Sted Hay, John McArthur and Cam McPherson had the famed mad-eyed stare and intimidated countless forwards.

But the mean streak didn't stop there and even half-forward flanker Ian Mort could mow down an enemy. Full-forward John Peck was a converted ruckman who could tough it out with the best of them and captain Graham Arthur was a low slung ruck-rover and forward who typified the nuggety talent of the side. The most brilliant players in the team were centreman Brendan Edwards and Ian Law. Edwards was a fitness fanatic who could run all day and the wispy haired Law was good enough to run third in the 1961 Brownlow Medal.

Coach Kennedy took the club to its first flag in 1961 and years later players remembered his ruthlessness. Half-forward Gary Young remembered the 1960 round that was postponed because of wet weather. Young heard the news on the radio and took his wife to the movies and when he turned up on Tuesday he heard that a number of players had turned up at the ground and been taken on a 15 kilometre run. His delight at missing that was shortlived as Kennedy asked all players who had turned up on the Saturday to move to one side of the room. It left Young and John Peck standing as a lonely group of two.

Kennedy said: "Off with your boots and socks and meet me on the oval in two minutes". He immediately took them on a 30-lap run and at the end asked for a sprint! Kennedy did it easily and by the time Young had recuperated sufficiently to display his anger, the coach had showered and gone home.

The Hawks dipped to ninth in 1962, but made the grand final in 1963. The next year Kennedy accepted a teaching appointment in the country, but he returned after a four-season break.

Kennedy was a master tactician. In the late 1960s and early 1970s he was criticised by the purists over Hawthorn's method of bulldozing the ball forward, but it was because Hawthorn lacked individual skills. Kennedy always insisted if there was a ball-up after a pack formed, then the player on the bottom should be a Hawthorn player and the ball should be under him.

His strategy was to leave Peter Hudson and the opposing full-back in one third of the field. It won Hawthorn the 1971 flag, but once Hudson was injured the Hawks reverted to an orthodox approach.

As a coach Kennedy was revered by his men. He was always reluctant to single out a particular player for criticism or praise and when something had to be directed at an individual he made sure it was done out of the earshot of officials or supporters. One year when Hawthorn lost the first eight games he called the players together and said they would have to do something quickly. They would run around The Boulevard at 5.30 the next morning in the depths of winter. As it was freezing cold, players turned up in beanies and tracksuits, but there to lead them was Kennedy in white singlet and bare feet. His theory was the team needed to suffer together and he was willing to set the example himself.

He retired from the Hawthorn coaching post af-

ter steering the club to another flag in 1976 and handed the reins to David Parkin, the logical successor. It was similar to his ascendancy to the throne to replace Hale. Such by then was the logical, ordered way of doing things at Hawthorn.

NICK AND BOYDIE: OUT WITH A BANG

John Nicholls was one of the game's all time champions - of that there is no argument.

He was also one of the toughest ruckmen of his time as any player who roughed up a Carlton player will testify. The steely Nicholls stare was legendary, and he was prepared to wait for the right moment to square off on behalf of his team.

But on August 5, 1961 "Big Nick" was on the receiving end of one of the most famous punches of all time. The Boyd-Nicholls incident has earned a niche in footy folklore, but it had its origins in an earlier clash between the two players.

Ken Boyd was a rough, wild customer who came from the tough environment of South Melbourne Technical School. There were no frills about his style, but he was South Melbourne to the core. "I would have paid them to play," he proudly said in later years.

He first played for the Swans in 1957 and had built a reputation by 1961. Murray Weideman, no slouch in the roughhouse department, said Boyd was the only man that scared him on a football field: "One day Ken evidently didn't see me and walked straight over me, stops and all".

In Boyd's first year he copped eight weeks for abusive language and fighting, and in 1959 he was outed for four weeks on a striking charge. In 1960 he was severely reprimanded for striking. It wasn't long before he was in trouble in 1961. In the fourth round against Carlton he was reported for striking Carlton rover John Heathcote and acting skipper John Nicholls. The Tribunal suspended him for three weeks on each charge.

Late in the return game at Princes Park, Boyd and Nicholls clashed again. Nicholls lay flat on the ground for nine minutes before trainers were able to get him to his feet and help him from the field. There were no reports because no one had seen the incident.

The next day Nicholls appeared on television and gave what Boyd described as a very one-sided account of the incident. Boyd contacted the newspapers to give his side of the story. He claimed Nicholls had threatened to kick him in the groin if Boyd bothered him during the match. Boyd had replied that if he did, Nicholls would get his head knocked off.

"Nicholls and I went for the bounce of the ball in the centre of the ground. I fell to the ground and two trainers rushed to my assistance. When I recovered I ran straight to Nicholls, turned him round, and hit him under the eye."

That prompted the VFL to call its investigation officer into action, and on August 25- 20 days after the incident, Boyd was charged with having assaulted Nicholls. Boyd and the South president, Ross Tait, issued a Supreme Court writ stating the VFL, or its investigation committee, was exceeding its powers in reporting Boyd. In addition Tait and Boyd sought an injunction restraining the the VFL or the committee from hearing or acting on the charge. But the action failed to prevent the committee going ahead.

Tait was criticised by the investigation committee over his comments "that a player was justified in retaliation". The hearing lasted for two hours, took another six minutes to decide the charge had been sustained and another 28 minutes to decide the penalty.

Nicholls said: "I remember little about the incident. I remember being hit, but I don't know by whom."

Mr McCutchan asked: "What effect did it have

on you?"

Nicholls: "I suppose I was stunned and it broke my nose".

Mr Jack Titus (Richmond): "You were supposed to have interfered with Boyd earlier in the game at a centre bounce".

Nicholls: "There was a ball-up in the centre - nothing particular happened".

The only one of the 11 witnessses to say he saw Boyd strike Nicholls was the emergency umpire.

Boyd was suspended for 12 weeks.

After the incident police had feared for Boyd's safety in getting off the ground and had suggested to coach Bill Faul that he take Boyd off. But Faul did not want to risk the chance of being left short if a player was injured, and refused. He did agree to play Boyd near the race so he could get off quickly.

Years later Boyd told veteran writer Jack Dunn, who was there on the day, that he was unworried by his dramatic exit that afternoon. "I got out that day and still lived to tell the story. I have no regrets over what happened. I took a course that was warranted."

Field umpire Jack Irving did not see Nicholls flattened, but said of the ball-up that triggered it: "They just went up with their feet out as ruckmen did then, hoping the other bloke would run into them. I cancelled out the bounce. Boyd went to the ground after they made contact with each other."

That was the end of Boyd's stormy, 60-game VFL career and shortly after he went to Wangaratta Rovers as captain-coach.

KEVIN MURRAY: THE IRON LION

Kevin Murray spent the greater part of his VFL career trussed up like an Egyptian mummy.

But that didn't stop him from becoming one of Fitzroy's, and the VFL's, greatest players. His back problems plagued him for years and he had to use a back brace to get through games. He injured the back

The Old Lion. Battle worn Kevin Murray has a breather at three quarter time.

he was thrust into the role of centre half-back and ruck-rover and his speed, strength and intuitive football brain led to success in these positions, too. In the latter part of his career the sheer cunning developed by experience meant that he could outwit younger opposition.

He was also as tough as nails and it was a foolish opponent who took him on in the strength department. One famous story concerns a game against Footscray in the early 1960s when a Fitzroy player sunk the boot into an opponent and Footscray's leader, Ted Whitten, raced in to deal out retribution. Murray rushed to the defence of his man and before long the two captain-coaches were wrestling on the ground. The two legends were face-to-face when Whitten said: "Kiss me!" and both broke up into laughter.

Murray captain-coached Fitzroy in 1963-64, but it was a lean time for the undermanned Lions who won only one game in the two seasons, ironically when Murray was away on state duties. In 1965 he backed a reform group at Fitzroy then was lured to a coaching job at East Perth, but after two years returned to the Lions. He skippered the team until 1972, then the captaincy was handed over to John Murphy.

In the meantime he had won the 1969 Brownlow Medal at the ripe old age of 31 and delighted the crowd at his presentation with probably the longest thank-you speech of all time. Most people thought his Brownlow chances had disappeared, but he was a worthy winner as he had always polled well, running second by one vote in 1960, equal second in 1962 and third in 1968. He finished in the top 10 votegetters eight times.

Fitzroy only played three finals during Murray's time at the club and by a strange quirk of fate he missed one of them, the 1958 first semi, through injury. He did not miss another game for Fitzroy until the time he retired.

His career record of games is nothing short of amazing. He played 333 day games and 17 night

in 1957 when he got a ride over the top of a pack which then moved from underneath and left him to fall flat on the base of his spine.

Yet his career was one of remarkable longevity and he did not miss a game through injury in his last 16 seasons of senior football. His 333 games, despite a two-season stint in Western Australia, are still a record for Fitzroy . For a while the tattooed and toothless champ also held the VFL games record.

The son of an old Fitzroy player, Dan Murray, Kevin made his debut before his 17th birthday after coming through the Lions' thirds. Funnily enough he had not been particularly impressive in his early teens, and had often gone home to tell his father that he was giving the game away. He soon made his mark as a half-back flanker and was a state representative by his third season.

Murray's long arms and big spring made him a great high mark even though he stood only six feet tall. After achieving early fame as a half-back flanker games for Fitzroy, 24 games for Victoria, six for Western Australia and 44 for West Perth - a total of 424 first-class games. "Bulldog" Murray was awarded an MBE in 1974 for his services to the game. He won the club's best and fairest award a record nine times and wore the Big V on 24 occasions - he won All-Australian selection while playing for Victoria and Western Australia, the first man to achieve it for different states.

Kevin Murray's love for the game meant he could not hang up the boots and he captain-coached Sandringham in the VFA for two years, in 1975-1976. Despite the ever-present back injury and a host of other ailments he continued to fill in as a reserve when the team was short of talent.

For all his ailments, Murray's knees never gave him problems and that, combined with the physical nature of his work in the building industry, probably explains how at the age of 47 he was still playing in a minor suburban league.

The boy who had considered giving the game away in his early teens was still in action three decades later.

LEN SMITH: MASTER TACTICIAN

Len Smith's career as a player and his statistical record as a coach are dwarfed by the feats of his brother Norm. But at Fitzroy and Richmond the name of Len Smith is revered as the architect of those club's high points in the post-war era. A quiet, humble man who was remembered for his sincerity and patience with young players, he was also one of the first coaches to advocate the play-on game.

As a player Len Smith was a capable defender who was discovered by Melbourne scouts when he was at Northcote. He only played 18 games for the Demons from 1934 to 1935 and was mostly used as a forward. After a brief return to Northcote for the 1936 season he was talked into having another crack

at the VFL and after Fitzroy tried him as a forward he eventually found his true niche at centre half-back. His career was interrupted by RAAF service, but in 76 games up to 1945 he built a fine reputation as a backman.

It was as a coach, however, that he would make his real mark on the game. He took on the Fitzroy under-19s coaching job just after the war and in the mid-'50s he nurtured a talented crop of kids who would form the basis of the club's future. Graham Campbell, Ian Aston, Wally Clark, Graeme Mackenzie and a brilliant defender named Kevin Murray were some of the boys to pass through his hands.

His back problems plagued him for years...he did not miss a game through injury in his last 16 seasons of senior football.

Many junior coaches produce finished players for the senior man to reap results and accolades, but Smith was given the chance to see his boys through to maturity when he was appointed senior coach in 1958. He immediately lifted the club from eleventh to a finals berth in his first year. It was an amazing effort considering the team had lost two stalwarts - Norm Johnstone and Bill Stephen - through retirement, and had gained only one new player - Keith Bromage from Collingwood.

Smith was a brilliant tactician and had the marvellous gift of being able to build confidence in his team. His style of speaking individually to players before the game was a departure from the traditional mass address that was the only form of communication for most coaches. He also master-minded a dazzling system of handball and slick teamwork that was ahead of its time. One of the more unusual aspects was the use of code words. For example the shout of "Brunswick" would indicate that a line of four players had to take up positions between the goal and the centre. This created increased space for brilliant flanker Owen Abrahams and resulted in many goals.

Smith's scientific training methods introduced circuit training by a physical training expert, Harvey

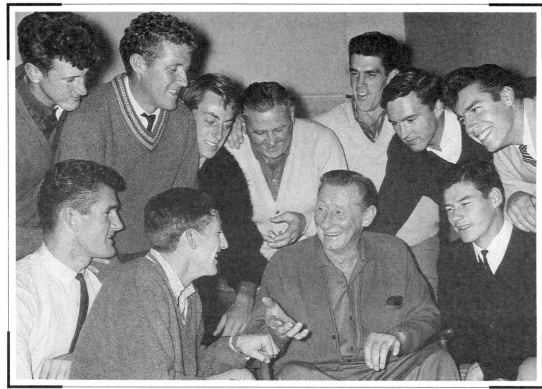

The oracle. Richmond's Len Smith was regarded as a footballing guru, not only to these Tiger players, but to a generation of coaches starting with Allan Jeans.

Cox, whose use of a weights and sprinting program was unheard of. Fitzroy's edge in fitness meant that the team had the capacity to finish over the top of the opposition and in 1960 this asset won the club many games and saw it rise to second place at the end of the home and away series.

Years later Allan Gale, a key player in this era, recalled how he had resented Smith at first: "He took over from a mate of mine, Bill Stephen, and I thought he was too soft, too sympathetic. I used to abuse players, he used to show compassion. I used to drink and he didn't. He didn't like many of the things I did. Once when we were trailing our opponents at half time, he said: 'Allan, you're captain, you've got to do something'.

"So I KO'd a bloke. After the game he took me aside and said: 'Allan, I didn't mean something like THAT'."

Although they were opposites in every way, Gale said Smith won him over to his way of thinking in just four or five weeks.

Another of Smith's players, Tony Ongarello, summed up his approach best when he said: "In some ways he hardly ever had to be a disciplinarian - people seemed to do the right thing for him anyway".

Len Smith was one of the first coaches to believe that handball was just as important a skill as kicking, and he devised a fast moving style that compensated for his team's lack of big men. The Lions were unlucky to go down by five points in the preliminary final of 1960 and narrowly missed a finals spot the following season.

His belief in the attacking possibilities of handball led to experimentation. He developed the idea of the flick pass - striking the ball with the open hand - as a quicker alternative to the traditional means of punching it with a clenched fist. Controversy raged over its legality, but the flick pass was a matchwinner for Smith. In this he was poles apart from his brother Norm who thought it was a blot on the game. The law stated the ball had to be held in one hand and hit with the other. It made no distinction on whether the striking hand should be clenched or open.

Norm Smith contended many players propelled the ball with the hand that held the ball which therefore constituted a throw.

In the end the flick pass was outlawed, but the innovative mind of Len Smith was unfettered by traditional concerns and always sought new means of improving football. In 1964 he mused: "After a succession of failures players have to be taught to regain their confidence. Perhaps a psychologist would be valuable." Years would pass before psychologists became a part of the VFL scene.

Smith resigned as Fitzroy's coach after a disappointing 1962, but after a year in the VFA as Coburg's coach he returned to the VFL at Richmond. He rebuilt the Richmond list with the accent on six-footers who had pace and long-kicking ability. Quieter in approach than his younger brother, he was nevertheless insistent on the way his football philosophy should be implemented.

Just as the 1964 season was about to start he fell ill with a heart attack, and although he was back on deck within a few weeks, the signs were worrying. The club was desperate to retain his unique knowledge and at the start of 1965 appointed Jack "Skinny" Titus as joint coach to ease Smith's workload. Four rounds into the season he had a heart attack and he decided he could no longer fly in the face of medical advice.

He stood down from the coaching post, but in his short tenure he had made a remarkable impact. He had laid the structure and created the style that would resurrect the Tigers as one of the great powers of modern times.

The heart problems that dogged him in latter years eventually took his life just before the 1967 finals series and the whole football world mourned the loss of one of its most creative thinkers. A few weeks later Richmond won the flag.

DOUG WADE'S MARK

The 1962 finals series was the setting for one of the most controversial umpiring decisions of all time.

Umpire Jack Irving's adjudication of a duel between Geelong's Doug Wade and Carlton full-back Peter Barry thwarted the Cats' bid for a flag and was the culmination of two weeks of razor-edge football.

Geelong and Carlton's home and away clashes in 1962 gave no indication of the closeness of the two teams that would emerge in September. Geelong had bolted to a 39-point win on the opening day and 11 weeks later the Blues reversed the result at Kardinia Park. But come finals time the clubs fought out two of the tightest encounters in League history.

The lead swapped four times in the final quarter of the preliminary final before Blues full-forward Tom Carroll levelled the scores deep into time-on. Then 1961 Brownlow medallist, John James, whose erratic 1962 form had seen him lowered to the reserve bench, pulled down a spectacular mark. James had played a magnificent game after replacing the concussed Gordon Collis in the second term.

He had the chance to win the game for the Blues and from a long way out he unleashed a big drop-kick. The distance was okay, but the accuracy was lacking and the ball went out of bounds and the final siren signalled the third tie in VFL finals history.

Controversy raged over an incident in which Carlton's Maurie Sankey had run far more than the legal 10 yards and kicked the second last goal of the match. The Press believed umpire Schwab should have pulled him up; had he been free-kicked Geelong would almost certainly have won the game.

The Cats' star full-forward Doug Wade returned to the side despite lingering doubts on his fitness. Wade had pulled his thigh muscle a couple of weeks before the finals and had only lasted for one and a bit quarters in the last home and away round before collapsing in agony after the thigh "went" again.

PAGE FORTY-EIGHT   *The Sun*   MONDAY, SEPT. 24, 1962

• Two pages
  of football
  —P.44, 45

THE FREE: UMPIRE WAS RIGHT —EXPERTS

WAS Umpire Irving right when he gave Carlton's Peter Barry a free kick against Geelong full-forward Doug Wade in the last minute of Saturday's League preliminary final at the MCG?

Irving set a record crowd of 99,203 roaring when he gave the free to Barry as Wade marked.

Had Wade been "paid" the mark he probably would have goaled and won the match for Geelong.

But umpire Irving ruled that he had held Carlton full-back Peter Barry, gave Barry a free kick and Carlton won 10-18—78 to 10-13—73.

● Former umpire Allan Nash says Irving was right.

"It was the most courageous decision I've ever seen made by an umpire."

● Kevin Hogan says Irving blew his whistle before Wade took the mark.

● Doug Wade said: "I did not interfere with Barry at all in going for the ball."

● Nearby Carlton players said that they heard the whistle before Wade's mark.

● **WHAT THEY SAY, PAGE 46.**

WADE, in front, jostles Barry in the start of a sequence of pictures taken from HSV7 videotape recording of the closing minutes of Saturday's replay.

Gretel is really fighting..

AUSTRALIA'S Gretel is staging the battle of the century to win the America's Cup from the United States.

On Saturday Gretel lost the fourth race in the series against Weatherly—but by only 26 seconds.

This was the smallest victory margin in the 11-year history of the race.

Now Gretel, which won the second heat, trails 1 in the series.

But the crew and the yacht still are out to make a fight of it in the fifth heat, which will be sailed early on Wednesday (Melbourne time).

● Expert comment on the series, and the chances—
Pages 4 and 38.

And RACING.

● Summer Fair headed for Cup— Page 42.
● Sky High too good — Page
● Quite Able's "comeback"—Page 42.
● All your racing details — P.
● See how they finished — P.

THE BALL approaches — and Wade runs forward a short distance to take the mark.

←LEFT: Wade gets the ball — and already umpire Irving's whistle has blown — against him!

BELOW: Wade hugs the ball, making sure of the mark, and still confident the kick will be his.

The Wade-Barry incident as depicted in *The Sun*.

The Cats gambled on his fitness and it paid dividends. The burly spearhead marked everything and booted three goals during a torrid opening quarter in which Geelong had to withstand a battering from the bigger Carlton side. Brownlow medallist Alistair Lord was flattened by Blue Ian Collins only moments after the start and star rover Billy Goggin was crunched soon after.

Carlton went into the last quarter holding a nine-point lead, but Geelong had pegged it back to a solitary point by the 11-minute mark. The Cats grabbed the lead 23 minutes into the quarter when Sutherland kicked a glorious goal.

John James whirled out of a pack to snap a magnificent goal at the 28-minute mark and restore a five point lead to the Blues. Geelong would not concede defeat and a magnificent solo effort by Frank Pomeroy forced the ball forward to Fred Wooller who chipped a pass to Wade.

The big Geelong forward held his position in front and outmanoeuvred Carlton full-back Peter Barry to take the mark at shoulder height to the thunderous roar of the crowd. With six goals and only one behind on the board surely he would land the 25-yard shot and seal Geelong's grand final berth. But it was not to be. Umpire Irving raced downfield and took the ball from Wade, ruling that he had interfered with Barry before the ball arrived.

After the game Wade told reporters: "I asked umpire Irving what the free-kick was for. He gave no answer, turned and ran away. I didn't give any interference."

It was Geelong's last chance as the siren rang seconds later.

Opinion was sharply divided on the free-kick. *Age* football chief Percy Beames wrote: "In penalising Doug Wade, Jack Irving made the most courageous decision of his career, but I believe nine times out of 10 Wade would have got away with his tactics. As I saw it, Wade left himself open to be penalised by dropping his hands down and behind him,

where they boxed Barry in while the ball was still 20 yards away. But for the rest he used his strong body magnificently and shrewdly in a move that was cleverly conceived and carried out. To me this piece of baulking and finessing represented one of the best individual efforts of the match."

FARMER AND BALDOCK: A PEERLESS PAIR

THE lead-up to the 1962 season was dominated by talk about two interstate recruits who came to Victorian football with unequalled reputations.

Graham "Polly" Farmer from Western Australia and Darrel Baldock from Tasmania were hailed by fans of Geelong and St Kilda as the men who would lift their clubs to glory. At Kardinia Park the membership increased by 2000 in anticipation of Farmer's arrival and it was said that 10,000 people had attended the opening practice match.

As ever, there were cynics who doubted the boom interstate recruits would make the desired impact. Farmer had turned 27 just before the 1962 opening round and Baldock, although only 23, was only five feet 10 inches tall - far too short for a centre half-forward in Victoria. Yet both were exceptional footballers whose styles added a new dimension to the game.

The huge pre-1962 build-up seemed to fall flat when both had less than satisfying first games. Farmer landed awkwardly at a first quarter boundary throw-in against Carlton and injured a knee. He was forced to spend most of the day resting in a forward pocket, but still managed to boot four goals - an amazing effort as he had damaged the anterior cruciate ligament in his left knee.

In Stephen Hawke's biography Farmer said the accident had happened because he was trying not to use his normal style of "riding" an opponent at throw-ins. "It was more or less a straight jump at the ball instead of using them as a springboard. Because of that I was taking up front position and as three of us flew for the ball I got knocked over and lost my balance, and as I came down my legs were tangled with Maurie Sankey and Graham Donaldson. They landed on top of me, and bang went my leg."

St Kilda's opening game was against Collingwood on Easter Monday, but disaster struck Baldock when he cracked a bone in the arch of his foot on the Thursday before the match. A trainer suggested the foot should be packed on both sides to take pressure off the injured area. But after about five minutes the packing had all moved inside the boot and was under the sore part of the foot.

Baldock's main memory of that match was relief at getting the game out of the way after five years of conjecture about whether he would play. He had only an average game and had to suffer the frustration of sitting out the next four weeks. But the year ended satisfactorily after St Kilda's selectors realised he could play centre half-forward in the VFL and he won the Saints' best and fairest.

Farmer's first season was not as happy. The knee problems restricted him to only half a dozen games in the first year. Despite that, he was one of the game's greats who made a huge impact in a relatively short career in Victoria from 1962 to 1967 in which he appeared in 101 games and kicked 65 goals.

Raised in an orphanage in WA he honed the natural skills of his game despite the fact that his left leg was shorter than his right. As an eight-year-old he practised handballing through a partly opened car window for hours on end. In 1963 he blossomed and finished second to Bob Skilton in the Brownlow Medal. He is one of the few men, of whom it could genuinely be said, altered the style of the game as his spearing 30-yard handballs became a form of attack rather than a means of escaping trouble.

Farmer's method of leaping slightly earlier than opponents and getting a "ride" at boundary throw-

ins fuelled controversy, but he was a master of ruck play and his clashes with John Nicholls were magnificent. He played in Geelong's 1963 flag side, captained the club from 1965 to 1967 and later coached the Cats from 1973 to 1975. He was the club's best and fairest in 1963 and 1964.

He left the Cats after captaining the losing team in the 1967 grand final. In his full career Farmer played a total of 392 games with East Perth, West Perth and Geelong and won the Sandover Medal in 1956 and 1960 as well as the Tassie Medal in 1956.

Baldock's was a truly unique career, studded with glittering moments and the honor of leading St Kilda to its only flag in 1966. As a youngster Darrel Baldock had no great vision of playing in VFL football, but his interest was stirred when he visited an aunty in Melbourne as a 16-year-old and after receiving detailed instructions from the aunt that he was staying with, Baldock set off by train for the MCG to watch the all-powerful Melbourne in a practice session.

At first he didn't think he could get into the ground. Every gate seemed to be locked and he finally saw a fellow walking in with his football bag. He turned out to be Ian McLean, a star winger, and Baldock told him that he had come to see Peter Marquis, a fellow Devonport boy who was one of Melbourne's defenders.

One thing led to another and within 20 minutes the young Tasmanian was training with the famed Demons under the eye of Norm Smith. He was signed by Melbourne on a Form Four and stayed to watch the Demons' second semi-final clash with Collingwood the following weekend.

The Form Four bound him to Melbourne for two years, but even in that time there were tentative (and not entirely legal) approaches from St Kilda. He signed with South to get other teams off his back, but by the 1961 carnival South's Form Four was about to run out. Baldock starred for Tasmania and immediately after the championships it was an-

> **Farmer's method of leaping slightly earlier than opponents and getting a "ride" at boundary throw-ins fuelled controversy.**

Polly Farmer spears out a handpass.

nounced that he had signed for the Saints. St Kilda had sneaked under the guard of a battery of clubs chasing his signature and had actually signed him before the carnival. By this stage Baldock had run out of things to do in Tasmania.

Three decades later Baldock is remembered as perhaps the greatest ball-handler of all time. His ball control and weaving was legendary and remains for all to see on a captivating bracket of film clips. Baldock said both attributes stemmed from his youth. History tells us that Don Bradman refined his skill by hitting a ball against a corrugated iron fence with a cricket stump. There was a Bradmanesque side to Baldock's early development as he practised kicking a ball hard against a brick wall and gathering it on the rebound. Baldock's talents would have been enough on their own, but coupled with brilliant centreman Ian Stewart they were irresistible. As with any form of magic there was no contrived recipe. The two champions did not deliberate over "set piece" moves before a game.

Baldock described the partnership: "There were no tactics. Timing was the most important thing because of my height. The ball had to come down quickly and providing the ball was kicked out in front I was right.

"That was a specialty of Stewie because he was such a magnificent kick of the ball. He'd look up and I was half way there. The greatest asset I had was reading the ball upfield."

While the Baldock-Stewart combination was the essence of the side, St Kilda had a galaxy of stars. The team made the 1965 grand final after a magnificent first season at the new home of Moorabbin and in 1966 St Kilda went one better by taking out the flag.

He went home to Tasmania in 1968 with 119 games and 236 goals to his credit. Almost two decades later he answered the call to coach his old club and was at the helm from 1987 to 1989. He suffered a mild stroke in his first season but continued in the job and helped lift the club's fortunes.

Famous foes - Polly Farmer and John Nicholls.

1964: GRAND GOALS

Grand finals are remembered for many individual highlights, usually associated with the winning teams.

The 1964 game between Melbourne and Collingwood evokes memories of a winner - Melbourne's Neil Crompton - but equally etched into the annals of the game is the name of Ray Gabelich who was part of the losing side that day. Both men were famous for goals they kicked in the dying stages.

Ray Gabelich was a massive ruckman who first attracted Collingwood's attention when he played for a visiting WA junior side. He came to Victoria in 1954 and spent the season with Parkside in the amateurs. The following season he appeared in Collingwood's senior team and soon developed into

a fine follower as his huge frame made him virtually unbeatable at throw-ins. He was a safe mark and a powerful, penetrating kick and was one of Collingwood's best players in the 1958 grand final win over Melbourne.

He won the Copeland Trophy in 1960 then shocked the football world by returning to WA side West Perth. He was set to make his fortune in real estate, but the credit squeeze sent the company to the wall and he was left with only his incentive money for West Perth of eight pounds per win. As the team won only eight games for the year it was hardly a windfall. He had already represented Victoria, but his greatest interstate triumph came for his native state in the 1961 carnival when he earned an All-Australian blazer and won the Simpson Medal for WA's best player in the state's carnival win.

He returned to Collingwood in 1962 and was made vice-captain. He took over as captain after Weideman's retirement in 1964 and led the Magpies to a grand final in his first year. He resigned the captaincy midway through 1965 because of injury problems, but was still an effective contributor and played his last game in the 1966 grand final and finished with a career record of 161 games and 43 goals. By then his bulky torso tipped the scales at over 17 stone. He later said the most difficult stint in his football career was a season in Darwin. "They had to pour water on me at the end of each quarter and during the game!"

Neil Crompton was a sporting all-rounder who represented the state in cricket and football. He was a handy, dedicated batsman for the Shield side and his 45 first class appearances yielded three centuries and an average of 31. He made his Shield debut at only 19 years of age. In that same year he played his first football game at Melbourne, but the competition for places as a rover and half-forward flank was intense as Ian Ridley and Frank Adams held down the roving spots and Hassa Mann and Geoff

Tunbridge were the forward flankers. Crompton lacked a yard of pace which didn't make his task any easier.

Starved of opportunities, Crompton headed to South Australian club Glenelg in 1961 and kicked plenty of goals as a half-forward flanker. Yet when the call came to return to Melbourne he was earmarked for a back pocket. Suddenly he found his niche and played every game in 1962. By 1964 he was regarded as the state's top back-pocket and won a big V guernsey.

It was on grand final day 1964 that Neil Crompton made his lasting impression on the game. He was a bit player in the first part of the drama when Collingwood's Ray Gabelich charged off on his solo run from the half forward line late in the final quarter. As all players had moved up field there was no one between Gabelich and the goals. His lone 50-yard run for goal became part of footy folklore. As the ball bounced from side to side the colossus was determined to ram home the goal and the heroic effort put his team in the lead with only moments to go. Crompton and other Melbourne defenders pursued him and Crompton yelled "Kick it! Kick it!" hoping that Gabelich would think the instructions were coming from a teammate and would muff the kick. Gabelich was too smart for that and he slammed through the goal that put the Magpies in front.

As Melbourne desperately tried to break through everyone crowded into the Demon forward line. Both Collingwood's rovers were there which left Crompton on his own. Coach Norm Smith had ruled that the back pocket player should never cross the centreline even if his opponent did. This time Crompton got to the centreline and looked towards Smith. Someone waved him on and a punch clear by Collingwood ruck-rover Kevin Rose landed in his arms as a couple of Collingwood defenders charged at him with their arms high above their heads to make him kick high for goal.

It has been said over the years that Crompton kicked blindly, but he insists he had a split second to line up the goals and that it wasn't just a wild kick. His roving days had included plenty of time around goals and that stood him in good stead. Collingwood made a last surge and Crompton heard a roar as the ball went over his head into the square. Fortunately it was a Melbourne mark - this time to Barry Bourke the full-forward who Smith had thrown into defence, and the Demons won by four points.

That night Crompton asked Norm Smith what would have happened had he kicked a point, and Smith said: "You wouldn't have got another game".

Crompton figured he was joking, but he wasn't quite sure at first. In later years he said Smith had been happy that he had shown initiative.

Chapter Twelve

1965-1969

Bombers, Breen and Barassi's Blues

Ron Barassi's standing in the VFL was best summed up by his nickname: Mr Football. Thousands of youngsters proudly sported his famed number 31 on the back of Melbourne guernseys and dreamed of leading the all-conquering Demons to another flag. They watched intently when his how-to-play football segment appeared on television.

So it was understandable when Melbourne fans were aghast when they read in December 1964 that Carlton had offered Barassi 3000 pounds a year for three seasons to become captain-coach. Barassi had rejected the offer and red and blue fans heaved a collective sigh. Surely he would not desert the Demons . . . his father had played for the club before losing his life in the war and Barassi had been virtually brought up by Melbourne coach Norm Smith. In short he WAS Melbourne.

But the relief was shortlived. Barassi accepted the Blues' offer early in January and immediately set about restoring the Blues to a position of power. Carlton had just completed its worst year in history, finishing tenth.

As Carlton and Melbourne faced a transition period three other clubs prepared for a new dawn at different homes. Richmond's move to share the MCG with Melbourne was prompted partly over a fear that the widening of Punt Road would chew through part of its ground. The Tigers need not have been in so much of a hurry to pack their bags as the roadwork did not start for another 25 years! North

Melbourne also decided to shift to VFA ground Coburg, but the move was not without its hassles as the VFL executive said the facilities weren't up to scratch.

St Kilda's move to Moorabbin required the most drastic amount of work and also caused the most controversy. A section of the club's members had not wanted the club to move and one even issued a court order to stop it. In the meantime the VFA expelled the Moorabbin club for its supposed treachery. The VFA club's oval had facilities that were little better than any average suburban ground. Grandstands and outer banking had to be created and workmen were still toiling with only days to go before the new season. The ground was situated in Melbourne's sandbelt region and opposition coaches were wary of the new surface. Bob Rose, whose Collingwood team was due to play the first game there, made a special visit to test the bounce of the new ground.

The opening clash between the Magpies and Saints drew a crowd of 51,370 to Moorabbin - a crowd that has never been equalled since at the Linton Street oval. St Kilda completed the fairytale start at its new home with a six-point win after a rugged, tight game and red, white and black fans hoped it was the start of a bright new future.

Melbourne seemed to make light of the loss of Barassi and retired veteran Frank Adams with eight wins in as many games. The faithful in the mem-

A new year, a new home. Darrel Baldock leads out his Saints in the first game at their new home at Moorabbin in 1965.

bers' stand were unruffled by the slender nature of the victories and contented themselves with the old axiom that good teams win tight finishes. Five of the winning margins had been two, three, four, six and eight points and instead of representing a team capable of always winning close games it was an indicator of a side teetering on the edge. In a strange twist of fate Melbourne's eighth win was recorded over Ron Barassi's Carlton, and was hailed as a victory for the master, Norm Smith, over the pupil.

On the Queen's Birthday, St Kilda blasted the veneer away and crushed Melbourne. The 61-point hiding was the biggest loss the club had suffered during Norm Smith's time as coach, and four weeks later the comittee shocked the football world when it sacked him as coach. He was reinstated after players spoke out but the damage had been done and Melbourne's reign as a VFL power was over.

It was reported that Smith had been incensed when the Melbourne committee had refused to back him against a writ issued by umpire Don Blew claiming that he had been libelled by Smith the year before.

Barassi's Blues had opened with a win against Hawthorn, but the Hawks had slipped as a power and would struggle for much of the year. The 1961 premiership coach John Kennedy had left the city in 1964 to take a headmaster's position at Stawell, and the side was only a shell of the combination that had been beaten by Geelong in the 1963 play-off.

Captain Graham Arthur had taken on the playing coach role in the 1964 season and decided to retire from the field prior to 1965. The Hawks' poor start convinced him to return as a player after only two rounds. Arthur ended a sorry season by being suspended for four weeks late in the year and critics poured scorn on the rule which prevented a suspended playing coach from going onto the field to address his team at the quarter-time and three-quarter-time breaks.

Carlton had improved considerably and was able to compete with the best sides in the competition. In front of a huge split-round crowd at Moorabbin the Blues levelled the scores three times during a hectic last term before they had to endure the agony of midget-sized Bruce McMaster-Smith, a Carlton reject, kicking a goal to win the match.

St Kilda was the club which had developed into a real power, and the Saints played their new home ground to perfection. The only time they went down at Moorabbin was early in the year against Essendon in a match where half-back Barry Davis was flattened in a fearful collision with St Kilda's Jim Read. Read was suspended for 10 weeks after the incident and returned to the side for the next clash with Essendon on the same day that Davis resumed after a fractured cheekbone. The heavy sentence reflected concern over raised elbows and forearms.

Another finals contender, Geelong had problems with Brownlow medallist Alistair Lord who was trying to cross to Tasmanian club Burnie as captain-coach. He was a last-minute inclusion in the Cats' team against Fitzroy and the reluctant champ was coerced into staying. He left the club at the end of the following year.

St Kilda was the glamor team of the competition with brilliant players all over the field. The side revolved around the chemistry generated between centreman Ian Stewart and centre half-forward Darrel Baldock. Stewart won the first of his Brownlow Medals this year, and was a player of unlimited skills and courage. The Saints had champions in Verdun Howell, Allan Morrow, Daryl Griffiths and the flamboyant Carl Ditterich. The Saints headed the league ladder after the home and away games for the first time ever.

St Kilda and Collingwood fought out a thrilling second semi-final in the heat on the MCG. Before a record crowd St Kilda notched a desperate one-point win and advanced to its first grand final since 1913.

Essendon had crushed Geelong in the first semi-final and repeated the dose on Collingwood in a preliminary final made famous by the Somerville incident. Seven minutes into the big game Bomber half-forward John Somerville was knocked unconscious 40 yards behind play and lay motionless on the turf at the feet of Collingwood's Duncan Wright, who was immediately rushed by Essendon players. Wright was later questioned by police and released a statement that said in part: "I have not been given a fair go in all the publicity about it. I want to say clearly that I am innocent in this affair and have done nothing wrong."

Essendon's momentum continued in the grand final and swept aside St Kilda's dream of a first flag. The Bombers careered away to a comfortable win. The Bombers had talent all over the field with a great centre half-forward in Ken Fraser and stars such as Jack Clarke, John Birt, Barry Davis and Hugh Mitchell. But it was the unfashionable duo of ruckman Brian Sampson and full-forward Ted Fordham who played the games of their lives. Sampson remembered: "We were fairly confident and went in as underdogs. Morrow was injured early in the game and Ditterich was always hard as you had to keep up with him." But Sampson revelled in the big-match atmosphere.

Attendances dropped overall, but that didn't thwart the interest of TV stations, and when the ABC entered the replay field in August all four channels were covering the game. There was interest from another area when the acting Premier, Sir Arthur Rylah, started an inquiry into the sale of finals tickets.

> Attendances dropped overall, but that didn't thwart the interest of TV stations, and when the ABC entered the replay field in August all four channels were covering the game.

The value of playing coaches was debated by the purists and the results of 1965 provided arguments for both sides. Barassi and Bob Skilton (South) made a good fist of it, but under Graham Arthur and Ted Whitten, Hawthorn and Footscray struggled.

St Kilda began 1966 keen to atone for the sad grand final result of the previous year and started by putting another nail in Melbourne's coffin. By the time St Kilda had won the first eight games there was extravagant talk that the team could go through undefeated. The Saints promptly lost the next two.

South Melbourne had been out of the finals for 20 years, but showed early promise with boom WA forward Austin Robertson prominent in the early stages. As had so often happened in the past the Swans could not maintain the momentum and fell away badly.

Once again the Coulter Law reared its head when Kyabram recruit Dick Clay was snared by Richmond after a tussle with North Melbourne. The matter of illicit signing-on fees was once again swept under the carpet. Controversy of a different sort surrounded Geelong, which had already been the centre of attention when it dumped coach Bob Davis and replaced him with Peter Pianto over summer. Pianto asserted himself early in the year when champion centreman Alistair Lord sidestepped an opponent and Pianto dragged him from the field.

Carlton had clawed its way from tenth to sixth in 1965 and recorded some impressive wins in 1966 despite losing Barassi through injury problems. It was rumored the Blues had been prepared to spend $40,000 to lure champion WA rover Barry Cable to Victoria, but the bid failed.

The big improver was Richmond. The Tigers had been kick-started by Len Smith and after illness forced him into retirement the club turned to former nuggety defender Tom Hafey. Late in the season Richmond moved to top place for the first time in 26 years. The Tigers had a big, long-kicking side that had been moulded to suit the open spaces of the MCG. With players such as "Bustling" Billy Barrot thumping the ball forward the yellow and blacks relied on all-out attack to outscore the opposition.

The top six teams met each other in a thrilling round 15 and after that only one win separated the top five. Geelong rolled Richmond a week later and nudged the Tigers out of the five, but in the final round it was St Kilda which looked like tumbling out of the finals race.

The Saints were struggling at home against Hawthorn and could not shake the determined opposition. Skipper Darrel Baldock, who had injured his knee a couple of weeks earlier, had been placed on the reserves bench, and when he was hurled into action in the third term he altered the course of the game. St Kilda shook off the cobwebs and steadied to seal the double chance. The Saints still had their problems as dynamic ruckman Carl Ditterich had been suspended for six weeks on the eve of the finals.

In the second semi Collingwood jumped St Kilda just as it had in the same game a year earlier, but this time it was the Magpies who took the honors in a close finish. Skipper Des Tuddenham was an inspiration with seven goals from the half-forward flank. The Saints accounted for their 1965 conqueror Essendon in the heavy conditions of the preliminary final and prepared for another crack at Colingwood. A big problem was Darrel Baldock's knee injury, and the Saint dynamo injured the joint in the last minutes of the Thursday night training session. Coach Allan Jeans immediately called in the rest of the team so the injury would be concealed, and although the champion took his place in the team he felt the knee "go" when he kicked the team's second goal early in the grand final.

The match was a classic thriller which was only settled when Barry Breen sent a wobbly punt through for a point at the 27-minute mark. There was jubi-

> During the year Victoria regained the crown as carnival champions it had lost in 1961 with a 15-point win over Western Australia in the final.

lation in the St Kilda camp when the siren signalled the club's first flag, but the Magpies could only feel heartbreak, and for coach Bobby Rose the one-point loss came on top of the four point near-miss to Melbourne two years earlier.

During the year Victoria regained the crown as carnival champions it had lost in 1961 with a 15-point win over Western Australia in the final. The injury-riddled side showed tremendous spirit and the team's versatility provided coach Allan Killigrew with plenty of options.

Fitzroy had been a struggling team for several years, and in desperate search of an upturn in fortunes moved to share Princes Park with Carlton. The Lions also changed the style of their guernsey, but the cosmetic alterations made no different to form.

The whole question of player recruitment was one which caused ongoing concern in the VFL boardroom. The VFA and the country leagues were tired of losing their best players without compensation in most cases. The VFA demanded the introduction of transfer fees for players going to League clubs and the VFL responded by scrapping the clearance agreement that had been in force since 1951. Next move in the bitter dispute was the VFA's announcement that it would ban Terry Alexander and Kevin Sheedy for five years after they had crossed to Collingwood and Richmond respectively.

On the country front the atmosphere was just as tense. The VFL's view was obvious in the *Football Record* which said the situation "is fast becoming chaotic, with country players, who are really hardly more than novices, asking fantastic sums of money to join VFL clubs". The League's preferred solution was a zoning scheme which divided the state into 12 zones with each one allocated to a club. The idea was for each club to control its zone for a determined period (three to five years) and be responsible for development of the game in that zone. No player could be recruited from outside the zone, and a transfer fee would be paid to the club of each recruit. The

Victorian Country Football League did not want the scheme, but it could not hold out forever and even though it was not passed by the VFL initially the scheme was voted in 12 months later. Zoning stayed in force for the next two decades even though the idea of rotating zones never materialised. Eventually it was replaced by drafting, a method suggested as an alternative to zoning even back in 1967.

The season started sensationally when Collingwood, which had lost its last match by a point, was pipped by the same margin against Geelong. Cats' forward Bill Ryan was given a penalty kick in the final seconds of the game. As the siren sounded and thousands of supporters ran on to the field, Ryan kicked into the man on the mark. Umpire Perkins ruled the Collingwood man had gone over the mark and gave Ryan another kick which he sent straight through the centre.

Amid all the discussions of clearances Hawthorn won the services of the biggest fish of all - Tasmanian star Peter Hudson. The high-scoring spearhead made his debut against rugged Carlton full-back Wes Lofts in the second round and finished the day with four goals out of Hawthorn's losing tally of six. Commentators gave the honors to Lofts, but from the moment Hudson doubled back behind a pack for a clever opening goal in the first term it was obvious he was a star.

Just as Hawthorn was heralding a new star, Essendon farewelled two of its greats as Jack Clarke and Hugh Mitchell were dropped after the second round and announced their retirements.

Carlton and Geelong were the early pacesetters and the Blues had a controversial win over St Kilda when the half-time siren failed to sound. Timekeepers furiously tried to signal the end of the quarter with the emergency bell, but because of the noise in the grandstand the umpire could not hear it. Play kept going and Carlton's John Gill scored a goal. In

> The VFL "is fast becoming chaotic, with country players, asking fantastic sums of money to join VFL clubs".

At last!
An emotional
St Kilda coach Allan
Jeans with skipper
Darrel Baldock
moments after the
Saints landed their
first flag in 1966.

The finals series was notable for brilliant, free-flowing football. Geelong, a pacy, talent-laden side finished all over Collingwood in the first semi-final, and then turned on a second half blitz to come from behind against Carlton in the preliminary final. John Sharrock, a traditional half-forward flanker with a lethal left foot, was the man who did all the damage in the third term and the star-studded Cats powered their way to a grand final showdown with Richmond. Carlton's limitations up forward had seen the Blues lose both finals games.

The Tigers had been convincing in their second semi-final win and the football purists expected a thriller in the grand final. That was exactly what was produced by these teams, both hell-bent on attack. It was a magnificent game played at a cracker-jack pace with spectacular marking and precision kicking under pressure. The great Richmond centreline of Dick Clay, Bill Barrot and Frances Bourke epitomised the height and long-kicking that had been sought by Len Smith and his successor Tom Hafey. Barrot had 27 kicks, many of them 70 yards, and was a constant source of drive. Another hero was Royce Hart, the electrifying young forward who capped off a great first season.

The lead changed four times in the last half hour before Richmond edged ahead. There was drama when Tiger captain Fred Swift marked a Billy Goggin shot on the goal line, but the flag belonged to the Tigers and they brought the premiership back to Punt Road for the first time in 24 years. The only touch of sadness was that ruckman Neville Crowe missed the game through a suspension incurred after a second semi-final report. John Nicholls, the man he was alleged to have punched, admitted years later that he had only been staging for a free kick. Oddly enough Crowe's replacement John Ronaldson was an unlikely hero with three vital goals.

A month after the grand final former umpire Harry Beitzel took a team to Ireland, Great Britain and the USA. The team was christened "The

the end it made the difference as the Blues won by five points.

Carlton excelled in close finishes during this season whereas St Kilda could not take a trick and tumbled down the ladder. The Saints did not shake off the cobwebs for a long time but then they managed seven wins in a row to mount a late challenge for the four.

Richmond meanwhile went from strength to strength and there were none of the slip-ups of 1966. The Tigers had been boosted by the inclusion of brilliant ex-Tasmanian Royce Hart who gave the attack added bite. Also enjoying a good season was Geelong and the Cats' full-forward Doug Wade, in the midst of his best season, bagged 13 goals against the Swans. He finished with 96 goals, well clear of the next best scorer Peter Hudson on 57. Wade wasn't the only player to kick a bag of goals in 1967 and St Kilda's "Cowboy" Neale kicked six goals in a dazzling quarter against Essendon and finished with eight for the game.

Galahs" and took on the best Irish teams at Gaelic football. County Meath, the All-Ireland champions, visited Australia for a series of matches the following year.

The surprise packet of early 1968 was Essendon. New coach Jack Clarke's training routines and match plan rejuvenated the careers of several older players. His merry-go-round forward line structure rotated Ted Fordham, Ken Fraser, David Shaw and others between the forward line and ruck-roving positions and caught many opposing sides unaware. Clarke's declaration that he wanted to "put more fun and enjoyment back into League football" was pooh-poohed by some critics, but he wiped the smirks off their faces when Essendon started the season by posting five wins in a row.

St Kilda had regrouped after the patchy efforts of 1967, and on the Queen's Birthday dazzled Essendon with an avalanche of goals in the first quarter. Skipper Baldock had struggled for much of the time in the early rounds, but he was at his best against the Bombers. A week later St Kilda plunged into controversy when ruckman Bob Pascoe was reported on a charge of kicking Geelong's John Sharrock. Pascoe was suspended for the rest of the year - equivalent to a 12-week sentence - and the Saints announced they would ban umpires from after-match functions as a result of the evidence given by a boundary umpire at Pascoe's hearing.

Hawthorn full-forward Peter Hudson had shown signs of his brilliance in 1967 and he became a dominant figure in 1968, regularly kicking huge tallies and steaming to the magical 100 goal mark by the 16th round.

The battle for places in the four was still open right up to the final round when St Kilda torpedoed Geelong and prevented Richmond from defending its title. The fickle nature of football was never better illustrated than in the first semi-final when Geelong reversed an eight-goal defeat and notched a seven-goal win over the Saints. A steady, methodi-

Saints Cowboy Neale, Alan Morrow, Brian Mynott, Jim Read and Rodger Head on a victory lap after the 1966 grand final.

cal Carlton overcame Essendon in the second semi, but the Bombers won the right to challenge again by dispatching Geelong in the preliminary final.

The grand final was a grim, dour affair which suited the workmanlike Carlton team down to the ground. The Bombers went into the match without skipper Ken Fraser who was injured, but had a bonus when teenage full-forward Geoff Blethyn kicked four goals in the low-scoring game which Carlton won by three points. Carlton's line-up did not have the all-round quality of future Blues' sides, which was testimony to Ron Barassi's coaching ability, but its smattering of stars were true champions. Much of the Blues' game was built around the ruck dominance of John Nicholls, and he had an able lieutenant in Sergio Silvagni. Adrian Gallagher led the group of small men who fed from Nicholls. Younger players such as Brent Crosswell and Alex Jesaulenko had already established themselves as top flight performers and winger Gary Crane and half-back John Goold were acknowledged as leading lights in their positions.

A rule change introduced prior to 1969 was the catalyst for a change in the whole style of football.

Peter Hudson clambers for the ball against Carlton.

Footscray's Ken Greenwood adopted the more traditional method of using an advocate and pleading not guilty. The tribunal also reacted in the orthodox way and suspended him for four weeks.

The Blues were also in the news when they slugged out a wild match with Collingwood in which Collingwood's Len Thompson and Ted Potter and Blues Ricky McLean and Peter Jones were reported. Collingwood bolted to a big win thanks to the flashy skills of John Greening who kicked seven goals, but the football world's attention turned to the tribunal hearing the following Monday night. The cases were tipped out due to a technicality when it was found that VFL delegates had not been informed of the reports immediately after the game and the reports were not made available within the time specified under VFL rules. The umpires were incensed and threatened strike action.

Collingwood figured in another headline-grabbing match against St Kilda when the Saints scraped home by six points. Wingman Stuart Trott had been St Kilda's best player, but he almost lost the game for his side when umpire Crouch took the ball from him for wasting time in the closing minutes. On the same day Peter Hudson booted 16 goals against Melbourne, only two short of the all-time League record and the third best by any individual.

Carlton captain-coach Ron Barassi briefly emerged from retirement as a player for one game against his old club, Melbourne. He struggled before hobbling off the field late in the day. One of football's great careers had ended.

Previous year's wooden-spooner North Melbourne started 1968 in brilliant form with wins from each of its first four starts. The bustling dynamism of "Slamming" Sam Kekovich powered the young side to the unexpected splash of success, but the Roos lost momentum when Kekovich injured an ankle in the fifth round and they only won four more games for the year.

Richmond struggled in a mid-season slump and

The rule penalised a player who kicked the ball out of bounds on the full and led to more direct and faster play. In the first year the lift in scoring was obvious, but the basic format of play did not change vastly. In the 1970s it would change markedly.

Carlton showed it had adapted to the new rule by kicking a new League record score of 30.30-210 in the second round against Hawthorn. The Blues would have fashioned an even bigger score if the brilliant Jesaulenko had not kicked 6.12 for the afternoon. The running battle between Wes Lofts and Peter Hudson continued in this match when Lofts was reported for striking the star forward. He was rubbed out for four weeks. Later in the year it became too much for Hudson, and he was reported for striking Lofts. He was given a reprimand.

Anyone who thought they had seen everything at the tribunal was in for a surprise when South's Arthur Budd waived the use of an advocate and threw himself at the tribunal's mercy. He escaped with a reprimand after pleading guilty under provocation while the other player in the incident, there was talk that coach Hafey's position was in jeopardy. That was enough to spur the Tigers who unleashed a big run towards the end of the year, and returned to the four only a fortnight before the finals at the expense of Hawthorn, whose percentage had never recovered from the early hiding from Carlton.

Hafey had the knack of getting the team to peak at just the right time and Richmond wiped the floor with Geelong to win the first semi by nearly 20 goals. The Tigers looked down and out in the preliminary final against Collingwood, but turned the match around and marched into the grand final.

They looked like continuing the run against Carlton, but the Blues hit back in the third term and actually went into the final quarter with a slender lead. But that was the end of Carlton's burst, and getting great drive from the first ruck of Mike Green, Mike Bowden and Kevin Bartlett the Tigers finished all over their opponents.

It was a year in which attendances had fallen away and VFL administrative director Eric McCutchan called on the press not to be so negative about the diminished crowds. Even the cheer squads went on strike when floggers and confetti were banned by the VFL.

As the game prepared for the 1970s there were plenty of vexing questions for administrators. The next decade would see developments proceed at a pace which would be too great for many of them.

ROYCE HART: A TASMANIAN TIGER

Writing an autobiography at the age of 22 is an exercise fraught with danger.

After all, it isn't exactly a ripe old age and when Royce Hart wrote his book there were plenty of raised eyebrows. The fact that he named himself as centre half-forward in a "best ever" team was generally regarded as a more than precocious piece of selfishness. But by the time he ended his career nearly a decade later Hart did not have to rate himself at the top of the tree - there were plenty of others who would venture that opinion.

Bruce Doull, a worthy foe in many a struggle, lowered his taciturn facade to rate Hart as his hardest opponent, saying "he could never be contained for a whole game".

Richmond brought him to Melbourne in 1965 as a 17-year-old, gangling tenderfoot for the price of a new suit, six shirts and a pair of shoes plus 20 pounds spending money. Amazingly Richmond had not even seen him play. The club had heard that he had done well for Clarence under-19s and as a rover in the state schoolboys team. An extensive gym program and a gradual introduction through the under-19s and reserves was the first step on the ladder of league football. He had received a good grounding in the under-19s under the coaching of Ray Jordon -"He showed me how to kick a drop-punt".

Hart was introduced to League football in the opening round of 1967. Thrust into the new role of full-forward, he starred, was a unanimous choice as recruit of the year, played in the state side and kicked seven goals against WA, played for the premiership team and even represented Australia in Gaelic football. It was a dream start, but the following years were not a letdown as he went from triumph to triumph.

He had lightning recovery, a great spring, vice-like hands and was a penetrating left foot kick. His balance was also superb, but his greatest asset was total and unwavering concentration. He would scramble after the ball in a pack until he secured it regardless of the danger. Hart's ability to kick the team lifting or matchwinning goal, usually after a soaring mark, was the hallmark of a champion. In 1969 he was paid $2000 to play for Glenelg in a grand final while he was in South Australia on national service. It was a far cry from the 20 pounds for crossing to the Tigers, but unfortunately he was knocked out in the first five minutes of the game.

One of his trademarks was the ability to launch himself from the side of packs. There was a popular misconception that he was taught the method by Len Smith, but Hart developed it by necessity in Tasmania when playing for Clarence under-19s as a short 16-year-old. "I was too light to mark in front and jumping from behind was no real value."

Royce Hart was an inspiring player in the 1967, 1969, 1973 and 1974 premierships, captaining the last two successes. In his last couple of years the strain on his knees led to three operations, but he was still a devastating and feared player. He stood aside as Richmond captain at the end of 1975 after four seasons. He captained Victoria and played for the state 11 times. Oddly enough he played for most of his career without contact lenses despite poor eyesight. "It didn't affect my marking, I just couldn't read the scoreboard!" he said.

His playing career netted 363 goals from 189 games from 1967 to 1977. Later he coached Footscray from 1980 until early 1982 when he was sacked in a particularly bloody manner.

That sorry exit could not tarnish the memory of Hart the player. His football story was indeed one worth telling.

Chapter Thirteen

1970-1974
Rebellion and revolution

The 1970s were a time of questions at all levels of society. More than ever before the status quo and the old values of authority were put to the test by the inquiring and rebellious new generation. Throughout the Western world the Vietnam War was the symbol of protest and division and Australia was no exception. A demonstration held in Melbourne led by Dr Jim Cairns MP was the largest held in Australia.

Opposition to authority would manifest itself in football too, and coaches would face increasing rebellion. Most footballers would grudgingly accept the orders, but in some cases players would stand firm. It even ended the careers of some, such as Russell Petherbridge who won the under-19 Morrish Medal while playing with St Kilda. Petherbridge refused to follow coach Allan Jeans' edict that he cut his hair and promptly left to play at Sandringham.

The haircut issue seems almost laughable 20 years later, but it seemed to be the testing ground of coaching authority. Ron Barassi had ordered that long-whiskered Blues have their hair cut and sideburns trimmed in 1969 and went a step further on the eve of the grand final by sending Brent Crosswell and John Goold, two of football's most elegant dressers off the field, back to the dressing room to change their socks.

Football's biggest revolt for years came on the eve of the 1970 season. The Bombers' five best players - Don McKenzie, Barry Davis, Geoff Pryor, Geoff Gosper and Darryl Gerlach - demanded pay rises and when they were denied they threatened to stand down from the practice match against South Adelaide. Eventually they played in the practice match, but then handed in their resignations and were not considered for the opening round team to play Carlton. The club threatened to split wide open as John Williams was elected captain. Four days later the row was settled and the rebels returned with one of them, Barry Davis, being elected the new skipper.

> **Football's biggest revolt for years came on the eve of the 1970 season.**

A few weeks before the Essendon showdown there had been a pay dispute at Collingwood, the bastion of tradition and the "play for the guernsey" ethic. Captain Des Tuddenham and star ruckman Len Thompson had walked out of the club after their contract demands had been thrown out by the committee. After three weeks they resolved the matter and went back into training, but Tuddenham lost the captaincy over the issue.

When the bread and butter business of football finally got under way the long downtrodden Fitzroy turned on a right royal display against Richmond before Queen Elizabeth and Prince Philip in a special Sunday match at the MCG. Little known names such as David Wall, Harvey Merrigan and Mike Andrews played the games of their lives and stunned the reigning premier.

But the Lions' joy was shortlived and in their

first game at their new Junction Oval they were slaughtered by a St Kilda team which created a new club record score. Fitzroy's veteran skipper Kevin Murray alleged after the game he had been kicked by a St Kilda player, but the League's investigator Jack Chessell found no charges were warranted.

The Lions were part of history when they played the first game at VFL Park against Geelong. The Cats drew first blood at the "thunderdome" with a 61-point victory. The 1970 season also marked the first time that all clubs played each other twice, but there were many other things which made this a historic year. Footscray champion Ted Whitten set a new VFL record when he reached 321 games and announced that he would retire. A rascal who could tough it out with the best of them, Whitten was above all a magnificent all-round footballer with every skill in the book. He now concentrated on coaching, but found that being on the other side of the fence didn't dampen his fire and he was furious later in the year when a prankster delivered 20 sheeps' hearts to the dressing rooms after a particularly poor effort against South.

Form was a factor which meant nothing in this topsy turvy season. Reigning premier Richmond started the year poorly and Hawthorn, which had just missed a finals place in 1969, lost its first seven games. South Melbourne, now coached by the famous Norm Smith, emerged as a finals prospect and Smith's old team Melbourne showed its best form for years.

The Swans had often begun well in previous years only to fade dramatically, and the pundits waited for the young team to falter again. But the speedy young side had more backbone under the wise guidance of Smith. Led by veteran rover Bob Skilton and centreman Peter Bedford, the talented group of small men created formidable opposition for all teams. It wasn't until a stirring one-point victory over ladder leaders Collingwood on the Queen's Birthday that the doubters were silenced. Rapturous Swans fans swarmed onto the ground before the end of the game and the game was delayed for several minutes. South lacked big marking players around the ground, but Smith crowded the centre bounces and relied on the ball hitting the turf to give his smaller players control. He relied heavily on Fred Way as the side's only recognised ruckman and the victory over Collingwood was even more remarkable as it was achieved without Way in the team.

Despite the loss Collingwood was the competition's dominant side, and the Magpies' most amazing win was the success over St Kilda when they came back after trailing by 52 points at half-time. Collingwood was gone half way through the final term when it needed six goals to win, but with a whirlwind finish and the benefits of some dubious umpiring decisions plucked the game from the fire. Hostile Saint fans pointed to the free-kick statistics after the game and wanted to know how Don Jolley could pay 34 frees to Collingwood and only 12 to St Kilda in the second half, including an amazing 16-4 ratio in the final term.

The four was settled well before the end of August when the Swans beat Geelong in a crucial match at Kardinia Park. In a hectic finish the ball slewed off Cats' full-forward Doug Wade's boot as he was having a shot for goal. It turned out the ball had been hit by an apple thrown from the crowd. The Swans thus made their first finals appearance since 1945. It was a sentimental occasion for skipper Skilton who had toiled so long without a chance to play in the September games and the red and whites were sentimental favourites in front of the record first semi-final crowd.

But sentiment counted for little in the match and St Kilda's bevy of tall men such as Ditterich, Brian Mynott and John McIntosh exploited the Swans' biggest weakness. An eight-goal last term sealed the issue. Collingwood won an electrifying second semi over archrival Carlton and there was drama at the tribunal when Blue Syd Jackson and Magpie Lee Adamson faced the music for striking each other. Jackson, an Aboriginal, said he had been provoked by racist taunts and both players escaped suspension. A couple of decades later Jackson confessed the defence was a ploy devised by Carlton officials.

The two teams faced each other again in the grand final and by half-time Collingwood fans were opening the champagne. The Magpies led by 44 points, Peter McKenna had five goals on the board and the Blues hung their heads in despair.

But fate intervened in the form of a small blond-haired nineteenth man and a masterstroke of coaching. Ron Barassi told his team to handball at all costs - even from the last line of defence if necessary - to break Collingwood's stranglehold on the flag. Barassi and his fellow selectors conferred at half time and Barassi wanted to immediately replace Bert Thornley with Ted Hopkins. The other selectors wanted to compromise and wait 10 minutes, but as the players were walking down the race Barassi made the snap decision and told the reserve to get onto the field. Hopkins launched the initial assault and then inch by inch they pegged back Collingwood until the Magpies succumbed under endless attacking waves.

By the time Brent Crosswell goaled late in the final term to wrest the lead for the Blues, Collingwood was finished and when Jesaulenko sent through a bouncing goal moments later their fate was sealed. The win had shown that handball could dictate a game and is regarded as a watershed in the annals of football. Barassi had not only won a flag, he had created a whole new approach.

Another feature of the 1970 season was the re-emergence of full-forwards. Peter Hudson's 146 goals was only four short of the all-time record and was his third successive century. Magpie heartthrob Peter McKenna was only three behind Hudson after narrowly missing the century a year earlier, and Alex Jesaulenko finished with 115.

A word in your ear! Carl Ditterich looms up on Carlton's Sergio Silvagni in the 1970 preliminary final.

The biggest shock over the 1970-71 summer was the swap of Ian Stewart and Billy Barrot. Stewart, who had won two Brownlows for St Kilda, had struggled to overcome injuries and an apparent lack of enthusiasm in 1970 and many people thought his best football was behind him. The temperamental Barrot had fallen out of favor at Richmond and when he expressed his wish to leave, the way was open for a deal between the two clubs. Stewart confounded the doubters when he won another Brownlow in his first year for the Tigers, but St Kilda got little value from the moody Barrot who did well in his first game with four goals then was taken from the field after only three quarters a week later and dropped. Disillusioned and on the outer, he crossed to Carlton for the latter part of the season.

The Blues recruited Barrot, and coaxed veteran ruck-rover Sergio Silvagni out of retirement to give them a lift in a year marked by patchy form which produced a blend of fine wins, such as one over a rampaging Hawthorn, and inexplicable losses. They

Ace centremen Billy Barrot and Ian Stewart contest a mark at Princes Park. Their swap between St Kilda and Richmond was a landmark in football history, but within weeks Barrot had been dumped by St Kilda and cleared to Carlton where he remained for half a season.

had gone down to lowly North at Arden Street in the first match and that was an indicator of the type of season they would have.

Carlton's hopes of a finals berth ended in bizarre circumstances when it lost to Fitzroy at Junction Oval in a fog so bad that the emergency umpire had to relay scores from one goal umpire to the other.

Carlton's coach Ron Barassi had grabbed the headlines even before the start of the season when

he ordered star rover Adrian Gallagher to do 20 push-ups because he had not trained at top pace. Gallagher said his new boots gave him blisters and refused Barassi's demands. He was sent off the field and suspended for the first match.

Gallagher wasn't the only VFL player to run into disciplinary problems either. North's flamboyant Sam Kekovich was dropped after failing to attend a training session because he missed a plane from Wagga after going there for the races.

South Melbourne fell away after the big effort of 1970 and for a while it looked as if the Ian Ridley-coached Melbourne would perform similar deeds in 1971. Melbourne won the first five games and faced Collingwood in a clash reminiscent of the great days of the past. About 80,000 people saw the Demons crushed, but the team managed to stay in the four until late July before being tipped out.

Hawthorn had been on the fringe of the finals for a couple of years and started 1971 in blistering form . The Hawks built a strategy around the amazing talents of Peter Hudson which involved the rest of the forward line moving downfield and leaving him one out with the full-back. His skill was so pronounced that no full-back could hold him and he could rely on the ball being shot out by star flanker Bob Keddie and the brilliant roving duet of Peter Crimmins and Leigh Matthews. Hawthorn was a power combination with strength equal to the 1961 flag side and had plenty of stars around the ground such as full-back Kelvin Moore, centre half-back Peter Knights and hard-working ruckman Don Scott.

Collingwood had looked like being the main challenger to Hawthorn for the early part of the season, but the Magpies were overtaken by St Kilda. The Saint full-forward Alan Davis sunk Collingwood with 10 goals early in the season and emphasised their right to second place with a decisive win at VFL Park when the clubs met again. The Magpies ended the afternoon in disarray when coach Bob Rose dragged captain Terry Waters and star goalkicker Peter McKenna from the ground. A few days later Waters resigned the captaincy and players pledged their support for Rose. He resigned at the end of the season, but still had the coaching bug despite his frustrations at Victoria Park and would return to the scene as Footscray's coach the following year.

St Kilda finished the season strongly, and although beaten twice during the season by Hawthorn, turned on a fierce last quarter in the second semifinal after plodding for the first three terms. Only a couple of wayward shots at goal in the dying moments stopped the Saints from taking the honors and Hawthorn's wobbly two-point win sowed the first seed of doubt in a team that had looked invincible all year.

St Kilda fought fire with fire in confronting Hawthorn's tactic of crowding the centre bounces and the ugly knot of players led to calls for a limit on players at bounces. Eventually it resulted in the introduction of the centre square, another innovation which boosted scoring. The idea was tried in a match between Fitzroy and Carlton in June and coaches Graham Donaldson and Ron Barassi agreed that it worked well.

The Saints earned another shot at Hawthorn with a strong win over Richmond in the wet. It was the first time the Tigers had lost a final since moving into the MCG. This paved the way for a bonejarring grand final which has earned a reputation as one of the toughest ever. St Kilda looked to have defied all the form of the year and was set to cause the upset until Hawthorn flanker Bob Keddie's four-goal last quarter turned the game. Keddie had been well-held by Gary Colling for the first three quarters, and even though St Kilda fought the game right out, the Saints were still seven points down at the siren. Hawthorn looked to be on the verge of a dominant era.

Season 1971 marked the end of the post-season night series which had been contested since 1956 by teams which had missed the finals. VFL president Sir Kenneth Luke died after governing an era of change. Ron Barassi retired as Carlton's coach with two premierships to his credit.

There was the usual share of unusual incidents and Ted Whitten came up with the novel approach of addressing his team by tape recorder before the Swans game. The Bulldogs won by two points. Umpires had been criticised for jumping into packs and one boundary umpire learned his lesson when he was flattened after colliding with Geelong's Doug Wade.

Full-forwards held sway again and in 1971 Peter McKenna was first to the century. A few weeks later Peter Hudson became the first man to kick four century tallies in a row, and ended the year by equalling Bob Pratt's record of 150 goals. He looked like passing the mark early in the grand final, but the combination of a heavy knock and the brilliance of Saint full-back Barry Lawrence restricted him to just three goals.

Two big breaks with tradition came in 1972 when the VFL sold its longtime headquarters Harrison House for $962,000 and announced there would be a final five. The finals series would now consist of seven matches and would see finals played at VFL Park for the first time. The VFL still had a long-term goal of playing the grand final at the Waverley stadium and announced plans to encircle the oval with grandstands by 1974.

Des Tuddenham and Collingwood parted company and he crossed to Essendon as playing-coach. For the first time in many years there were two playing coaches, Tuddenham and Carlton's John Nicholls, and their success would cause a rethink on the value of captain-coaches.

Hawthorn's ambitions of a long reign were running high in the opening round of 1972. Hudson had booted eight out of nine and looked quite capa-

> **Two big breaks with tradition came in 1972 when the VFL sold its longtime headquarters Harrison House for $962,000 and announced that there would be a final five.**

ble of kicking 20 for the day. But all the Hawks' fantasies came to an abrupt end just before half-time when he collided with Melbourne's Barry Bourke and was carried off on a stretcher. Any hopes of an early return were soon dashed. He was out for the year and later had an operation on the knee.

With Hudson sidelined Peter McKenna led the way as the VFL's top goalkicker, but injury marred the latter part of his season. A new member of the "ton" club was Bomber spearhead Geoff Blethyn, who played in hardened spectacles.

Essendon developed a streak of iron under Tuddenham and became a serious contender for a finals berth. Tuddenham returned to Victoria Park with his brash, aggressive young team before a Queen's Birthday crowd of 42,000 people, but the home side had a lethal forward in McKenna who kicked 13 goals. The Dons also couldn't match Carlton later in the year when the Blues turned on a dazzling performance to kick 13 goals in a row at one stage. Jesaulenko kicked five of them in 11 minutes.

At the other end of the ladder North Melbourne was determined to shake off its loser image, and was reportedly set to embark on a massive recruiting drive. In the meantime the Roos were having ongoing traumas with truculent Sam Kekovich and when he failed to turn up for a reserves game the burly star was suspended indefinitely by the club. One of North's more novel recruiting campaigns came to a deadend when 37-year-old Ted Whitten shelved plans to make a comeback with the Roos. By season's end the club had pulled off the biggest recruiting coup of all when it convinced Ron Barassi to pick up the threads of his coaching career. They went one better by also appointing Norm Smith to a specialist position. Smith had sacked himself from the South coaching position after the committee had called for applications for his job.

The tribunal was kept busy all year, and one of

> The tribunal was kept busy all year, and one of the most newsworthy cases involved a charge of misconduct against Brent Crosswell.

the most newsworthy cases involved a charge of misconduct against Brent Crosswell by umpire Ian Coates. Coates told the tribunal Crosswell had struck him, and although it suspended him for four weeks the tribunal said Crosswell had not struck the umpire deliberately.

There were a couple of wild games in which there were no reports. Twenty-six Essendon and Melbourne players slugged it out in a fierce brawl, but no numbers were taken. There were no reports when Collingwood star John Greening was felled behind play at Moorabbin, but the VFL called for an investigation into the incident that left him unconscious for several hours. St Kilda half-back Jim O'Dea was suspended for 10 weeks, and the Saints were rocked by another incident a week later when an opposition Footscray player, Stephen Boyle, lost the sight of an eye. Within three weeks the Saints had slid out of the five.

Early in the year St Kilda had whipped leading club Richmond, but now had to scrap with Hawthorn and Essendon for the last two places in the five. Essendon had to beat Collingwood in the final round as Hawthorn and St Kilda fought it at Glenferrie. St Kilda, now restored to full strength after a spate of injuries, accounted for Hawthorn. As the game finished earlier than the Essendon-Collingwood clash, the Hawks had to rely on Essendon being beaten to keep a finals place, but inspired by Tuddenham the Dons lifted and won by five points.

Essendon and St Kilda met in the historic first final at VFL Park and 52,499 people saw the Saints reverse the two defeats they had suffered at the hands of Tuddenham's team during the year. St Kilda rolled Collingwood a week later, and after seeming to have been dead and buried, now loomed as a major premiership threat thanks to the drawn second semifinal at VFL Park between Richmond and Carlton.

The second semi had been a hard, tight game and the Saints sat back for an unexpected breather while the Tigers and Blues slogged it out again in the replay. Just when the cards seemed to be falling into place for St Kilda the team was struck by injuries and influenza, but with a few minutes to go in the preliminary final the Saints held the lead. Carlton popped through a couple of last-gasp goals to save the match, but entered the grand final as rank outsider against the classy Richmond.

Carlton restructured its line-up before the game and went for a policy of all-out attack. The result was a welter of goals from both sides and the biggest scoring grand final of all time. Carlton never looked threatened and scored 28.9-177 to 22.18-150. The Tigers' score would have won any other grand final. Jesaulenko kicked seven goals and Robert Walls and John Nicholls booted six each.

The win was a triumph for captain-coach Nicholls who had copped plenty of flak over his waning influence as a player. In the second semi he had suffered the indignity of having his hair ruffled by a rampaging Kevin Sheedy, but in this match he parked himself in a forward pocket and dictated play. Throughout the year Nicholls had used Jesaulenko in the centre, but he employed him as a full-forward in the pressured atmosphere of the finals.

An end-of-season series of matches between state premiership clubs in Adelaide would normally have evoked only minimal public interest, but West Australian Mal Brown ensured plenty of headlines when he took on a batch of Carlton players with both fists blazing.

The VFL's decision to allow players to leave a club without a clearance after 10 calendar years' service sparked a summer of intense speculation. The rule would later be changed to restrict automatic releases to clubs outside the VFL, but in late 1972 some of the biggest names in football swapped colors.

North Melbourne had given a hint that it was prepared to go all-out for success by recruiting Barassi as coach and now the Roos grabbed Geelong's Doug Wade, Essendon's Barry Davis and South's John Rantall to boost their side. There was no way a team could have expected to gain such readymade champions in an instant, but North made the most of the new rule and immediately transformed its status from chopping block (one win in 1972) to finals aspirant. North had an energetic president in former star Allen Aylett, the best fundraiser in the game in Barry Cheatley and, of course, Barassi.

The Roos were innovative and forward-thinking. They had Lady Cilento, an expert on diet, address players before the season.

As North chased 10-year players, other clubs galvanised themselves into action. Melbourne spent the most on one man when it netted Carl Ditterich for a reported $62,000. The Demons also payed St Kilda $20,000 plus two players - Robert and Bruce Elliott.

At Collingwood the 1972 Brownlow medallist Len Thompson announced he had retired and the Magpies also looked like losing another ruckman, Graeme Jenkin, to Essendon. Eventually Jenkin stayed, but his hopes of being number one ruckman were jolted when Thompson came to terms with the club. The 10-year rule had caused chaos and the predicament of Footscray typified the shambles that had developed. The Bulldogs lost rover George Bissett to Collingwood at a cost of $9,000 and had to recruit Carlton's Adrian Gallagher for $24,000 to replace him. VFL directors, who had voted it in to avoid court action under restraint of trade laws, were severely embarrassed by the shemozzle.

When the season finally got under way coaches tackled the new 45-metre centre diamond rule. Hawthorn's style of crowding the centre had been a major catalyst to its introduction, and coach John Kennedy stunned purists in a practice game in Adelaide when he lined up 16 men outside the dia-

North Melbourne had given a hint that it was prepared to go all-out for success by recruiting Barassi as coach.

mond and sent them charging downfield. He didn't pursue the tactic in a VFL game.

Collingwood again dominated the first part of the season with 14 wins from the first 15 games. New chum North Melbourne scored a sensational win over the Magpies at VFL Park when full-forward Doug Wade kicked a goal after the siren following a mark and a 15-yard penalty. The Roos made a big run for the finals and had strengthened their side by more than just the 10-year players. Ex-Brunswick star Wayne Schimmelbusch and Sandgropers John Burns and Richard Michalczyk added to the team's depth.

Footscray mates Bernie Quinlan and Barry Round. Years later the two close friends would share a Brownlow Medal - as players for Fitzroy and Sydney respectively.

Hawthorn was still in contention for a finals place late in the year, but as in 1972 lost a vital game at home to St Kilda. The Hawks produced a desperate trump card the next week when Peter Hudson returned for the do-or-die clash with Collingwood. He arrived in movie-star style by helicopter after flying in to Tullamarine from Tasmania, and although he was carrying considerable excess poundage and lacked pace, it was obvious the football brain was as alert as ever.

Stumping on one leg, he had two goals on the board within four minutes. He wanted to come off then as his knee reacted to the pressure, but there was more to come. He had six goals by half-time and finished with 8.3 for the game taking care of four different opponents along the way. It was "Boy's Own" stuff, but sadly for Hawthorn it wasn't enough to win the game. The Hawks missed the five and contemplated their future at their new headquarters at Princes Park.

During the year the ill-fated Footypools betting scheme was launched, but despite being revised to make it more attractive the scheme was given the thumbs down by the football public.

The pace of the game meant collisions could cause serious damage and none was more brutal than the incident involving North's Sam Kekovich and Carlton's Brent Crosswell. Crosswell ended up in hospital for two weeks after his nose was smashed and doctors struggled to stop the bleeding.

Physical confrontation wasn't restricted to players either and Ron Barassi was in hot water when he came to grips with Essendon's playing coach Des Tuddenham during a quarter-time break. He was given a severe reprimand and Tuddenham a warning by the Tribunal.

Barassi's North missed the finals, but it had been a hugely successful year for the club. To cap off the season, Keith Greig became the first Roo to win a Brownlow.

Collingwood, which led the ladder and only lost three times for the season, promptly lost both finals in another inglorious September display. Star full-forward Peter McKenna was not picked for the preliminary final against Richmond and the club said he was "ill". Later McKenna denied that there was anything wrong with him and controversy again brewed at Victoria Park. McKenna was replaced by 16-year-old youngster Rene Kink. Kink kicked three goals, but it wasn't enough to save the Magpies from being bundled out by a Richmond team inspired by

Royce Hart. Hart was carrying a knee injury and was placed on the bench as a precaution. When his team lagged by six goals at half-time he was thrown into the fray and turned the game around.

The Tigers entered the grand final intent on revenge for the humiliating loss to Carlton a year earlier. The game got off to a sensational start when Carlton captain-coach John Nicholls was up-ended by Richmond's Laurie Fowler. Later in the quarter the Blues' star full-back Geoff Southby was flattened by Neil Balme. The incidents left Nicholls groggy for the rest of the day and Southby did not return after half-time. Richmond led by four goals at half-time and despite a Carlton fightback, eventually won the flag by 30 points.

Richmond was a powerful and worthy premier. It had great players and household names in Royce Hart, Ian Stewart, Francis Bourke, Kevin Bartlett and Kevin Sheedy and coach Hafey had built a reputation of being able to mesh " malcontents" from other clubs into his team structure. The 1973 flag side included Robert McGhie (Footscray), Stephen Rae (St Kilda), Ian Stewart (St Kilda) and Paul Sproule (Essendon) as well as Wayne Walsh who had originally been a Tiger before crossing to South and then returning to Punt Road.

History was made at the tribunal during 1973 when television evidence was accepted for the first time. St Kilda made the breakthrough in its defence of rover Ian George, but the landmark move made little difference to the result as George copped a two-week suspension.

Over the following summer the decision was made to form the VFL Players' Association to protect players' rights. It was a significant move which was not welcomed by many clubs, and even as football enters the 1990s the thought of a players' union grates with many officials. Although the player traffic was nothing like the hectic criss-crossing of the previous year there was still plenty of activity and Graeme Jenkin at last crossed to Essendon in a swap

deal with John Williams and South's John Pitura announced that he wanted to join Richmond. The seemingly interminable Pitura saga dragged on for more than a year. During that time he briefly returned to South and played several games before winning a clearance the following season. He never regained his top form at Richmond and fans wondered whether it had all been worthwhile.

Richmond was never one to rest on its laurels on the recruiting front and unveiled its latest acquisition - the controversial West Australian Mal Brown. It wasn't all plain sailing for the Tigers. Ian Stewart had doubts over whether he wanted to continue and even a petition from hundreds of fans did not sway him at first. He came back, but after seven games decided he had had enough.

The Tigers had a fight on their hands at the League table too, when president Ian Wilson and administrator Alan Schwab criticised the League over TV rights and VFL Park. Wilson was censured by fellow directors, but there was a widespread feeling that the strongest on-field club was trying to run the show on the other side of the fence as well.

North's frustration at being toppled by lowly South on the opening day bubbled over when Ron Barassi was reported by a boundary umpire for abusive behaviour. The Roos fought back strongly in the next weeks and surged to the top with some big wins. One of the more sensational efforts included a 10-goal burst by Sam Kekovich against South.

Big improver for the year was Footscray which had it best season for many years. Carlton had started the season poorly, but in the later weeks fought out an engrossing battle with the Bulldogs for fifth place. When the two teams met in a showdown at Western Oval in round 19, Carlton threw away its chances with atrocious kicking for goal. The Bulldogs had an inspiring leader in Laurie Sandilands and had a good group of recruits such as Ray Huppatz, Kelvin Templeton, Ted Whitten junior and ex-Melbourne man Greg Parke. Footscray made the finals for the

"More serious was the ugly brawl at Windy Hill on May 18. The incident snowballed and involved most players, plus officials, umpires, police and spectators."

Richmond committeeman Neil Busse restrains Graeme Richmond after the Essendon-Richmond brawl.

first time since 1961, but was overrun by Collingwood in the elimination final.

Richmond, usually a slow-starter, began well. Coach Tom Hafey could only shake his head in amazement when two of his players, Ricky McLean and Kevin Morris, were stranded on Port Phillip Bay all night after their boat's engine failed. Morris had to withdraw from the senior side for the big game with St Kilda.

More serious was the ugly brawl at Windy Hill on May 18. It began just before half-time when Mal Brown tangled with Essendon's Graeme Jenkin. The incident snowballed and involved most players, plus officials, umpires, police and spectators. Essendon fitness adviser Jim Bradley was knocked out and had a broken jaw, and Richmond's Brian Roberts was injured by a flying beer can. A VFL investigation resulted in Bomber officials Bradley and Laurie Ashley being suspended for six weeks each. Essendon defender Ron Andrews was outed for six weeks, Richmond's Mal Brown was suspended for a week and teammate Stephen Parsons went out for four. A couple of days later Tiger director Graeme Richmond was fined $2000 and suspended until the end of the year, but both actions were later withdrawn. Parsons and Richmond were later charged by police over the brawl, but were cleared.

The suspensions united the club and officials claimed there was a vendetta against the Tigers by the other clubs. The siege mentality was a potent force in Richmond's quest for back-to-back flags and the Tigers entered the finals as raging hot favorites. North Melbourne was a clear second and had been strengthened by interstate recruits Barry Cable and Malcolm Blight. The Roos won through to their second ever grand final appearance with a fighting win over Hawthorn in the preliminary Final, but looked out of their depth against the finals hardened Richmond.

Critics wondered whether the arrogant Tigers were the best team of all time. They bristled with talent on every line. Hafey had developed a balanced and settled unit which looked capable of a long stay at the top of the table. Professional and close-knit, the Tigers were the dominant team of the era with four flags in the space of eight seasons.

TUCK AND MATTHEWS: A LETHAL COMBINATION

Physically there could not have been two men more different. Leigh Matthews, squat, short legged and barrell-chested, and Michael Tuck, lean, sinewy and gnarled.

Yet the differences in physique proved there is no physical formula for longevity in football as both men enjoyed remarkably long careers. Matthews and Tuck led Hawthorn during the club's greatest sustained era of success and embodied the qualities that made the Hawks the envy of other clubs. Leigh Matthews played the game in a totally fearless manner, but believed the words of his famous coach John Kennedy who said anyone without fear was either superhuman or stupid. Real courage was being able to overcome that fear.

Leigh and his brother Kelvin who also played VFL football were raised on the right football principles by their father Ray who coached country side Langwarrin and later Frankston under-17s. The brothers showed out at Chelsea and it wasn't long before Leigh was under the scrutiny of VFL recruiting officers. He joked in a self-deprecating way about his lack of pace and high marking ability, but there was no-one who had better judgment or anticipation. At five feet 10 inches and 13 and a half stone he had an unusual build for a rover, but he was a powerhouse who left a trail of crumpled bodies and reputations in his wake.

He wasn't an unfair player....just totally single minded in making the ball his only object. When he landed an unfortunate punch late in his career that floored Geelong's Neville Bruns the case went to court and it was a disappointing way for Matthews

Hawthorn's Michael Tuck beats St Kilda's Jeff Dunne to get his kick.

to end his playing career. He caused a huge controversy in West Australia when he legitimately ran through Perth hero Barry Cable in a state match.

Early in his career he was nicknamed "Lethal" and it was a tag that applied to his goalscoring capacity as much as his playing style. When he first joined Hawthorn, Matthews teamed up with the terrier Peter Crimmins in the roving duties and spent the greater part of his time in the forward zone. After Crimmins' tragic death, Matthews took over the top spot and late in his career he returned to forward line with telling effect. One figure indicates his stature in the game. He won eight best and fairest awards at Hawthorn in an era when Hawthorn was the dominant club in the competition. He captained the Hawks from 1981 to 1985, a reign which included the 1983 flag. He had already been a member of the 1971, 1976 and 1978 premierships.

In 1986 his football career entered a new phase when he became coach of Collingwood and started on the path that culminated in breaking the most famous drought in League football. When the Magpies won the 1990 flag the club's president proclaimed Matthews coach for life, but "forever" is not a word that figures prominently in the coaching lexi-

con and in 1995 Matthews career at Victoria Park came to its end.

The Coodabeen Champions parodied many tunes in lauding VFL footballers, but none was more suited than the "Old Man River" lyric adapted to describe Michael Tuck's football career. Tuck just kept flowing along as one of the game's most valuable yet often unheralded players. A wiry player, he was deceptively athletic and in the early 1970s when there was a competition called the VFL Olympics he displayed his talent. Many League players doubled up as pro runners, but Tuck always won the 400 metres event with ease.

John Kennedy, his first coach, recalled that Tuck looked too skinny at 10 stone (63kg) to make the grade. Kennedy did observe that Tuck was always strong for his body weight, that he had exceptional ball-handling skills and could run all day. Over the years he managed to add a couple of stone to his playing weight, but the results of a gym program and extra food didn't make much difference. While the bulk did not come, Tuck was able to add strength to his body and that made him an even tougher proposition.

He was tried as a full-forward in his early days, and was used as a winger and defender before he found his niche as a ruck-rover. Eventually he became the best of his type in the League. Tuck captained Victoria and took over the reins at Glenferrie after Matthews retired, but strangely never won the club's best and fairest. He came second on six occasions.

When he first came to the Hawks Tuck had the appearance of a country bumpkin in his loose fitting shorts and big plumber's boots, but in time he came to epitomise the quiet, hard-working approach that was the club's trademark. Never a man for many words he was acutely aware of the need not to let people down, and his dry sense of humor made him immensely popular.

The constancy of Tuck's footballing style was mirrored in his approach to life. For 14 years he drove the same battered old Holden that had first transported him from his father's dairy farm in Berwick. The bushy beard that adorned his chin in later years added to the good ol' country boy image.

Hawthorn's opening ruck combination of Don Scott, Tuck and Matthews was the most feared in the League and fuelled the side. Tuck was a member of seven premiership sides - four of which were as captain. After the 1991 success Tuck wanted to continue, but Hawthorn said it was time to pull stumps and the loyal Tuck gritted his teeth and called it a day.

TED WHITTEN: MR FOOTBALL

Whenever the bar room talk turns to the greatest player ever to play Australian Rules you can be assured the name Ted Whitten will be at the forefront. Along with that enormous ability Whitten was also a larger than life personality.

Whitten was undoubtedly Footscray's most famed player and men of all teams who played with or against him regard him as the finest all-round footballer of his era. Whitten was a prodigious kick, a flawless mark and had ground and hand skills that were unequalled. He could play in any position on the field and was such a brilliant player that a magazine poll to pick the best player in each position on the ground resulted in him coming out on top both as a centre half-forward and centre half-back.

He developed his skills as a youngster in the streets of Yarraville and played his first games with local club Braybrook in the Footscray District League's under-17 competition. On Sundays he would play open age football for Collingwood amateurs in a competition renowned for its toughness. The Sunday team was coached by Charlie Utting, a former Collingwood star who urged him to try out at Victoria Park, but the Magpies cast an eye over him and said he needed to build up his body strength. "Come back in a few years, when you put on a stone or two" was the advice ringing in his ears as he left

Ted Whitten in 1964. From a 'Mobil Football' card

Victoria Park, but Footscray had other ideas and invited him on the end of season trip to Tasmania. The next season he was playing for the Bulldogs, the team he had supported all his life.

In his first game he confronted the fearsome "Mopsy" Fraser and had an instant baptism when he extended his hand in the customary manner. Fraser kicked him straight in the ankle! Moments later Whitten got to the ball first and heard the threatening Fraser say :"Don't do anything silly kid!". Whitten recalled in later years that he stopped dead in his tracks and Fraser cannoned into him to give away a free. As he lined up for goal Fraser warned him that kicking a goal would be a big mistake. Whitten sent his first kick through for a goal which enraged the volatile Fraser. Whitten ended the day being carted off on a stretcher just before three-quarter-time.

It wasn't long before Whitten's genius became

obvious to the whole League and the nation. Footscray reached the finals in his first year and Whitten was doing National Service training. It looked like he would be unable to play because of army duties, but Prime Minister Menzies over-ruled his defence minister and cleared the way for Whitten to line up in the team.

Whitten had tremendous flair but his showmanship and sharp tongue often incurred the wrath of umpires. That probably explained why he never won a Brownlow Medal. Although his best Brownlow placing was a fourth, they knew his worth at Footscray and he won the club best and fairest four times. The first of those was in the club's premiership year of 1954. Whitten was one of the best players in the grand final win and the following year made his Victorian debut. It was an association that would span 29 appearances, and endures into the 1990s when he lovingly ruled the roost as chairman of selectors.

From the outset he cherished wearing the Big V and even risked serious injury to make his interstate debut. He had been hit in the eye a week before the side was selected and was told that he only had to perform reasonably in the following match to be selected. A doctor told him he could be blinded by another knock in the eye, but he played anyway. Late in the game he received a tremendous whack to the eye, but realised it was not the injured one. Sporting two shiners he made his state debut.

In early 1957 Footscray sacked Charlie Sutton, who had captain-coached the club to the flag, and replaced him with Whitten. It was a difficult time for the 23-year-old Whitten as he met early resistance from older players, but in the end his leadership and inspiring football won their confidence. He stammered and stuttered through his first address before Sutton appeared at the door. The room went dead quiet as the little man walked across to wish his replacement good luck.

The innovative Whitten got his team to perfect the flick pass. By 1961 he had a young team in the grand final, but the Bulldogs were overwhelmed by Hawthorn. "We had a side that was just capable of winning a few matches a year and we needed to try something different," he recalled in later years. In Whitten's opinion the 1961 team would not have even made the finals if not for the flick-pass. Whitten's lightning reflexes meant he could mark and fire out the ball before his feet even touched the ground.

Charlie Sutton took back the reins as non-playing coach for two years in 1967-68 then Whitten resumed as captain-coach until the end of his playing career. He retired as a player early in 1970 after breaking the long-standing VFL games record of 321 held by Dick Reynolds.

His coaching career came to an end after the 1971 season, but he never lost touch with Footscray or with football. When the Bulldogs had a coaching crisis in 1978 he helped stand-in coach Don McKenzie and maintained his media involvement.

Whitten had the rare mix of tremendous skill and unlimited toughness. Whenever one of his Bulldogs was on the end of rough treatment, "E.J." would be there in a flash to even the score. But few opponents took it to heart and his popularity was universal. The football community was shocked to hear of his battle with cancer and there was not a dry eye in the house when he was driven on a lap of honor around the MCG before the 1995 state of origin game. A few weeks later, "E.J" was dead at just 62 years of age. A tide of grief overcame the football world.

He had lived life to the full and had truly been a towering figure. In an interview recorded on the Coodabeen Champions Legends tape a couple of years before his death, he said: "A lot of people have said, and I hear them say to others, if you had the chance to turn the clock back and start again, would you like to change anything? My answer is 'No' - I was quite happy the way it went."

Even with eyes shut Jesaulenko could outwit the opposition.

JESSA: A TOUCH OF MAGIC

"Jessa" is a nickname instantly recognisable to football fans all around Australia, but in truth it belongs to a man whose name is Alex Esaulenko.

Immigration officials inadvertently added the "J" when the family arrived in Australia and it has stayed there ever since. Jesaulenko became one of the most famous names in football and will remain so as long as the game is played.

Alex Jesaulenko was a footballing genius who undoubtedly ranks among the best to have played the game. His ball-handling wizardry, cat-like balance and spectacular marking thrilled crowds for one and a half decades.

Born of a Ukranian father and a Russian mother in Salzburg, Austria, he could have turned his skill to any ball sport. When he was four his parents migrated to Australia yet he was drawn to soccer, then

rugby, as a youngster. He did not play Australian Rules till the age of 14, and then ran down the field eluding opponents and kicking a goal before he was informed that he needed to bounce the ball. As a teenager he chauffered visiting Geelong stars Polly Farmer and Alistair Lord around Canberra and told them one day he would make VFL football.

North Melbourne actually won the race for his signature only to discover that ACT players could not be signed, and in the end he went to Carlton after acting on the suggestion of his wife's father who was president of the Manuka-Eastlake club. Despite a relatively late start at the age of 22 his coolness under pressure and tremendous ball-winning ability made him an instant star in the VFL. He started as a centre half-forward and came third in the Brownlow in his first year, a placing he earned again in 1970.

Jesaulenko then went to full-forward and kicked

115 goals in 1970 to become the first Blue to top the ton. It was an achievement all the more remarkable by the fact he played a number of games that year at centre half-forward and even spent time on the flank.

Early in his career he harbored a quiet ambition to play in defence and when back problems reduced his leap he transformed into a half-back flanker and succeeded brilliantly, as he did with everything else in his career. Strangely, it was in that first year as a defender in 1975 that he won his only best and fairest at Carlton.

His time at Princes Park was not without its tribulations. He applied for an open clearance when a pay dispute was unresolved in early 1977, but greater ructions lay ahead. Early in 1978 Carlton's coach Ian Stewart quit and after nearly a month of deliberating, Carlton turned almost reluctantly to Jesaulenko. President George Harris admitted later that he didn't think Jesaulenko would make a coach, and most observers thought Jesaulenko was too much "one of the boys".

Yet he guided the side to a first-up win and to a place in the finals. At first he had declared that he would retire as a player upon his appointment, but then decided to keep going and by 1979 he had the Blues in a grand final and despite being carried off with a broken bone in the ankle late in the game was there at the end to receive the premiership cup - the last man to captain-coach a VFL club to the flag. It was his fourth flag after the successes of 1968, 1970, and 1972.

Carlton's most bitter argument in history split the club in two. Jesaulenko sided with president George Harris and when Harris was ousted Jesaulenko went too. Several clubs wanted him and in the end he chose to go to St Kilda as a player only. Two weeks into the season St Kilda sacked Mike Patterson and installed Jesaulenko as coach and the old magic lifted the Saints to a draw in their first game and a win the next week. But times were lean at St Kilda and the club never rose above 10th place in Jesaulenko's three years at the helm.

After that Jesaulenko coached in Queensland and back in his native Canberra and had seemingly drifted into football's backwater when Carlton dramatically recalled him as coach in mid-1989 to replace Robert Walls, and yet again the Carlton hero led the side to a first-up win. The magic was still there and the prodigal son had returned with a vengeance. But Carlton had little patience when results did not come and he was sacked straight after the 1990 season although he had managed to halt the club's decline. Despite the setbacks Jesaulenko's standing as one of Carlton's favorite sons could never be tarnished.

Chapter Fourteen

1975-1979

North, night football and Rocky

The influence of television on the game had grown considerably by 1975 and the advent of color TV heightened the emphasis.

Color sets achieved phenomenal sales, and sport of all description became an increasingly marketable commodity. Satellite coverage of international sporting events became commonplace and the VFL introduced its properties division to cash in on the spin-offs from TV exposure. Clubs began to chase big companies for the all-important sponsorship dollar, and Richmond set the trend by signing Carlton and United Breweries as major sponsor for $50,000. But Channel Seven threw a spanner in the works when it said it would not televise games if sponsors' logos were plastered all over jumpers. The TV station was beginning to have a larger say in proceedings, but was knocked back when it tried to push for a pre-season night competition.

Clubs introduced colored shorts for all teams to spruce up the game for the TV audience, and the new season got under way with the restricted centre area altered from a diamond to a square. The tribunal came down hard on offenders after a torrid first round, but a week later the football world was stunned when Footscray's South Australian recruit Neil Sachse suffered horrific injuries in an incident at the Western Oval. Sachse became a quadriplegic and it was the worst injury in the VFL's history.

The tribunal had its busiest night of the year after the savage Essendon-Carlton clash at Windy Hill

when eight players were outed for a total of 14 weeks. The Bombers had a difficult year and struggled after captain-coach Des Tuddenham broke his leg in June. At the end of the year Tuddenham was dumped as coach.

Richmond was still agitating at the VFL table, but reneged on a threat to take the VFL's clearance rules to court. Finally the Pitura case was settled and he was cleared to the Tigers, who were then fined $2000 for trying to win his services without South's permission.

The VFL rubbed its hands with glee when 77,770 people crammed into VFL Park to see the Anzac Day clash between Carlton and Essendon. Not so happy were the fans caught in the one and half hour traffic snarl leaving Waverley. The League directors voted against Sunday games, but the seed had been sown.

It was a year which saw yet another impressive crop of interstate recruits, and the most outstanding, and flamboyant among them was Collingwood's Phil Carman. Wearing a flashy new pair of white boots the former South Australian blitzed St Kilda with an 11-goal performance late in the year that sank St Kilda's finals chances and kept the Magpies alive. He missed eight games after breaking a bone in the foot during the state game yet still managed to finish only three votes behind the Brownlow winner.

> The League directors voted against Sunday games, but the seed had been sown.

Mark of a champion. One of hundreds of fingertip marks pulled in by Footscray's Gary Dempsey.

Outsiders put this down to the after-effects of the Pitura case. The club had traded Brian Roberts, Graham Teasdale and Francis Jackson for the South man and it was said to have damaged team morale. Roberts, affectionately known as "The Whale", was one of the club's true characters and he showed that he also had more than a little football ability when he was best afield for the Swans in his first outing in the new colors.

Clubs had always had trouble beating Geelong at the distant Kardinia Park, but St Kilda struck a different hurdle when the team bus broke down on the way to the ground and forced a late start to the game.

Hawthorn finished on top of the ladder after the home and away games, and Hawk fans main interest in the closing weeks had centred upon Peter Crimmins' game bid to regain a place in the team. The courageous little rover had played in the early matches, before entering hospital for cancer treatment, and in the end he was unable to make the team. Hawthorn narrowly beat North in the second semi, but the Roos gained another chance when they rolled Richmond in the preliminary final.

From the outset North's little men ran rings around a bigger, leaden-footed opposition and Hawthorn showed an unusual lack of discipline. North's Keith Greig, John Burns and Barry Cable were brilliant and the side had a big contribution from Brent Crosswell, who had looked to be a light of other days when he crossed from Carlton earlier in the year. John Rantall played a key role in tagging Leigh Matthews and the shutdown was typical of the way the game unfolded.

North bolted to its first flag by almost 10 goals, and it was yet another notch in Barassi's belt. He was freely dubbed "Supercoach" by the press and the tag was justified. North excelled at the fast, play-on game that had its genesis in Carlton's famous 1970 grand final win, and the VFL's decision to introduce two field umpires was an indication of the pace of the modern game.

North's campaign to improve on its second placing in 1974 started on a lacklustre note as the Roos lost the first three games. They even dropped champion full-forward Doug Wade and tried to turn around the losing trend before it took hold. Gradually the Roos clawed their way back to third place and put themselves in with a chance. They beat Richmond in a mid-season grand final rematch, and although the Tigers were still powerful they seemed to lack the killer instinct of the previous two years.

Teams which had struggled for years to make a mark on the VFL scene showed rapid improvement in 1976 and helped to make it one of the most evenly contested seasons of all time. After 15 rounds Collingwood, lying in the uncommon position of bottom place, was only two wins out of the five. The Magpies stayed there and collected their first wooden spoon after a turbulent year in which the club tried every possible way to destroy itself.

A player revolt brewed over contracts even before the first match and coach Murray Weideman threatened to resign early in the year after a dispute with president Ern Clarke. Then former captain Wayne Richardson was stood down for four weeks by the club committee, breaking a personal sequence of 128 consecutive games.

Coaches grabbed more than their usual share of headlines in 1976 and it started when John Nicholls announced his shock decision to quit Carlton's top post on the eve of the opening round. David Parkin and Alex Jesaulenko were both touted as contenders for the job, but both missed out. Ironically each man would later lead Carlton to premiership success, but that was a long way off and former Melbourne player Ian Thorogood ended up guiding the Blues to the top of the list at the end of the home and away games.

Thorogood was one of three first-year coaches to lift their sides into the finals as Rod Olsson (Geelong) and Bill Goggin (Footscray) also steered their teams into September. Olsson's Geelong came from no-where this year and much of the success was due to the big goalkicking effort of full-forward Larry Donohue.

At the end of the previous season Donohue had played only 22 games in three years and weighed a hulking 17 stone, yet a rigorous summer fitness program led to him booting 105 goals and topping the goalkicking list.

South's new coach Ian Stewart began his reign by sacking ruckman "Whale" Roberts over his train-

Len Thompson, Brownlow Medallist in 1972, marks strongly against Melbourne.

ing habits. Roberts, who had run seventh in the Brownlow only a few months earlier, tried to win a clearance back to Richmond before eventually drifting out of the game. Stewart's year also included being disciplined over criticism of umpires, but his young side managed to score the occasional impressive win and none gave him more joy than beating his old club Richmond by eight points. For the first time in three decades the Swans beat Collingwood twice during the year.

Stewart's old mentor Tom Hafey was another who landed in hot water when he abused a field umpire at half-time during a game, and after Hafey was fined a paltry $150 by the League the umpires demanded an apology from Richmond. A strike of umpires was only averted by a special meeting at VFL House.

South's new coach Ian Stewart began his reign by sacking ruckman "Whale" Roberts over his training habits.

Reigning premier North Melbourne had an action packed year both on and off the field. On the ground North fashioned a couple of amazing victories. The Roos were reduced to 17 men in the final term against Essendon, but overcame a strong breeze and got home. A week later Malcolm Blight turned on a mercurial last quarter against Carlton with three goals in time-on including a ball-bursting goal after the siren to snatch the points. Erratic forward Sam Kekovich toyed with the idea of trying out for gridiron team the Los Angeles Rams before deciding to stay put, but then injured himself in a car smash.

In mid-August North's plans suffered a jolt when coach Barassi was involved in a road accident in the country and was laid up in hospital with chest and leg injuries. His friend, St Kilda Brownlow medallist Neil Roberts, was injured more seriously in the crash, but both eventually recovered. Barassi was even back by the finals, on crutches, and when his side put in a disappointing first quarter he drew a huge gasp from the crowd by hurling a crutch to the turf in anger.

No team typified this rollercoaster year better than St Kilda. The Saints could not string victories together and usually followed the destruction of a top team with an inexplicable loss to a lower side. They staged one of the more amazing comebacks of the year against Hawthorn at Princes Park after trailing by 14 points to 58 at one stage in the second term. The resurrection was sparked by the KO of tiny rover Paul Callery in a pack. Callery lay motionless on the turf and the crowd lapsed into hushed silence as it realised that he was badly injured. He

had to be revived by trainers and could have died on the ground.

Incensed St Kilda players thought he had been hit by the opposition, but it turned out that he had accidentally collided with teammate Gary Colling. Still, coach Jeans wasn't about to question the reason for motivation and the Saints clawed their way back into the match before eventually cruising to a handy win. In true character the Saints lost the next game to bottom side Fitzroy.

Hawthorn entered the finals primed for a big assault on the flag and crushed North and Carlton in the first two weeks. The Roos pipped Carlton by a point in the preliminary final, but did not have the all-round talent that had taken them to a flag a year earlier. Hawthorn held the whip-hand from the start despite wayward kicking and North could not break the Hawks' hold on the flag. Hawthorn had conclusively proved its superiority in the finals and had inspiring leaders in Don Scott and Leigh Matthews. With no apparent weakness and several improving youngsters the Hawks were assured of a big say for a long time to come. Coach John Kennedy said the win had not been motivated by revenge although he conceded he had felt the humiliation of the 1975 loss.

Collingwood had never finished last in a VFL season and decided that tradition had to be abandoned in the modern era. Tom Hafey had been the subject of endless back-stabbing at Richmond and he finally decided to reject the club's contract. A chance meeting between Hafey and Collingwood president John Hickey had convinced Hickey that the club had a chance to win his services and in October 1976 Hafey signed a three-year contract to become the first non-Collingwood player to coach the club. He insisted on fierce discipline and relentless training and it wasn't long before the results started to show. The players loved him and developed a team spirit that had been missing at Victoria Park for years.

Keith Greig swoops on the ball to elude Hawthorn's Leon Rice. North and Hawthorn staged many titanic battles from the early 1970s.

The Magpies had not recruited extensively, but three new boys, Rick Barham and West Australians Stan Magro and Kevin Worthington, became key players. Hafey also rekindled the enthusiasm of players like Len Thompson and the Richardson brothers who had seemed to be on their last legs. By round six, when Collingwood inflicted the biggest hiding ever on Carlton, the ghosts of 1976 had already been laid to rest. The black and whites finished on top of the ladder at the end of the home and away games and thus completed the biggest turnaround in VFL history by going from last to first in 12 months.

There were plenty of other attention grabbers in this season which was marred by the wettest June in 118 years. Grounds were quagmires and the VFL even cancelled reserve grade curtain-raisers to ease the pressure. There was talk of postponing one round but 10 of the 12 clubs voted in favour of going ahead

with the round. A helicopter was used at the Albert Park ground to dry it.

South Melbourne prospered under the coaching of Ian Stewart. The triple Brownlow medallist was often unorthodox in approach and executed a master-stroke when forward Graham Teasdale was so depressed by his drop in form that he wanted to go home to the bush. Stewart tried the springheeled Teasdale in the ruck and the move was such a success that Teasdale won the Brownlow and the Swans made the finals. Half way through the year South came to an arrangement with Geelong to lease fullback John Scarlett for the remainder of the year.

The VFL moved quickly to outlaw future leasing deals. South's interstate recruiting plans hit a snag when South Australian David Young had to threaten to take out a Federal Court action under restraint of trade action before he could play. In the

Let's adjust that headband. Phil Carman offers a hand to Bruce Doull in 1978.

choice of letting the point stand (thus giving a draw) or having another kick. From 30 metres out he was a certainty to score and would probably kick a goal, yet the man who had sunk Carlton in a similar situation the previous year, inexplicably, missed.

Much of the early-season interest focused on Peter Hudson's return to Hawthorn. Hudson left the comfort of life running a Hobart tavern to pick up the threads of his career and achieved his target with stunning success. Hudson passed 100 goals yet again and the Hawks under new coach David Parkin finished only one game behind Collingwood. The Hawks even managed an amazing scoreline of 25.41-191 against St Kilda - an average of one scoring shot every one and a half minutes.

Night football resumed with clubs competing for $200,000 prizemoney during the season, but there were plenty of injuries in the wet conditions. Richmond's Peter Laughlin and Collingwood's Russell Ohlsen suffered badly gashed knees due to exposed sprinkler heads. The VFL, meanwhile, was more concerned about facial injuries and asked clubs not to allow photographs of players with head injuries.

In the finals series the thrills came thick and fast. Collingwood continued its form of the home and away series and steamed into the grand final with a two-point win over Hawthorn in the second semifinal. But the Magpies paid a big price when the brilliant Phil Carman was suspended for two weeks on a striking charge.

North Melbourne crushed a flat Hawthorn in the preliminary final and the Roos faced Collingwood in the grand final. The Collingwood dream of winning its first flag in 19 years looked certain to be realised with only half an hour to go when North, with only four goals on the board, trailed by 27 points. Barassi swung defenders David Dench and Daryl Sutton into attack and in a flash the move paid dividends. By the 23-minute mark North had shot to the lead by seven points and it seemed Collingwood was finished. But at the 32-minute

end the Croweaters relented, but it was a sign of things to come. Melbourne captain Stan Alves was embroiled in a bitter wrangle to win a release to North Melbourne before winning his clearance in the middle of May and Richmond's Kevin Morris was targeted by Collingwood after walking out on Richmond.

North Melbourne's ever-active recruiting team was always on the alert for new talent, and there were rumours that the Roos were prepared to spend $100,000 to win a clearance for West Australian Ross Glendinning. At the other end of the scale the club severed its often troubled link with Sam Kekovich. He crossed Barassi once too often at training and was given his marching orders. He was snapped up by Collingwood early in June.

The Roos' clashes with Hawthorn had become highpoints of the era and the two sides fought out a titanic struggle at boggy Arden Street. Hawthorn led by a point when North pushed the ball forward for Malcolm Blight to kick a point. He was pushed after kicking as the siren rang and was given the mark the Magpies made a last surge and the bony frame of Ross "Twiggy" Dunne pulled down a mark in the middle of a huge pack and goaled to tie the grand final for only the second time in history.

In the replay North skipped away early, but Collingwood dragged itself back into the game with four goals just before the long break. A gripping third quarter went goal for goal until the final minutes when North kicked clear. Even then Collingwood refused to go down and was back to within 12 points by the nine-minute mark of the final term. The Magpies kept fighting to the bitter end, but North answered every challenge and won its second flag.

After many years of discussion the grand final was televised live to a huge audience throughout Australia. It was estimated that seven out of 10 Victorians watched the game and the VFL agreed to another direct telecast of the replay, but stressed the situation would be reviewed each year in future and was conditional on the match being a sell-out.

The major innovation in the rules for the 1978 season was the introduction of interchange reserves players which meant that players could return to the field after having left it. Some coaches such as Ron Barassi and Rod Olsson tried to use it has a tactical weapon to change ruckmen, but the novelty of that approach soon wore off. The game's huge drawing power continued to snowball and attendances topped the three million mark for the first time.

North Melbourne looked to be at the peak of its form under Barassi in the early part of the season. An already strong team had been bolstered by the versatile brilliance of WA powerhouse Ross Glendinning, but a mid-season slump of four losses in a row stunned coach Barassi and cast doubts over his team's capacity to reach the grand final for the fifth year in a row.

In the opening part of the season wooden spooner St Kilda looked to be the big improver. Former Richmond ruckman Mike Patterson took over as coach and soon showed his liking for aggres-

sive big-man power. Carl Ditterich and Jeff Sarau were two of the hardest men in football and the addition of costly WA recruit Garry Sidebottom along with speedy ruck-rovers Russell Greene and Trevor Barker, made the Saints' ruck squadron the most feared combination in the game. After six rounds St Kilda had risen to sixth place and kicked a new club record score.

An intensely physical game against Essendon exploded into controversy when three St Kilda players were reported and two Bombers carted off on stretchers. Essendon officials called St Kilda "Animals" after the game and lodged a complaint that Carl Ditterich had struck Terry Cahill during the game. St Kilda started legal action over the "Animals" jibe and for a couple of weeks a war of words raged between the two clubs. Eventually all actions were dropped.

The Saints had a potent side when they could get all players on the field, but injuries and suspensions revealed there was no depth at all. Fitzroy was another team which promised much in the early weeks only to suffer a series of heartbreaking near-misses. St Kilda sunk to the depths in a mid-season slump when Carl Ditterich went into a self-imposed exile and then Footscray thrashed it with a new VFL record score.

They broke the run with an unlikely, and controversial, win over North thanks to Robert Elliott's goal which many North players believed was touched. Several Roos had to be restrained as the umpires were escorted off by police, but the result stood and St Kilda's finals hopes kept flickering. The Saints had a chance up until the last round when they blitzed Carlton with devastating aggression at Moorabbin in front of a huge crowd.

The Blues had endured a season of astonishingly mixed fortunes. New coach Ian Stewart resigned af-

The VFL's attempts to play Sunday games were knocked back by the State Government. The League devised a way to get a foot in the door by playing two senior Sunday matches in Sydney.

Agony for Alex Jesaulenko in the dying stages of the 1979 grand final. The Blues' captain-coach badly injured his ankle and had to leave the field, but he soon experienced the joy of his side winning the flag.

ter only three games because of illness and Sergio Silvagni stood in for the next few weeks while the committee pondered the coaching position. In the end Alex Jesaulenko was chosen, almost reluctantly, and he tackled the task of lifting the side, eleventh with only one win from six games, into a credible finals contender. A first-up win over Collingwood was a great tonic and the Blues proceeded to win 13

of their next 15 games. Jesaulenko rekindled their enthusiasm and comradeship, but the other finals sides took note of their susceptibility to the physical game when St Kilda dismantled them in the last round.

Carlton got past Geelong in the first week of the finals, but Collingwood turned on the heat a week later and put the Blues out of contention. Ron Barassi celebrated his 50th game as a player or coach in the finals, but his North Melbourne side had a troubled finals series, losing Peter Keenan through a suspension after the second semi, then losing Brent Crosswell with a broken arm.

In the grand final Hawthorn's Mike Moncrieff booted two goals in the opening three minutes and the Hawks ran North ragged in a half-hour of football that set the Roos back on their heels. They fought back gamely, but all day it was an uphill battle and they could not get the breaks. In the end Don Scott and Leigh Matthews turned on the power and were aided by Peter Knights who had been sent up forward to recover from an injury and chipped in with two quick goals.

A much reported "leak" of the Brownlow Medal result tinged the end of the season with drama, but North's Malcolm Blight was a worthy winner. His happiness was shortlived as he spent much of the grand final cooling his heels on the interchange bench.

The VFL's attempts to play Sunday games were knocked back by the State Government and at one stage Carlton president George Harris even suggested the VFL play a Sunday game regardless. The League devised a way to get a foot in the door by playing two senior Sunday matches in Sydney and telecasting a reserve grade match on each of the other Sundays. The Commodore Cup was known derisively as the Comedy Cup by those cynical fans who saw it as yet another move to saturate the football market and force smaller opposition, the VFA, into the background. The VFA relied heavily on

Channel 0's TV coverage for publicity and income.

There was a hitch when the South Melbourne council stopped the VFL from playing its Commodore Cup games on the Albert Park ground and the matches had to be switched to Moorabbin. The VFA wasn't the only sporting body feeling the pinch and the Victorian Cricket Association was angry when the VFL season kicked off with a game on March 31, the earliest starting day ever.

Trying to invade Sydney was nothing new and the League had shown its missionary zeal as far back as 1903 in playing games for premiership points in the harbor city. North and Hawthorn played there in front of 31,000 people in June of 1979 and five weeks later Fitzroy and Richmond met on the Sydney Cricket Ground.

The legal profession assumed an ever-increasing role in the game and the VFL was jumpy about clearance regulations being tested in court. Carlton started Federal court proceedings to win clearances for two players from West Australian club Subiaco, but the case was settled out of court. Carlton was on the receiving end, too, when rover Rod Ashman took the club to the Federal Court to win a release, but he eventually dropped the bid and stayed at Princes Park. Carlton lodged a complaint with the VFL that North and tried to poach Ashman.

On the field Carlton made sure there were no false starts this time around and dominated the season with 19 wins from the 22 games. The Blues were amazingly consistent under Jesaulenko and had strength and speed all over the ground.

It was a time when the "Rocky" theme song echoed through dressing rooms across the land and clubs threw money around as if there were no tomorrow. North Melbourne went for broke in the recruiting stakes and in the first game fielded big names such as ex-Footscray Brownlow Medallist Gary Dempsey and high-priced interstate stars Russell Ebert, Graham Cornes and Kevin Bryant.

The public's perception of the VFL as high-

handed and greedy became an increasing feature of the football world and touchy VFL chiefs moved to censure the VFL Players' Association after it published a cartoon in its newsletter which depicted the League as greedy pigs. The cartoonist, Carlton player Rod Galt, was unrepentant even after being rebuked by his club president George Harris.

St Kilda was one club concerned with more earthy matters and when the team was on the wrong end of the biggest hiding in League history the Saints called a crisis meeting. The Saints had lost many players through retirement or transfer over summer and a first round win over reigning premier Hawthorn papered over the deficiencies. They were laid bare at Victoria Park when Collingwood bolted to a 178-point victory. Among the goalkickers in his debut that day was 17-year-old Peter Daicos.

South was another club in the depths of despair and members raised a petition calling for for an extraordinary general meeting to elect a new committee. The Swans were in dispute with star ruckman Graham Teasdale and rumors circulated that he was available to a club willing to spend $250,000. Carlton reportedly offered $200,000.

Former Saint Carl Ditterich took over the coaching post at Melbourne at the start of the year and was in top form until suspended. As a result of Melbourne's protests the VFL scrapped the outdated rule which prevented playing coaches from addressing their side on the field during suspensions. Ditterich discovered more of the reasons that coaches tore their hair out when he had trouble with Phil Carman. The two clashed at training and Carman was told to meet the coach afterwards for a discussion. He chose not to turn up and was promptly dropped for the next game. The big coach still had a sense of humor and when he fronted the tribunal, for once as a victim, he said: "You get a different reflection on life from this side of the table".

Playing matches in Sydney prompted suggestions that a club might be relocated there, but Fitzroy, considered a prime candidate, announced that the club would remain at Princes Park. A few days later the Lions emphasised their will to succeed and racked up a record score of 36.22-238 against Melbourne.

Essendon looked anything but a finals prospect in a 96-point loss to Fitzroy early in the year, but mounted a big run for the finals. When the Bombers reached the elimination final they found Fitzroy was just as merciless as it had been earlier in the year and the Lions won by 75 points.

The Lions had done well to reach the final, but Carlton and Collingwood were the dominant teams in September and they met for the flag on a wet and bleak afternoon. The conditions suited the desperate, hard-working Collingwood and the Magpies had Carlton in deep trouble when the Blues had not scored a goal 19 minutes into the second term. Carlton hit back with four goals just before half-time and set the scene for a titanic second half. Captain-coach Jesaulenko was carried off with an injury half way through the last term, but his side had the will-power to carry on without him.

In the last moments of the game Blue dynamo Wayne Harmes miskicked into attack then charged for the ball and punched it back into play just before it crossed the boundary line. It landed at Ken Sheldon's feet and he slammed through the crucial goal. Collingwood fans still say the ball was over the line when Harmes reached it but the argument is to no avail as Carlton entered the record books as premier.

Many clubs had plunged heavily into debt, but it was still surprising news to hear that St Kilda had accumulated debts of more than $750,000. The Saints sought salvation in the form of trucking magnate and ex-player Lindsay Fox who took over as club chairman in early September. The whole board stood down and other members of staff were dismissed including general manager Ken Murphy. Fox announced: "There's going to be the strongest discipline that you kids have known since your old man

probably smacked you across the backside." One of his moves was a decree that all Ballarat-based players had to shift to Melbourne and the Saints lost the services of star half-back Val Perovic, who refused to move to the city and was cleared to Carlton.

The Saints could only look at clubs like Carlton with green-eyed envy. The Blues were well administered, had virtually unlimited player depth, and had a premiership-winning coach. Everything, it seemed, was rosy in the Princes Park garden. All that was about to change in dramatic circumstances that would have been unimaginable when Alex Jesaulenko and "Percy" Jones proudly hoisted the premiership cup.

ROOS ON THE HOP

Getting a team off the bottom is a herculean task. Rising from rock bottom to top in five years is something else again.

North Melbourne did just that with the right blend of a sharp administration, the right coach at the right time and the ability to use a one-off rule to the maximum. North Melbourne is remembered as the prime beneficiary of the 10 year rule that enabled players to become free agents if they had a decade of service, but it should not be forgotten that the opening was there for any other club if they had demonstrated the same drive and flair as Allen Aylett, Ron Joseph, Albert Mantello and co.

In order to erase North's image of being perennial battlers, Aylett and his committee generated an aura with the willing assistance of the press. Aylett recalled: "That charisma captured attention," recalls Aylett. "We were very conscious of that and we set out deliberately to create our own publicity. If there wasn't a story we created one." Aylett says opposition clubs were wary of North's splurge on players and a coach. "They were saying things like 'where are they getting the money...under the gasometer!"

The VFL signalled its intention to introduce the

10 year rule in July 1972 and by September 1972 it was law. Ron Barassi still marvels at the way in which North did its homework - "They found that there were 22 players eligible under the 10 year rule and they interviewed all of them within 48 hours of the law being passed."

Within a week North had signed John Rantall, Barry Davis and Doug Wade. Aylett admitted that North had sounded out some of their key targets even before the law was passed, in contravention of VFL regulations. The only one they missed out on was Carl Ditterich. "Within four months of negotiating with him, Ditterich's price went from $7,000 to $20,000."

Rantall's loyalty to South Melbourne made him a hard nut to crack. Former South coach Norm Smith, who North were seeking for a place on the selection committee, had told Barassi they should do everything possible to get Rantall. North signed the trio, and at the same time set the wheels in motion off the field for a resurgence. Finance director Barry Cheatley introduced special memberships to raise funds and North set the scene for other clubs in areas such as grand final breakfasts, president's luncheons and gold pass coteries.

"North Melbourne started the ball rolling with football inflation. Over the period from 1973 until now, football payments and costs have gone up by a rate 10 times normal inflation." Despite that, Aylett had no regrets, and believed that it is merely part of progress.

Barassi rejects the notion that the 10 year rule was the sole reason for North's advance to the flag. "It should be pointed out that in the case of Wade and Rantall many people thought they were too old when we recruited them. The quick rise was due to a tremendous administration...they were just fantastic. They put up their houses as security and did everything you could ask for."

Barassi also reacts to any suggestion that he considers he made the difference. "It's stupid to think that you can do it without good players. I get very irked about it when people suggest that. As if I think it is me that was responsible." Barassi is quick to point out there had been plenty of groundwork at North before he arrived and that Brian Dixon deserves credit for the two years he had at the helm. Aylett agrees: "Dicko was from the successful Melbourne ilk. He became unpopular at the end at North, but that was unfair to him because he was only unpopular for doing the right things."

There had been plenty of speculation over Barassi getting back into coaching and he had admitted openly that he had itchy feet. Albert Mantello had made the first approach on North's behalf when he arrived at Barassi's furniture business and asked for a second hand desk. "I told him we didn't have second hand desks and he started kicking at the leg of one of the desks then told me that this one was second hand." Barassi agreed to sit down with North for a chat. He wrote in his column in *The Sun* that he would be discussing plans with North over bacon and eggs

David Dench was a dashing defender in North's halcyon era. Here he has a heated exchange with umpire Kevin Smith.

the next day. Over breakfast North offered Barassi
$35,000 a year - and also provided a $50,000 loan.
He signed on a paper serviette that was souvenired
by Albert Mantello.

North came from last to sixth place in 1973 - a
huge jump. Davis won the best and fairest, Rantall
was second and Wade booted 73 goals. Next year
the Roos went further and made the grand final, but
were humbled by Richmond who won comfortably
by 41 points. Barassi gave them a blast at the after-
match function at the Southern Cross - "I'm not
proud of you today .. I am afraid some players did
not show enough desire to win ..Today we tasted
the ultimate in defeat in the ultimate match and I
hope it stays with you until next year."

Aylett says North had been optimistic about its
chances in the 1974 grand final. "We were hoping
like anything that we would win it and were naturally very disappointed to lose. But I called a meeting for 7am the next day so we could focus on 1975.
We knew it would have been great to win it, but all
that we had done and had learned was terrific. We
just kept going full bore."

Early in 1975 North lost several games and as
Aylett wrote in his book "Barassi was out of control". Barassi was launching attack after attack on
the players and Aylett called a meeting at his home
to tell him to ease off. He did and the club turned
around. Barassi remembered: "You find that any administration will get toey about whatever coaching
methods you are using when you lose games. Their
rationale is that if it's not working then it must be
wrong." Allen Aylett says the criticism was accepted
by Barassi. "I've always had the suspicion that because we were contemporaries as players it made a
difference and he accepted it more readily than he
would have from others."

North turned the crisis around because everyone involved had a unity in their purpose. A couple
of months later that willingness to work for the common good had its ultimate reward.

Chapter Fifteen

1980-1984

Send lawyers, guns and money

Off-field upheavals are nothing unusual in football clubs when factions try to unseat non-successful administrations.

But Carlton's internal war over the 1979-80 summer was fought only a couple of months after the Blues had won a premiership, and the public bloodletting stunned the football world.

The trouble had its genesis in the middle of 1979 when a series of reports in *The Age* cast doubts on the financial position of the club and the capabilities of its president George Harris. The row simmered until the Carlton annual meeting in December when Harris announced he would resign as president and his backers pushed for him to head a six man board replacing the current committee.

What really struck at the heart of Carlton fans was Alex Jesaulenko's announcement that he would not return unless Harris got his way. Three months of bitterness, acrimony and even a touch of farce came to a head at a special meeting in the appropriately confrontational setting of Festival Hall. Former city councillor Ian Rice had taken over as caretaker president and at the crucial meeting a move to reinstate Harris was outvoted by 1241 to 480. Jesaulenko's mate Peter Jones had been appointed coach and the Blues' legend departed Princes Park bound for St Kilda.

Jesaulenko was not the only legend causing heart palpitations among his fans as Tiger stalwart Kevin Bartlett stood out for 10 weeks in a pre-season con-tract dispute. South Melbourne showed less sentiment when it sacked veteran defender John Rantall who had to cross to Fitzroy to break the VFL games record. Coaches dominated the football news in the early part of the year and none was more ruthless than Footscray's Royce Hart who sacked a succession of players that could not measure up to his tough pre-season training schedule. One of the unlucky ones was teenager Brian Wilson who later won a Brownlow Medal.

Jesaulenko had said when crossing to the Saints that he was content to be just a player, but from the moment he arrived there was speculation that he would take over as coach from Mike Patterson. After two losses the axe fell swiftly on Patterson, whose demise had been sealed in the Hawthorn game when two St Kilda players ran into each other in front of the St Kilda chairman's enclosure and the snake-eyed stare of Lindsay Fox. The Richmond-St Kilda clash suddenly assumed greater status and in a stirring match the Saints tied with the home side. A week later they pipped Essendon at Moorabbin and Jesaulenko was hailed as the saviour, but the success was shortlived for the battling club.

The St Kilda-Essendon match had been notable for much more than Jesaulenko's first win as the Saints' coach. Phil Carman, turning out for his third club Essendon, was reported for striking St Kilda's Garry Sidebottom and head-butting boundary umpire Graham Carbery. Many people thought that he might

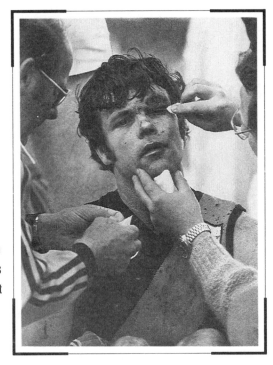

It took a lot to stop Richmond's Francis Bourke. Bloodied at three quarter time, he undergoes running repairs.

Collingwood's finals woes had become almost a September ritual, but the Magpies' horror transferred to July when they lost the night grand final to North Melbourne in bizarre circumstances as Kerry Good marked after the siren and goaled to give the Roos a three-point win.

The end of the season was dominated by news of coaches, as the start had been. David Parkin and Barry Davis quit the Hawthorn and Essendon positions and Ron Barassi decided that his time was up at North which immediately raised speculation that he might return to Melbourne when Carl Ditterich announced that he was finished.

Carlton's Peter Jones told the press he would have to guide the Blues into the top three to keep his job. In the end they only missed top place on percentage, but hefty losses to Richmond and Collingwood ended the Blues' finals campaign and Jones's coaching career. He was replaced by ex-Hawthorn man Parkin.

Jones was involved in the unusual spectacle of an onfield fight between coaches when he jousted with Richmond's Tony Jewell at the quarter-time break of the qualifying final. There was no verdict in the coaches' battle, but the Tiger players had too many guns and bolted to a win.

Richmond had won 11 games in a row during one golden burst, before a shock loss to South in the last home and away game lengthened their odds. The Tigers had a big, strong and talented side with a strong goal-to-goal line and an abundance of scoring firepower. They relied heavily on centreman Geoff Raines, centre half-forward David Cloke and century goalkicker Michael Roach. Mark Lee and Dale Weightman were a fine ruck/rover duet and ageing stars Kevin Bartlett and Francis Bourke had all the guile that could accumulate over years of service.

Bartlett's career had been rejuvenated when a loss of pace saw him shifted from a roving commission to the new role of half-forward flanker and in

cop a life suspension, but the mammoth 20-week disqualification was still the biggest sentence in memory.

Pre-season trauma had caused many people to wonder whether Carlton's performance would suffer, but the Blues started in fine fettle and went win for win with the improved Richmond. Carlton dug into its coffers to make a $200,000-plus offer to St Kilda for captain Garry Sidebottom and then snared Melbourne veteran Greg Wells for $100,000. St Kilda retained Sidebottom, but his form deteriorated and he went to Geelong the next year.

It was an era of wheeling and dealing for players' services with clubs frequently parting with ludicrous sums to try to achieve instant success. None of the swaps typified the ruthlessness and speed of the transactions as much as the Russell Greene case. Greene, a talented St Kilda footballer who lacked off-field discipline, was exchanged for Hawthorn pair Mark Scott and Tony King on a Friday night. When he ran into his friend Steven Icke in the car park outside the North-Hawthorn game Icke thought he had come to the wrong ground.

the grand final he dazzled Collingwood with a record-equalling seven goals. Richmond powered to record breaking 81-point winning margin and left the Magpies in tatters. Collingwood had been the first side to reach a grand final from fifth place, but the effort had drained it by grand final day.

Recruiting and legal wrangles dominated the summer and spread into the heart of the 1981 season. Fitzroy official Leon Wiegard even joked that the VFL's new headquarters should have been built in Queen Street - the heart of Melbourne's legal fraternity.

South Melbourne fought long and hard with Carlton to win a clearance for young Port Melbourne ruckman Stephen Allender. Finally he was cleared, but the club was also fined $20,000 on a poaching charge. It had seemed at one stage that the VFL permit rules would be tested under restraint of trade laws, but yet again this was averted. Along the way the argument descended to such a low level that Carlton moved to have South expelled from the League and South replied by taking legal steps to have Carlton president Ian Rice jailed for contempt of court!

North lashed out in a buying splurge reminiscent of the 1972 outlay, but this time the crop of interstate recruits Peter Spencer, Peter Jonas, Phil Kelly and Kym Hodgeman was nowhere near as productive as the crop a decade earlier. Only Hodgeman could be said to have reached the heights.

An interstate recruit with another club, St Kilda, provided the biggest sensation of the year. West Torrens defender Doug Cox was the centre of just another clearance hassle in the weeks leading up to the start of the season when the Saints finally gained his services free of encumbrances because he was in the army and could transfer without strings. Eight weeks into the season Richmond filed papers with the VFL that claimed Cox was residentially bound to the Tigers because of an old Mildura address.

The VFL ruled Cox had been an ineligible player

As his capacity for roving began to wane, Kevin Bartlett slotted into the role of a goalkicking forward. Here he heads Carlton's Des English and teammate Michael Roach in the hunt for the ball.

for all eight rounds and stripped St Kilda of the two wins that it had registered. St Kilda, incensed at the ruling, took out a Supreme Court injunction so Cox could play the next game, ironically against Richmond the following Saturday. Richmond looked like trampling St Kilda in the early stages of the game and the Saints showed none of the aggression their officials were displaying off the field. Eventually they mounted a comeback, but the Tigers kicked clear at the end.

The game was to prove costly for Richmond in the long run because big centre half-forward David Cloke injured his knee, and was absent for the next 11 weeks. Richmond's little men revolved around

Cloke's strength and his loss was a key factor in the club falling from the five.

In the aftermath of the Cox affair there was chaos with St Kilda president Lindsay Fox threatening to check the qualifications of every Richmond player. The matter was finally settled out of the court and sanity prevailed when St Kilda's points were restored. In hindsight many of the actions by clubs and the VFL seem to be those of bodies hellbent on self-destruction.

The climate of confrontation also applied to dealings between the VFL Players' Association and the League with a pre-season strike only narrowly averted. The League couldn't thwart the umpires' strike in round 19 and for the first time in memory replacement umpires from reserve ranks were actually cheered at some grounds. The umpires had walked out over the VFL's refusal to consult them or pay extra for Sunday games. The dispute was settled in time for the following round, but the bitter taste remained. In many ways the uncompromising non-conciliatory approach mirrored Australian society at the time as the Liberal government and unions came to halts over industrial disputes.

Another contentious point was Sunday games. For several years the VFL had waged a relentless campaign that naturally provoked savage opposition from the VFA which had pioneered Sunday games. Finally the State Government relented and allowed two "trial" Sunday games, but even then the VFL struck a snag in its own ranks when Collingwood refused to be part of either of the games. The Magpies came to the party in the end and were part of the initial Sunday fixture against Essendon which drew a crowd of 62,000.

As ever, all clubs started the season with sparkling hopes, but some didn't have to wait long to fall flat on their faces. Footscray lost Kelvin Templeton, a decisive and universally acclaimed

> **One of the most interesting faces among the new coaches was Essendon's leader Kevin Sheedy.**

Brownlow Medal winner the year before, with a knee injury in a pre-season night match and he didn't play again that year.

Over at Melbourne the faithful looked to the returned coach Ron Barassi for a miracle, but it never came and even the supercoach could not raise his side to more than its solitary win for the year. At one stage Barassi said it might take eight years to fulfil his plan for the club to again become a power. Although history records that he would not be at the reins in eight years time, the comment was prophetic.

One of the most interesting faces among the new coaches was Essendon's leader Kevin Sheedy. The former Richmond star had long been touted as coaching material and on the night before the first game he spent five hours writing individual letters to each player. The Bombers went down narrowly in that game, but had a disastrous start to the season with only one win from the first six games and Sheedy, as is the wont of young coaches, even contemplated a return as a player. Then came an amazing transformation which netted a stunning 15 wins in a row. The Bombers beat everyone, everywhere, including a victory over Hawthorn in the first match in Brisbane for 29 years. That was part of the VFL expansion interstate.

Essendon's most celebrated win came against Carlton after the Blues had held a 26-point lead at the 20-minute mark. Blues skipper Mike Fitzpatrick tried to hold up play by taking an excessively long time to take his kick and the ball was taken from him by the umpire. Essendon stormed home and with two goals to Neale Daniher deep into time-on pulled off an unthinkable victory. The Bombers had the double chance in their grasp until the final round when Geelong brought the great run to an end. A week later Fitzroy administered the coup de grace in the elimination final although the match was far tighter than the equivalent game two years earlier.

The VFL was reminded of the difficulties of future interstate competition when the Victorian team to play in Perth had to cross the Nullarbor in two light planes because of a national pilots' strike. Hawthorn star Michael Tuck even had to travel in the luggage compartment and not surprisingly the Vics lost the game.

More fortunate was WA star Brian Peake. Geelong won his signature after a seven-year chase and when he decided to cross to Victoria in mid-season he was flown to Tullamarine where a helicopter immediately whisked him away to Kardinia Park to join his new teammates for a training run. The champion Sandgroper played a key role in the following Saturday's mammoth win over North Melbourne and was a handy player for the Cats even though he was given the unkind tag of "Past his" Peake by the more cynical fans.

The team humbled by Peake and the Cats, North Melbourne, had its own headaches and late in the year it all became too much for captain-coach Malcolm Blight who resigned and handed over the coaching job to Barry Cable. Relieved of the burden Blight promptly kicked 11 goals the next week.

Carlton, boosted by interstate stars Peter Bosustow and Ken Hunter, and restored as a cohesive unit by new coach David Parkin, finished the season on top of the ladder ahead of Collingwood on percentage. The Blues clinically disposed of Geelong in the second semi-final with the much vaunted pack of little men running riot and the tight-knit defence stifling the Cats.

In the first semi Collingwood had ended the hopes of the vastly improved Fitzroy and although not the most skilled side ever to grace the field, the Magpies had too much tenacity and will-to-win for a Geelong side that was freely conceded to have more talent man-for-man. The Cats did nothing to dispel their "country hick" image when an official forgot to tell Garry Sidebottom that he was to be picked up by a bus and he missed a seat and therefore a place in the team.

Geelong moved heaven and earth to secure highly credentialled West Australian Brian Peake.

Collingwood coach Tom Hafey extracted everything possible from his team, but Carlton had brilliance all over the field and the gulf between the two teams was too great to bridge in the grand final. Evergreen defender Bruce Doull rightly won the Norm Smith Medal for best afield and skipper Mike Fitzpatrick led from the front in the 20-point win. Alex Marcou, Phil Maylin, and David Glascott were the most prominent of the fleet of small men. For Parkin it was a triumph which matched his 1978 flag success with Hawthorn.

Yet he, like every other coach knew the fickleness of the job and the point was rammed home on the last day of September when Tony Jewell resigned from the Richmond position to avoid the sack. Just 12 months earlier he had coached the Tigers to a record-breaking grand final win. Richmond maintained its ruthless image early in 1982 by refusing to release Jewell to fill in as North's reserves coach for three weeks while the regular coach was ill.

Richmond changed captains even more frequently than coaches and when David Cloke was appointed to the position he became the sixth Tiger skipper in six seasons.

Legal action was still the flavor of the day in the lead-up to the 1982 season and WA club Subiaco sued Hawthorn over its recruitment of Gary Buckenara. It wouldn't be the last time Buckenara was the centre of a legal wrangle, but he soon showed he was worth the bother and was one of the season's best recruits.

Coaches expressed dissatisfaction early in the year with the more rigid application of marking laws which required players to clearly mark the ball and not juggle it and then drop it as had been the case in the past. The umps also clamped down on head-high tackles and Essendon's Ron Andrews was the first man to be suspended for flattening an opponent. The Tribunal did have its lighter moments such as the report of Swans reserves runner Ray Ball for baring his backside to express his opinion of the field umpire.

All the pre-season drama had centred on South Melbourne's move to Sydney, and Bulldog fans were rocked to hear the VFL had offered to do a feasibility study of moving the club to Brisbane or the Gold Coast at no charge.

Second and third-placed clubs of the previous year, Geelong and Collingwood, fell away alarmingly and the Magpies' plight drew most attention. Plagued by injuries the club recruited 28-year-old Preston full-back Gordon Towan as one of the measures to stop the rot. Then after eight losses in a row

Collingwood dropped a bombshell by sacking coach Tom Hafey. Under Hafey's guidance the Magpies had played off for the flag three times, but failure to bring home the ultimate reward counted for everything and the man who had the best coaching record since the great Norm Smith was sent packing.

There were bomb threats before the Magpies' next game, but under stand-in coach Mick Erwin they took the points. A huge storm was brewing off the field and the hostility had an effect on players. The Magpies made little improvement in the latter half of the season. A reform group titled "The New Magpies" announced its intention to challenge the commitee. Businessman Ranald Macdonald led the group which included former stars Len Thompson and Terry Waters. Late in the year Collingwood members were surveyed on whether they would prefer to see Leigh Matthews, Don Scott, Len Thompson or Mick Erwin as the next coach. As Matthews was still a Hawthorn player the Hawks were incensed and ordered other clubs to stay clear of their champion.

A few days after Hafey's sacking, his former Richmond protege Royce Hart was "demoted" to the assistant coach position at Footscray. The wording may have been different, but the result was the same as the Bulldogs turned to veteran ruckman Ian "Bluey" Hampshire to fill the role.

Controversy seemed to dog certain players during the year and violence erupted at Essendon when Ron Andrews tangled with Melbourne full-forward Mark Jackson whose erratic behaviour and on-field antics were starting to lose their novelty. Beer cans rained down on the goalsquare melee and Jackson threw one of them back into the crowd. He was censured by the Melbourne administration and Andrews was suspended for two weeks by the Tribunal.

All clubs were hit hard by a flu virus in July and August, but a bigger blow came when the State Government said it would demand the clubs pay backdated payroll tax. For some already embattled clubs teetering on the edge financially, this loomed as a disaster.

Meanwhile the Sydney venture was not without its highs and lows and not long after the Swans had won the night grand final the club was embarrassed by the leak of a committeeman's report which said coach Ricky Quade was not flamboyant enough to lead the club's Sydney push. The committeeman resigned, but it was yet another disruption. The Swans made a run for the five and still had a chance with two weeks to go to the finals, but they fell away.

Essendon, which had promised so much the previous year, again bombed out in the elimination final. It was the fifth time in 11 seasons that the club had lost the opening final, and indeed the Bombers had not tasted success in a final since the 1968 preliminary final. The club had started with the crucial loss of injured skipper Neale Daniher before the start of the year and many players who had built big reputations were not up to scratch in 1982.

The real power sides for the year were Carlton and Richmond. Carlton started the year slowly with a draw against Fitzroy then a big loss to Essendon. Carlton could not master Essendon during this time when all other teams were easy fodder for the Blues. Essendon had a big team and Sheedy's tactics stopped Carlton's running flow which was the basis of the Blues' strategy.

Carlton's lack of size around the field meant that Parkin had to use a running game and he did so with great effect. It was brought undone by a ferocious Richmond in the second semi-final. The hard-hitting Tigers were back to their 1980 form and the 23 point win stirred the old spectre of Carlton's vulnerability to physical pressure. Some of that talk was countered when the Blues overcame Hawthorn in the preliminary final, but it could only be dispelled by a win over Richmond.

The opening of the grand final was one of the fiercest for years and brawls erupted all over the field. Oddly enough it was Carlton's big men such as skip-

per Mike Fitzpatrick and Warren "Wow" Jones who spearheaded the Blues' effort. The aggressive Jones, who had wanted to leave the club earlier in the year, immediately showed Richmond's Mark Lee who was boss. Richmond tried hard all day and the result was still in the balance as the clock ticked into time-on, but a couple of late goals by the Blues sealed back-to-back flags - a triumph for coach David Parkin.

There was the usual summer cattlemarket of players between clubs, and the newly formed VFL Appeals Tribunal was designed to hear both sides of a dispute and decide the size of transfer fees. The new Collingwood administration netted Richmond stars Geoff Raines and David Cloke plus interstaters Gary Shaw and Greg Phillips. For a while it seemed that disgruntled Swans brothers Shane and Paul Morwood would also move to Victoria Park, but Paul had his mind set on joining St Kilda. Poaching allegations surfaced against the Magpies when Carlton star Wayne Johnston was approached by wealthy black and white fans, but the charges fell through because the contacts were not Collingwood officials.

Coaches at three clubs had their problems in the early weeks for a variety of reasons. New Geelong coach Tom Hafey faced a heavy list of injuries and Footscray's Ian Hampshire had to contend with rumors that he would be replaced by Michael Malthouse. Hampshire stayed in the job and Footscray had a reasonable season, but history would eventually confirm the basis of the rumors when Malthouse took the reins later on.

At Melbourne Ron Barassi locked horns with 1982 Brownlow winner Brian Wilson and when Barassi removed him from the ground Wilson gave the thumbs up sign to the coaching box and stood next to the interchange bench, with arms folded, for the next 15 minutes.

> On April 24 Judge Crockett of the Supreme Court ruled that the Swans' refusal to clear Silvio Foschini to St Kilda was a restraint of trade.

Peter Bosustow soars in the Princes Park goalsquare to take one of the great marks of all time against Geelong, 1981.

In a season studded with controversy the last week in April stood out not only for its immediate impact, but also for the long-term effect on the game. On April 24 Judge Crockett of the Supreme Court ruled that the Swans' refusal to clear Silvio Foschini to St Kilda was a restraint of trade. It was the decision which the VFL had dreaded and had been averted in other cases by a series of out-of-court settlements. The decision effectively pulled down the whole system of rules governing players' transfers and clearances. Foschini even admitted that he never thought the case would go the distance, but there was an even bigger shock ahead for VFL officials the next day when Paul Morwood ran onto the field for St Kilda. Morwood had also been fighting for a clearance from the Swans, but with the clearance rules in disarray St Kilda went ahead and played him.

St Kilda chairman Lindsay Fox and manager Ian Stewart copped flak from all directions and there were calls for St Kilda's expulsion from the League. There was unrest among all clubs and the running of the competition was thrown into chaos, but in the long run it was a turning point which forced the VFL to revamp the entire transfer and recruitment rules. Feeling ran especially high between St Kilda and the Swans, but the match a week later did not boil over into violence.

The madness of exorbitant player payments knew no bounds. Collingwood had been one of the biggest spenders and was stunned when Allan Edwards, who had been bought for $100,000 just before the clearance deadline in 1979, announced his retirement. He was convinced to return later, but the Magpies never received a satisfactory return on their investment.

VFL president Allen Aylett canvassed the possibility of another team moving to Sydney, but the Swans were having enough trouble on their own and early in May the club's executive director, Brian Dixon, was sacked from his $90,000 job after refusing to resign.

On the field Richmond, already weakened by the loss of star players through transfers, had a terrible string of losses and there was reported to be internal turmoil at the club. A strange manifestation of the discontent was the sacking of the club doctor! Coach Francis Bourke was said to have been unpopular with a number of key players and he looked like joining the long list of discarded Tiger coaches. The Tigers also threatened to take the VFL's zoning system to court because the club believed it had been hard done by in being allocated the Sunraysia zone.

> Fanciful talk of a National League being formed now assumed more credibility.

About the only happy event in Richmond's year was Kevin Bartlett reaching 400 games. No-one had reached the quadruple century mark in the game's history and fans marvelled at the durability of the wispy-haired champion.

Reigning premier Carlton had its troubles rekindling enthusiasm and struggled to establish a foothold in the five. The Blues met Essendon in the elimination final and the Bombers continued to have the "wood" over Carlton and ended a horror stretch of elimination final losses. The brashness of the Essendon side was typified by tiny rover Tony Buhagiar who threw Bruce Doull's trademark headband over the fence! Essendon sent the game Fitzroy out of the finals race, then exposed all of North's flaws in a preliminary final hiding.

But that was the end of the Bombers' glory. On a bright September day they were humiliated by a machine-like Hawthorn side whose only hiccup was the early injury to star forward Gary Buckenara. In the end Hawthorn's dominance reduced the game to boredom. Hawthorn's team play and movement of the ball was nothing short of awesome and middle-sized players such as Colin Robertson, John Kennedy and Russell Greene lacerated the Essendon defence. Captain Leigh Matthews booted six goals and was an inspiration to the side.

Coach Allan Jeans admitted he had been worried that he may not have been able to rekindle the older players' desire after the successes of the Parkin-Kennedy era. He knew he could not improve the traditional Hawthorn virtues of chasing, tackling and going in for the ball, but concentrated on developing the team's ability to run the ball out of defence. The development of men like Gary Ayres, Chris Mew and Russell Greene was vital in this area and it paid dividends in 1983.

Fans at that "one day in September" wondered how long the grand final would stay at the MCG. The VFL's avowed intent to stage the match at VFL Park had been made obvious from the moment the 212 acres of land at Waverley was purchased in 1962.

By 1983 the VFL had decided to pursue the issue more strongly and entered into heated discussions with the Melbourne Cricket Club. At first the VFL wanted to lease the MCG, but the MCC refused to agree. Victorian Premier John Cain bought into the argument in December when he announced that if the two bodies did not come to quick agreement about the 1984 grand final he would use legislation to ensure the game stayed there. The VFL huffed and puffed about Government intervention, but the vast body of the football public wanted the grand final at the MCG. Besides, VFL Park had a smaller capacity for crowds and could not match the public transport access of the cricket ground. At the same time there were surface problems at VFL Park that required a $125,000 repair job.

In other ground moves before the 1984 season, North Melbourne successfully applied to play four home games at the MCG. It was the forerunner to North becoming the third resident club at the ground.

It was a time of great self-examination, on the surface at least, by football authorities. A "task force" was created to examine the direction of the sport, but it ran into problems when the VFL initially limited its power. Later the VFL backed down on its stand against the task force.

Fanciful talk of a National League being formed now assumed more credibility. Carlton's new high-profile president John Elliott held several secret meetings to discuss a new competition, and North Melbourne floated a proposal that a new competition should include nine Victorian teams, two from Western Australia and South Australia and teams from Tasmania and Queensland. By August it was reported that six financially sound clubs - Collingwood, Carlton, Essendon, Melbourne, Hawthorn and Richmond - were contemplating a breakaway league. Finally the League called all presidents together and they unanimously voted to stay under VFL control the next year.

But all that was far from the minds of the teams as they lined up for the opening bounce of 1984. Full-forwards were again the big talking point with Carlton's interstate debutante Warren Ralph starting his career with nine goals. The most appetising part of the day was the double act performed at Moorabbin by two young men about to make a huge mark on the game. Essendon's Paul Salmon and St Kilda's Tony Lockett each kicked seven goals and although they had made their debuts the previous season this was the match when they gave notice that they were future stars.

The gigantic Salmon posed nightmarish problems for full-backs who could not match him in the air. He dominated the first part of the season and was bang on target for his 100 goals until he injured a knee at Victoria Park.

Geelong made a flying start, but as was their habit so often, the Cats failed to produce the goods later on. Much of the early season impression was due to the forward work of two men who had been written off in the football world. The much-travelled Mark Jackson, surely now on his last chance at his fourth club, kicked nine goals in the opening round, but it was the form of another recruit which dazzled commentators. Gary Ablett, a richly talented footballer whose wayward manner had seen him dumped by

Glorious night. North veterans Keith Greig and Wayne Schimmelbusch embrace after North wins the 1980 night grand final.

Hawthorn, produced a special brand of magic for the Cats under Tom Hafey.

Collingwood again departed from tradition in its appointment of South Australian John Cahill as coach. Cahill had an astute football mind, but his lack of VFL experience was a problem. Still the Magpies performed well and were involved in two of the more hectic finishes in the early part of the season. Against Carlton they gained a reprieve when fullforward Ralph missed a set shot from only 20 yards out, but at Footscray the indiscretion of Graeme Allan kicking across goal cost the Magpies dearly. Simon Beasley marked comfortably and goaled to snatch a win.

It seemed that just about everyone, including judges, was sick of football litigation. When the WA League and two of its clubs took St Kilda to court over the release of Phil Narkle and Phil Cronin, the Supreme Court judge, Mr Justice Kaye, adjourned the case saying there were more important cases than football ones.

Football's own court, the Tribunal, had a busy year as usual and the most sensational incident involved a frequent customer, St Kilda's Robert Muir. Muir was reported seven times after flattening former teammate Val Perovic, headbutting Bruce Doull and using threatening behavior towards umpire Kevin Smith. He was outed for 12 weeks, thus ending a turbulent VFL career. Muir's tribunal visit may have received all the attention, but teammate Glen Middlemiss also tasted the body's displeasure on the same night and was on his way to an amazing record of five separate appearances there in senior ranks. Just for something different Steve Macpherson was fined $1000 for striking Swans runner Graeme Bond.

The financial desperation of clubs was an ongoing concern and St Kilda's desperate plight was well known in VFL circles. The extent of the trouble be-

A great Carlton skipper - Mike Fitzpatrick gets his kick ahead of South's Robert McGhie.

came obvious when it was announced that a scheme of arrangement would be necessary to keep the club afloat. An accountant in charge of the scheme, David Crawford, said the club could be wound up if football creditors including former players and coaches Jack Clarke, Barry Breen, Bruce Duperouzel, Jeff Sarau, Alex Jesaulenko and Allan Jeans did not accept the offer of 22.5 cents in the dollar. Other creditors were offered 7.5 cents in the dollar. There was even doubt that St Kilda would survive to meet Hawthorn in the scheduled round 14 game, but the club survived when creditors accepted the scheme. It didn't prevent a 17-goal hiding from the Hawks, but the Saints were happy just to be alive.

The VFL and the State Government were constantly at loggerheads over a number of issues, but the League did get one concession when it was permitted to stage two Sunday finals for the first time. East Melbourne residents reacted angrily to the plan,

but the finals went ahead anyway.

Football betting was also an issue during the year with a new scheme of predicting winning margins. There was uproar when four players had to withdraw at the last minute from the Carlton team that had been heavily backed against St Kilda. The Saints pulled off the upset of the day on the boggy Moorabbin ground and had to withstand allegations that the ground had been watered to increase the home side's chances. The Saints were at the centre of more controversy when they sacked Tony Jewell on the spot after he said he would retire at the end of the year and was critical of the club's administration. Caretaker coach Graeme Gellie immediately led the team to a win, but that was only a brief respite in an otherwise dismal year.

Without doubt the fairytale story of the year was Fitzroy's amazing burst. A constant target of rumor about their financial woes, the Lions were a hardy group of battlers. They were last with only one win after round nine and even with four weeks left to the finals still sat in tenth place. But the fairytale came to an end when Collingwood destroyed them in the elimination final.

Cahill's Magpies were to suffer a worse fate a couple of weeks later. Essendon pulverised the black and whites and by half-time thousands of Collingwood fans were streaming to the carparks and headed for home with the scoreboard reading 17.6 to 3.6. The eventual difference of 133 points marked the biggest humiliation in finals history.

Now Essendon faced Hawthorn, the team which had so conclusively beaten it 12 months earlier, and there was an added sideshow when police investigated a "mystery substance" inhaled by the Hawks during breaks between quarters. It turned out to be a harmless mixture of ammonia and eucalyptus oil and an embarrassed Essendon had to apologise for the incident.

It was Bombers fans who were calling for the smelling salts in the opening moments of the grand final when Hawthorn slammed on three goals which left the Bombers bewildered. The Hawks went into the final term leading by just under four goals, but Essendon could sense that they were flagging. Some inspired moves by Sheedy turned the game around completely. Defender Paul Weston was an inspiration at centre half-forward and Leon Baker opened up the Hawthorn defence with a series of streaming forward moves. It was his goal that put the Bombers in front but in typically Hawthorn style the lead was snatched back with a goal by Peter Curran.

On this day Essendon would not be denied, and the nine-goal last quarter powered the Dons to a stirring victory. The bitter memories of the previous year were all but erased.

The Swans Fly North

The Victorian Football League had always regarded Sydney as a "heathen" football city, but also with a hint of envy. Sydney, Australia's largest city, represented a challenge and if the VFL could establish itself there the code of Australian football would become truly national.

However, there were only half-hearted efforts to take the VFL competition to Sydney up to 1979 when the League played two home and away matches at the Sydney Cricket Ground. These matches were known as "The Sydney Experiment" and the aim was to determine whether to establish a new League club in Sydney. The first of these matches was played between 1978 grand finalists Hawthorn and North Melbourne and attracted 31,391 fans. The VFL was delighted and League president Dr Allen Aylett waxed lyrical about what he described as "the enormous possibilities" of having a VFL club based in Sydney.

The VFL then commissioned its corporate planner, John Hennessy, to prepare a report on the prospect of establishing a club in Sydney. This report, tabled in 1980, suggested a Sydney club would have

10,000 members within three years of establishment and attendances in the first year would be an average 17,500. The VFL reacted by appointing former St Kilda club president Mr Graham Huggins as a specialist consultant in Sydney, with the specific aim to talk with prospective sponsors, supporters and other interested parties.

At this stage the VFL seemed prepared to launch a new club from scratch, as it later did with the West Coast Eagles and the Brisbane Bears for the start of the 1987 competition. However, two existing VFL clubs had already realised the potential of wiping out debts and becoming successful with a new start in Sydney. Fitzroy and South Melbourne expressed interested in migrating north as early as 1978.

Fitzroy's flirtation with the Sydney experiment was brief, its involvement stopped dead in its tracks by a leak to the media. Fitzroy had already had talks with the VFL over a possible move, but media disclosures forced club supporters to express their disapproval and club directors later publicly announced the Lions had abandoned the idea of shifting north.

This left a clear path for South Melbourne, one of the League's founding clubs. The Swans had desperate financial problems throughout the 1970s and a dwindling support base led most club directors to the view that a shift to Sydney would be preferable to extinction. South had last won a premiership in 1933 and had played in only two finals series since its last grand final appearance in 1945. It had finished a creditable sixth in 1980, but it was floundering in a sea of red ink that threatened to drown it.

Club directors, therefore, approached the VFL in 1981 about the possibility of playing its home games in Sydney the following year. The football media again got wind of the move and South supporters reacted with a ferocity to match their anguish. Ironically, South was drawn to play

> The Victorian Football League had always regarded Sydney as a "heathen" football city,

Collingwood in an "experiment" match at the SCG on July 26, 1981, not long after news of the possible move had broken. A "Keep South at South" movement already had been formed and club directors received anonymous death threats. A protest meeting was held at the club's Lake Oval ground and supporters vowed to "fight forever" to keep the club in Melbourne. Battle lines were drawn.

The Swans' first official "home" match in Sydney was against Melbourne at the SCG on Sunday, March 28, 1982.

Club president Jack Marks went on television at half-time during the Swans-Collingwood match in Sydney to explain the reasons for the suggested move. His plea for common sense thinking fell on deaf ears and the club was split down the middle. The Keep South at South (KSAS) movement gathered momentum, but Marks and his co-directors took heart not only from the Swans' 18-point win over Collingwood in Sydney, but also from the 22,238 attendance.

The South directors therefore took their next step in the battle to shift to Sydney. It was a critical move and one that ultimately saw the defeat of the KSAS movement. VFL directors, on the Wednesday after the Swans' win over Collingwood, voted in favor of an application from the South Melbourne committee to play its 11 home games at the SCG in 1982. That vote proved critical, as any change had to be voted for by a three-quarter majority of League directors. The KSAS group, despite its frantic attempts to reverse the decision to shift to Sydney, was never able to overcome this problem.

South played out the 1981 season in a fog of trauma. Its last game at the Lake Oval was in the final round of the season, against North Melbourne. Just over 6000 fans watched the Swans trudge from its old home. Sadly for South supporters, North Melbourne defeated the Swans. Meanwhile, shots were being fired from both sides. The KSAS pinned its hopes on an extraordinary meeting of members scheduled for September 22, although group leader John Keogh claimed that Sydney interests had been "buying up" club memberships.

The combatants faced each other at the Caulfield Town Hall on the night of September 22. Placards were waved, banners were draped over chairs and a red and white army of supporters chanted against the very suggestion of a move from Melbourne. The KSAS group won control of the club by just 10 votes, but could not overthrow the VFL decision to allow the club to play its home games in Sydney in 1982.

Keogh wrote to members: "It is with great personal sorrow that I must advise you that I and all other members of the board consider we must accept the VFL decision to play 11 games in Sydney in 1982 on a trial basis, and we will continue to fight on your behalf to ensure that South will have a definite say as to where it plays in 1983 and thereafter".

The KSAS group, now in control of the club with Keogh as chairman, obviously believed it had lost a battle but had won the war. It might have acknowledged that it had to play home games in Sydney in 1982, but it was convinced it would return to the Lake Oval from 1983. The group had not counted on the strength and determination of the players, who had backed the move to shift to Sydney. In fact, 19 senior players walked out on the club and started making preparations to play with rival clubs.

The KSAS group faced the prospect of having a football club without footballers. The "rebel" players backed the old committee's decision to appoint former club captain Ricky Quade as coach, whereas the KSAS group had appointed another former club champion in John Rantall as coach. Most players wanted Quade as coach, but Rantall also had his supporters. The players even had an end-of-season trip to Asia with Rantall the official coach.

The situation became critical and in December, 1981, there even were fears that South Melbourne would self-destruct. The League at one stage warned it would make plans for a 1982 without the Swans if the warring did not stop. The VFL even intervened to make peace, only for hostilities to re-open after each meeting.

Then, at a meeting on December 11, Keogh stood down as chairman in favour of well-known racing broadcaster and life-long club supporter Bill Collins in an attempt to defuse the situation. A new board was formed and the VFL fully expected that a meeting on December 20 would settle the issue once and for all. The 19 players refused to accept Rantall as coach and it was thought the meeting on December 20 would see Rantall replaced as coach by Quade.

However, Rantall was reappointed and players left the Lake Oval horrified. Rover Steve Wright, a tremendously loyal clubman, was in tears and had to be consoled by teammates. The civil war had only intensified, especially as several board members resigned after the meeting. The VFL, through Dr Aylett, intervened by insisting Rantall step down as coach in favor of Quade and the plans to play in Sydney would go ahead.

Rantall did resign, Quade was appointed, the striking players returned to the club and the Swans migrated north for the 1982 season, not temporarily, but permanently.

The peace plan was put into operation on Christmas eve, 1981, but the Swans' first years in Sydney were anything but peaceful, especially as there was still considerable bitterness from diehard South Melbourne supporters. However, there was now no turning back and the club was launched at a lavish ceremony at the Opera House on February 24, 1982. At this stage the club's official name was still South Melbourne, but everyone would now know them as the Sydney Swans, even if they still lived and trained in Melbourne. The Swans' first official "home" match in Sydney was against Melbourne at the SCG on Sunday, March 28, 1982.

The weather was perfect and South Melbourne, officially to become the Sydney Swans the following year, was expected to triumph. After all, Melbourne had won just one game (against Footscray in the opening round) the previous season. The Swans had finished ninth with eight wins. Coach Quade later confessed he was physically ill just before the start of play; the pressure on everyone connected with the move was enormous.

The Swans ran onto the ground to the roar of 15,764 fans. Football history was about to be created and the Swans certainly seemed to sense that they simply had to win this match. They cruised away from Melbourne in the first half and looked set for a comfortable win, only to face a desperate Melbourne challenge in the last quarter. Melbourne gradually whittled away the Swans' big lead and Swan captain, 1981 Brownlow medallist ruckman Barry Round, had to stretch himself across the half-back line to repel what seemed to be constant Melbourne thrusts. The Swans eventually won by 29 points (20.17-137 to 16.12-108) and the celebrations threatened to be spectacular.

Prominent Sydney identity Lady Mary Fairfax opened her magnificent Darling Point home to selected Swan guests, who wined and dined the night away as if a cloud would never cross the Swans' sky in future years.

No one who celebrated that night could have known that the Swans' problems were in their infancy. The Swans might have finished a highly creditable seventh (with 12 wins) and might have won the night premiership in 1982, but Sydney's streets were not paved with gold.

Sydney failed to attract the corporate and spectator support in 1982 that it envisaged and by season's end the club was in dire financial difficulties again. In fact, the Swans' operating costs were estimated at being $900,000 more than if they had stayed in Melbourne. Naturally, there were moves to recall the club, but a Sydney group won control

> **Sydney failed to attract the corporate and spectator support in 1982 that it envisaged and by season's end the club was in dire financial difficulties again.**

at the club's annual general meeting in September, 1982. The Swans from there were destined to remain in Sydney.

Former champion winger and former Victorian Government minister Brian Dixon was appointed executive director, but his appointment failed to inspire the Swans in 1983 and the red and white finished only one rung from bottom position with just seven victories. Fans were difficult to woo and recruits were reluctant to shift to Sydney.

The Swans also faced a major crisis when several players refused to join the shift to Sydney. Classy rover Silvio Foschini and Paul and Shane Morwood also decided to stay in Melbourne, although their brother Tony elected to shift. Foschini became involved in the greatest football courtroom battle in VFL history and the Morwood brothers eventually won releases, through different means. Shane Morwood wanted to play with brother Paul at St Kilda, but when the Swans refused to clear either of them, he elected to join Collingwood. The Swans agreed to that move, but refused to negotiate with St. Kilda. Paul Morwood eventually played for St Kilda against Geelong at VFL Park without a clearance, sparking one of the greatest controversies in VFL history. Angry VFL delegates met the next day to discuss the issue and there was even talk that the Saints would be drummed out of the competition. However, the Swans finally relented and cleared Morwood to prevent further damage to the League's image. The Foschini case proved to be an even more explosive issue.

Foschini had made his debut with the Swans in 1981 as a 17-year-old schoolboy and his goalkicking exploits from the forward pocket won him instant acclaim. When the Swans played in Sydney in 1982 he was the club's number one drawcard and was idolised by Sydney fans. However, he insisted he would not shift to Sydney with the rest of the team for 1983

> It seemed increasingly obvious to some VFL officials that there was little or no hope for the Swans unless the club was privately owned.

and wanted to remain in Melbourne with his Italian family.

The Swans believed St Kilda had suggested this stance and refused to even discuss the possibility of clearing Foschini to the Saints. However, the Victorian Supreme Court, in a momentous decision, ruled that refusing Foschini a clearance was a restraint of trade and the VFL's permit regulations came tumbling down.

Foschini was granted a clearance to play with St. Kilda and lined up for the Saints against the Swans at the SCG on April 24, 1983. Foschini upset the Swans by kicking the first goal of the match, but then rarely touched the ball. As Paul Morwood also was playing with the Saints, there were genuine fears that the match would be a bloodbath. There were several scuffles, especially in the second half, but both sides carried out instructions to play the ball. The Swans defeated St Kilda, but it was of their few victories, on or off the field, that year.

Dixon was sacked during the season and the Swans were eventually forced to seek further financial assistance from the League. In fact, the League appointed an eight-man board to run the club and an arrangement was put into place to settle debts.

The Swans limped through the 1984 season with even more off-field drama and trauma following the mid-season resignation through illness of coach Quade. He was replaced temporarily by chairman of selectors Tony Franklin before South Australian state coach Bob Hammond was enticed to take over for the second half of the season.

The Swans continued to mark time and finished tenth in both 1984 and 1985. The players had battled enormous odds, but needed fresh inspiration. And it came in the unlikely form of private ownership and a flamboyant doctor who liked to tell everyone that he flew pink helicopters. A new era was about to dawn for the Swans and the VFL, but again there were enormous difficulties and again the Swans almost sank into oblivion.

It seemed increasingly obvious to some VFL officials that there was little or no hope for the Swans unless the club was privately owned. The possibility of private ownership of a League club had been mooted at least a decade earlier and the subject raised from time to time in the interim. However, no positive steps were taken until marketing consultant Bob Pritchard raised the possibility with the League's marketing consultant Jim McKay of owning the Swans.

Pritchard was discreetly led to believe the League would entertain this prospect and he immediately embarked on an ambitious plan to seek private ownership of the Swans and therefore irrevocably change the face of Australian football. Pritchard's ambitious scheme eventually reached the ear of that flamboyant doctor, Geoffrey Edelsten.

At that time, in 1985, Dr Edelsten was one of Sydney's most highly-publicised medical practitioners. He had pioneered to concept of luxury reception rooms and his name became a byword for opulence. The Pritchard-Edelsten team early in 1985 forged ahead with its plans to buy the Sydney club and meetings were held with VFL officials. Other buyers entered the scene to cloud the issue for Pritchard and Edelsten. One group was led by South Australian millionaire businessman Basil Sellers and another by leading Melbourne businessman Richard Pratt who, surprisingly, was an avid Carlton fan.

Pratt soon bowed out of the race and it became clear the VFL would have to choose between Edelsten and Sellers. At one stage it seemed the Sellers group would take control, until Edelsten upped the ante. He seemed determined to win control of the Swans, no matter the cost. Edelsten's offer eventually reached an estimated $6 million and the League announced on the night of July 31, 1985, that Edelsten had made the successful bid.

The Swans had an owner and Edelsten made the most of the publicity he had been given by making a typically flamboyant entrance to the Carlton-Swans match at Princes Park the following day. His wife Leanne on his arm, he walked around the inside of the ground to the cheers - and the boos - of the fans. He was welcomed at Carlton's official pre-match luncheon and was even promised the full support of the Carlton club. Carlton then thrashed the Swans to convince Edelsten that there was a lot of work to be done, on and off the field.

The VFL might have nominated Edelsten as the owner of the Swans, but the question of exact ownership was not revealed for some time. In fact, Edelsten's bid was highly dependent on financial support from business colleagues and it was eventually disclosed that the Swans' licence to compete in the competition had been bought by Powerplay International Limited through its subsidiary company Kemsit Pty Ltd. Meanwhile, Edelsten pressed ahead with his plans for the 1986 season.

Former Richmond forward John Northey was sacked as coach after just one year in charge of the beleaguered Swans and Edelsten immediately set his sights on Essendon premiership coach Kevin Sheedy. The Bombers were still celebrating their 1985 flag triumph when Edelsten approached Sheedy. It was just six days after the grand final and Edelsten cornered Sheedy in a lift at Melbourne's Southern Cross hotel where both men were guests at a luncheon organised by the Roaring Forties Club, a group of prominent businessmen.

Sheedy rejected Edelsten's offer and the doctor shifted his attention to former Hawthorn champion Leigh Matthews, who also declined the invitation. Edelsten then approached former Richmond, Collingwood and Geelong coach Tom Hafey, who was officially appointed the Swans' coach on October 14. Hafey must have been impressed by the quality of Edelsten's recruiting as it seemed the Swans would have a completely new combination for the 1986 season.

At a special meeting at the Sydney Hilton on October 2, Edelsten announced he had signed Melbourne's Gerard Healy, Richmond's Maurice Rioli and Tim Barling and others. The Swans later signed Geelong trio Greg Williams, David Bolton and Bernard Toohey and Essendon's Merv Neagle.

The new-look Swans were launched under a blazing sun off Sydney Harbor on February 20, 1986. Just over a month later, the Swans defeated North Melbourne by 25 points at the MCG. The Swans, under Hafey, were about to enjoy rare onfield success. Off the field, the club's problems continued and on July 1, 1986, Edelsten resigned as chairman to be replaced by former Sydney Lord Mayor Doug Sutherland. The Swans finished the season in second position, but lost narrowly to Carlton and Fitzroy in the finals.

The Swans also made the finals in 1987, but again lost both finals matches, this time to Melbourne and Hawthorn by huge margins. Following the defeat by Melbourne in the first semi-final, club general manager Ron Thomas blasted the players for their lack of commitment and vowed there would be changes in team personnel for the 1988 season. All was not well with the Swans and it later was revealed that Powerplay was in financial difficulties following the share market crash of November, 1987.

The League again had to intervene in the Swans' affairs and a net was cast for a new owner. The VFL bought the Swans for the token sum of $10 and the club eventually was bought by a consortium led by Sydney businessman John Geraghty, who became club chairman, and media personality Mike Willesee, who became club president.

The Swans, who did not even know if they would survive the 1988 season and at one stage had no cash reserves for even medical equipment, had a brand new start in 1989. Hafey was sacked and was replaced by former Carlton reserves premiership coach Colin Kinnear as the club tried to forget the trauma of the previous year.

The Swans, in the space of eight years, had shifted from Melbourne to Sydney and had been in the hands of two groups of owners (not to mention temporary ownership by the League itself). Yet, through it all, the Swans showed remarkable onfield tenacity to win a hard core of fans in the harbor city. The Swans discovered almost too late that the streets of Sydney were not paved with gold, but they at least survived Australian football's greatest, and probably bravest, adventure.

Chapter Sixteen

1985-1989
A national consensus

An end to the confrontationist society was one of the main philosophies of Bob Hawke's Labor Government when it came to power early in the 1980s.

In VFL circles the idea did not catch on, even though changes in clearance rules reduced the flow of money from football clubs into legal coffers. It was an era when chequebook football reached crazy extremes.

Just after the 1984 season, a new and ominous form of litigation was tried by Collingwood utility player Andrew Smith when he issued a summons against Footscray's Steve Macpherson claiming $100,000 damages for injuries received in a pre-season match in 1983.

This was one question which probably hadn't even occurred to the task force headed by David Mandie which was looking at the whole spectrum of League affairs. Mandie's thoroughness meant that he was often doing too good a job for the liking of the VFL and the task force was gagged from commenting on its controversial report. One suggestion of the task force was that a five-member board of management take control of the game.

By December, 1984, it was announced that Jack Hamilton would be the full-time Commissioner and Graeme Samuel, Peter Nixon, Peter Scanlon and Dick Seddon would be part-time commissioners. In all this the ordinary fan on the terraces felt more and more alienated and there was a brief rally to the call for a VFL Supporters' Association. The disillu-sionment would be reflected in people turning away from the game.

As the task force ploughed on relentlessly there was more than usual turbulence among VFL coaches. John Cahill gave up the Collingwood job to return to Adelaide and North and the Sydney Swans were also on the prowl for new coaches. The names of Barassi, already coaching Melbourne, and John Kennedy were bandied about by the Press, and other clubs such as St Kilda had coaching hassles, too.

The Saints appointed former star Darrel Baldock as coach even though he was still a Tasmanian Member of Parliament and would have to fly to Melbourne each week. In the end the huge uproar in Tasmania and the impractical nature of the exercise led Baldock to resign the St Kilda job before he had started. Loyal Graeme Gellie was given back the position he had vacated.

North pulled off a coup when it coaxed John Kennedy out of retirement to coach the club, and Collingwood caused a surprise when Bob Rose was reappointed to the job which had caused him so much heartbreak in his first stint. The Swans opted for the quiet, thoughtful skills of John Northey ,the former Richmond half-forward and Richmond appointed Paul Sproule.

Meanwhile, the link with Irish Gaelic football was resurrected and the Irish part-timers were roughed up and beaten 70-57 in the first Test in

The mighty Gary Ablett heads skyward over Footscray opponent Neil Cordy and short-term teammate Mark Jackson.

Cork. By the second time around the Irishmen were awake to the men from downunder and won 80-76. Aussie coach John Todd warned Irish umpire John Moloney that if he manhandled them again they would "hit back". Despite this diplomatic approach, the Aussies' style won the hearts of the locals and they came home with a 2-1 winning record.

The VFL's brand new commissioners didn't have to wait long for a big problem to grapple with: they had to decide whether to sell the financially embarrassed Sydney Swans to private enterprise. The team put its talents on show for prospective buyers in the opening round when it crushed St Kilda by 110 points at Moorabbin.

There was no let-up for the Saints a week later when Carlton steamed to a 140-point win. General manager Ian Stewart made a public apology to fans and chairman Lindsay Fox accepted responsibility, but it made little difference and the Saints went down for their third humiliation against Richmond. Many people wondered whether the Saints would win a game, but on Anzac Day they confounded the critics with a fighting win over Fitzroy.

On the following weekend the televised Sunday reserves game, usually nothing more than a slight diversion, produced the headline of the month. Collingwood seconds player John Bourke was reported for kicking the field umpire and also sinking the boots into Swan Pat Foy. He was suspended for 10 years and despite Collingwood lodging papers with the Supreme Court claiming he was denied natural justice, Bourke remained on the outer until reprieved after the 1990 season by Tribunal chairman Neil Busse.

One of the VFL's biggest names, Leigh Matthews was embroiled in a clash which exposed the cumbersome nature of the VFL's judicial system. After three tame quarters the Hawthorn-Geelong game exploded with Geelong's full-forward Mark Jackson the catalyst. A series of vicious brawls broke out, then late in the quarter Matthews clashed with Geelong's Neville Bruns. Bruns went down with a broken jaw and Matthews went down in the square-up with a broken nose. The VFL took two weeks to complete its investigation and eventually asked for Matthews and Geelong's Steven Hocking to front charges. Matthews had his registration and permit cancelled for four weeks for "conduct unbecoming a VFL player" and Hocking was cleared. Two days later Matthews was charged with assaulting Bruns and was later found guilty of assault. It was an action which tarnished the record of one of the game's fine individuals.

> One of the VFL's biggest names, Leigh Matthews was embroiled in a clash which exposed the cumbersome nature of the VFL's judicial system.

Through all of the trauma happening in other circles Essendon continued to build an aura of near-invincibility. It seemed the Bombers, having endured the trauma of repeated elimination final losses and a grand final hiding, had used the 1984 reversal over Hawthorn as a springboard for an era of total domination. No side since the glorious Melbourne days of the 1950s, apart from perhaps Richmond in the early 1970s, had looked to be so absolutely flawless and overwhelming.

The big-man power of the peerless Simon Madden and his aggressive partner Roger Merrett was a key to the side and the return of Paul Salmon offered insurmountable height up forward. Around the ground the Bombers had powerhouse footballers in Tim Watson, Terry Daniher, Leon Baker, Mark Harvey and Mark Thompson. On occasions even Sheedy's eagle-like vigilance did not prevent complacency and the game against lowly St Kilda was an example. The Saints trailed by 44 points, but slashed the gap with a seven-goal burst in 12 minutes. Even that was not enough to faze the Bombers who steadied and won, but at least it showed other sides they were human.

Essendon entered the grand final as hot favorite after a convincing second semi-final win against

Hawthorn. The Hawks surprised with the grand final strategy of recalling veteran David O'Halloran to mind the gargantuan Salmon, but from the outset it was apparent that they were undermanned.

Hawthorn threw everything at the Bombers in a physical opening that included a brawl involving every man on the field, and for a brief time Essendon looked unsettled. But by half way through the term the Bombers had regained composure and led by nine points at the change of ends. Dermott Brereton, playing a magnificent lone hand at full-forward, kept the Hawks in the match until half-time, but after that Essendon picked up the game by the scruff of the neck and never relinquished control. The 11-goal burst in the final half hour buried Hawthorn. It was the last appearance in the 340-game career of Leigh Matthews and he commented that Essendon was the greatest team he had seen.

About the only cloud on the Essendon horizon was the report that Sheedy had been offered a huge sum to coach the Swans. Big-spending new owner Geoffrey Edelsten was on record as saying that he wanted someone more flamboyant than John Northey, but in the end Sheedy stayed at Windy Hill and rejected an offer said to be worth $1.5 million.

Essendon may have dominated the season, but Footscray deserved high commendation. The Bulldogs rose to third under the astute coaching of Michael Malthouse and also produced the Brownlow medallist, Brad Hardie, and the top goalkicker, Simon Beasley. The Bulldogs produced a high quality, determined brand of football and were helped by a good run with injuries. Eight of their players appeared in all 25 games.

In October, 1985, the VFL recommended a radical set of plans that would change the competition forever. The main recommendations were the introduction of a 14-team national competition in 1987, replacement of the zoning scheme with a national draft, and the rejection of private ownership of Melbourne clubs but the possibility of merger as a last resort.

Over summer the Melbourne-based clubs battened down the hatches and prepared for the storm of Dr Edelsten's cheque-book assault. Astronomical figures were being suggested as it was said the Swans were prepared to pay $580,000 for Essendon's Simon Madden, and that they had already forked out $250,000 to regain Paul Morwood from St Kilda. The Sydney club missed out on Madden but netted Merv Neagle (Essendon), Gerard Healy (Melbourne) and the Geelong trio of Bernard Toohey, Greg Williams and David Bolton.

The coaching merry-go-round saw four men swap seats with Tom Hafey going from Geelong to the Swans, John Northey coming to Melbourne from Sydney, and Robert Walls and David Parkin, by a circuitous process, swapping jobs at Fitzroy and Carlton. In another interesting move Leigh Matthews was appointed assistant coach to Collingwood's Bob Rose.

For Parkin the culture shock of going from the big-spending Carlton to the financially straitened Fitzroy created a new set of coaching circumstances, but he seemed to have adapted straight away when he guided the team to a 50 point win in the first game. One of the many people sinking the boots into the Lions was former VFL president Allen Aylett who predicted a couple of months earlier that 1986 would be the club's last in the VFL and they would possibly merge with Melbourne.

Fitzroy wasn't the only club under the financial hammer. St Kilda's troubles were well known, Footscray needed more onfield success to get out of the mire and Richmond announced a big sponsorship by brewing magnate Alan Bond which it hoped would save the club.

But the real shock came when it was announced that Collingwood's finances were in bad shape. Here was the club which despite all its grand final woes

> In October, 1985, the VFL recommended a radical set of plans that would change the competition forever.

Brownlow Medallist Robert DiPierdomenico gets his kick in the 1986 grand final.

had the biggest following in Australia. The newly introduced salary cap, a rule limiting the amount each club could pay its players per year, posed a huge dilemma for the Magpies who had spent freely in the previous couple of seasons. Players such as David Cloke, Mike Richardson and Geoff Raines did not come cheap and all players were asked to take a 10 per cent pay cut in January so the Magpies would not have to unload footballers. Coach Bob Rose and his assistant Matthews accepted the cut in a show of good faith, but the players wouldn't have a bar of it.

Champion Peter Daicos, recovering from a knee operation, said he would quit the club, but eventually he was talked into staying. Then popular 10-year player Peter McCormack was sacked to keep the club within the salary cap.

After the Magpies lost the opening two games players were told they must take a 20 per cent pay

cut. Geoff Raines, a costly buy from Richmond, refused and was promptly dropped. He and Mike Richardson would be cleared to Essendon later in the year. President Ranald Macdonald said the club's financial position had worsened by $300,000 after losing the first two games plus a loss in the night competition.

Two days after yet another loss, Rose and Macdonald quit and chief executive Peter Bahen was sacked. Leigh Matthews took over as coach saying he would make no promises whatsoever. The Magpies turned to the younger players and they repaid the confidence. By late in the year the side had a chance for the finals, but was pushed aside by Fitzroy, the club which had moved to Victoria Park as co-tenant and ironically was regarded as poor relations.

The League introduced a new rule before the 1986 season under which players could be reported for wasting time, and while it was a noble philosophy the implementation was not easy. First man reported was Essendon's interstate recruit Brenton Phillips and the unusual result of the hearing was a $500 fine for the Bombers for not telling him about the rule beforehand.

Essendon started the season in dynamic style with a 10-goal win over Collingwood and then a 16-goal thrashing of Geelong. A hat-trick of flags was there for the taking if you believed the talk around town, but in the Geelong game there was a sign of things to come when Paul Van Der Haar broke his ankle. The following week claimed Tim Watson for the season and Mark Harvey also went down in the eight-point cliffhanger win over Footscray. The Bombers and Blues fought out a classic game on Anzac Day before Carlton took the points. Along the way Essendon suffered yet another long term casualty when Darren Williams broke his leg.

> The League introduced a new rule before the 1986 season under which players could be reported for wasting time.

From that point Essendon produced a mixture of hot and cold football that drove coach Kevin Sheedy to distraction. In the end the Bombers just made the five and many people wondered whether the introduction of high-priced Collingwood malcontents Raines and Richardson had a disruptive effect on morale. Essendon cleared Steve Carey and Peter Bradbury, two fine clubmen, to stay within the salary cap provisions and it was an action reminiscent of Richmond's release of Brian Roberts in the 1970s.

A matter of concern to the VFL was the increasingly nasty habit of eye-gouging. Umpires adviser Bill Deller said it was becoming serious and North's Jim Krakouer was the first man to face the tribunal. He was cleared of the charge, but a month later the problem re-surfaced when Essendon and the Swans met on the Queen's Birthday. Four players were subsequently asked to appear before the VFL on charges of "conduct unbecoming". Swans Rod Carter and David Bolton and Bombers Trevor Spencer and

Brian Wood faced an extraordinary meeting of the Tribunal at Channel Seven in a precursor of the "trial by video" approach which was to become more prevalent.

It was a year that saw several clubs adopt desperate measures to shore up their finances. Collingwood launched a national campaign to raise $1 million, Footscray restated its determination to remain in the western suburbs, and Fitzroy drew a crowd of 3000 people to Festival Hall who pledged money to support the club. St Kilda held a rally of supporters to raise enough cash to stay afloat and the miraculous turnout even sparked the team to a 75-point win over Richmond the following Saturday.

The ugly spectre of merger loomed as a possibility for some clubs. Fitzroy and Melbourne actually got to the negotiating table and St Kilda also made tentative overtures to the Lions before being convinced by the successful supporters' rally that they could go on alone.

At League headquarters there was a change at the top when Jack Hamilton retired and Ross Oakley took over as chief commissioner.

In the first week of the finals reigning premier Essendon met Fitzroy, the team which had been threatened with extinction for months. A tight, hardfought game in wet conditions was finally decided by a running goal from Fitzroy's Mick Conlan with only 45 seconds left for play. Game, heroic Fitzroy had captured the public's sympathy and fervour. Coach Parkin had a team bonded together by the threatening talk of the League's big-wigs and the club possessed unlimited spirit. It also had two of the best footballers in Australia in Gary Pert and Paul Roos and an ageing, but still mightily effective, full-forward in Bernie Quinlan. Ruckman Matt Rendell and bustling forwards Doug Barwick and Mick Conlan gave great drive.

When the Lions met the Swans in the first semi-final it was a clash of opposites. The Swans had money, flashiness, and hype - all factors absent from the Lion den. Fitzroy did have the overwhelming support of the crowd, but for the best part of three quarters it seemed the Sydneysiders would win the day. Fitzroy was undaunted and four goals in eight minutes amid teeming rain set up a last-quarter fightback that snatched a memorable five-point victory and bundled Sydney out of the finals race.

Hawthorn, rolled by Carlton in the second semi, faced Fitzroy in the preliminary final and although they never gave in, the Lions saw their dream evaporate under the weight of Hawthorn's clinical professionalism.

The Hawks restructured their team and their strategy for the grand final and Allan Jeans plotted a path that snuffed out the Blues' chances from the earliest stages of the match. Hawk full-forward Jason Dunstall goaled from their first attacking move and relentless smothering and tackling stopped the Blues developing their flow. Smarting after the consecutive grand final losses to Essendon, Hawthorn was in no mind to let its prey off the hook.

Hawthorn had a great goal-to-goal line of Chris Mew, Chris Langford, Terry Wallace, Dermott Brereton and Dunstall and had tremendous talent all over the field. The Hawks' win was hailed by the average fan who saw Hawthorn as "the family club" and Carlton as everything they despised about the modern game. The Blues meant big business, big money and faceless men sipping cocktails in corporate boxes. That feeling was strengthened after the game when Carlton's millionaire president John Elliott ridiculed Hawthorn's homespun image and its famed after-training barbecues.

Hawthorn president Ron Cook told the story of the previous grand final when the committee's postmortem concluded Jeans should become full-time coach and enlist the help of a psychologist. When he rang Jeans, the veteran coach said he had a couple of things he wanted to say. One was that he should devote more time to the job and the other

was that he would like a psychologist to help with the players! Cook was amazed, but the tale accurately depicted the unity of purpose and approach at the club.

League football braced itself for the biggest changes in its history. As the executives of the two new clubs, West Coast Eagles and Brisbane Bears, set about constructing teams, the other clubs prepared for recruiting raids.

Hawthorn immediately showed that no favors would be granted when it went to court to prevent the Eagles winning the services of Paul Harding and Gary Buckenara. Harding had originally signed with the Hawks then signed with West Coast when the new club sprung into existence. Buckenara, a native West Australian, had wanted to go home. In the end Hawthorn kept both men and showed that for all the homespun image the club had a will of iron and streak of ruthlessness.

The Brisbane Bears cobbled together a collection of hand-me-down players with some respectable purchases such as Brad Hardie, Phillip Walsh and Mark Williams. No-one expected the team to begin with a victory, but ex-South Australian Mark Mickan guided them to success over North Melbourne on the opening Friday night at the MCG. After the match the Bears had to sing the club song from photocopied sheets. The other new chum in the VFL, the West Coast Eagles, powered home with a nine-goal-to-one last quarter that destroyed Richmond in Perth.

A week later the Eagles played excellent football to go within five points of Essendon at Windy Hill in a titanic game. Many football people wondered whether the Eagles would prove to be too great a power once they got together and it was suggested that two teams from the west should have been introduced to divide the Sandgropers' strength.

Back in Victoria coaches like Tony Jewell, now

> **League football braced itself for the biggest changes in its history.**

had built a game suited to the smaller confines of the Sydney Cricket Ground. Full-forward Warwick Capper was the darling of the local crowd with his spring-heeled marking and goalkicking skills, and the Swans had a fleet of talented medium-sized and small players who kept pumping the ball forward. Greg Williams and Gerard Healy knocked up getting possessions and rovers Stevie Wright and Barry Mitchell were terriers around the packs. A fighting seven-point win over Carlton was a highlight and late in the year the Swans claimed the unusual record of kicking three 30-goal-plus scores in a row.

The Blues sat at the top of the ladder in the mid part of the season before going down in Perth by three points. Early in the year they had suffered the tragedy of Peter Motley's shocking car accident. A fine defender who had been one of the few men to hold his head high in the 1986 grand final debacle, Motley survived the horrific crash, but it ended his football career. Defender Des English was forced to retire because of a battle with cancer and plight of their two teammates had a unifying effect on the Princes Park team.

Carlton had its share of drama on the field during the year and no finish was tighter than the game against St Kilda which hit the front 29 minutes into the last quarter after a stirring fightback. Milham Hanna goaled just before the siren to snatch a one-point win for the Blues. Carlton had appointed Stephen Kernahan as captain at the start of the year after only one season as a player. Kernahan had come from South Australia with a huge reputation and his brilliant high marking at centre half-forward made him a power. He responded magnificently to the captaincy. The Blues had great defenders in Stephen Silvagni and Jon Dorotich and coach Walls surprised many people by using the game's "enfant terrible" David Rhys-Jones in a defensive role for much of the season.

Hawthorn, as always, was a leading light and the talent of Jason Dunstall and Dermott Brereton in

Up and over. Hawk John Platten takes a spectacular spill.

back at Richmond, had more to worry about. The Tigers' series of last-quarter fade-outs was enough to drive him to despair, and Footscray's Mick Malthouse wasn't much better off after three hidings in the opening weeks of the season. Stories of internal discontent and possible extinction began to circulate, but the Bulldogs scared off the swirling vultures by a stunning reversal in beating Hawthorn. Powered by rover Brian Royal who kicked six goals, the team began a string of wins that would place it in contention for a finals berth.

The Sydney Swans were the early pacesetters and

attack was enough to kick winning scores in most games. The Hawks had a good run with injuries for most of the year, but in the closing weeks the problems with Dunstall, Chris Mew and rover Richard Loveridge threw the side out of gear.

By the latter rounds the coveted top three places were safely held by Carlton, Hawthorn and Sydney with the Blues having a stranglehold on top position. Interest shifted to the fight for a berth in the five and the unlikely name of St Kilda emerged as a chance. The Saints, a long-time chopping block, had shaken off their loser image under coach Darrel Baldock who had finally arrived in Melbourne to take on the job he had rejected a couple of years earlier.

Headed by an unstoppable full-forward, Tony Lockett, and a brilliant young Western Australian Aboriginal, Nicky Winmar, the Saints had a talented band of young players who struck a purple patch late in the year. They crunched Melbourne and rolled fourth side North before edging out Footscray in an emotion charged game at Moorabbin where Lockett kicked his 100th goal then followed up with the matchwinner a few minutes later. St Kilda's coach Darrel Baldock had suffered a stroke a couple of days earlier and his team played inspired football. Just as the mathematicians were calculating permutations by which St Kilda could make the finals the dream ended abruptly at the hands of bottom side Richmond. Saint fans had some consolation when Lockett tied for the Brownlow Medal with Hawthorn's John Platten a few weeks later.

With St Kilda out of contention another "Cinderella" team came into the reckoning. When St Kilda thrashed the Demons a few weeks earlier onlookers would have given only one of the clubs a hope of reaching the finals and it certainly wasn't Melbourne. The Demons had not contested a finals series for 23 years, and had been on the brink of merging with Fitzroy less than 12 months earlier. A fundraising campaign had focused on the wish to give brilliant skipper Robert Flower one last chance

Happy Blues. Steve Kernahan holds the 1987 premiership cup.

to play in the finals, and by the last round the Demons had to beat fellow contender Footscray and hope that Hawthorn accounted for Geelong.

Melbourne accomplished its part of the task, but had to wait on the result at Kardinia Park and fans clustered around transistors as the game went down to the wire. When Jason Dunstall kicked a goal with 30 seconds to go the Demon fans went wild. Their battling team was in the five.

Their entry into the finals gave a new spark to the competition and all hearts were with Flower, the classic champion making his finals debut after 270 games. Any thoughts that just getting there would be enough for Melbourne were soon dispelled. The three most experienced players, Flower, Greg Healy and Brian Wilson, had worked off the field to unite the team and it showed in the elimination final when it overwhelmed North Melbourne to record a huge win by 118 points.

A whole new set of possibilities opened up because of Hawthorn's slaughter of Sydney a day earlier. The Swans, shell-shocked and in disarray, lost 100-goal full-forward Warwick Capper and winger Merv Neagle with injuries and a big crowd flocked to the MCG for the Sunday final to see if the Melbourne phenomenon could continue. Melbourne jumped the Sydney team which offered surprisingly meek resistance as it lost its fourth final in succession to complete two miserable years of September failure.

Melbourne was now the flavor of the month, but hardened observers predicted the dream would come to a rude end now the side had entered the VFL's silk department. Hawthorn and Carlton, the two clubs which stood between the Demons and a flag that had been unimaginable a month earlier, were battle toughened finalists and paid scant attention to the hype of a new up-and-comer.

For all that, it was Melbourne which held the lead for most of the day against Hawthorn in the preliminary final. Going into the final term the Demons gripped a 22-point advantage and it seemed even the gods were on their side as the wind had changed at quarter-time, meaning they had the advantage for three quarters. Hawthorn had made wholesale changes to its team and gradually began to peg back the Demons who started to play safe. With only a minute to play the Hawks had crept within three points.

Buckenara received a free-kick 50 metres out from goal with only seconds to go. Few people heard the siren, certainly not Melbourne ruckman Jim Stynes who desperately ran across Buckenara's path to pick up a man. The umpire awarded a 15-metre

penalty which put Buckenara within easy range and he made no mistake. The tears flowed on both sides of the fence as Melbourne came to grips with the lost hope. Ironically Melbourne would have entered the grand final without two stars as Flower and Wilson were injured during the game.

In an era of machine-like, production line football Melbourne's heroic finish had looked like penetrating the status quo. On grand final day it was back to Hawthorn and Carlton, meeting for the second year in a row and for the Hawks it was the fifth successive appearance in the play-off.

Hawthorn coach Allan Jeans had never seen his players more exhausted than after the preliminary final and the club also had the worry of full-forward Jason Dunstall who had missed the game. Dunstall was named in the team but when they burst through the banner his muscular frame was not to be seen. From the outset the Hawks faced an uphill battle in the hot conditions, and with Brereton struggling to overcome the effects of injury and the attentions of Carlton's Rhys-Jones, the much vaunted attack was blunted.

Carlton burst out of the blocks and received tremendous drive from Wayne Johnston whose brilliant first quarter was punctuated by a report for striking Robert Dipierdomenico. Robert Walls had welded a side with greater discipline and had more options than the Hawks. The Blues looked more durable and Walls had introduced seven new players into the 20 that lost the previous year. By game's end the Blues had won by 33 points and grabbed their 15th flag.

Hawthorn had fought it out to the bitter end as was expected, but hit an unforeseeable snag only weeks after the grand final. Veteran coach Allan Jeans suffered a brain haemorrhage and was forced to stand down. His replacement was Alan Joyce, a former player who had been the club's football director. Jeans said he would return in 1989, but many people were prepared to write him off as a League coach. They would be wrong.

> The 15-metre penalty was replaced by the 50-metre penalty. Players also had to kick the ball when receiving a free, and if the player handpassed, it meant a ball-up.

Just after the end of the season Christopher Skase's Seven Network clinched a TV deal worth $30 million over five years. The station had lost the VFL rights to ABC in 1987 and after a season in the wilderness returned with new commentators and a brighter, spruce approach. Some people wondered whether the public would tire of saturation coverage with more games scheduled on Friday nights and Sundays.

For several clubs the 1987 season did not end until early November following international tours by Carlton, Essendon, North Melbourne, Melbourne, Sydney Swans and Hawthorn and an Australian team competing in a composite rules series in Ireland. A Bicentennial Carnival of state sides in February and the Panasonic Cup played exclusively pre-season meant little rest for footballers.

Players, umpires and spectators had plenty of problems coming to grips with the new rules introduced for the 1988 season. The vexed question of preventing players from delaying the game had been addressed in confused manner by the reporting of players, but now the 15-metre penalty was replaced by 50-metre penalty. Players also had to kick the ball when receiving a free, and if the player handpassed it meant a ball-up.

The Brisbane Bears' entry to the national competition in 1987 had not been without its trauma and the northern club attracted plenty of headlines again in 1988 when it grabbed glamor Sydney full-forward Warwick Capper for a reported transfer fee of $400,000. The record fee will never be broken unless League clearance rules change in the future. Also netted in the Bears' trawling expedition were Fitzroy's Scott McIvor, Hawks Rod Lester-Smith and Rodney Eade and Essendon strongman Roger Merrett.

There was also trouble at home for the Bears when the club agreed to stay at Carrara and incurred the wrath of the Queensland Australian Football League which wanted the club in Brisbane. Constantly heavy rain early in the season didn't help the Bears' preparation either and the VFL shifted a Bears-Eagles clash from sodden Carrara to Subiaco Oval.

It had been obvious for years that the VFL wanted to even up the competition, but stronger clubs baulked at the idea calling it "football communism". The West Coast Eagles prepared a detailed submission which resulted in them gaining the first five choices from Western Australia in the 1988 draft.

Much of the opening round attention focused on full-forwards. Warwick Capper was unsuited by a drenched Carrara, and back in sunny Melbourne the Brownlow medallist Tony Lockett opened his new campaign by being the first player to be booked by an emergency umpire. He was outed for three weeks and the new-look VFL Tribunal assumed more menace than ever before. A week later Melbourne's Rod Grinter flattened Footscray's Terry Wallace and even though he was not reported the VFL called in its special investigator to view the incident and Grinter copped a six week holiday.

Field umpire Ian Clayton was banished to the country over the incident and all umpires were made fully aware of what lay in store if they did not report players.

Field umpire Ian Clayton was banished to the country over the incident and all umpires were made fully aware of what lay in store if they did not report players. One non-violent report was that of St Kilda's Stewart Loewe, the first man in 64 years to be reported for shaking a goalpost! He was fined $1000.

There was always something new at the Tribunal and Geelong's Martin Christensen introduced a rare element - honesty - when giving evidence against Justin Madden, the man alleged to have struck him. Carlton's general manager Ian Collins criticised the Geelong man for his lack of "player ethics".

The troubled Swans were put up for sale by owners Powerplay in yet another downward twist to the endless saga of the Harbor City club. The Swans were

Gerard Healy was good footballer when he went to Sydney from Melbourne, but by the end of his career he was regarded as a great one.

marked on the final siren, needing to kick the goal to win the match and chaos erupted when Bears fans jumped the fence and twice prevented him from taking the kick. Brisbane's Mike Richardson sat on a teammate's shoulders in the goalsquare to provide further distraction and when Beasley finally took the kick he missed after having kicked seven goals straight for the afternoon. Footscray was justifiably incensed at the farcical shambles, but could do nothing to change the result.

St Kilda had been in the depths of despair, but pulled off an amazing last-gasp win over Geelong at Kardinia Park thanks to a match-winning goal by Nicky Winmar. The Saints then knocked off top side Melbourne and with full-forward Tony Lockett now back in devastating form took the game right up to Hawthorn.

The Saints showed their best football for years, but could not hold the Hawks in the later stages. The backline had been depleted when captain Danny Frawley was sensationally knocked out behind play by Dermott Brereton. Brereton took charge in the dying stages, but was later suspended for six weeks. Just as the Saints looked like fulfilling their promise Lockett broke his ankle in the Footscray game. His season was over and so, effectively, was St Kilda's.

At the same time as St Kilda fell away, Richmond began to bloom. Kevin Bartlett's young side had only two wins from the first 11 matches, but stunned reigning premier Carlton. Two weeks later they took the points against the Swans in Sydney and the world started taking notice of youngsters such as Greg Lambert and Tony Free. The Tigers at least were able to catch a flight home from Sydney. A fortnight later St Kilda had to wait in Sydney for two days because Tullamarine airport was closed by fog.

Footscray, constantly under the hammer because of its financial problems, revealed it could not make necessary improvement to its ground without VFL assistance.

defeated by Melbourne in Sydney for the first time and the Demons racked up their fifth win in succession. A week later the VFL bought the Swans for a nominal fee of $10 and installed a 16-man board to run the club until a satisfactory owner was found. The Swans had debts of $3.5 million yet the players' spirit could not be questioned and they notched a fine victory at Geelong in the midst of the turmoil.

To some Sunday TV viewers sitting next to their fires, the fortnightly game telecast from sunny Carrara might well have come from another planet and that air of unreality was never more apparent than in the clash with Footscray. Simon Beasley

By late in the season the top four clubs - Hawthorn, Collingwood, Melbourne and Carlton - had established themselves, but there were seven other contenders for the last finals place. Among these was West Coast, a fine performance in the club's second year, even though the team struggled to win in Melbourne.

The colorful Dermott Brereton returned after his suspension and immediately made his presence felt by charging through the pack at the opening bounce against Melbourne and bowling over anyone in his way. The following week he marched through the Essendon three-quarter-time huddle, bumping a couple of stunned opposition players as he went. Essendon coach Kevin Sheedy laughed it off by saying: "He's just another mad Irishman!".

The plucky Swans, despite all their hardship, scored a coup by beating Carlton and the players also won a handsome return when they backed themselves with $1000 at odds of five to one against. The brilliant quartet of Gerard Healy (on his way to a Brownlow), Greg Williams, Barry Mitchell and David Murphy fuelled the win.

A feverish struggle for the five now opened up another possibility as Melbourne's form deteriorated. On the morning after round 21 there was another sensation when Channel Seven highlighted two incidents involving veterans Warren "Wow" Jones and Terry Daniher. The Saint big man subsequently fronted a specially convened tribunal hearing and was suspended for four weeks, thus ending his career despite two subsequent re-hearings. Daniher received a suspended sentence. The incidents stirred the argument about "trial by video", a controversy that would rage even more brightly the next year.

Melbourne shook off its lethargy and sealed a finals place by beating Carlton in the final round. That left a mathematician's delight in the Sunday clash between Footscray and West Coast. The Eagles had to overcome their appalling Melbourne record and could still get in even if they lost by less

than five goals. Footscray had to win by around 10 goals to get in, but if they won by six to seven goals Essendon would sneak in on percentage. The Eagles ended the calculations by winning easily.

Hawthorn stormed into the finals as red-hot favorites, but a thrilling elimination final caught the public's imagination. West Coast skipped away early, but Melbourne fought back and a snap by Garry Lyon in time-on gave the Demons the lead. The Eagles' Wrensted missed tragically in the dying seconds and Melbourne held on for a two-point win.

A rejuvenated Melbourne romped past Collingwood in the first semi-final then stunned Carlton in a hard fought preliminary final. Now the Demons faced their 1987 nemesis, Hawthorn in the grand final.

But there would be no last-minute sensation such as the Buckenara-Stynes incident to decide this game. Hawthorn quickly took control and dominated. With machine-like precision the Hawks dismembered Melbourne, which looked out of its depth. The victory was so comprehensive it was hard to imagine that a few months earlier many people had said the Hawks were getting too old. Michael Tuck, Russell Greene, Robert Dipierdomenico were all the wrong side of 30, and Peter Russo, Peter Schwab, John Kennedy and Gary Ayres weren't far behind. Yet the club had blooded new men such as Tony Hall, Scott Maginness, Andrew Gowers, Robert Dickson and Dean Anderson to build its future.

The advent of the draft system meant an eerie quiet over summer compared with the frenetic horsetrading of the past. Bottom side St Kilda swapped its first draft choice with Hawthorn in exchange for Hawks Paul Harding, Robert Handley and Peter Russo. The Hawks were able to look to the long-term and picked an 18-year-old from the country. St Kilda, on the other hand was desperately in need of experience and jumped at the chance of getting three readymade players. Harding, who had been the centre of a court battle between Hawthorn and the Eagles a couple of years earlier, gave St Kilda a great season and Russo proved handy. The VFL's draft was beginning to unfold in just the way it had hoped and when Footscray, St Kilda and the Swans headed the list after the first game it looked like a bumper year.

It was also soon evident that it would be a bumper year at the Tribunal with 12 reports on opening day, and clubs showed their first sign of resistance when Collingwood tried twice, unsuccessfully, to have Craig Starcevich's case reopened.

There had been much speculation over summer about Tony Lockett's recovery from a broken ankle and some of the more exotic theories had him written off as a virtual cripple. A 13-goal effort in a practice game against Essendon showed he was capable of more than just standing and when he kicked nine goals against the Bears it was obvious he was back in business. He followed that with a sensational 10 goals against Carlton in the second round which included a drop-punt goal only 45 seconds before the final siren to win the game.

The Blues' slide continued with a third consecutive loss and everything at the club was put under the microscope. Rumors concentrated on player-coach friction, committee in-fighting and too much emphasis on big business. The corporate dollar was becoming the all-important factor on a wider front and ordinary fans felt cheated when thousands were turned away from the Collingwood-St Kilda and Essendon-Carlton games on the Anzac Day weekend.

It was farcical that the MCG was not used on either of these days and the lame-duck excuses offered by the VFL and the home clubs were treated with disdain. Collingwood and Carlton said ground switches would have hurt their sponsors. The Blues were also desperate for a win, but despite a flying finish it did not come against Essendon. During the

> The Cats took out their frustrations on St Kilda the following Saturday by kicking the fourth highest VFL score of all time in a 35-goal avalanche.

week the Blues had resorted to using rugby union coach Alan Jones to motivate the team.

Geelong made a flying start to the season, but most people were wary of making extravagant predictions about eventual success as it had often failed to deliver in similar circumstances. Certainly coach Malcolm Blight seemed to have found the right recipe this time around, but the old doubts surfaced when the Cats squandered a sizeable lead to go down to Fitzroy by a point.

Still the Carlton woes continued. There was little sympathy from the rest of the football public when the Blues lost their fifth in a row, the club's worst start since 1899. In the meantime one of the game's true champions, Terry Daniher, celebrated his 250th game by playing a key role in the win over St Kilda. "He's the only person at Essendon I've ever threatened to fine if I saw him at training," quipped coach Kevin Sheedy after the game.

Geelong had developed a dazzling brand of football and put it on show against the mighty Hawthorn to build a lead of 56 points by late in the second term. The Cats did slacken, but Hawthorn's comeback was magnificent. Gary Ayres seized control in the centre and powered the Hawks to a 64-point turnaround and an amazing victory. The Cats took out their frustrations on St Kilda the following Saturday by kicking the fourth highest VFL score of all time in a 35-goal avalanche.

The Bears had a constant battle to make an impact on the competition and turned in a lamentable effort against Geelong, kicking only 2.12 to three-quarter-time and going down by 129 points. Much of the criticism aimed at the club was also directed at costly full-forward Warwick Capper. The much-maligned Capper sunk Carlton with a late goal at Princes Park, but the full ramifications of the kick did not become apparent until a few days later when the Carlton powerbrokers sacked coach Robert Walls and chairman of selectors Wes Lofts.

Walls was replaced by Carlton legend Alex

Jesaulenko who had taken charge in similarly dramatic style mid-season 10 years before.

St Kilda had problems of a different nature. The Saints had made their best start to a season in 16 years, thanks largely to brilliant full-forward Tony Lockett, but the grand dream of the Moorabbin faithful unravelled against the Eagles when the big full-forward was reported. Lockett, with 70 goals from nine games, was on course to break the season goalkicking record of 150 and perhaps collect another Brownlow, but it all went down the drain when he was suspended for four weeks. When he came back he injured a groin and missed the closing part of the year. The Saints won the next match to be out of the five on percentage, but fell away from there.

The Geelong doubters began to think that maybe the Cats would be a power at long last when the magical Gary Ablett blitzed Collingwood in the wet at the MCG then repeated the dose on Essendon at the same venue.

Sydney had copped rain every weekend for five months, but up to this stage Melbourne had been blessed with fine conditions. The weather turned nasty and even the MCG's normally perfect surface began to show the strain. The Hawthorn-Bears clash was moved from there to VFL Park so the Cricket Ground could recover in time for the interstate clash with South Australia. Conditions were worse at Windy Hill where Essendon won 3.10 to 3.5. The match aggregate of 51 points was the lowest in any VFL game since the 1927 grand final when Richmond and Collingwood could only manage 38 points.

Coaches, as ever, occupied the hot seats of VFL football and an ill-timed leak at St Kilda told the world that Darrel Baldock would be returning to Tasmania in 1990. A couple of weeks later the Bears sacked Peter Knights and installed Paul Feltham.

Back in Melbourne the MCG looked like a beach as it had been covered with sand to soak up the mud.

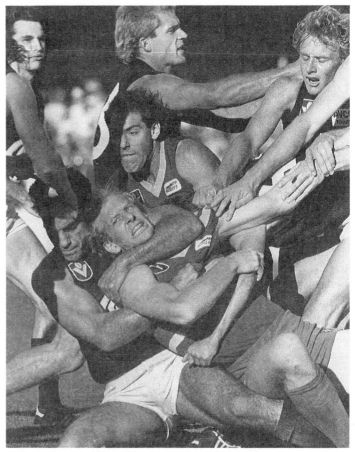

Possibly around the neck? Carlton's Jon Dorotich applies a less than legal tackle on Bulldog forward Simon Beasley.

The top four sides - Hawthorn, Essendon, Geelong and Melbourne - were safely ensconced, but Collingwood's place was under threat from Fitzroy and North Melbourne. The Magpies tumbled out of the five in round 19 when they were pipped by North. Fitzroy, which had edged into the Magpies' place, stayed there only seven days after Collingwood rolled it at VFL Park. The Lions' agony was compounded by a serious knee injury suffered by star forward Richard Osborne.

Collingwood held its place in the five and met Melbourne in the elimination final. For the second year in a row the Demons ended Collingwood's run, but found themselves on the outer when Geelong demolished them in the first semi-final. The Cats then steamrolled Essendon by 94 points in the biggest turnaround of all time. Only 13 days earlier Essendon had humiliated the Cats by 76 points.

The stage was set for a classic grand final between Hawthorn and Geelong. The Hawks started as favorites, but everyone recalled the dazzling burst by Geelong against them in the Princes Park game earlier in the year and wondered whether the Cats could sustain that brand of football for four quarters.

There was a sensational opening when Gary Ablett opened the scoring with a goal after just 19 seconds. Dermott Brereton, in an action which was virtually becoming a trademark, tried to charge through the centre at the bounce and was thwarted by Mark Yeates. Brereton had wrought havoc against Essendon in the second semi-final and to lose him would be a tremendous psychological blow. Even his detractors had to admire the way he soldiered on in the forward pocket kicking two goals in a great Hawk opening of eight goals.

An injury-ravaged Hawthorn held a six-goal lead going into the last quarter and that looked enough to seal the flag. Surely even a side of Geelong's firepower could not bridge that sort of gap in the last quarter of a grand final against such quality opposition. But with 10 minutes left there were only two kicks between the sides thanks to the brilliance of Ablett and the spirit of his teammates. When the final siren sounded Hawthorn was clinging to a six-point lead.

It was a triumphant comeback for Allan Jeans after his serious illness and a testimony to Hawthorn's indomitable commitment after suffering a number of serious injuries in the game. Wingman Robert Dipierdomenico's effort of playing on with a punctured lung typified the determination, but it was later revealed that Geelong had also suffered injuries in this classic, but tough, game.

The dust had hardly settled when it was announced that Footscray and Fitzroy would merge. The deal would virtually obliterate Footscray and it sparked a wave of anger and emotion. There had been talk of mergers since a VFL think-tank session in Hobart three-quarters of the way through the season, but the news that it would actually occur rocked the public. In the end the Bulldogs survived thanks to a public uprising of supporters.

At a time when there was a public perception the game was being ruled by corporate wheelers and dealers this was a victory for the average supporter whose opinions had so often been trampled in the dust. It was a timely reminder for the League's hierarchy that the change of name from Victorian Football League to Australian Football League could not erase the tradition of years gone by.

That, after all, was what the game was all about.

THE NATIONAL HURDLES

The League would like to believe that football's move to a national competition was prompted by a pioneering spirit and a realisation that the game needed to expand.

In truth the League's growth from the suburbs of Melbourne would not have gone ahead without the existing clubs chasing the quick-fix of instant dollars from licence fees.

Western Australia and South Australia were always Aussie Rules states, but the advances into Sydney and Queensland broke new ground as rugby was the dominant force. Oddly enough rugby took over as No.1 sport in Western Australia way back in the 1880s, but the commitment to the old English game was fickle and when Fremantle Rugby Club was convinced to change codes it was a turning point. The Fremantle name was a strong force throughout the development of Western Australian football. Gold strikes in 1892 changed Western Australia irrevocably and many of the greatest Victorian footballers headed West to try their luck on the fields around Coolgardie and Kalgoorlie.

Even the mightiest of them all decided to pull up stumps and chase his fortune on the other side of the continent. Albert "The Great" Thurgood was to Essendon and the VFA what Gary Ablett is to Geelong and the AFL today. It was no surprise that this giant of the game dominated in Fremantle's side.

The goldfields competition was extremely strong and half of the early WA representative sides were made up of goldfields players.

Western Australia churned out quality footballers for years and Victorian clubs constantly raided their stocks. By the early 1980s most of the WA clubs were broke and relied on transfer fees to survive.

In 1986 WA officials jumped at the chance to enter a composite side in the national competition and the West Coast Eagles were born. South Australia, on the other hand, would have nothing to do with such a deal and steadfastly refused to be part of the new AFL. There was a rich heritage of football in Adelaide that extended as far back as 1860 and through the South Australian history there was a constant thread of resentment towards the bossy and arrogant Victorians.

Like Fremantle in WA, the Port Adelaide Football Club was a long term and pivotal player in the story of South Australian football from the moment it was formed in 1870. In 1877 Victorian club teams Melbourne and St Kilda made the trek to Adelaide and in 1888 Norwood played South Melbourne for the "Championship of Australia" and won. One of the prime objectives of the Victorian Football Association upon its formation in 1877 was to arrange games between Victoria and other colonies. On July 1, 1879 Victoria thrashed a South Australian team by 7.14 to 0.3 at East Melbourne Cricket Ground in the first intercolonial clash.

There was nothing more satisfying to South Australians than beating the cocky Victorians and a wariness of all things Victorian surfaced in 1986 when the VFL went national. South Australia refused to hop in bed with its arch rival, but the whole scenario changed in July 1990 when Port Adelaide made a bid to join the AFL. The SANFL was horri-

fied at first, but then realised it could be left out on a limb and formed its own proposal to join the AFL. In September 1990 the AFL clubs voted 13-1 in favor of the AFL signing a deal with the SANFL. The Adelaide Football Club was up and running within two weeks and Port Adelaide was left to ponder its fate.

Of all the interstate clubs that have joined the AFL, Brisbane has had the hardest road to hoe. The side was cobbled together in a state with little football heritage and in its short history seems to have been frequently treated in a hap-hazard and thoughtless way.

Last century the game prospered in Brisbane for a brief time and was popular in some of the mining settlements. For reasons that remain unclear, the game did not maintain its original foothold despite the fact that exhibition matches in Brisbane have been sprinkled through the years. Essendon and Geelong even met for premiership points at the Brisbane Exhibition Oval in 1952.

The process of bidding for a licence in the national competition was a tangled and unsatisfactory affair. There was a suggestion that Fitzroy may relocate to Brisbane, but the move faltered and the licence was eventually granted to syndicate formed by the QAFL and former actor Paul Cronin. Entrepreneur Christopher Skase stepped in to assist with finance, but it was revealed three years later that the original $4 million licence fee remained owed to the bank that had loaned it to Skase.

A rag-tag collection of cast off players launched the club and the puzzling decision to play home games at Carrara on the Gold Coast was something that thwarted the Bears' acceptance and years passed before the club adopted its rightful home in Brisbane.

Because of its chequered career, Brisbane's rise to a finals place in 1995 had perhaps greater significance than the initial finals appearances of West Coast and Adelaide. The Bears had conquered the rockiest road of all to make the grade.

Chapter Seventeen

1990-1996
A national obsession

The name of the Victorian Football League had been an anachronism for several years and from the start of the 1990 season the competition was played under the more appropriate banner of the Australian Football League.

The change of title did not mean that life became any easier for some of the newer chums in the competition that spanned the continent. The owner of the Brisbane Bears, Quintex, collapsed as its head, Christopher Skase, was the first of many corporate high flyers to bite the dust.

Early in January, Brownlow medallist Brad Hardie told the club he would "not take part in any further physically demanding exercise" until he received his salary for the previous season. There was immediate speculation he would return to Footscray and the AFL launched an inquiry into a $50,000 cheque made out to Hardie's fiance by the Footscray Fightback Foundation which was alleged to have been drawn from funds raised to keep the club alive. Hardie returned to the Bears, but a week later the AFL fined him $5000 and fined the Bulldogs $10,000. As well, he was banned from playing for Footscray until after the 1993 draft.

Brisbane's troubles did not only centre on Hardie. Twenty-five senior players went on strike before the season in protest against the club's off-field operation and forced club chairman Paul Cronin to resign. So great were the club's problems that the AFL withdrew it from the pre-season competition, but relief came when Queensland millionaire Reuben Pelerman was awarded the licence to run the Bears and pledged to spend $2 million a year for the next five years. One of Pelerman's first moves was to fire coach Paul Feltham.

Back in Victoria there were several clubs feeling the pinch and three Fitzroy players were sacked after Lions players refused to accept a seven per cent across-the-board pay cut.

As usual the soothsayers were predicting that Hawthorn would wane as a footballing power, but there was no sign of that in the opening round when a 12-goal barrage from Jason Dunstall set the scene for a 115-point win over Geelong in the grand final rematch.

On the same weekend Footscray looked overawed by the tumult of the off-season and was comprehensively thrashed by St Kilda. Tony Lockett (10 goals) was in the driver's seat.

Lockett and Dunstall were the two biggest name full-forwards, but North youngster John Longmire grabbed a share of the limelight with a dozen-goal bag against Richmond. The Tigers looked woeful and even early in April looked set for a long, depressing winter.

Knee injuries to a succession of star players dominated the headlines throughout 1990 and some of the biggest names in football went under the sur-

> The 1990 season was played under the more appropriate banner of the Australian Football League.

The powerful Darren Millane was a key force in Collingwood's rise to its first flag in 32 years. His tragic death a year later stunned the football world.

geon's knife. Some like Gary Ablett and Tony Lockett were able to re-emerge later in the season with varied success, but others such as Andrew Bews were sidelined indefinitely. There were a number of serious injuries that dwarfed the imposing list of knee casualties. Brisbane's Andrew Taylor ruptured his spleen and missed two months when Jason Dunstall fractured his skull in a freak collision with the knee of Melbourne's Earl Spalding.

Another interstate club hit the skids when the Sydney Swans owners predicted a loss of $1 million following a fall-off in corporate and crowd support and told players to take a 20 per cent drop in salary.

One of the most vocal "anti cut" individuals was Bernard Toohey who responded with a magnificent game in the nine-point win over Geelong and snarled: "I hope there's not too many owners here tonight," to a TV reporter after the game.

The tension between the AFL and the South Australian League had led to the scrapping of the state of origin clash between Victoria and South Australia because the South Australians intended to put some of the revenue towards a player retention scheme aimed at keeping the best local players in Adelaide. Instead, the Vics lined up against a "New South Wales" side concocted under a dubious set of eligibilty rules and in an appropriate end to the farce were beaten by 10 points.

Football in general was shocked by the tragic death of former VFL Commissioner Jack Hamilton in a car accident. The former Collingwood player and administrator was one of the most respected men in the sport.

Meanwhile Hamilton's old club was gradually looming as a premiership threat in a season that saw an overall levelling of the competition as the effects of the draft began to grip. The Magpies had a young side with plenty of runners and a sprinkling of genuine stars such as Peter Daicos, Gavin Brown, Graham Wright and the fiercely competitive Darren Millane.

Coach Leigh Matthews knew the ways of premiership sides from his days of glory at Hawthorn, and he had welded a potent unit at Victoria Park.

While Matthews coolly went about achieving his aims there was nothing but torment for other League coaches. Malcolm Blight's frustration at Geelong's inability to reproduce its 1989 form boiled over and resulted in a $1500 fine when he criticised umpires after three of his players were reported. Blight was in the news a fortnight later when he chastised star full-forward Gary Ablett for trying to play football without training.

As Geelong struggled to find form its grand final opponent of 1989, Hawthorn, began to show cracks which threatened to cut short its unprecedented run of grand final appearances. After luring veteran centre half-back Chris Mew out of retirement coach Allan Jeans commented that desperate times needed desperate measures. Hawthorn had trouble getting its best 18 onto the field and just as Jason Dunstall returned - complete with protective helmet - Dermott Brereton broke his ribs. Brereton made an astonishing return two weeks later wearing a specially padded vest under his guernsey and kicked 11 goals against the hapless Richmond.

The non-Victorian clubs had a year of remarkable contrasts. News of more bizarre off-field happenings continued in Brisbane when owner Reuben Pelerman sacked coach Norm Dare and then had the decision reversed by his board of directors three hours later. The West Coast Eagles had a more edifying year and looked a far more solid and formidable combination under the coaching of Michael Malthouse.

But by far the biggest sensation came when news broke of the AFL's discussions with South Australian club Port Adelaide about joining the national competition. Years of bitter debate with the South Australian National Football League had produced nothing but angst for the AFL which had finally lost patience. The AFL announced its recommendation for Port Adelaide to join the League, but there was feverish debate on both sides of the border. Many Victorian clubs were doubtful about the wisdom of the move and Adelaide clubs expressed white hot anger.

Glenelg began court action to block Port Adelaide's shift and then the cornered SANFL announced it would enter a composite team in 1991 but would really prefer to hold back until 1992. AFL directors hedged their bets by delaying a final vote as long as possible and eventually it was announced the composite SA side would join the League in 1991.

When the public gaze was averted back to the field it could see that an engrossing battle was taking place. Footscray, inspired by a stunning last-minute goal by Steven Kolynuik, snatched a fairytale victory from top side Collingwood at the MCG and moved to within a gasp of the top five.

Unfortunately the Bulldogs could not keep the momentum going to seal a finals spot and cap a remarkable comeback from the point of near extinction. Doubts were raised over Collingwood's flag credentials when the Magpies went down narrowly to Essendon before a huge Sunday crowd at Waverley in a match that was televised live within Victoria.

At the other end of League affairs Richmond bared its soul and club president Neville Crowe announced that unless $1 million was raised in a special campaign the Tigers would fold. The money was eventually gathered by the October 31 deadline placed on the club by its bankers.

Hawthorn skipper Michael Tuck established a new League games record when he passed Kevin Bartlett's mark in the final round, but a week later he suffered the despair of his side bowing out to Melbourne in the first week of the finals. It was the first time in nine years that the Hawks had not reached the grand final. It would prove to be the end of an era in another way as coach Allan Jeans stood aside to let Alan Joyce take the helm.

A thrilling tie between West Coast Eagles and Collingwood in the first week of the finals threw the AFL into chaos. Peter Sumich's last-minute miss put the finals back a week and led to calls for extra time provisions in drawn finals.

Collingwood bolted home in the replay, but that was not the end of the plucky Eagles who fought back to reach the preliminary final. Tired and jaded after a disrupted flight due to an airlines dispute, the Sandgropers were beaten comfortably by a patchy

Football in general was shocked by the tragic death of former VFL Commissioner Jack Hamilton in a car accident.

Essendon, but came out of the match with newly earned respect from the Victorian public.

Collingwood, so often the bridesmaid in grand finals since 1958, now entered the play-off as clear-cut favorite. Essendon started well with the towering Paul Salmon taking ominous early marks, but before long the Magpies had the upper hand. A wild brawl after the quarter time siren resulted in the KO of star forward Gavin Brown and that fuelled an even stronger effort from the black and white unit. After so many reverses in premiership contests Magpie fans were never sure of the result until the final minutes, but in truth Essendon was gone by the early stages of the second half. Powered by an inspirational skipper in Tony Shaw, Collingwood stormed to a 48-point victory and unleashed a flood of emotion and celebration that had never been equalled.

> Players and fans had to acclimatise to the changing surrounds at the MCG where half of the ground was closed due to the construction of the new Southern Stand.

Magpie barrackers rejoiced in their club's accolade as the first AFL premier, while the army of Collingwood haters on the other side of the fence shook their heads in despair at the death of a tradition of Collingwood failure.

Football was about to alter dramatically with the change to a final six and there was even talk of a split of the competition into two eight-team divisions.

Prior to the 1991 season Geelong fans had more immediate concerns than the competition's structure. Gary Ablett stunned them with the announcement of his retirement. He did not specify reasons and the Geelong community - which had suffered through the Pyramid Building Society collapse and job losses at Ford - had yet another wave of misery to contend with. Not until 13 weeks into the season did Ablett announce his imminent return as suddenly as he had proclaimed his retirement.

Another superstar, St Kilda's Tony Lockett, suffered a bad back injury in a pre-season game when a West Coast player cannoned into him. It turned out he had fractured a wing vertebrae in his back despite St Kilda maintaining a farcical line that his back was just badly bruised. The supposed "bruise" kept him on the sidelines for six weeks.

A chronic wrist injury forced Sydney's Brownlow Medallist Gerard Healy into retirement at the age of 30. Collingwood took the punt that the wrist would come good and drafted Healy with choice No.59 in the March draft.

The arrival of Adelaide as the AFL's 15th team created a bye for the first time in almost seven decades. The effect of the bye was earnestly debated in 1991 with many people saying it broke a team's continuity, but in time coaches would regard it as a bonus rather than a hindrance.

Adelaide made an amazing start to the season by rolling the reigning premier Hawthorn by 86 points in the Crows' debut game. On top of that the Hawks lost Dermott Brereton for five weeks after he was found guilty of striking Chris McDermott.

Players and fans had to acclimatise to the changing surrounds at the MCG where half of the ground was closed due to the construction of the new Southern Stand. Three construction company workers were employed for each game to retrieve the ball whenever it went over the fence.

Struggling Fitzroy played three of their home games in Tasmania and as usual, Collingwood president Alan McAlister had advice for anyone who wanted to hear, and even for those who didn't. He told Fitzroy it should move to Tasmania full-time if it hoped to survive. Four weeks into the season the Lions launched a tin-rattle campaign and fans were told the club had to raise $800,000 by the end of June or face extinction. McAlister had enough to worry about in his own backyard as Collingwood's premiership hangover matched the scale of its 1990 celebrations. Coach Leigh Matthews played down the hangover theory at first, but changed his mind when his side lost six games on the trot.

Other coaches grumbled about the need for extra men on the interchange bench when several teams had to keep players on the ground when they were injured. One player who suffered a terrible injury was Gareth John and there was no thought of keeping him on the field when his larynx was crushed in a freak incident as he collided with Simon Madden's knee. The young Swan could have died, but fortunately was rushed to hospital in time.

Brisbane at last played games in Brisbane itself rather than on the Gold Coast. It was only four matches in 1991, but it was a move in the right direction. Other non-Victorian teams had varying fortunes and West Coast's awe-inspiring form prompted calls for a second team from Western Australia to diminish their strength.

The AFL had announced that finals could be played interstate for the first time and the possibility of meeting West Coast in Perth sent shudders down the spines of Victorians. The vocal Collingwood president McAlister announced his club would simply refuse to play a final there.

Adelaide was busy coming to grips with the demands of playing on foreign turf, and when thrust into the cauldron of St Kilda's home ground at Moorabbin they shrivelled under the heat. Tony Lockett celebrated his return by goaling in the first 30 seconds of the game and powered his team to a club record winning margin of 131 points. Also back in the team was Nicky Winmar after serving a suspension from the previous year and he was little behind Lockett in effectiveness. Lockett's 12 goal bag

was followed by hauls of 10 and 11 in succeeding weeks and was the impetus for St Kilda's re-appearance in the finals after an 18 year drought.

Kevin Sheedy made sure interstate visitors did not get any breaks and for his team's clash with Adelaide the windsock was missing. When the Eagles arrived at Windy Hill they discovered the windsock was tied down. Sheedy pleaded innocence: "I don't know how to tie knots!"

The tribunal was tied in knots as it agonised over the report of Sydney champion Greg Williams. The Brownlow Medallist was making his 12th appearance before the league judiciary and the Swans asked that Neil Busse stand aside as chairman because he would be prejudiced against Williams having heard so many charges against him. Busse heard the charges, Williams was suspended for four weeks and Sydney was fined $2000 for its comments about Busse.

Crowd control was a problem that almost affected the result of the Essendon-Melbourne game. Melbourne's Steven Clark received a free kick just before the final siren with his side trailing by six points. Before he could take his kick the siren blew and fans raced onto the ground so Clark had to take the kick amid a sea of people. In the goal square Essendon barrackers helped their defenders stop the ball from going through, but as it turned out the torpedo punt just fell short.

Demon president Stuart Spencer said if the first person to touch the ball was not a player then the game should be declared a draw. For Clark's part he believed he was right in trying to take the kick as quickly as possible. "The longer you wait, nerves probably get to you more. I've had a few kicks from that area and rated myself a chance."

The broad shoulders of mighty forward Tony Lockett carried St Kilda to a finals berth for the first time in 18 years. Although his career was punctuated by injury and suspension Lockett was a prolific goalkicker with the Saints.

Mind games. Geelong coach Malcolm Blight adopted the unusual tactic of providing Adelaide with an impromptu guard of honor at the start of this match in Adelaide.

West Coast's Karl Langdon was attacked by a spectator as he left the field at Princes Park and the AFL hurriedly scratched around for a solution. It ran an advertisement warning fans they may have to watch games through cyclone fencing if behavior did not improve. There was also a directive to club coaches and other officials to refrain from inflammatory statements likely to incite opposition fans. Certainly there had been some problems, but it seemed that the AFL's knee-jerk response was excessive.

A week later there was a controversy of a different nature over a last minute kick. This time it was over dubious umpiring decisions which gave Adelaide's David Marshall and Rod Jameson the chance to kick goals in the last minute and steal a game from the battling Fitzroy. Lions officials were ropable with the umpiring of Anton McKernan and must

have had some grounds for complaint as McKernan was dropped for the next game.

In their short history the Eagles had established a record of enmity with Melbourne and the saga continued at half-time of their game at the MCG when Melbourne's Allen Jakovich had a verbal clash in the players' race with John Worsfold who was not even playing in the game. Jakovich had been opposed to his brother Glen and surrounding players had been treated to presumed obscenities in their native Slavic tongue.

There was more drama when the tribunal was presented with the bizarre charge against Chris Lewis of having bitten his Melbourne opponent Todd Viney. Lewis was rubbed out for three weeks and Viney had an AIDS test. The case raised the profile of the AIDS issue which had previously been given little attention.

The first use of a final six system produced a well-contested series. Probably the best game was played on the opening Sunday between St Kilda and Geelong at Waverley. Tony Lockett celebrated St Kilda's long-awaited return to the finals with a nine goal performance, but Geelong won a thriller. It was a costly day for the Cats, though, with Gary Ablett being suspended and without him Geelong went down to West Coast in the preliminary final. Hawthorn won the 1991 flag in the one and only Waverley grand final, but the pointer to the future was the presence of West Coast in its first play-off. These were changing times and the interstate threat was looming large.

Traditionalists were also surprised to see the Brownlow go to a former Irishman who had been spotted playing Gaelic football and had been "manufactured" into an Aussie Rules star. Melbourne's Jim Stynes was a dominant player throughout the 1991 season and was a worthy winner.

Tragedy struck Collingwood Football club just days after the 1991 season had finished. Darren Millane died instantly when his car ploughed into a truck in South Melbourne and the Magpies grief was immense. Tough, talented, and a great team man, Millane left a gap at Victoria Park that was impossible to fill.

Coaches were always looking for new ways to bond players, but one training routine made Adelaide the butt of endless jokes during summer. At a pre-season camp the Adelaide players were told to walk over a bed of hot coals and defender Nigel Smart bravely decided to be first man across. After a couple of steps on the 400 degree celsius pit he screamed and was pulled away in agony with badly blistered feet.

One of the biggest dramas of the 1992 season came before the season had even opened. Greg Williams, who had been rejected by Carlton as a young man, was lured back to Princes Park from Sydney with an offer said to be worth more than $200,000 a year. By a complicated swap arrangement Carlton forwards Simon Minton-Connell and Peter Sartori went to Sydney and Fitzroy respectively and Fitzroy's Darren Kappler transferred to Sydney. The AFL put the deal under the microscope and Williams revealed he had been part of a plot in Sydney to bypass the salary cap rules. One false contract had been lodged with the AFL while the real one meant Williams was the highest player in the competition.

Williams was de-registered until April 30 and fined $25,000. The Swans were fined $50,000 with half the amount suspended. Carlton was bitter over being denied use of a player who had committed his offences two years earlier, but most fair-minded supporters considered it was fair enough considering the way the Blues had snared one of the competition's best footballers. Williams often struggled in his first season with Carlton and played under the added strain of chronic knee problems.

Williams shared the spotlight with Collingwood when the Blues and Magpies attracted 83,262 people to the MCG for the Magpies' centenary match. There was no icing on the cake for the Magpies who lost the game and subsequently lost captain Tony Shaw for three weeks on suspension. Apart from Carlton, the big winner was the new Southern Stand which won universal acclaim from football fans and set a new benchmark for football viewing. Later in the year a Friday night game between Essendon and Collingwood attracted 88,066 to the MCG and Essendon was convinced that its decision to play all 12 home games at MCG was a correct one. Collingwood also played four of its home games there in 1992 and moved towards more permanent residency.

Another club with a new footballing home was Hawthorn which played all of its home games at Waverley. The Hawks made a smooth transition from Princes Park, but St Kilda fans reacted more

> **The first use of a final six system produced a well-contested series.**

savagely when their board pushed for the Saints to leave their beloved Moorabbin oval. In the end the emotive issue was put to a vote and the financial opportunities persuaded the red, white and black faithful to make the move. Ironically St Kilda's best win for 1992 came at Waverley in the type of conditions that had prompted the "Arctic Park" tag. In a game marred by a fierce hailstorm St Kilda beat West Coast by 75 points thanks to the "twin towers" - Stewart Loewe and Tony Lockett.

An incident early in the season cause plenty of debate. Collingwood's Craig Kelly flattened Swan Ben Doolan with an elbow that knocked out three of Doolan's teeth. Kelly earned a five match suspension, Doolan came under fire for not wearing a mouthguard and Sydney trainers were accused of not acting quick enough to save Doolan's teeth.

Collingwood re-established itself as a finals contender and St Kilda, with its dazzling core of four of the best players in the land, became a glamor team. Reigning premiers Hawthorn on the other hand, experienced a season of wildly fluctuating form. Paul Dear, the 1991 Norm Smith medallist, had an individual season that was a microcosm of his club's performance. He was dogged by injuries and then was suspended for four weeks over a controversial tripping incident that left Footscray's Peter Foster with a broken leg.

"Trial-by-video" became one of the year's most contentious issues and consistency was often queried by clubs. Tribunal regulars such as Rodney Grinter and Tony Lockett made appearances with Grinter copping six weeks over a clash with Greg Williams. Lockett seemed to be balancing on a tightrope after much publicised wrestling incidents with a succession of opposing defenders. On a day when he kicked 15 goals against Sydney, "Plugger" took time out to counter the attentions of full-back Craig Nettelbeck whose head was gashed on the fence.

> "Trial-by-video" became one of the year's most contentious issues and consistency was often queried by clubs.

Lockett said after the game: "I won't tolerate being pushed around" and the AFL issued guidelines to umpires over reporting instances of wrestling. Mild mannered Fitzroy forward Richard Osborne was surprisingly the first victim of the new ruling and he was supended for a week after an incident with Melbourne's Haydn Robins.

The issue of mergers had been dormant since the disintegration of the Footscray-Fitzroy marriage in 1989. Carlton had made a tentative move to merge with North in 1991 and Carlton's executive director Ian Collins re-ignited the idea by suggesting: "There's always a possibility of it being reactivated." He said Carlton was prepared to change its name to Carlton-North Melbourne and become the Kangaroos.

A club that had seemed down for the count a couple of years earlier was Footscray, but the Dogs had a remarkable season under the coaching of the committed motivator Terry Wheeler. The Dogs won 16 of their 22 games to finish the home and away round in second position and their ruckman Scott Wynd won the Brownlow. Their campaign ended in the preliminary final when they were gunned down by the free-scoring Geelong. The Cats forward line was built around the potent talent of Gary Ablett, Barry Stoneham and Bill Brownless and racked up some big scores including a new AFL record 37.17-239 against Brisbane.

At the other end of the ladder the AFL had an ongoing headache with the disappointing form of problem children Sydney and Brisbane. Sydney, after losing Williams prior to the season, lost its last 15 games in a row and looked to be in tatters. The club was also involved in a tangled dispute with the AFL over the two match suspension of Barry Mitchell which had resulted from video evidence and the verbal evidence of Essendon's Sean Denham. Sydney successfully won a court injunction to enable Mitchell to keep playing and in an embarrassing move the AFL set aside the disqualification and

Mitchell did not miss a match.

It was a year when full-forwards amassed huge tallies. Lockett's 132 goals was only bettered by Jason Dunstall whose best game return was 17 against Richmond. His season's bag was 145 goals and was just five short of the all-time record. Normally Hawthorn could be expected to be in more than one final and give Dunstall the chance to surpass the Hudson/Pratt mark, but in 1992 the Hawks were dismissed in the first week when they went down valiantly to West Coast at Subiaco.

With their previous year's conquerors out of the way, West Coast now had a clear view to the 1992 flag. It wasn't all plain sailing in the early stages of their grand final showdown with Geelong, and the Cats twice established four goal breaks in the second quarter. But then the Eagles hit top gear and the breakneck speed of winger Peter Matera set them on course for a runaway win. For Eagles' skipper John Worsfold hoisting the premiership cup was a dream come true. For Victorian fans who lived in dread of interstate competition it was a nightmare.

An imminent reign of dominance by West Coast was foremost in the thoughts of the football public, but changes by other non-Victorian clubs were also important for the game on a long term basis. The Brisbane Bears finally cut their ties will the ill-fated Carrara ground to locate themselves wholly in Brisbane and both the Bears and the Swans became membership based clubs after having been privately owned. Sydney's financial problems continued to make news in 1993 and early in the season they pulled a surprise by sacking Gary Buckenara and convincing Ron Barassi to take over as coach. Adelaide made a surge in their third season and looked to have the potential to build a successful era.

It was Adelaide which precipitated the downfall of North coach Wayne Schimmelbusch after the Crows slaughtered North by 147 points in a pre-season Fosters Cup game. Ex North player Denis Pagan took over after a long apprenticeship coaching under-19s and reserves teams. At the time of his appointment to the North senior job he was coaching Essendon reserves, but he knew the Arden Street scene well. Of North's 52 senior list players he had coached 38 at junior level.

Pagan turned North's fortunes around in 1993, but a fair slice of credit also had to go to Wayne Carey who emerged as a modern superstar. North held top place on the ladder for much of the season with the powerhouse Carey at the helm. Carey was just one of the brilliant individuals who captured the AFL spotlight. The amazing Gary Ablett seemed to lift to even greater heights as the season progressed. Fourteen goals in a losing team against Essendon prompted his coach Malcolm Blight to say it was the best individual performance he had ever seen. Commentators rapturously wondered whether 1993 crowds were witnessing the greatest footballer of all time.

Ablett and Dunstall were joined in the ranks of century goalkickers by Adelaide's flamboyant heart-throb Tony Modra. The high-leaping spearhead was the darling of crowds at Adelaide's Football Park, but in time the adulation would create huge pressures for the young man.

Clubs desperately sought to maximise their recruiting harvests and player values sky-rocketed to ridiculous levels. Sydney's Barry Mitchell was up for grabs and Collingwood snared him at a reputed price tag of $1 million for five years. Meanwhile Tim Watson decided to have another run with Essendon after a year of retirement. Watson was still only 31 years old and despite having copped his fair share of injuries, was confident he could make a success of the comeback.

The pre-season competiton began in farcical circumstances in February with the Waverley ground in an atrocious state. Large replacement clods of turf were easily shifted and Carlton's Luke O'Sullivan

> The issue of mergers had been dormant since the disintegration of the Footscray-Fitzroy marriage in 1989.

injured his knee so badly he was forced to miss the season. Angry AFL boss Ross Oakley watched in bemused silence after the game as young children happily tossed loose chunks of the oval into the air. Later in the year the attempts to rehabilitate the ground with sand prompted the comment from Tony Shaw that it was "like playing on the Sahara".

Carlton's captain Stephen Kernahan could not blame the ground surface when he was the centre of attention at the MCG in the second round. Kernahan marked just as the siren sounded with Essendon and Carlton dead level. All he had to do was register a score, but the kick from 40 metres slewed out of bounds. Nine days later he made amends when his side was four points behind Hawthorn with only minutes to go. Kernahan's goal won the game for Carlton.

St Kilda travelled to Victoria Park in the knowledge they had not beaten Collingwood there for 17 years. With Tony Lockett out suspended and Robert Harvey off the ground with a thigh injury in the second quarter it was hardly the scenario for an end to the drought, but the brilliance of Aboriginal stars Gilbert McAdam and Nicky Winmar gave the Saints a win. The stylish Winmar copped a barrage of racist abuse from the Collingwood crowd and when the siren sounded he lifted his jumper and pointed to the color of his skin to show his pride in his race.

The racism issue was handled tactlessly by Collingwood president Allan McAlister and even some quick back-tracking did not remedy the matter. It was an issue which had never really been brought out into the open before and the ramifications would echo for years. In lighter vein, a Darwin Aborigine placed a curse on the Magpies.

On a personal note Winmar had been the outstanding player in the competition until this stage, but he was to be involved in an even bigger controversy within days. He had been unhappy with the club over what he said was inadequate treatment for a shoulder injury in the 1992 finals and a hitch in contract negotiations had been simmering for weeks. A new personal manager had issued an ultimatum to St Kilda on the eve of the clash with Carlton and the Saints had rejected it and withdrawn Winmar from the team. The whole matter degenerated into a farcical soap opera for the next three weeks and even though Winmar returned, St Kilda's season was left in tatters. Eventually the whole sorry affair would cost coach Ken Sheldon his job.

Another Aboriginal player assumed centre stage during Winmar's self imposed exile. North's Adrian McAdam booted seven goals in his first game and 10 a week later. He bagged another six in his third appearance and fans wondered why no side had recruited him earlier. When it came to McAdam's turn to play at Victoria Park he was inspired to a nine goal performance by the sight of an Aboriginal flag in the midst of the outer crowd.

The arrival of McAdam turned heads, but there were other, less orthodox sides of football that left people open mouthed. On a day at Geelong one home team fan waved a frozen flathead in the air every time Geelong scored a goal. Perhaps it had something to do with the fact that cult figure commentator/fishing guru Rex Hunt was in the broadcasting box for 3AW.

There was no laughter in Sydney when a sickening collision between Swans' teammates Dale Lewis and Richard Osborne resulted in Osborne going into convulsions. An ambulance came on to the arena to rush him to hospital. Osborne stopped breathing as he lay on the SCG turf and was advised by doctors to retire, but he decided to play on.

Football's attention shifted to Sydney again in tragic circumstances when AFL executive commisioner Alan Schwab was found dead in a Sydney hotel room. Schwab had just embarked on the project of rescuing the ailing Swans. The football world was united in its grief.

The Swans ended a horror 27 game losing stretch by rolling Melbourne and the man who led the charge was Osborne, just five weeks after he had almost died on the same piece of turf.

The advance of the Crows prompted huge interest in South Australia as Channel Seven's Adelaide management discovered when they considered delaying the telecast of the Crows-Eagles game so the evening news could be shown at its normal time. The result was thousands of phone calls and faxes plus a death threat for the program director!

Dermott Brereton was also saying his piece and when he criticised Hawthorn's selectors for dropping premiership stars Tony Hall and Gary Ayres he was fined $12,000 by the club. It was the start of a chain of events that would eventually see his departure from the club.

Fitzroy's Darren Wheildon found himself in hot water for a different reason. He was dropped for not turning up for a handball competition on a TV sports show. Wheildon had kicked eight goals the previous week and when he returned to the team he was in trouble again as he was reported for shaking a goal post while a team mate was having a shot at goal. He was fined $750.

Hard luck story for 1993 was that of Geelong. The Cats had to achieve the unenviable task of beating West Coast in Perth in the final round to have a chance of getting into the finals. They did the job despite the last minute loss of champion on-baller Garry Hocking with back spasms, but other results didn't go the way the Cats wanted and they missed out.

Night football at the MCG was a big winner in 1993, but traditionalists were aghast when they heard the AFL's plan to play a final at night. Some reactions were predictable - Alan McAlister said Collingwood wouldn't have a bar of it - but on Saturday September 4, there were 79,139 fans who voted with their feet to watch Essendon confront Carlton in the qualifying final. The Blues won a cliffhanger by two points, but Essendon rebounded to knock off West Coast a week later.

North Melbourne's Wayne Carey emerged as a superstar in the mid 1990s. Here he boots clear of Tony Liberatore.

The Bombers trailed Adelaide by 42 points at half time of the preliminary final and Victorian fans braced themselves for a grand final invasion of Crows faithful. But it wasn't to be. There had been just a hint of a turnaround late in the second term, but only the most optimistic Essendon fan would have predicted the amazing comeback that transpired. By the time exhausted veteran Tim Watson goaled deep in time on Essendon had sealed an 11 point miracle.

Essendon never let Carlton get away to a start in the grand final and the 1990s version of the baby Bombers powered to a tremendous victory. Oddly

Every move you make. North's Mick Martyn attends to star Cat Gary Ablett.

eyebrows, but it was nothing compared to the uproar over the decision to stage an eight-team finals series in the 1994 season just when the final six system had been fine tuned. In addition to more teams in the finals there were more umpires on the field as the pace and added demands of League football led to the introduction of a third umpire. One of the intentions was to combat behind the play interference by defenders on forwards and although that area seemed to improve early in the year it was neglected later on. Lastly the cause championed by Essendon coach Kevin Sheedy was finally resolved when the interchange bench was extended from two to three.

The need for a second team in Perth was addressed early in the year and the AFL approved an entry package for a Fremantle team that would take the field the following year. Existing clubs believed the new team should start from scratch, but Fremantle wanted concessions. In the end they did not get the draft concessions they wanted after a compromise was agreed to.

This was the year when it became obvious to everybody in football that nothing was sacred as far as the corporate dollar was concerned. A sponsor's name had been emblazoned on the ball in the 1993 finals and in 1994 Carlton announced it had signed a five year agreement with a telecommunications company under which Princes Park would be called Optus Oval.

Big names Dermott Brereton and Peter Daicos found themselves leaving the clubs they had called home. Multi-premiership hero Brereton left Hawthorn and Sydney snapped him up with an eye to his marketing appeal. It was a big gamble considering Brereton's immediate past which had been restricted to a handfull of games amid a succession of injuries. He soon wished that he didn't attract attention, as a TV crew sent to take footage of him in his new colors caught him standing on the head of Hawthorn's rookie Rayden Tallis in a reserves prac-

enough the club's strategists had groomed the team for a flag two or three years down the track, but they weren't arguing with the unexpected flag. Youngsters like Dustin Fletcher, Rick Olarenshaw, Joe Misiti, Mark Mercuri, and Gavin Wanganeen represented the Essendon of the future. Wanganeen had won the Brownlow Medal a few days earlier and in an odd twist to the racism debate his fellow Aboriginal Michael Long won the Norm Smith medal for best player in the grand final.

For 1994 there was more of everything in the AFL. More teams in the finals, more field umpires and more interchange players. The creation of a final six system in 1991 had caused plenty of raised tice game. He was suspended for seven matches.

Daicos was dropped from Collingwood's list and his popularity was obvious when he ran a lap of honor before the Collingwood-Carlton game. He resisted the invitations from other clubs and opted for retirement.

Once the season got under way Tony Modra dispelled concerns about his attitude with a 13 goal bag against Carlton. It was record opening day effort for an individual. On a more unusual note Melbourne stalwart Jim Stynes turned the clock back 80 years by wearing a cap during the game played in the hot, sunny conditions at the MCG. Nobody could accuse Stynes of being a softie - it was his 150th game in a row.

Few coaches could achieve a record to match that sort of longevity. Footscray's Terry Wheeler found that out when he was called aside by club president Peter Gordon during a selection committee meeting prior to the round three match and was told he would be replaced as coach. His job went to Alan Joyce, the man who had been deposed as Hawthorn coach several months earlier and was the son of a former Footscray player. Wheeler had every right to be pround of his record: "I believe I have been able to take a team which was on the brink of extinction and bring them right back into the hearts of many football people".

While Footscray had buried Wheeler as coach, the Carlton president wanted to fill in Waverley park. John Elliott said it was too expensive too run and the land should be sold for $50 million. At the same time he said Carlton was keen to expand Optus Oval.

Meanwhile there were signs at last that Brisbane was gathering strength. For the first time all four non-Victorian teams played at home in the one round and all won. At the other end of the ladder Richmond plunged into controversy when the club's business manager, the extroverted Mal Brown delivered a tirade in his role as a TV panellist, decry-

ing the way the club was run. "The people who make decisions are tired and don't contribute. You can't blame the players and the coach entirely. It comes from the top."

The statements began a chain reaction that saw the resignation of general manager Cameron Schwab and four board members. Richmond convincingly won its next month and thus began a remarkable turnaround that eventually put it within striking distance of the finals.

North Melbourne was a pace-setter in the early weeks and every team pondered how to stop the rampaging centre half-forward Wayne Carey. Geelong's Tim McGrath, a former under-19 teammate of Carey, volunteered for football's toughest job and he was able to put a halt to the North man's run. West Coast, on the other hand could not contain him, but won anyway. Carey took 15 of his team's 45 marks.

Carey had his share of run-ins with umpires, but another forward, Tony Lockett, was responsible for one of the year's biggest sensations. When he came steaming out downfield for the ball Lockett was an irresistible force and for Sydney's Peter Caven coming the other way, there was no chance of going unscathed. There was no chance of Lockett evading video scrutiny either. One estimate was the TV stations replayed it 90 times in the next few days. Lockett was suspended for eight weeks and the fact that he had played one of the most amazing individual games of all time was forced into the background. Lockett kicked 11 of his team's 16 goals and thanks to him St Kilda won by a point after trailing by 48 points early in the last quarter.

Collingwood's Gavin Brown had more luck with the tribunal. Initially found guilty he was exonerated when a re-hearing viewed amateur video tape. The only other instance of a tribunal decision being reversed was in 1989 when Paul Van Der Haar's suspension was overturned. When Wayne Carey fronted the tribunal for the fourth time in 1994 he was suspended for three games and the Kangaroos were incensed because AFL operations manager Ian Collins said before the hearing that it was annoying to keep reviewing the same players.

Adelaide's campaign for 1994 had been a patchy one and coach Graeme Cornes was under increasing pressure. On the day that Columbian soccer star Andres Escobar was shot dead for letting in an own goal, a Crows fans sported a banner that read "Cornes for Columbia". The Crows tried to show a strong hand when they dropped Tony Modra because he had missed a training session, and the cynics said it was easy to be tough when the side was only about to play the hapless Swans. It turned out to be a miscalculation as the Swans won by 12 points.

Talk of merger reared its head again and this time the linking of Melbourne and Fitzroy had more authenticity than previous speculation. There were strong reports that the two clubs had met at AFL House to draw up final plans. Brisbane put up its hand as a merger candidate if Fitzroy was willing, but nothing eventuated. The League's much heralded five year plan did not break any new ground, but it made the point that clubs had to prove in advance that they were financially viable and this pointed directly at Fitzroy.

A huge dust-up just before the finals earned censure from the AFL for Footscray and West Coast. The trouble flared as players were leaving the field at half-time and ended with Eagle Peter Sumich convulsing on the ground. The AFL's investigations officer decided that no-one had a case to answer, but AFL operations manager Ian Collins had told the clubs they would be fined and no players would be charged. Then eight players were told they would be charged. The Bulldogs were furious and successfully sought an injunction to have the hearings delayed until after their first final. Details of the Collins "deal" were revealed at the court hearing. West Coast's five players were cleared as were Footscray's

> There were two issues which dominated media time and column space in 1995 - racism and mergers.

three men a week later - although defender Danny Southern was fined $10,000 for applying a headlock. The whole affair was an absolute shambles.

The eight team finals series provided another first in the opening week. North and Hawthorn were tied after the completion of four quarters and the game went into extra time. Taller and younger than their opposition, the Roos scored 3.5 to nothing in the extra 10 minutes and ran out decisive winners. Carey was an inspiration when it mattered. A couple of hours later the night clash between Footscray and Geelong also ended dramatically with the much maligned Billy Brownless goaling after the siren to grab the game for the Cats.

Carlton was the biggest disappointment of the finals series after finishing second at the end of the home and away games and when the Blues crashed in both of their finals, the question mark was put against coach David Parkin and several of his senior players headed by Brownlow Medallist Greg Williams.

A tight finals series continued when Geelong won its way through to the grand final thanks to a last minute goal by Gary Ablett. It was a heartbreaking finish to the preliminary final for North's Mick Martyn who kept the champ under a tight reign for four quarters. After such an evenly contested series it was logical to expect a tight grand final, but after the first quarter West Coast was invincible. Geelong's loss of Garry Hocking early in the game did not help either and West Coast methodically and mechanically ground down the Cats. Dean Kemp, Guy McKenna and Chris Waterman maintained a constant supply to their forwards and the Eagles surged to an 80 point win. The result highlighted the difficulty of winning four finals and Geelong went the same way as Collingwood (1980) and Melbourne (1988).

West Coast's all-powerful display was conclusive proof that the strength of football in WA needed to be spread to a second team. Under coach Gerard

Neesham the Fremantle Dockers showed from the outset in 1995 that they could play an attractive, innovative style of football. It came at a time when the Michael Malthouse coached Eagles were often accused of being boring and over-regimented. Fremantle recruited established players Ben Allan and Scott Watters to lead the side and the team's "chip and draw" game caused plenty of comment. The Dockers would hold on to the ball and even stop dead at times, so they could lure defending players and then chip the ball over their heads.

There were two issues which dominated media time and column space in 1995.

Racism and mergers alternated as the leading items and many followers of the game grew disillusioned with the focus shifting so often from the actual football. The racism debate had begun in 1993 with Nicky Winmar's show of pride and it burst forth again when Essendon's Michael Long revealed he had been called a "black bastard" by Collingwood's Damian Monkhorst. Ten days later, the AFL called the two players together for a meeting to resolve the issues then announced that no penalty would be handed down. Long was clearly not satisfied and after it was disclosed that Monkhorst had not apologised to him the pair was again brought together four days later. This time there was an apology and Long was placated.

All of this unfolded at a time when the AFL was forming a players' code of conduct. Racism contin-

Rejected by Carlton in his youth, Greg Williams eventually found his way back to Princes Park via Geelong and Sydney.

ued to bob up as an issue and by season's end the AFL was calling for fans to dob in fellow spectators who were dishing out racial abuse.

AFL Commissioner Graeme Samuel ignited the merger debate in May and it gathered momentum at a rapid pace when a war broke out in Rugby League ranks between the Kerry Packer-backed Australian Rugby League and Rupert Murdoch's proposed breakaway super-league. The AFL pushed things along by offering a $6 million enticement to any clubs that took part in a merger so they could introduce Port Adelaide as the 16th club in 1996.

Fitzroy was the club that for years had been under the hammer. Poor both in terms of money and success, they called upon former hero Bernie Quinlan to step in as coach, but the drain on their playing resources left them with a group of kids plus others whose time had expired with other clubs.

One interesting recruit was Footscray's Doug Hawkins who gave his all in his 18th season of League football. Fitzroy had good ground to complain that the draft rules and concessions to interstate clubs had effectively raped the Lions. Gary Pert and Matthew Armstrong had departed and one of the last straws was the departure of Paul Roos who had long been a champion and stalwart of the cause.

Roos went to Sydney as part of a recruiting campaign that was made possible by the interstate concessions to Sydney. Even with those provisions in place Sydney still managed to get their sums wrong and was unable to fit Ross Lyon, its No.1 February draft choice, into the salary cap.

Another challenge was convincing star schoolboy Anthony Rocca, brother of Collingwood spearhead Saverio, to play for Sydney. The Swans had already stitched up their prime target - St Kilda's super full-forward Tony Lockett who had come out of contract at the end of 1994 and was at first courted by Collingwood before moving north at a reputed cost of $1.2 million. Big "Plugger" had his interruptions to 1995 that included a duodenal ulcer and ongoing knee problems, but in full flight he was still unstoppable as the hapless Fitzroy discovered when he booted 16 goals straight against them.

He could have smashed Fred Fanning's 18 goal record if he had not spent 12 minutes on the bench after a mixed up message from a runner. Lockett thought he had been told to "cool it" on the bench and when coach Barassi saw him leaving the field he thought he had been sent off under the blood rule.

That rule was one of several that was not always well accepted in 1995. There were calls for it to be streamlined to minimise disruption to games, although there was one odd case of an umpire being forced to leave the field when he suffered a blood nose when colliding with a player. Field umpire Geoff Caulfield did not get much crowd sympathy when he trotted off the field.

Penalties for abusing umpires were stepped up and a number of fines were placed on players. Those players found guilty were also made ineligible for the Brownlow Medal and the harshness of that ruling was apparent when Brownlow favorite Nicky Winmar was cited by an over-technical Anton McKernan.

Football's era of "political correctness" extended to fining clubs over melees and the new rule speci-

> The AFL tried to enhance state of origin football by allowing a vacant Saturday for the games rather than hold them mid week between rounds.

fied a maximum fine of $50,000. It was inspired by the pre-game melee between Essendon and Collingwood late in 1994. First two clubs to be carpeted in 1995 were Essendon and Melbourne whose round three tangle earned them a fine of $15,000 each.

Geelong surprised the football world when it announced the club would have three co-captains-Gary Ablett, Ken Hinkley and Barry Stoneham - after Garry Hocking resigned the post. Most of the captaincy duties landed on Ablett's shoulders as Stoneham was sidelined all year through injury and Hinkley had persistent back and leg troubles.

Richmond, meanwhile lost its skipper in different circumstances when Tony Free injured his knee so badly that it required a reconstruction. The Tigers were undaunted by a shocking run of injuries that included top full-forward Matthew Richardson who crashed after pulling up quickly to avoid the fence at the small Sydney Cricket Ground. The AFL ordered the Swans to increase the gap between boundary line and fence by a metre.

Initially there were sceptics over Richmond's qualifications as a genuine finals contender, but the Tigers just kept on going and a heart-pumping draw with Essendon sealed their credibility in the eyes of the football public.

The AFL tried to enhance state of origin football by allowing a vacant Saturday for the games rather than hold them mid week between rounds. On a cold wintry day at the MCG the crowd of 64,000 people thrilled to the sight of Gary Ablett and Tony Lockett sharing the goalsquare and the two champions turned on a fitting performance to give the Vics a runaway win.

Prior to the match the crowd saluted the great Ted Whitten, a prime mover in keeping interstate football on the map, and now suffering from cancer. There was not a dry eye in the house as Whitten was driven around the MCG on a lap of honor. Sadly the disease would claim "Mr Football" within a matter of weeks and the whole football world was overcome with grief.

With Victorian based clubs under threat, St Kilda launched a tin rattle. The Save Our Saints campaign aimed to raise $1.5 million by October to evert the threat of merger. The campaign seemed to spur players and the Saints knocked off top teams Geelong and Richmond to add to the scalp of Carlton which had been collected earlier in the season. The Saints were also able to hang on to three of their best players - Nathan Burke, Robert Harvey and, eventually, Stewart Loewe - despite speculation that the trio would move on when they came out of contract at the end of the year.

Fitzroy plunged into further despair when Bernie Quinlan was sacked just three weeks before the end of the year. It was rightly condemned as an unnecessarily abrupt end for one of the club's favorite sons. The Lions' old coach Robert Shaw was not having a much better time of things in Adelaide. The Crows' inability to win in Victoria was costly and when they defeated St Kilda it was the first time they had succeeded in Victoria since winning the 1993 qualifying final against Hawthorn. That simply wasn't good enough to earn a finals place.

The battle for finals went right down to the wire. Brisbane's latter half of the season had made everyone sit up and take notice and it was achieved in the unusual circuumstances after Robert Walls had announced his decision to quit the coaching job midway through the year. Led well by gnarled old veteran Roger Merrett, Brisbane had a talented young side that charged into the finals. The Bears knocked off another finals contender, Melbourne, in the Friday night game of the final round, but had to sweat on Collingwood losing the Sunday match against Sydney. Well served by midfielders Paul Kelly and Derek Kickett, full-forward Tony Lockett kicked six goals in the second half to give a fine send off to retiring coach Ron Barassi.

The Bears produced a valiant performance in the opening week of the finals against Carlton, and as it turned out they were the only team that could get close to the Blues in September. Carlton easily beat North, and took another step in erasing the bitter memories of their 1994 fadeout.

Inconsistent West Coast and Essendon both fell by the wayside after being touted as premiership chances, and Richmond's courageous run came to an end against Geelong. It set up the prospect of a mighty grand final, but as had happened so often in recent times it was a one sided affair. Geelong tried to physically intimidate Carlton early in the day, but the Blues, who had lost just two games all year, were not about to roll over. Veterans Steve Kernahan, Peter Dean and Greg Williams were supported by the younger brigade headed by Anthony Koutoufides and Ang Christou.

In the background there was talk by the AFL of staging a night grand final in future. It was all too much, said the traditionalists, but they had said the same thing 99 years earlier when the little mark was abolished and behinds were credited in the scoring.

Football's one constant has been its evolution, sometimes fast, sometimes slow, but forever on the move.

> In the background there was talk by the AFL of staging a night grand final in future. It was all too much but they had said the same thing 99 years earlier when the little mark was abolished and behinds were credited in the scoring.

NO SHADES OF GREY

There is a theory among some historians that Aboriginal people invented the game that was the basis of Australian Rules Football.

That may or may not be true, but anybody who has thrilled to the delights of a Winmar, Farmer or Kickett in full flight will not have much difficulty in accepting the premise that the Koori affinity for the game is so deeply ingrained that it extends back sev-

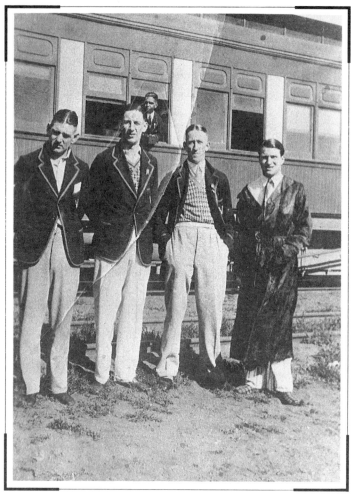

The man in the background, Doug Nicholls was a groundbreaker for Aboriginal players in League football. Here, he is poised with his box Brownie camera as the 1935 Victorian team takes a break during its train trip across the Nullarbor. In the foreground are Albert Collier (left), and dapper Carlton man Keith Shea in the smoking jacket.

eral generations. The hypothesis suggests whites may have stolen the idea of footy as we know it from the original inhabitants of this continent.

In South Western Victoria it is known that a game was played with a "Football" made from opossum skin filled with crushed charcoal. The ball was kicked with the instep of the bare feet and players flew high to catch the ball. The word describing this was "amarkum" which may contain a clue to the origins of the word that describes the distinctive act

of catching the ball that is peculiar to our own game.

Historian Geoffrey Blainey in his book *A Game Of Our Own* says it was possible that the white founders of Aussie Rules may have picked up the style by watching the native Australians in action. Blainey rules out a direct link to the creation of Australian Rules as we know it, but there are plenty of people willing to debate the issue.

The origins of the game will continue to be debated in academic circles, but the influence of Aboriginal players on the 90s game is beyond question. As the number of aboriginal players in the national league has increased, so too has the dimension of an associated problem - racism.

So why do Aboriginal players shine so brilliantly at Australian Rules? One theory is the genaeological development of a muscle in the foot that was due to the hunter/gatherer nature of Aboriginal life. Another interesting aside was a test done with top white and aboriginal footballers at a Teal Cup carnival a few years ago. Sixteen different shaped stones were placed on a chess board and each player was given time to look at them before they were covered over. When putting the stones back into place the white boys could only manage an average of three out of the 16. On the other hand the Aboriginal teenagers averaged around 11 in the correct placing. It was an illustration of how to envisage an overall picture of what was in front of them in much the same way as the famed trackers of the Northern Territory.

That quality of peripheral vision is the same that gives Aboriginal players the time to assess the best option when delivering the ball upfield. It is something that gives Aboriginal players a special quality.

In today's highly mobile society players move more freely between states than in the early days of the game. Part of this movement has brought gifted Aboriginal players across the Victorian border. Although it is generally accepted that Fitzroy's Doug Nicholls was the first Aboriginal player to appear in League football, that assumption may not necessarily be true.

Fitzroy can lay claim to the first regular Aboriginal player to make his mark at the top level. There may have been others, but it seems Tom Banks was the first Aboriginal to hit the big time. The words written of him many years after he had retired would not be acceptable in today's society, but in 1944 they were meant to be a compliment.

Lal McLennan, a player, official and eventual president of Fitzroy, wrote: "Banks although dark of color, was an absolute white man....

"Banks was a magnificent footballer. A great captain, he was the senior vice president and really was the executive head of the club."

It is likely that Banks was raised by a white family after being adopted as a baby, as was the practice in those days. Even several decades later Aboriginal children were taken from their natural mothers and farmed out to white families. The Fitzroy area has had a connection with the Aboriginal community as the early Aboriginal missions were built in nearby Collingwood. Banks, though, wasn't a local boy, as he was born in Maryborough in 1867 and came to Fitzroy from Bendigo in 1888. He decided to join Fitzroy because his old school friend Con Hickey was there.

It is not clear where the two had been schoolmates, but it seems likely that it was in Fitzroy. Banks did not take long to establish a fine reputation as a footballer. He was rated as one of the best players in the state by commentators and could play in any position on the field. Not only that, he was a tremendous leader and captained Fitzroy to a flag as well as leading Victoria to success in an intercolonial match against South Australia.

He announced his retirement from the game after leading the team to the 1895 VFA pennant, but club supporters and officials wouldn't let him go that easily. Banks was cajoled out of retirement in 1896 and even played 10 games in the first year of League football in 1897. He remained a key figure behind the scenes at Fitzroy for many years and his football brain was instrumental in future successes.

Another Aboriginal player who made it to League ranks in the early days was Joe Johnson. In just three seasons with Fitzroy he played 55 games that included two premiership appearances. Carlton had the chance to become the next club to field an Aboriginal player in 1927 when a young Doug Nicholls trained at Prince's Park.

But after six weeks the Carlton hierarchy dumped him giving its reason that his black skin smelled. Nicholls withdrew to the less demanding environment of the VFA with Northcote. He spent five of his prime footballing years there, before Fitzroy approached him to have a second try at League football.

Small and compact, he had electrifying pace that had been developed as a pro runner. In 1934 he came third in Fitzroy's best and fairest award behind Brownlow winners Haydn Bunton and Chicken Smallhorn and a year later he made the Victorian team. Nicholls' efforts in football, as in other walks of life, should have blazed the trail for other Aboriginal people and for other League clubs to follow. But over the next three or four decades only a handfull of Aboriginal players appeared in League football.

Eddie Jackson's six seasons at Melbourne from 1947 left an indelible mark on the memory of those who saw him. Jackson had tremendous all-round skill, balance and reflexes. Years later he was still getting a kick in bush football with Thornton.

In the same era Essendon fielded one of the great Aboriginal footballers in Norm McDonald. Like Nicholls he was a pro sprinter and once ran second to his teammate Lance Mann in the Stawell Gift. McDonald played 128 games from 1947 to 1953, and had the magical ability to rise to a big occasion . He was a star performer in the premierships of 1949 and 1950 and in 1951 he was the Bombers' best and fairest.

Perhaps the greatest of all Aboriginal players was Graham "Polly" Farmer who revolutionised the na-

Essendon's Gavin Wanganeen - the first Aboriginal player to win a Brownlow.

ture of the game in Victoria. The Geelong champion, who described himself as "quarter" Aboriginal, introduced handball as a weapon and made an immediate impact when crossing to the Cats from Western Australia in 1962.

His second placing in the 1963 Brownlow was the best by an Aboriginal footballer until Gavin Wanganeen's win in 1993.

Farmer had to face racial taunts in his time and once described the racist comments as being equal to any physical pressure. In 1970 the League tribunal acknowledged the extent to which racial abuse could affect a player when it exonerated Syd Jackson on a striking charge in the second semi after he stated he had been racially abused. Ironically Jackson admitted two decades later that he had been advised by Carlton to use the racism defence as a strategy to beat the charge.

There were a few other Aboriginal players in the 1960s and 1970s such as Footscray's Charlie Stewart, South's Elkin Reilly, North's Bert Johnson, Rich-

mond's Derek Peardon, and of course the volatile Saint Robbie Muir, but the rich vein of Aboriginal football talent was not properly tapped until the start of the 1980s. The Krakouer brothers, Jim and Phil, led the way for a batch of talent that included Brian Peake, Maurice Rioli, Wally Lovett, Michael McLean, Troy Ugle, Les Bamblett, Phil Egan, Phil Narkle, Chris Lewis, Michael Mitchell, Kevin Caton, Derek and Dale Kickett, Russell Jeffrey, Nicky Winmar, Greg Gilbert and Adrian McAdam, Michael Long and Gavin Wanganeen.

Opposition jealousy prompted racist remarks directed towards Aboriginal players and those with the shorter tempers often reacted savagely. Jimmy Krakouer and Robert Muir were two who frequently found themselves facing tribunals, but all Aboriginal players endured it. For many years racism was an issue which the game's governing bodies turned their back on, but it flared into a matter of wider concern early in 1993 on a landmark day at Victoria Park, Collingwood.

After being taunted all day by the Collingwood cheer squad St Kilda's Nicky Winmar lifted his jumper and pointed proudly to the color of his skin. The gently spoken Winmar was an unlikely focus for the national uproar that followed. He spoke for all Aboriginal players when he reflected in later times: "I remember it being there for so many years. You just get sick of it. We just go out there to play football and it did affect me a lot in my junior years."

By 1995 the AFL formulated a code of conduct for players that specifically identified racism as an offence. An incident involving Essendon's Michael Long and Collingwood's Damian Monkhorst hastened calls for action and the League's handling of such a delicate issue was not all it could have been. Some people believed the AFL had gone from one extreme to the other in tackling the problem, but if that was the case it was excusable. After all, the imbalance had been tilted the opposite way, against Aboriginal players, for far too long.

NIGHT FEVER

A generation ago night football was a sideshow at which non-finals teams fought out a "compensatory premiership".

By 1995 there was a strong push by the AFL to conduct the game's showpiece - the grand final - under lights. It was the most graphic illustration of the popularity of night football and how far this version of the game had progressed. Night football is a version of the game in itself and through football's history it has attracted its own share of publicity both good and bad.

It is unarguable that night football has proved a big drawcard for the major games staged at the MCG. The crowd numbers speak for themselves, but most people would be surprised to hear that night football was first played in Melbourne more than a century ago. The first match was played under a "stream of electricity" on Wednesday, August 6, 1879 between the Collingwood Artillery and East Melbourne teams at the MCG. In fact it has a place in the overall history of Victoria as it was the first commercial use made of electricity in the state.

The teams used a ball that had been painted white so it could be seen more clearly by players and spectators, but it had to be cleaned every so often when it became too muddy. There was an even bigger problem when the ball burst during the game.

The special lighting system was set up by a Professor Pepper "and the lights were of the large clear glass type suspended from poles erected around the arena". Despite the cold, wet weather the game attracted a healthy crowd of 10,000 people. Another game was played the following Wednesday between Carlton and Melbourne which drew 7,000 people and Blues' champion George Coulthard a sporting hero of the day, booted all three goals for his side which overwhelmed Melbourne who only scored a solitary goal.

A third night match took place on August 28 between Essendon and Melbourne, this time on the East Melbourne ground which drew a 10,000 crowd. The third game was hampered by the lights going out on several occasions, and in other matches there had been "black spots" where it was difficult to see players.

As the years passed there were several more flirtations with night football. There was an exhibition match between South and Richmond in 1935 at Olympic Park, a VFL versus VFA game on Show Night at the Royal Melbourne Showgrounds in 1936 and a number of night games at Brisbane in the 1950 ANFC Carnival. Essendon and Geelong met for premiership points under lights at Brisbane in 1952 during the League's round of matches played across Australia to promote the game.

Night footy was put on the backburner for many years until it was revived in the mid 1950s. One of the current concerns in the night-time finals debate - the behavior of crowds after an extra intake of alcohol - was a problem which surfaced in those days at the old South Melbourne ground.

The lighting at the South ground didn't help keep the behavior nice on the playing side of the fence. The notoriously gloomy areas in the front of the bowling green and in the forward pocket near the scoreboard were the backdrop for some fearsome incidents.

The first night game between St Kilda and South Melbourne was a torrid affair and after the dust had settled three players and a trainer had been reported. An all-in melee in the third quarter resulted in police and trainers racing in to try and separate the combatants. All 36 players were gathered at on end of the ground. *The Sun* described the evening: "Incidents of sly elbowing, kneeing and punching flared sensationally in the third quarter after South Melbourne half-back flanker John Elder was smashed to the ground when play was 60 yards away".

There is a theory among some historians that Aboriginal people invented the game that was the basis of Australian Rules football.

Bob Skilton was the first casualty of the game, and recalled the night: "I lasted two minutes before my elbow was broken. When I went to hospital I was sitting in the casualty section wearing my footy gear. I remember a bloke walking around with a transistor listening to the game and telling me how lucky I was not to be playing because they were all involved in a punch-up!" Skilton laughed when he recalled how "lucky" he was to be nursing a broken elbow.

Skilton said the lighting of those days cannot be compared to that which is used now at the MCG. "It really is like comparing night to day," said Skilton. Apart from squaring up old scores the matches didn't provide much appeal for the participants. Ted Whitten admitted in Ken Piesse's *Complete Guide to Australian Football* that "you had to have eyes in the back of your head. I was no Robinson Crusoe. I was letting them go too."

The night competition in those days included only the teams who had missed out on the finals. Jaded and weary after a long season, the players did not relish the thought of fronting up for more matches and the story has been told of a game when Richmond's Royce Hart kicked a match-winning goal late in the evening, only to be confronted by an angry teammate Mike Green.

"What do you think you're doing? Do you want us to be back here next week too?" demanded Green.

The novelty of night games was popular with the sporting public especially the locals in South Melbourne who would head to the ground straight after 6 o'clock closing. The bar trade wasn't just restricted to spectators either and it was said the pre-match preparation of many players would include a counter tea on the way to the ground.

In the first year of competition, 1956, the crowds averaged over 20,000 per game and the final between South and Carlton attracted 33,120 people. In that first series there was plenty of work generated for the tribunal and latter day AFL commissioner Albert Mantello was one of the men nabbed by umpires.

Mantello was reported twice for striking Essendon's Jack Clarke who would comment in later years that the action on the other side of the fence was often more chaotic than what was happening on the field.

The first season was so successful that the League included all 12 team for the 1957 series, but it was dogged by bad weather with two games cancelled because of rain. After that year it returned to the format of the eight teams who had missed out on the finals. The night series played until 1971 and the Thursday night matches were broadcast by 3DB's Lou Richards and Ron Casey interspersed with the announcement of the League teams for the day finals.

After a six year lapse the night series was revived in 1977 at Waverley. As modern day fans are aware it has evolved through several stages that initially involved games being played during the same weeks as the day time season through to its current structure as a pre-season competition.

In 1985 the first games for premiership points were played under lights at the MCG. Gradually it has become an accepted part of the football calendar and in a way it was only a matter of time before the idea of night finals bubbled to the surface. As with anything different, footballers devise ways and means to overcome new problems. Think back to the late 1970s and you will recall the "battle paint" worn under the eyes by Don Scott and co, and there were also a number of players who experimented with gloves.

The first night time final was played in 1993 when 79,139 people witnessed a cliffhanger qualifying final between Essendon and Carlton at the MCG. Admittedly the Bombers and Blues had big followings, but during the afternoon North Melbourne and West Coast had drawn only 29,147 people to Waverley for their elimination final.

By 1995 there was a further ground-breaking move when the preliminary final between Carlton and North Melbourne was staged under the MCG lights. A night grand final was but a step away.